Y0-BCE-442

AFRICAN CONGRESS

Congress of African Peoples, Atlanta, 1970.

AFRICAN CONGRESS

A Documentary of the First Modern Pan-African Congress

edited with an Introduction by

Imamu Amiri Baraka (LeRoi Jones)

William Morrow & Company, Inc., New York 1972

Printed in the United States of America.
Library of Congress Catalog Card Number 78-159735

**Kitabu Kweusi Kwa
Queen Mother Moore**

Introduction

The September 1970 meeting of the Congress of African Peoples in Atlanta, Georgia, was one in a growing historical tradition of international gatherings of Pan Africans, in so-called modern history, beginning with the four meetings called by W.E.B. Du Bois down to the Manchester Conference (the fifth Pan Africanist Conference) in 1945, pulled together by George Padmore and Dubois, in which the phrase "Pan Africanism" first got put into common circulation. In most recent times, the Black Power conferences, held in 1966 (Washington, D.C.), '67 (Newark, N.J.), '68 (Philadelphia, Pa.) were the immediate forbears, as well as an international meeting in Bermuda in 1969. All these meetings were part of the same historical and contemporary dynamic, the movement for international African liberation, which is Pan-Africanism at its broadest!

The veil of controversy which is thrown over our movement by our enemies is only to hide the simplicity of what we intend! The Pan African movement encourages African people wherever they are in the world to understand that they are brothers and sisters, families, communities, nations, a race together, bred in common struggle, brought forth from, and a result of common history, and in the circulating combustible of our racial memory, we all strive for a common future; a people united, independent, basing our claim to national and international sovereignty upon a unified, independent mother Africa, whose freedom, then, would automatically raise the level of Africans' lives all over the planet.

The Congress remanifested in contemporary application the ideas of great Africans like Blyden, Garvey, Du Bois, Casely Hayford, Nyerere, Nkrumah, Touré, Elijah Muhammud, Malcolm X. But now we understand the great "synthesis" that men like Hayford spoke of, the need to combine the views of Africans living on the continent of Africa with the ideas of Africans living in the West, or wherever outside the continent, to produce the contemporary African education, technology, politics and economic development necessary to unify and liberate all of us together!

To this 1970 meeting came African men as diverse as Hajj Abdoulaye Touré, Guinea's Ambassador, and the late Whitney Young, who just before his death had, like Dr. King before him, begun to see the need for all black men to work together whatever their smaller view. The tone of operational unity, which the executive council of the Congress tries to emphasize, was ubiquitously apparent. Minister Louis Farrakhan delivered a strong message from the messenger of Islam, the honorable Elijah Muhammud, to an audience in which was seated the wife of our slain leader, Malik Shabazz. Julian Bond, Mayor Hatcher, Imari from the Republic of New Africa, continental African Liberation Army spokesmen, Breadbasket's Rev. Jesse Jackson, SCLC's chairman, Rev. Abernathy, newly elected black mayor, Kenneth Gibson from NewArk, all came and participated and delivered addresses that fixed the consciousness of all of us and all of them, at a higher level. The body of thought was high, and the vibrations of such a gathering are sufficient in themselves to generate whole epochs of new dynamic movement among Africans.

It is the ideological theme of all the Congress's activities that all Africans are part of the same racial, cultural, political, historical, emotional body, and that even though some of us might see the progress of the whole as being achieved in one way, and others of us might have more special views, it is still the duty of the body to be in constant intercommunication one part with the others, or there will be minimum movement all around. This is the basis of what Maulana Karenga called "Operational Unity": Unity without Uniformity. It is this way of thinking that allows the Urban League's National Executive Director to exchange views frankly with a Minister Farrakhan or a Kenneth Gibson to reflect on the concepts of more orthodox Pan Africanists. There is health in such an approach. It is much like the united liberation front of the Vietnamese people, called "Viet Cong," in which all walks of Vietnamese people unite themselves, whether they are Catholics, or Buddhists, socialists or speak of free enterprise, unite themselves around ideas which are mutually beneficial to all, ideas that finally will liberate all. So that like the old Fanti intellectuals, they can then have "peace" . . . peace in which they can sit and listen to their own varied counsels, and eventually shape a future designed to enhance the lives of all Vietnamese.

The exchange of varied blackness, the coupling of seemingly antithetical approaches to national and international African liberation—these are the kinds of dynamic that are set up at such a meeting as the 1970 Congress, just as this spirit has been kept moving at each of the great Pan African Congresses of the past.

In the eleven workshops, which covered Black Technology, Economics, Education, Communications, Creativity, History, Law & Justice, Community Organization, Political Liberation, Social Organization, Religious Systems, the emphasis was placed upon the development of institutions. Since Africans can only defeat white supremacy by creating alternative institutions which in actuality will be the replenishment and reorganization of inert traditional African institutions (of course redefined by our confrontation with western traditions and technology, but African nevertheless, and able to deal in the contemporary world, and able to answer the needs of the contemporary African wherever in the world). We sought to answer the questions: What is a contemporary African Political Institution (the answer, in this case, was an International African Political Party able to run candidates for elections, build schools and housing and hospitals, or fight a war!), What is a contemporary African Economic Institution, and so on in each area. And the strongest sentiment heard at the Congress was that we had all passed through the time for rhetoric, that we had been steeled and inspired by the words of our leaders, but now we must be on the move for the actual transformation of the visible world. There was the feeling that revolution (actually the international liberation of Africans) was the causing of real change, not reference to change. And the revolutionary was he who actually brought change, not those of us who simply continue to say what is wrong but can bring no way of realistic change! And in the year that has passed since the Atlanta meeting, the talk at the various regional meetings has been about the continued creation of *prototypes*, realistic models, which can be exchanged and locally customized, upon which we might be building these critically needed institutions.

Even though the future of the organization called the Congress of African People is bright, it is nevertheless of great value simply to have been responsible for calling the Atlanta meeting, to initiate the seventies, and begin a new decade of continued struggle toward total liberation! The thousands of young and old Africans, neophyte and conservative Africans, all were bathed in the communal spirit of continued but renewed commitment. The last part of the sixties saw perhaps a divisive spirit among young and old Africans caused in no small part by attempts to reassert so-called "radical" European definitions into the African struggle. This cannot be done, with any benefit to Africans. Groups that fantasized about the overthrow of the American goverment brought about by coalitions of Europeans and Africans were themselves made to realize that it is only the movement of the International African Community that will be able to change this world. And the Congress was the gathering that represented this ideology and motive, no matter how diversely expressed, back to the world at large, at full strength. It demonstrated that for the next decade there have been real gains made through the analysis and study and practice of principles learned at the feet of our fathers, the great initiators and continuers of the Pan African tradition.

And as the seventies begin with the unsuccessful attacks of Europeans on Guinea and momentarily successful attacks on Uganda, as well as the continued harassment and oppression of those of us who call for African Liberation wherever else in the world, this present volume will provide a kitabu kweusi, a black book of direction for the decade to come, and hopefully past that. There will be more and more Pan African Congresses meeting until we meet with the frequency of a completely operational international political mechanism. There will be Congresses until we meet in Congress as one people, whether in Harlem or Johannesburg, whether resisting the oppression of Israelis or Quakers, one people, one flag, one leadership, one identity, purpose and direction.That is the vision of the Pan Africanist, and that is the duty and commitment of the organization called the Congress of African People.

IMAMU AMIRI BARAKA
NewArk, August 1971

Contents

BOOK I: SPEECHES

Hayward Henry

Twenty-seven-year-old chairman of the Congress of African Peoples. Hayward Henry is also a member of the Harvard University Department of Afro-American Studies and chairman of the National Black Caucus in the Unitarian-Universalist Church. He has been long associated with the push for black liberation during the sixties.

All power to African people now and forever more. . . . Now I want everybody to say that after me. All power . . . to African people . . . now and forever more. . . .

What time is it?

Nation time.

What time is it?

Nation time.

What time is it?

Nation time.

And why did we come to Atlanta? . . . to labor for a nation. Why did we come to Atlanta? . . . Why did we come to Atlanta? . . . Well, all right. . . . Now I want you to do one other little thing which I think is central to what we're here in Atlanta for this weekend. I want to deal with four brief areas of concern that are non-negotiable and unequivocal for our people's liberation, and I want you to repeat them after me.

African people must govern themselves.

African people must provide for themselves.

African people must respect themselves.

And African people must defend themselves.

Well, all right now. What time is it? (Nation time)

What time is it? (Nation time) . . . what time is it? . . . (Nation time) Well, all right.

I had to get that out of my system because a lot of brothers and sisters who heard that there was something called a Congress of African People said, all them foreigners are coming from across the ocean somewhere, and they didn't see themselves as part of the African world and did not necessarily see themselves as allied with the struggles of our people, wherever those struggles may be occurring locally, nationally and internationally.

But in the last three and one-half years of our struggle, we have indeed witnessed a very sharp, a very decisive turn. We're not always sure where we're going with that turn; we're not always sure that we have the answer; we're not always sure that we have the correct style and approach; that's why we create a congress, to bring ourselves together to do a critical analysis of what those new directions imply and the specific kinds of action that we as a people must take.

Just a word of background for those of you who are not aware. Several months ago a meeting was called in the city of Washington, D.C., in which better than 250 Black organizations were invited to plan the next steps which we as a people should take for our empowerment. And it was at that meeting in Washington, D.C., that several kinds of decisions were made. Number one, the international Black Power conference which was chaired by Brother Roosevelt Brown, the distinguished Roosevelt Brown, which was scheduled for July 8th was canceled because the government of Barbados placed restrictions on the scope and dimension of the conference: namely that Europeans or their descendants should attend. It is obvious that you cannot discuss Black Power in the presence of Europeans or their descendants, but it is also obvious that their representatives are sometimes present even when they are absent.

But nonetheless, that conference was canceled . . . the time for calling conferences was over. This is not a conference, Brothers and Sisters, this is a congress. And because that level of thinking was going on in the minds of those persons who were in Washington, D.C., we decided to pull what was the National Conference on Black Power and the International Conference on Black Power together, as a reflection of our awareness of a universal and international nature of our struggle.

We decided that we wanted to come to Atlanta, Georgia. Nationalism and Pan-Africanism would be our theme. Nation time and laboring for a nation would be our specific focus, and building institutions would be our direct mission.

And thus we spent the last three months meeting with people in Atlanta, planning, coordinating, to have this meeting come into existence. And many people said to us that we could not do it, they said to us, you cannot have a national meeting in three months' time. They said, you cannot have an international meeting in one year's time. And this is but the first day of this meeting, and all you beautiful African people are here, and of course we are especially glad that you are. But there were also many brothers and sisters who said that they didn't want anything to do with this business called a congress, because they were so sure that it would not happen. But when many people saw that we were for real, we were suddenly inundated with requests for involvement, participation and input, and by that time, we had made all of our basic decisions, and one of the major decisions which we made was to put together a coordinating committee, a committee that represented something, represented constituencies, mobilities, not just individuals, and I would like to read to you the names of the persons who are on the coordinating committee—those who are present and those who are not, and many of those who are absent are still in the process of planning for tomorrow and the subsequent days: The chairman of finance, Brother Richard Traylor, who is the administrative executive of the Black Affairs Council; the chairmen of program, Brother Roosevelt Brown and Brother Imamu Baraka, who most of you know as LeRoi Jones; head of public relations, Uniworld Group Inc., Bill Cherry and Sonny Carson from Brooklyn.

By the way, if any of these brothers are present, would they please stand until I have completed this list. I know Brother Roosevelt Brown is here, so he will stand up. . . . I see he did an African . . . on us, he disappeared.

And on the national coordinating committee from Atlanta, Brother Julian Bond, Honorable Brother Bond, who was the chairman, and Brother Father Bob Hunter, who has done such a tremendous job that I would like to personally thank him . . . and other members of the coordinating committee equally as distinguished. For instance, Brother Dr. John Cashin, who we affectionately call Governor Cashin because he's running against that little Hitler down there in Alabama. You'll certainly be hearing from him again, as one of the luncheon speakers. Brother Carlton Goodlett, who is not here, who is an editor and publisher; Brother Lou Gothard of the United Service Organization (U.S.O.) who is also the chairman of exhibits and concessions. I'm sure you'll see him running around from time to time, but he may not be up here on the podium at the moment. Brother Leonard Harrison, affectionately known as "Shubeedoo" from that great wilderness in Kansas. Where is Shubeedoo? He did an African thing too. Brother Dr. J. L. S. Holloman, immediate past president of the National Medical Association; Brother Reverend Jesse Jackson, head of

Operation Breadbasket, who will be with us as a major speaker; Brother Hugh Lane, who is not here at the moment, but he is the executive head of the national scholarship and service fund for Negro students, commonly called NSSFNS; Brother John Lewis, who was former chairman of S.N.C.C. and who is presently executive director of the voter education project, and of course a very lovely and charming lady who we know as Queen Mother Moore, who is not on the podium at the moment, but you certainly will see Queen Mother. And you have no doubts that that is Queen Mother.

Brother Zayd Muhammad, who is not on the podium at the moment because he is the brother who is chiefly responsible for securing our meeting; Brother Gerald Robinson, formerly executive head of the Black Caucus of the National Association for Community Development; Brother Chuck Stone, who is the immediate past president of the National Conference on Black Power and is a noted author about matters relating to Black politics; Brother Imamu Sukumu, who is head of the National Involvement Association based in San Diego; Brother James Varner, who is with us. Brother Varner, where are you? All right, and Brother Preston Wilcox of Afram Associates and the National Association of African Educators.

Now let me give you some brief information about the kinds of decisions which were also made in reference to what kind of meeting we wanted here in Atlanta. Basic to our decision was that what we wanted to do was to pull together intensive problem-solving sessions as the real heart of this meeting. Problem-solving sessions in which brothers and sisters will engage in problem definition and problem solution, not rapping for freedom.

We wanted to put together the kind of workshop which would be headed by persons distinguished in our struggle in that particular area, and workshops which would truly offer some reasoned attempts to plan and strategize for liberation, rather than to continuously act to crises, although to be Black is to be in a state of perpetual crisis.

The workshops which we put together were in the following areas, and if the coordinator or co-coordinator is present or on the podium, would he please stand.

The area of economic autonomy, and of course this is all on your program as you register, which will deal with land, labor and housing. Brother Robert Brown who is head of the Black Economic Research Center and Brother Dunbar McLaurin who has coined the phrase called ghettonomics. I know Brother McLaurin is here; he perhaps may be meeting with his resource persons.

In the area of political liberation, including electoral politics, repression, genocide, relationship to liberation struggles on the continent, the isles or wherever, Brother Imamu Baraka, who was principally responsible for the recent victory in Newark.

In the area of . . . well all right, come on y'all (APPLAUSE) . . . in the area of creativity the very distinguished Brother Larry Neal whom I am sure you have read, if not read, read of.

In the area of religious systems, the distinguished Black nationalist theologian, Reverend Albert Cleage, who due to illness . . . will not be with us, but fortunately that workshop was to also be coordinated with Brother Dr. James Cone, author of the book called *Black Power and Black Theology.* Brother Bill Land, who has principally been organizing shrines of the Black Madonna, will also be a coordinator there.

The area of education which will be dealing with what education means to Black people in terms of our protection, survival, liberation in the forms that it should take is being chaired by Brother Preston Wilcox who is also a member of our coordinating committee.

And the area of history we are most most most pleased with because we got perhaps two of the most, and I'm going to take a political risk in making this statement—two of the most distinguished Black historians in the country, who also have three of the other most distinguished Black historians in the country as persons in their workshop. I am of course referring to the noted historian, Brother John Henrik Clarke . . . and Brother Yosef ben-Jochannan . . . and those of you who think that history is dull and irrelevant, you ought to go to that workshop and learn something.

The area of law and justice, which deals with survival, institutions, prisons, narcotics, which will also be dealing with setting up mechanisms for Black people to survive, the legality and oppression of this system, and will also concentrate on the particular role of Black lawyers to Black political activists and will deal with how we arbitrate conflict in the Black community, is being headed by the very distinguished lawyer, Brother Ray Brown.

And of course we've got a new kind of workshop. Black technology. And those people who do not think that technology has anything to do with nation-building, but let them try to build a nation, they'll find out soon. . . . Oh, we don't have many technical friends tonight, do we? . . . Physics, engineering, chemistry, biological science, medicine, psychology, technology, etc., is being headed by Brother Ken Cave and I may point out that one of the things that that workshop will be considering is the feasibility of an Institute of Black Technology. . . . As you will read in the ideology statement, one of the principal concerns of that workshop will be how we develop total technical capacity of Pan-Africa wherever that is.

The area of communications and systems analysis—for those of you who don't know what that word refers to, it's simply information control. How do you generate and develop and interpret your own image of your own self to whomever you want to interpret it to will be headed by the distinguished Brother Lou House of "Black Journal," and the distinguished Brother Tony Brown of "Black Journal." . . . I see Brother Brown standing over there and of course the filming crew that is principally involved here is "Black Journal," so you can look for us after this congress.

The area of social organization which will deal with social institutions, family, American institutions, brothers and sisters, their roles, responsibilities in relationship to each other, the welfare of the community is being headed by Sister Amina Baraka and being co-coordinated by Sister Brenda Dash.

In the area of community organization which will be dealing with general community organizing and principally how we develop united Black fund-raising, to fund Black organizations ourselves wherever those organizations are in our communities or countries, and organizing brothers and sisters in some of the more difficult and oppressive areas will be headed by Brother Lou Gothard.

At the moment I will not continue the comments that I had intended to make. I will return after the next person, Dr. Ralph Abernathy has come before us.

Ralph Abernathy

Clergyman and civil rights leader. Previously Financial Secretary and Treasurer for Southern Christian Leadership Conference. Recipient of numerous awards. Associated with Dr. Martin Luther King, Jr., in all phases of nonviolent civil rights movement, including nine jail sentences. Presently Chairman of the Southern Christian Leadership Conference.

Brother Yates, the Congress of African Peoples and my Brothers and Sisters: It gives me a great deal of pleasure this evening to bring greetings to you assembled here for this magnificent gathering of brotherhood in the city of Atlanta, and I am pleased that this first Congress of African Peoples is taking place here in the south and in Atlanta for several reasons.

Firstly, Atlanta is a city where black people have struggled and toiled with age old racism, segregation and discrimination for more than 300 years.

Secondly, Atlanta is a city where young black people rose up and paved the way for student activism throughout the south in the early '60's. It was in Atlanta where the world acclaimed black scholar, W. E. B. Du Bois studied, educated and toiled for his people.

It was in Atlanta that Sherman marched down his Peachtree Street and those of the confederacy realized that it was all over. It is in Atlanta today that we come for this congress.

It was in Atlanta that the foremost prophet of the twentieth century, Dr. Martin Luther King, Jr., was born, but it will be here in Atlanta that we will say to a racist society that you may have been able to kill the prophet, but I'll be dogged if you will kill the dream.

It was in Atlanta on last evening that Muhammad Ali established the fact that he is the heavyweight champion of the world.

And that as black people we will not sit idly by and let a white racist establishment rob him of that title. He won it in the ring, and if he loses it he will lose it in the ring. He established last evening that he has more power in his fists than the white man has in his bank downtown.

Indeed, it is Atlanta today where black people with a sense of dignity move on rapidly as never before for brighter horizons. Atlanta is the hub of the southland. The southland where Mr. Eastland resides; where Strom Thurmond lives, where Herman Talmadge and Dick Russell reside. Those are the individuals who must assume the major responsibility for the murdering of our black brothers ten thousand miles away from American soil. We serve notice on you that we will put an end to war Mr. Thurmond, or we will adopt the Abernathy draft system, and that is we will start drafting from 65 years of age down, rather than from 19 years of age upwards. And once fabulous Ronald Reagan of California; Strom Thurmond of South Carolina; Dick Russell of Georgia realize that they may have to protect themselves with a grenade in a foxhole ten thousand miles away, you're going to hear a different message all the way from Tricky Dick's White House to Lester Maddox' state house.

It is here in the southeastern United States where more than 51 percent of the black population still resides. We have sweated and toiled and we have died on this good earth and it is my opinion that if there is to be any salvation for the American society, if there is to be any new breath blown into this destructive civilization, if capitalism as a system is not to continue to ravage three-fourths of the world, then black people who have chopped the cotton, tilled the soil and suffered injustice, intimidation and assassination will be the new and creative leadership in the vanguard of America's salvation. We gather here today at the threshold of a new decade, and we serve notice on America that it will never be in the future as it has been in the past.

We gather here today with the fires of human hatred and violence fresh on our memories. We gather here today with mementos of the gallant and saddened struggles of a heroic people. Yes, we enter this decade of the '70's witnessing ominous signs of decay, destruction, and brutal inhumanity to man. These are destitute and crisis-packed times. We as a people are in need of expression of solidarity and of unity. Black people and poor people. People of the third world must gather together to exchange ideas, to seek out new directives and understanding. We must build a new movement that encompasses black Baptists as well as Black Panthers. Black preachers as well as black teachers. And then we must move beyond these shores. We must find the formula for unity that encompasses the concerns of our brothers on the African mainland and our brothers who struggle daily for life in southeast Asia. We must find the unity that encompasses the chicanos and the Puerto Ricans.

Indeed, we must find the unity that encompasses the wealth of struggle of all oppressed people.

Yes, these are days to grapple, to find a true spirit of solidarity and of common thought, but let the record show that there will not be unanimity this week, for it is cruel to expect unanimity from black people when you have never achieved that even with the white people of America.

Through the years many deceptions, tricks have been played upon our people, tricks like the Emancipation Proclamation. Separate but equal education. Fight a war and win your freedom. But each time we've come back, we've said, we know that there is something better. It is for that something better that we meet here in Atlanta for tonight.

John Cashin

An Alabama dentist, who is founder and chairman of the Black National Democratic Party of Alabama, which captured effective control of three Alabama counties: Greene, Macon, and Lowndes. Cashin ran for governor of Alabama and polled 16 percent of the statewide vote in a campaign against George Wallace, designed primarily to get out the vote for other NDPA candidates.

I feel it is necessary to give a little history of the National Democratic Party of Alabama, a party which is now on the ballots of Alabama only because we began working at an early stage, perhaps a lot earlier than some other of our brothers and sisters. It was impossible to get along and work within the white system, especially when *they* control the party system. And in the State of Alabama we had a one-party system. That one-party system saying white supremacy for Alabama.

The major accomplishment over the years was to beg and finally force . . . the regular Democratic party to remove the white supremacy motto from its emblem. So that's just one minor consideration in what may or may not lead to this political revolution.

But now given that which I've told you, the reason for it was that we found very early that we could not work for liberation and equality of our people within a white-controlled institution, so then came the idea that we would have to do it ourselves, and this is a lesson . . . within ourselves. The sooner we learn that and really know it and believe it, we could then get down to business, because until you get to that realization you are wasting your time, believe me. Your salvation comes from within yourself. Institutions that control . . . and its . . . the elimination of white tokenism in the State of Alabama. It was not an easy fight at all. As a matter of fact, I wish I had one of these pins—I had a little button with the eagle symbol on it—I have quite a few of the things in my briefcase with the emblem on it. The emblem on the ballot is an eagle.

This was our first real big fight; when we chartered the National Democratic Party of Alabama, we felt that we had to have an emblem on the ballot, our home. We started off trying to get a donkey to ally with the national Democratic party, but through some means of co-option and chicanery we were told that we could not use the donkey emblem because of a white group trying to subvert what we intended to accomplish. Actually there was no cooperation with us. They pretended that they were our friends, and were asking to be included in the chartering of the National Democratic Party of Alabama and when they found out that our plans for filing our party and our charter and our emblem with the necessary forms were to take place on December 15, 1967, would you believe that on December 12, 1967, they got together a hastily contrived donkey emblem, took it down to the Secretary of State, and when we went down to file we found someone else already had the donkey. Now that's the kind of friends we had.

However, we went back and got another emblem and on January 12th, we filed with an eagle, and that eagle has become symbolic. That eagle cost us two Supreme Court cases to be certain that it went on the party of the—on the ballot of the State of Alabama. And the reason for the great fight, your own emblem on that and having your own party on the ballot, is that it's the only real answer to this tokenism. It's the only real solution because until we get our people into office wholesale, our problems are not even going to begin to be solved. As I said, the white-approved tokenism will take another hundred years to run its course and be of any practical benefit whatsoever. Even though Blacks are elected to office, to public office with both Black and white support, most of the time we find when they're elected along with white support they give their loyalty to the whites who supported them and forget about their identity with and their responsibility to the Black community.

But, however, as I said, the eagle on the ballot by-passes the hundred years of separate but equal education. I don't guess I should say the hundred, let's just say the hundred years or seventy-five years. Anyhow, generations of a separate but equal educational system that has resulted in my state or plantation an educational level among Black people of somewhere between the third and the fourth grades. For whites it's not that much better, but it's nearly twice—better than twice. The educational level in Alabama for whites is somewhere between the eighth and ninth grade. This means of course that our people are functional illiterates through no fault of their own because we did not have control of the educational process. It was whites who deliberately created the situation of what they thought was a completely ignorant electorate, one that could be easily molded and controlled, controlled through ignorance and fear and intimidation. However, that little eagle on the ballot by-passes all of that. The 1965 voting act where the illiteracy tests were thrown out and all a person had to do was mark an X—he didn't have to be able to read or write or even sign his name—the Federal registrar put masses of Black people on rolls who were truly functional illiterates.

And now, indeed, they can cast their votes in the right way for their own people. For their own salvation, because they don't have to read or write, all they have to do is see the eagle emblem on the ballot and mark X under it. That's a beautiful way. Because if we nominate our candidates to the ballot by county convention, we don't have the right to hold a primary at state expense. We nominate by county convention and state convention. The masses of the Black people in Alabama do trust that eagle party leadership despite what you have heard about the great boosting among the Alabama press of certain so-called Negro political leaders. The white press fails to mention the fact that these political leaders, these Negro political leaders that they're boosting are in the main state employees who have collected their living from the State of Alabama, every month there's been a paycheck from the State of Alabama, and I'm well tuned in to the psychological phenomenon of he-whose-bread-I-eat-is-whose-song-I-sing.

But of course we don't control the press in Alabama, we don't control the news media. It's up to our brothers and sisters outside to understand the situation that we are in, but believe me, our people do have confidence in the leadership of the National Democratic Party of Alabama which puts representative candidates on the ballot.

Since 1969 we had the results of our second Supreme Court case. Our first case came as the result of the Secretary of State's disqualifying all of our candidates after we failed to be recognized at the 1968 Democratic Convention in Chicago, if you want to call that a convention. I'm beginning to wonder some about the Democratic party—and the national Democratic party or Democratic National Committee or whatever you want to call it. I'm beginning to have some doubts of whether or not it can indeed respond to the needs of our people and perhaps a third party of course may be the answer. I don't know yet, but right now we know what our course has to be. As I said, they used the nonrecognition by the national party in Alabama as justification for disqualifying all of our candidates, so we went to the Supreme Court. And two weeks and two days before the general election, in November of 1968, the Supreme Court ruled us on the ballot, and we had two weeks and two days to put together a statewide campaign; we had to come up off the floor. As a matter of fact, we had to come out of a hole, because we were exhausted, physically, financially, emotionally, just drained of any strength. Well, however, that Supreme Court decision on October 19, 1969, yes, 1968, put fifty-eight local candidates of the National Democratic Party of Alabama on the ballot. In an heroic effort, we put together a statewide campaign, and would you believe we elected twenty-four of those fifty-eight candidates the first time out?

And that's what the straight ticket voting will do. It would have been impossible to mount an individual campaign over such a short period of time. Now for the second Supreme Court case. After the Supreme Court had ruled us on the ballot, two weeks and two days before the general election, in a county called Greene County . . . we had our strongest slate of candidates. We had four candidates for County Commission, which is the controlling board of revenue in Greene County, and two candidates for the Board of Education which controls the biggest budget, since the Board of Education in Greene County is a large business. It's close to a two-million-dollar budget for the year, the largest business in the entire county. We had already had one Black man on the Board of Education, a Reverend, and if we elected those two, we would have had a three-to-two majority, and if we elected the four County Commissioners, we'd have had a four-to-one majority; both of them are five-member boards.

So the probate judge of Greene County in an historic decision, in order to counteract our move, just plain and simply left the candidates off the ballot. Now that is really something, isn't it? That's what white power is. Just plainly and simply left the candidates off the ballot, despite the Supreme Court ruling. Our people called me on election day and said we don't have anybody to vote for. I said there must be some mistake, check all the districts; they checked every ballot, every voting place, and sure enough they were not on the ballot. So to get to the head of the matter, I called the probate judge's office and he said, "You are right, they're not on the ballot." And I said, "But the Supreme Court ordered them on there." He said, "Have you seen that court order?" and I said, "Yes, indeed. Not only do I have a copy of it—I just finished reading it before I called you." And he says blatantly and emphatically, in probably the most disrespectful manner that one could say in his dignified position, "Well I have a copy of that court order too and in my opinion they're not legally qualified."

So, off to the Supreme Court again we went, and in a special ruling, March 25, 1969, we were told that indeed a new election had to be held in Greene County, Alabama. Now I'm developing this so you can realize the turmoil and the strife we went through and you'll see the end results, because when the Supreme Court ordered a special election on July 29, 1969, where the NDPA, the eagle candidates, had to be on the ballot, and of course the white candidates were on the ballot under the emblem of the rooster, the regular emblem of the rooster. We had the classic confrontation in Greene County between white and Black and we got our votes out in a rash of straight ticket balloting; we swept the election, six out of six, just in marking those X's we swept it just like that. And this is the only county in this country that is really now controlled by Black people other than perhaps you might want to say Macon County, Alabama, which has a kind of coalition—kind of a Black and white thing. But I think they're learning their lesson now. It might be a little late, but they're learning their lesson now.

Hancock County, Georgia, I understand, has a semblance of control but I understand that the white members of their board seem to be causing quite a bit of trouble. If indeed they are, they're carrying through the same pattern that they are in Greene, because the remaining whites on the boards we find we can't get along with them. We find again that the two out of the five on the Board of Education are constantly at work to frustrate whatever programs the three, the Black majority, intend to impose and tend to elicit. We find that the one remaining white board member of the Board of County Commissions is the probate judge indeed and because he is the only carry-over from the preceding administration, he's the man that signs the paychecks, and he is the titular chairman of the Board of County Commissioners. He has used the same probate judge that left the men off the ballot. He has used his position to attempt to frustrate anything and everything that the Black members, the Black majority of that board tries to effect.

Now I want this to become a lesson to you. Because as I said, we have tried at every step to get along with these people. We tried back in the '62, '63, '64 and '65 era. We tried to nudge our way into the mainstream; we tried to, shall we say, take our place by, shall we say, allowing the moral suasion of the great moral leader, the spiritual white leaders to prevail. But however, that didn't do one bit of good. They exposed themselves, hypocritical from the very beginning. We could not crack it, we had to go our own way. And now finally have majority control in a county that is 81 percent Black by their own figures (81 percent Black by their own figures means it's closer to 90 percent Black).

Where we have a functioning majority on the boards of governors, they still attempt to frustrate everything we do, so what's the cure for that? The cure for that is another election, and it's going to be cured on November 3rd, 1970, because we will have a Black probate judge who will be chairman of the County Commission. He should be around here sometime today. We're also going to take those other two positions on the Board of Education. Then we can fight among ourselves, with a Black majority fighting against a Black minority, but anyhow the decision will be made by Black folks. And again I would like to say (I've said it to so many of you as individuals, but I want to emphasize the position that we are taking) that I am not just a candidate for governor trying to satisfy myself on some wild ego trip of running against the monster, George Wallace, in Alabama. Surely it's a job that needs to be done, so I've got guts enough to do it.

Okay, so much for my ego trip. What I am saying is that I am leading a ticket, a wholesale soul folks. We've got over 175 candidates scattered out all over the state. Our major effort is going to be in twenty-one counties in the state, twenty-one counties and there are twenty counties in Alabama that have a 50 percent or better Black population, along the east and the west Black belt, right across the center of Alabama. These are the counties in which we are active in order to make representative government a reality. I am leading a ticket of grass roots Blacks and believe it or not, there are a few whites we have too. Those who have accepted their role, and accept the fact that they're definitely or inextricably linked to the destiny of the freedom of the Black man. However, the whites are not in control. It's very important. They are working within the structure, working within the system of the eagle party but they are not in control. They do not determine the course of the eagle party.

I would like to say to you something about the importance of taking over courthouse government. Now there's a fairly good chance that I can beat George Wallace as the governor of Alabama, there's a fairly good chance. If our strategy goes through, the main thing we need is money right now to effect our strategy. We do not need sophisticated theoreticians to come down and tell us how we can run the thing though. If any of you would wish to come and take part in this occasion, of November 3rd, 1970, you would be quite welcome. As I said, we have been on the firing line long enough to know, as I said before, that our salvation truly will come from within ourselves, and we can use your help. . . . You'll have to go along with our strategy because we have survived and we have the measure of wholesale success that exists no other place in this country, regardless of what you hear about other parties, regardless of what you hear about Black empowerment, regardless of what you hear about nation-building. The only place that it is truly alive is in the Black belt of Alabama. Now understand that. Grass roots people who have learned a lesson under the most trying circumstances, the most hostile circumstances that exist in this entire nation. Freedom has taken root and is growing right now. If you wish to be a part of it, please, we welcome all of the help that you can give. We're not going to be so arrogant as to say that we cannot use your ideas, but we are saying that overall strategy dictates that we must stick to our original strategy of getting out people to organize communities, to get them registered to vote, and this is the essence of any election, getting the people registered to vote. And getting them out on election day, so that they can mark that one X. This way we're doing it wholesale.

Kenneth A. Gibson

First Black Mayor of Newark. Formerly a city engineer, Gibson has been long active in civic activities to better the lives of Black people in Newark.

Thank you very much.

I want to thank all of you for the really tremendous welcome that I've received and I want to thank you all for being here because I consider it an honor to be invited to speak to you, for many reasons.

First of all when I looked at the program and saw what you were trying to do, I felt that you really must have thought something of—either Ken Gibson, or NewArk, New Jersey—to invite me down here. I looked at all the distinguished guests, all the distinguished Steering Committee, and all the distinguished participants. And I wondered whether or not it was Ken Gibson you were inviting or whether it was just the Mayor of NewArk, or whether or not you were just inviting another Black man. I came to the conclusion that you were inviting a new Black mayor, so I accepted on that premise.

I want to talk to you just briefly about one or two things. I'll start off with one, dealing with my campaign in the city of NewArk. I ran for mayor in the city of NewArk in 1966, for the first time. And in our city you get on the ballot by petition. That means, you get signatures of registered voters and that qualifies you to run for mayor. There's no primary. You get enough signatures, you're on the ballot. So we don't have one or two candidates for the mayor of NewArk, we have six, like we had in 1966, or we have seven, like we had in 1970. Imagine seven candidates for mayor of the city of NewArk!

We had a very strange campaign. It really began with the Black political convention that was run by the Black community and the Puerto Rican community in November of 1969. I've told you this because I think you should get a lesson from it. We ran a convention to select, to pick candidates—Blacks and Puerto Ricans—to run for mayor and all council seats. We didn't have a candidate for every seat, but we tried. Imagine the Blacks and Puerto Ricans getting together to select candidates. This is what happened in NewArk, New Jersey.

Of course I came out of the convention as the candidate for mayor, and we had candidates for the councilmen seats. What has happened is that I have become mayor, and listen, three Black candidates were elected to NewArk City Council because of that unity—because of that convention, and because we didn't allow people to separate us during the campaign.

And I want to indicate to every one of you who intends to get involved in political organization to remember that trick. What they want to do is get you to organize in a disorganized fashion. When you get yourselves together they gonna come to you and tell you how bad the guy is down the street—because he combs his hair different than you; because he may dress different than you; maybe he goes to a different church than you; then maybe, he doesn't go to church at all. But if he can be used in the Black political organization that you form, you better use him because they're not going to help you one way or the other.

Now Brother Malcolm X said, "We better get into the closet and settle our differences." Because, "We don't catch hell because we are Baptist or Methodist, or Catholic or Muslim, you catch hell because you are Black." Then if you forget that, you're going to end up with a very strange situation.

Any of you that sleep through the message may have to continue to sleep on like Rip Van Winkle because you'll never wake up. People had better stop dreaming in our society, stop talking about dreams. This is a real world we live in; and the only reason you sleep is to rest so you can fight some more the next day. You don't go to sleep to dream and think about a better world that doesn't exist. You better get rid of those dope-pushers in your communities because they're selling you a dream too, and trying to keep you asleep while you're walking around. Sleep at night, then they give you a pill so you can sleep all day. Get rid of the dope-pusher, as Bernie McCain says, "if you have to move on them yourself." Now I've said throughout my campaign in the city of NewArk that you can't sleep because sleeping in our society gets you no place. But I ended most of my speeches by saying quite frankly, "If you gotta sleep, sleep; but the only thing that comes to a sleeper is a dream."

You know, I got two written speeches here: one, written by a fellow in NewArk, and another written by one of my aides in Atlanta. I haven't read a word from either one of them yet because I have a couple of things I have to tell you first.

You have to understand if you're going to talk about economics in our society that you do not achieve economic power by winning an election, you achieve political power. . . . Give me a more simple definition of self-preservation and survival than that. My father taught me that from the time I could understand what he was saying, and he never went past the first grade. And you don't have to go get no

B.S. and B.A., M.S., M.A. Ph.D. I think you ought to get it, don't get me wrong, but don't tell me you need them to understand what survival and self-preservation mean.

If any man allows his children to go hungry in the richest country in the world, while people are eating steak down the street, there is something wrong with him. In 1970 Black people will have to come to grips for the basic facts of survival. You have to understand that nobody is going to take care of you—of you, and people like you. We have to understand that nobody is going to deal with our problems but us. We have to understand that nobody is going to deal with the realities. And the realities and the basis that we are talking about—those realities—are the basis of nationalism. And so, nationalism is simply the expression of our recognition of the fact that in the final analysis it is Black people who must solve the problems of Black people. . . . You don't catch hell because you live on the East Coast, or West Coast or Alabama, or Mississippi. You catch hell because you are Black.

But we need an organization that is dedicated to political activity to organize around the form of a nation. This is a new Black politics. It is a Black politics focused around an internal form; focused inward on the development of relationships between ourselves and on the development of ways in which we can begin to assume responsibilities for our *own* survival. Focused in on the development of Nation. We need a Black political organization. Maybe we need a Black political organization along the lines of the Black political party of the one-party African state. We need an organization which will be a need for us to do as Malcolm X said—"Get in the closet and settle our differences."

So if Nation is the direction, then a Black political organization is a functional basis—a functional basis, an operational basis around which the Nation must begin to exist in real terms. In the 1970's if we are to survive, think about it, if you are to survive—*we*—you must become responsible for your own existence. We must recognize the reality—the reality—that in the final analysis only Black people will solve Black problems. We must recognize that internal organization—internal organization—in other words, Nation, is the necessary form of our survival.

Nation time! Nation time!

And I want to say in closing, Brothers and Sisters, that I'm going back to my home town tomorrow, Enterprise, Alabama—"Boll weevil capital." I'll tell you one thing about that trip. My father left Alabama becuase he had to leave, in order to survive. When I told him I was going back to Alabama, he called me up yesterday. My father never asked me for anything. He never had to. And I never had to ask him for anything. But he asked me for something yesterday—the first time in his life. He said, "Would you mind if I met you when you got there?" See, a lot of you young people don't know what it means. My father had to leave Alabama, and he left when he was making eight dollars a week, with a family to support, and no way to make a living.

The Mayor of Enterprise, Alabama, called me up yesterday and asked me could he, could he—he asked permission to have a press conference with me. And I told him, "Sure, that's all right. I don't mind sitting down and having my picture taken with you." . . . He said, "What time are you going to arrive?" I said, "I'll be arriving in Dothan at about ten o'clock in the morning." He said, "I'll have a car there with a driver to pick you up." I'm hoping that the chauffeur is white. Now those of you that are a little bit older understand what this means to my father. Because I'm going to take my father to lunch with the Mayor, and I'm going to let my father do the talking. . . .

Jesse Jackson

National Director of Operation Breadbasket, the economic arm of the Southern Christian Leadership Conference. From Chicago, Jackson directs the activities of Operation Breadbasket in sixteen cities. He is a veteran of the sit-ins and protest marches of the early 1960's and a protégé of Martin Luther King, Jr. Jesse Jackson responds to the urgency and impatience of the Black movement today with a militant but nonviolent call for Black power based on Black economic and political organization.

What time is it? What time is it? What time is it? What's happening? What's happening? What's happening? Land is changing hands. What's happening? What's happening?

Brothers and Sisters:

After our first Congress of African People I think that we ought to be quick to thank at the very outset the men and women, those known and unknown, who made it possible for us to be here tonight. The concept that we are an African people is not a freak term that was grown out of nothing, rather it came out of struggle and out of men and women who are dead. And I think that we ought to stop at this point before we go any further and whether your God is Allah, Yawa, or Buddha or Zen, or God Jehovah—it really doesn't matter—at least you can be respectful to the creative power that has brought forth these powers that have heightened our consciousness. And for Medgar and Malcolm and Martin, and indeed our twenty-seven Black Panther brothers who have paid the supreme sacrifice to make America wake up. I would like for us to take a minute to bow our heads in silent meditation for the lives that those brothers have given in order that we might be here tonight a more conscious people. Thank you.

Tonight I would like to deal with: "We got to go home but we can't take the short route." When some of us speak of going to Africa we speak of a ten-thousand-mile journey and we speak of the Pan American Airlines: That's the short way home. And some of us speak of Africa in terms of history. We speak of four hundred years ago, and the way some of us can jump across the pages of history without reading details: That's the short way home. In our new fashion outfits of dashiki and hair styles, ties and handshakes, we say we are tuned to what's going down, therefore, we are an African people; but I argue, Brothers and Sisters, that is the short way home.

The long way home, the long way home is psychological. The long way home is not new looks, necessarily, but it is a new mind. I want to bring a few facts to your attention now to premise my thoughts upon. One is that many of us say that there is a conspiracy going on by white people to eliminate Black people and we call that process genocide. But most of us are not very sure, but every once in a while now we get some evidence that some police have shot some brother. But you need to know that Pan-Africanism itself was a reaction to a program of genocide, not a feeling about genocide. In 1875, a group of white people got together. They didn't call it the white power conference. They didn't give themselves away like we have to do sometimes and expose our "hole card." They called it the International Geographical Congress. Sounds rather academic, and you were thinking that they were talking about geography in general. But in Belgium, Cecil Rhodes, whom the Rhodesians were later named after, along with King Leopold from Belgium was organizing a Geographical Congress to split up the territory of Africa. It was a program where white people actually got together and set out on their journey to conquer the African Nation. Militarily they succeeded. America wanted to get involved in the splitting up of Africa just as the French did in Algeria, just as the Belgians did in the Congo. It was not because of America's humanity that she didn't, but because America had seven million Black slaves on her own shores and at that time there were no airplanes. Having two oceans to protect her, developing isolationist policies and thereby deciding that rather than go through with the program of reconstruction that America would colonize the seven million slaves on this continent, America couldn't quite resist the total temptation and therefore sent an Ambassador, Sanford, to Belgium. That's how America got involved in the Belgium area. And even as late as the Belgian crisis in which Lumumba was involved, America was still involved as a result of the 1875 International Geographical Congress.

The name of the game, for those of us who think it's a new game, the name of the game has always been land! That ain't nothing, but land is unconscious energy and land ain't going nowhere. The first problem is not to say that land is what we need for a revolution; it is to organize the man on the land who is conscious energy. However, one of the first moves of these colonizers is to make the man on the land as unconscious as the land itself. If the man is walking on a cloud with his arms trapped with dope he is unconscious. Therefore, rather than the man who would be conscious subjugating the land, the man is swallowed by the land. Anybody who makes any contribution at all toward making us conscious is helping the revolution. Anybody who understands that we need land understands that we need a revolution. The question is, What are we willing to give up for it? It is easy to say we'll give up a life because we know that is not likely to happen as frequently as dealing with giving up cigarettes—poison weed; giving up liquor, giving up sleeping pills. Now you know every once in a while we have these Malcolm fits. We like to take us one or two of his quotes out of context, but I don't ever hear us talking about the discipline of his life style. I don't hear us talking about the new man.

Martin made his contribution because when he got his Ph.D. he didn't go to the National Council of Churches and start writing memos. He didn't go to New York and hide up in one of them offices and start writing books about things he thought about. He went directly to Alabama where many of our parents have run from. That's where he ran to. When the lady came with the hurt toe he didn't deal with the woman's toe—he dealt with the bus company.

Somebody says, "But Reverend, they are gonna lock us up." Say: "But until you come to grips with overcoming the fear of jail, police, court, money, bullets, you will not be conscious enough to take the land."

Many of us who escaped the Southern land, the Southern ground, to run up to the Northern sidewalks, ran because we had more consciousness and our consciousness was rent with fear, rent with fear! I want you all to hear me now. "I hope they win down South." "I went down there for a vacation." "The South sure is changing." Oh no, South ain't changing. Land don't move. Black people change. Revolutionaries are realistic. I don't know why Martin wouldn't tell them to shoot the white folks. When Martin went to Alabama, Black folks wouldn't talk back to white folks. Whipped our wives, refused to answer the questions of our children 'cause we was scared to confront white folks. Our individual fear was expressed as we talked under our breath. Therefore, the man brought forth a collective courage. So we marched en masse 'cause we was scared. See, I was born down here. I was taught to be scared of white folks and all my neighbors were taught to be scared. And when we asked, "Why can't we sit in the front of the bus?" others told us, "The back going where the front going." Others said, "The white folks don't want to sit with you, you don't have to sit with them." "The blacker the berry, the sweeter the juice." Furthermore, "Black is earnest." Niggers was scared of the crackers. Niggers was scared.

After about eight years of direct action, while our collective courage expressed itself, then our individual consciousness, symbolized in Malcolm, began to rise. For in the South you talked about Dr. King and you talked about Floyd McKissick and you talked about Jim Farmer. You talking about Black men leading crowds, confronting white folks at the door. But emerging in Harlem was a man by himself, a man with a new consciousness—but even that consciousness wasn't in the abstract. He was a part of the "Black Legacy." Now if we just want to trap all this great history of ours in one or two phrases and spend all of our time dealing with everything except why was Martin and Malcolm shaking hands and smiling while some of us were still trying to make a decision as to which one of them we wanted when both of them belonged to us. Why? Why?

I want to deal with going back home and Pan-Africanism because I believe it is the penultimate protection and security for our people. I believe strongly in Pan-Africanism. But before I began to talk about believing in it I had to study it. See, 'cause now when I was in South Carolina and I heard Pan-Africanism I thought they was talking about putting an African in a pan, see? I didn't know no better, see? Just like some of us still think that's what it means. In 1919, when they had the first Pan-African Congress it was called to stop the genocide. Pan-Africanism was conceived to stop genocide. That has always been the number-one agenda, number-one item on the agenda of Pan-Africanism. Between 1919 and 1945 they were only able to have five Pan-African Congresses because the same white European groups that had the Leopold meeting used government monies to break up and jail the Pan-African leaders. Ain't no accident. This is—tonight and this weekend—in reality the Sixth Pan-African Congress. We ain't just meeting in the abstract. We are standing on the shoulders tonight of great Black men.

Pan-Africanism was conceived to establish some means of cooperation between all the peoples of Africa and African descent. Pan-Africanism states that all the previous barriers of culture and language and politics and religion must fall and give way for our concern for race and descent. Pan-Africanism realizes that we are the sons and daughters of the raped and the rapist. Therefore, we are brothers and sisters, not by skin color (we go from high yellow, near white, to base black and some of us have gotten light enough to try to intimidate each other based on something we hated until about six months ago—black skin). But we ain't brothers and sisters based on skin color alone. We are brothers and sisters based on experience—common experience and common suffering. All of us have been embarrassed by whitey. Pan-Africanism would seek common aims of progress for all the Black Africans. But I think perhaps the most significant phrase that I found when reading Du Bois some time ago—Du Bois said, "We are going to have to work," and he said, "We are going to have to work in independent units." The beauty of Pan-Africanism is that it captures the best of two worlds, for on the one hand you live here and most of you ain't going to Africa. Most of you all was scared to come South. But to be planted here and realize your political and psychological and genealogical relationship in Africa means that you aim to be like great Africans of the past rather than great white men of the past. It means rather than having as your goal to be a little white man when you grow up that your goal become wanting to be a big Black man. That rather than being the headwaiter at the hotel or the chief bartender you want to be a king, you want to be a queen, you want to be an ambassador, you want to be a world leader. We in a trap right now 'cause we in the belly of the whale. Big white whale—we in his belly. Moby Dick Nixon—we right in his belly.

There are a lot of forms of escapism and one of the interesting forms of escapism is a rhetoric thing, this thing about, "I ain't gonna get involved because I don't want to be in the system." You think being unemployed means you ain't in the system? That just means you in the unemployed part of it! Ain't nobody talking African all day and sleeping in the Regency [a downtown Atlanta hotel] at night not in the system.

What time is it?

Now you might argue that since you believe in some creative form of democratic socialism that you don't believe in the system and that morally you are not of the system but economically you're in it. If you rode down one of these interstate highways coming over here you rode on the prerogative of the highway system. So let us not escape and categorize each other in bunches by saying: "He got a job, he in the system and I ain't," therefore you're self-righteous and clear. All of us are trapped. Now since all of us are trapped, now let all of us decide together how to get untrapped. One of the things that you have to recognize is that when you realize that you are in the whale rather than on the outside of the whale, you might have some advantages. That's why Brother Nyerere said not too long ago if you are concerned about coming to Africa even if you got a skill don't come with no attitude. He didn't even mention those who ain't got no skills. He didn't even discuss that. You all ain't hearing what I'm saying, are you? He say even if you got a skill, you know you can stick your arm down in the ground and take some oil out. Even if you can do that, don't come with no attitude; and he never did discuss at all them ain't got no skills; those that can't make sand and water into brick—he didn't discuss, those that can't mine oil, those that can't set up a communication system, those that can't set up a transportation system—he never did get around to dashikis and naturals. He never did get around to that.

Now I know that Pan-Africanism is so exciting until most of us are apt to try to escape to Africa rather than to go to Africa. I argue that there are four stages between us and Pan-Africanism (and I don't want to argue how many years it's gonna take because it's gonna be determined by what you do when you leave the congress). If you know that you can't really get to Africa by airplane and you really can't get there by boat but you must get there psychologically and intellectually, then at least you are on your way even without buying a ticket. There are four steps: The first step is *personalism.* The second step is *localism.* The third step is *nationalism.* The fourth step is *internationalism,* or to make it mellow—Pan-Africanism.

Let us deal with step one. When you look at Martin or Malcolm or Nkrumah, think of them in three categories. One category that you look at I call the three I's: intelligence, integrity and involvement. Follow me now: Malcolm was not a scolder, he was a scholar. You see, when he was a pimp nobody cared about him. When he turned his jail cell into a library and wrestled with the great ideas of history, he became significant. Martin had a Ph.D., a developed mind. Nkrumah a B.S. from Lincoln University; Bachelor of Theology; Master of Science from the University of Pennsylvania—lacks only his dissertation to get his doctorate. These men had developed minds: Castro, a lawyer and a Ph.D.; Che Guevera a Ph.D.; Ho Chi Minh, Ph.D.; Jomo Kenyatta, Ph.D.; Mao Tse-tung, three Ph.D.'s. Teach what you don't know and you can't lead where you don't go! I would have to be the first to admit I got a great concern for Black history. We need a sense of psychological self-esteem. We need to know where we came from. But if you don't attach a great feeling for Black future onto Black history, it's a trap.

Want you to follow me now: talking about personalism. Then they had integrity. They didn't talk one thing and do another. Malcolm didn't talk about stop using dope, he stopped it and then stopped other people from using it. That's integrity: closing the gap between what you say and what you do. Now if you been hanging around here twenty, twenty-five, thirty years and ain't smacked one, ain't shot one, ain't burned one building (when I was down home they used to say bugs in the bakery get a bun, bugs in me get none!), ain't no need for us to be asking each other about how mean we are. We got to love each other. Ain't no need trying to intimidate each other—looking mean. Looking mean don't make you meaningful. We got to love each other. That's why I ain't compromising on Black. On Black crime: Ain't no excuse for it. I believe in all them theories about the social causation of juvenile delinquency but if you are really mad, fight the man that castrated your daddy and raped your mama, if you are really mad. Murder is murder, lies is lies, dishonesty is dishonesty. Some of us should learn that lesson by now. Black man walked in Marcus Garvey's outfit one day and a few days later the C.I.A. had a spy on him. Black can be beautiful but it don't have to be. Dr. King went to give a Black woman an autograph one day, a few seconds later he had scissors in his chest. Black can be beautiful; it don't have to be. Malcolm stuck up his hand one day and said "Brothers," nigger blew him away. Black can be beautiful; it don't have to be. Mboya stepped out the drugstore one day, Black men blew him away. Black can be beautiful; it don't have to be. It's good as a race. It's poor as a religion. Once we deal with the whole category of intelligence, recognize that anybody really concerned about Black people would develop their minds, we go to deal with integrity. That's why when a man has integrity he can close the gap between what he says and what he does. If he can also think then he can lead.

Martin said what we ought to do is cut the margin of profit off the bus company. We ought to launch an economic cold war. Well, somebody say, "Well, Martin, what shall we do?" He say, "Well, my position is based upon having read history, that it is better to boycott even though we gonna have to suffer." Papers picked up nonviolence but it's really economic cold war. The bus company never recovered and he won the victory. What was the psychology, Brother? What was the psychology? How did he win? Some of us are so busy calling the movement feminine we can't deal with that in the national headquarters of the Ku Klux Klan. We won by figuring out a method of using the whitest words to trick him. Martin argued that men could ride the bus anywhere. Everybody said that's right. Black people can't; therefore, they are not considered people. All Black folk agreed. Some white folk agreed. Some disagreed. It's a nine-to-one ratio that makes you have a solid one and a split nine. We started the sitdown movement in 1960. We were looking for somebody to stand up in the South and tell it. Martin said people use the rest room when they have the urge. People use the library when they want to read. People use hotels when they are sleepy. All Black people agreed. Some whites agreed, some disagreed. Solid one split nine. That's what you call divide and deceive. I am talking about the need to get the intelligence and the integrity; then you can think—that's how them seeds open up. You ain't staying in the Regency tonight because white folks had a change of heart! You staying there because Stokely Carmichael and Rap Brown and Julian Bond and John Lewis offered their lives that Black people might have a right to stay there. Hell, it ain't no use in reading ancient Black history and don't know recent Black history. We'll be walking around ignoring beautiful alive Black people; spending all of our time worshiping great dead Black people. The people walking in our midst we ought to be glad to see. Some of them are tired now. Some of them shell-shocked. Some of them can't take it no more. When we were somewhere hiding and growing up. So we pick up where they left off—that's our responsibility to history.

When you look at Malcolm's integrity first you are talking about the ability to change his mind intellectually. We found him one place, he ended up another, because he was not scared to grow. He changed religions. He changed philosophies. His mind expanded. It takes an honest man to say I have changed, I have grown, I'm different now, and some of us are trapped in Malcolm part-one and won't deal with part-two.

What time is it? What time is it? All right.

Let's go to step two. If we got personalism, if we got intelligence, if we got integrity, if we are involved, what is step two? Localism. Let's look at Gary, Indiana, or Cleveland, or Newark. Most of you here are familiar with Amiri Baraka, and I think that perhaps if you would deal not just with his poetry but his politics you might see why Ken Gibson is Mayor of Newark tonight. Brother Baraka and I had a meeting in Philadelphia, trying to figure out how we could put together a convention in the Black community—to bring off solidarity. Then Brother Baraka flew to Chicago and brought Ken Gibson with him. We had several meetings there. Then the group of us flew to Newark and had meetings there. What were we discussing? How did we pull Newark off? Remember Du Bois said if you want to get engaged in Pan-Africanism you got to start where? With independent units. Newark is a unit. Cleveland is a unit. Gary is a unit. Is your unit organized? Have you taken over your unit? Are you escaping the government, talking 'bout the man can do it all? Talking 'bout we can win? You got a choice. If you got your personalism and you really ain't scared of the man you will seize the government rather than have a seizure before you get to it. Seize it. Take it over. Brother Baraka said, "Reverend, I'll tell you, I think we got a tough problem on our hands." And I said, "I don't think it's too tough 'cause we got a majority of Black people." He said, "No, say we got a majority of Negroes and colored people and they ain't ready to take on Addonizio 'cause some of them scared of themselves and some of them scared of each other and mostly all of them scared of white folks. How can we develop a program to seize Newark?" I said, "Well, Brother, maybe we ought to deal first with some unkind realities." Listen to me now, I said "some unkind realities." Most of us can't organize 'cause we don't want to deal with the truth about where our people are. See, you got to deal with where we actually are and then deal with where we got to go.

Now point one: The slave child referred to as colored, or Negro—sometimes as Black—got five basic characteristics. Don't care what community you in—whether you in New York, Seattle, Miami or Texas—number one: We are scared. Uh huh. You think I'm lying? Go on out there to take the man and see how many follow you. Christians, start attacking Jesus too fast! Conservatives, let one of us get a house *and* a car. Patriotic, let Black radicals start burning flags! And Democrats, let somebody come through as our savior in the form of a Republican. Let him come. Now I didn't say that's good, I said it's real. Scared, Christian, patriotic, conservative, and Democratic. Now your job might have to be to reverse all of that but you first got to know that that's where he is. So then Baraka said, "Well, we got to deal with the fact that them preachers got our people and I don't dig preachers." I said me neither. I say me neither but if we want Newark and they got the people we got to get them. So the people in Newark were in three categories. I'm talking about localism. They were either in church, in school, or at the ball game. So, Baraka—since he had his personalism, since he was secure and since he wanted Newark—he went to some churches; went to some schools; and went to some ball games. He went to where the people were. You can't be so hung up in your thing till you can't go where the people are. You got to go where the people are.

Now let me move on to nationalism 'cause that word was thrown around so long I thought nationalism meant wearing a robe. I didn't know it was an economic concept. I mean I just didn't know no better. If you get your local unit in Newark; in Cleveland; and East Orange; in Fayette, Mississippi; you are ready to join the train of nationalism. In other words, if you get your localism—your independent unit—and hook it up to a locomotive you are ready for "Nation time." Don't be talkin' 'bout "Nation time" if you ain't organized your unit. And if you're hangin' around the Black community in America and you don't like Whitney for one reason, and Roy for another, you don't like Ralph for another, you don't like Huey for another—when you finish ain't nobody left but you. A strong personalism will give up some of this bullshit to organize the necessary. The necessary. (I'm sorry, Queen Mother, I meant animal defecation. I didn't mean to say bullshit.)

Nation time!

What do we do? First, we observe the weakness of the enemy. Now, if you're in the belly of the whale, don't go running around up in the whale bluffin' when he got all them various organs to squeeze you and can't nobody else in the belly help you. If the man gives you thirty years that just means he will see you in the year 2000. That's what that means. If the man breaks in and shoot you at five o'clock in the morning that just means we get mad and give you a "rep" in death; but that's all we can do. It ain't that we don't love each other but we are in his belly and that's reality. Hell, Russia won't take him on in a hot war. That don't mean Kosygin is scared. It means he has faced the military reality that this man can bury Russia and is crazy enough to do it. Mao Tse-tung won't take him on with nine hundred million

Red Chinese. Don't mean he scared, that he won't. It means he's facing a reality. So don't let the man always call your manhood by setting you up and you kill one of them and they kill forty of us and then you feel gratified. Uh-uh! I want you all to hear me now. It don't mean we scared because we choose our method of warfare. Any intelligent man when he has a choice, chooses the ground he fights on and the technique. Now I said if you intelligent, follow me now. If I was in the whale's belly I wouldn't bluff him because the whale might get scared, or mad, and go out in deep water and start drinking it and if he does, that means you drown. That don't mean the whale drowns. That means he gets his systems flushed out. He'll keep on swimming. And now within a technological economy dealing with the economics of uselessness, where machines are replacing men, he can almost do it. That's why we must remain economically useful. We must have so much chemistry and physics tied up, so much communications and transportation tied up till he can't flush us out without destroying himself. If the man threw sixty million of us overboard four hundred years ago with his bare hands and with sticks, what will he do with napalm? Don't mean you scared! You know when I was in school we had to get our little "rep" together 'cause we thought man was muscle. . . . We didn't know it was mind. So we used to push little fellows around every once in a while, you know, just so we could keep our "rep." Like them fellows do. So every once in a while me and my "rep" be goin' down. Wouldn't have no P.R. or nothing, and see what you do is you do just enough to let him slap you so that you can justify kicking him, good. That's what you call suckin' a man in. Man suck us in close enough to our .22 and we say, pow! We kill one. Then he step back and say I told you that ain't good: tat, tat, tat! And we ain't got too much tat-tat-tat, see. We got to deal with that. But one thing you can do with the whale, you can grab him by his testes. You can grab him by his testes. You can grab him by his nuts. You can do that. You can do that. You don't have to worry 'bout Moby Dick's tail. You don't worry 'bout Moby Dick's head and all his big shoulders. If you just grab him by them fruits you can steer him to shallow water. Now, as I move on in my speech tonight I want to deal with what we can do with them vitals. What we can do with them fruits. What we can do with them.

Number one, they say we're twenty million. We are safely forty million. Who are we? Biologically we're the sons and daughters of the raped and rapists. Who are we? Psychologically we are confused because we are the well-trained people. Lot of funny kind of colors. African roots and American fruits and perverted by European brutes. Strange kind of people. That's why it's so hard to organize us.

Question is, Do we have power? Yes. We got more power relative to the American economy than Russia, China, or the European Common Market. I want you think with me now: We got more power relative to America's economy than Russia, China, or the European Common Market. Number one, we're the chief labor base. America is built on our shoulders. That is a strategic position. Russia ain't got that position; China ain't got that position. We are his consumer market. We buy the margin of profit of every major item produced and sold in America.

What am I saying? I'm saying that if you get your unit in Newark, and I get mine in Chicago, you get yours in Texas, you get yours in Seattle: One day somebody will say, "It's Nation time." One day. I ain't talkin' 'bout going home just saying, "*Habari gani*" and "*yebo.*" I'm talking 'bout go back home now and organize your economic unit.

And we say in forty colonies. I didn't say in ghettos. See, ghetto is a sociological concept that assumes that we are voluntarily staying somewhere for social reasons. We live in a colony based upon economic presupposition. And we ain't judged based on good and evil, intelligent or unintelligent—we've always been judged based on profit and loss, asset and liability. And once you get your economic definition, if in forty markets you say we don't want Dixie crystal sugar, you can run Nixon into Castro. Think about it! If in forty markets we don't buy a hundred General Motors cars, we can close down the plant. Margin profit ain't but 4 percent; they say we spend forty billion a year in the economy. We spend forty billion dollars but we got credit cards. That means in a nine-hundred-billion economy we spend about two hundred billion dollars. You snatch two hundred billion dollars out from under the American economy, it will collapse. But we have to do it by ourselves. When we move, the white people who are jealous of us and standing right across from us, they move too. So if Blacks strike so the poor white get mad and strike. Some might say that that ain't relevant. Yes it is, because of the forty million listed as poor, twenty-eight million are white. Numerically more white than Black, percentage-wise more Black than white, and they are fighting over jobs and we are fighting over jobs and there are no jobs—we can *back* into a revolution.

We can shake the foundation of the economy. (Talking about developed minds now.) If one day we say all white folks who building schools in our area can't build them no more—construction would be in trouble. If we say one day white bankers got to get out of the colony, the economy is in trouble. If we say one day we gonna build the rest of our roads—huh? I don't mind having two school districts, but it ain't just based on Black children sitting on one side of the tracks and whites on the other. If we have two systems I want our side of the budget and school board, not just the students. See, that's the liability.

See, in the city of Chicago, say we gonna keep two school systems—54 percent Black; well, time we say we want two school systems white folks say yes. Now since we gonna have one of the school systems, we want 54 percent of the budget and 54 percent of the school board and they say, "You all mind integrating with us?" You don't have to beg the cracker; if you get his nuts you don't have to beg him.

Lastly, internationalism. Internalism, really! You know we call it Pan-Africanism. That's gonna be when we stop dealing in lip service about Africa and start dealing in ship service with Africa. When you can talk to the leader of Tanzania and say we want your coffee in forty markets—nation speaks to nation; and inter-nation is internationalism. Ain't no wise African leader gonna do nothing but respect us when we can say, "Brothers in South Africa, we will boycott United Fruit Company until you get a liveable wage"; they say, "Well if you do that for us then we will allow you to come on such and such proposition,"—you can deal. You first got to work. First you got to work on your own mind, then your brothers in your independent units, then you got to hook up with the nation.

Finally all this don't mean a damn if we don't get a new value system. A new value system, Brothers, 'cause once we get Pan-Africanism we want to use it to save the world. We ain't no brutes. We want Mother Africa to be proud of her sons and daughters. It's always good when your parents can say my sons and daughters are helping somebody. I want Mother Africa to say that a new consciousness arose in my children across the sea. It's always good to go back home and say, "Mama you don't have to work no more"; say, "Daddy you don't have to work no more."

I see Brother Hatcher sitting over here. One Saturday morning while we were having our meeting, Dick [Mayor Richard] Hatcher's daddy came up and said: "We enjoyed this meeting this morning." Said, "Reverend, I want to give thirty dollars to Breadbasket."

I said, "Well we appreciate it very much."

He say, "I always told Dick that he wasn't inferior. I always told Dick he was somebody—even when I was on welfare. I always told my son, 'My son, don't you give up.' "

Then Mr. Hatcher said, "Son, I wanna give you thirty dollars. Will you please take this pen and write the check for me. I can't read nor write."

Y'all don't hear what I'm saying. I'm saying that from the least of us, in the wombs of our mothers, are sons and daughters, leaders and kings. Illiterate men and women producing mayors and kings! I want everybody to go to medical school that got the aptitude, but I want you to be a doctor for public health, not personal wealth. We want some new doctors. I want everybody who can to go to law school. We want lawyers who will secure justice, not just a judgeship. I want everybody to go to law school who can. I want preachers to go to seminaries and learn to prophesy not to profiteer. Train your minds but get your value system in order.

The reason I enjoyed looking at those women do their thing tonight, I'm proud of the fact tonight I was born in South Carolina. Georgeville Timberman [Senator Strom] Thurmond never meant for me to be able to read or write, and furthermore, even the colored people in our community didn't want me to be born because they say I was born out of wedlock. But my mama got a new new sense of identity long time ago and Mama said, "My son may be illegal by y'all's legislature and y'all's city council but he ain't illegitimate. He's real, he's mine, he breathes, he breathes." Yo baby may be illegal but he's not illegitimate, he breathes. That's why the mother from Hickory Hollow Swamp—she got to be a heroine, Mother Moore, because she was a woman who said, "Yes I got fourteen children and I'm not gonna destroy them through the distortion of abortion. Life is too beautiful. They may be illegal but they're not illegitimate—they got potential. I know y'all laugh at me," the woman said, "because my destitution, not my desire, my destitution has given me to prostitution. So what!

"My only commitment
To life is that
Since I got the will
And nature has given me the skill,
My baby will
Never see a hungry day."

What time is it?

Whitney Young, Jr.

Before his recent death, Whitney Young was National Director of the Urban League. A long-time veteran of the civil rights movement, he is the recipient of numerous awards.

Delegates and Friends to this Congress of African People: Brothers and Sisters all:

I first wish to commend the organizers of this congress for this effort to bring together people who may have come from different lands, even different cultures and languages, but who share together a common racial heritage and, most important, the common experience of being victims of oppression, exploitation and discrimination.

Our meeting together here in Atlanta is important, both in its substance and its symbolism; for I would hope by our very presence, in spite of shades of differences which may appear in our backgrounds, even in our ideologies, that we are saying loud and clear for the whole world to hear that we are through publicly bickering among ourselves for the entertainment of other folks—that instead, we are moving toward a new unity based on those things we have in common and our desire not just to survive, but to survive with equity and dignity for ourselves and for our children.

No more than this do we seek—but with no less will we be satisfied.

I am particularly pleased that we are joined in this conference by some of our African brothers and sisters who can share with us accurate and first-hand accounts of their problems and their opportunities—and most important, how they perceive the way in which Black Americans can be most helpful in their struggle to overcome generations of exploitative colonialism and imperialism. Here, in this conference, if we permit ourselves a minimum of arrogance and a maximum of humility we can all learn from each other. No one among us has a monopoly on wisdom. By sharing collectively from our background of actual experiences we can take a major step toward unity in objectives—and perhaps even in methods. I am confident that we can reflect a maturity that tolerates differences of opinion and that we can disagree without becoming disagreeable.

Because this is an international conference I anticipate much will be said about the continuing plight of Black citizens in America; and for those who will read and hear of these remarks and will retort with a certain degree of accuracy that however bad our plight is here, Black Americans are still far better off here than anywhere else in the world, I feel an important clarification is in order:

1) This is a claim that can be made with equal accuracy for all other ethnic groups in America—most of whom have been here a much shorter time than Black Americans. It is irrelevant and meaningless—because Black Americans measure their status and condition not by the standards of other countries, but by American standards. Our claim to this is undergirded by almost four hundred years of blood, sweat and tears in the building of this country; our contributions, our sacrifices—although American education and literature have consciously ignored them—are fact and legend.

2) Our expectations are greater, for America promised more to its citizens. America was born and created as a haven for the oppressed, "the tired, the poor, the lonely hearts longing to breathe free." Its Declaration of Independence, its Bill of Rights, its Constitution and all of its slogans rationalizing wars are filled with claims and cries of Justice—Freedom—Liberty—Equality. America promised to be the "melting pot" of the world.

The significant and continuing tragedy of America is that more than any other country it has, in fact, both in natural resources and manpower, the opportunity to live up to its promise. What it has lacked up to now is the morality, the vision and the courage of its leadership to achieve that objective.

3) Another somewhat unique dimension with which Americans are presented—although apparently in increasing jeopardy, is the ability to express profound and, I fear sometimes profane, criticism of its public and private officials at the highest levels. This will be evident, I am sure, in many remarks at this conference, as well as in the public speeches, writings and publications of those of us who feel wronged in this society. To those who have traveled throughout the world this is a concession we all know is not universally enjoyed.

And now, lest you think I have forgotten, let me deal as briefly as possible with the subject matter I chose for my discussion with you. First, because I feel it is my area of greatest competence; second, because as necessary as inspirational oratory is to our struggle and as much as I admire those of you here who are masters of that art, I know that that brand of philosophical discussion is not my personal style; it is not the means by which I can best communicate with you; and, third, because I was impressed and am taking literally the statements of the planners of this conference, that we must move from pure rhetoric to a discussion of those things which we consider concrete, important and crucial, if we as a people are to achieve true and self-determination, dignity and equity.

That subject is *Power*—real Power—*The Realities of Power.*

I would here today analyze four possibilities from the standpoint of timing and effectiveness—but most important from the standpoint of their realism for our struggle.

1) *Fire Power*—namely, the capability of producing, possessing and controlling superior weapons of destruction and the manpower to deliver them. This has been the most effective and quickest means of acquiring power since the beginning of man. All nations and societies have attempted it. Those who actually had it were successful, at least physically and temporarily; those who didn't were destroyed, even though they retained moral superiority—whatever comfort that may be for the deceased.

While acts of violence produced temporary fright and fear, and even some minimal programs, the overall result has been by far much more death and destruction for the victims of oppression, the mobilization of more effective means to suppress and the rise of a public attitude which develops and condones further vindictive, if not unconstitutional, measures of surveillance, apprehension and incarceration.

Conclusion: A technique to be rejected as an effective instrument, useful to the masses of Black people. I certainly reject it, for a society which will kill its own as we saw at Kent State will not hesitate to kill those it regards as alien. This is not to be confused with self-defense, in which I do believe, or Gandhi's Nonviolent Civil Disobedience, which I believe to be effective only where the oppressed are overwhelmingly in the majority.

2) *Economic Power*—in simple terms the ability to control the production and delivery of goods and services. It is the possession of money and the power to decide how that money is distributed, whether through investments or employment. One can be tempted at a meeting like this to speculate on the fact that more than two-thirds of the peoples of the world are nonwhite, and to go from there into the romantic notion that somehow economic power is in similar proportion. Obvious to everyone here, this is far from reality. But this present gross mal-distribution does not eliminate it from being if not *the* most realistic goal toward which we as a people should aspire, then at least in today's world society, the *single most important* factor that determines, motivates and conditions the behavior of those who would continue the oppression of Black people.

To a degree we have already witnessed the changes in attitudes and practices which were influenced by economics: Martin Luther King and the Montgomery Bus Company; Ralph Abernathy and the Charleston, Memphis and Atlanta garbage and hospital workers strikes; Leon Sullivan and the Philadelphia merchants in the Black community; Jesse Jackson and his Operation Breadbasket. The threat of economic consequences, as well as any moral reason, has encouraged many national corporations to improve their practices and cooperate with groups like the Urban League, Urban Coalition and National Alliance of Businessmen. Many companies who have only a slight interest in African citizens suddenly, for very good economic reasons, are establishing installations in Africa and so for the same reasons are rethinking their holdings in South Africa.

Conclusion: The acquisition of power through economic means by African peoples of the world is essential and crucial to our basic objectives, but it will be achieved only through careful, analytical and unemotional planning and cooperation over a period of many years. It will, to any elementary student of economics, have to concern itself with institutions outside of the Black community, as well as those within. For, as an example, if all the businesses in Harlem (America's largest Black community) were owned and operated by Black people, it would meet less than one-fifth of the employment and economic needs of its people. The Black community *must* aspire for power through investments and policy positions in management of the economic institutions which dominate America and greatly affect the social and economic development of African people the world over, as well as seek control over its own local institutions. For a historically economically disadvantaged people, this will enhance, if not require, collective and cooperative action, as well as individual effort. Formation of cooperatives and credit unions, which have been used effectively by other ethnic groups, labor unions and the like, must be pursued and implemented. The rather successful efforts of the Black Muslims in Chicago is one example of such cooperative effort. To assume that the needed economic development can take place for Black people any more than it has for whites without major government subsidies, public capital and private transfers, is to reflect economic naïveté and to invite economic disaster. We must support legislation at all levels toward this end, whether or not initially it is labeled socialistic by its critics.

This would include supporting an updated Urban League Domestic Marshall Plan, now being developed, and the A. Philip Randolph Freedom Budget. We must not shy away from terms such as reparation, indemnification, preferential treatment, etc.—but rather put them in their proper and just context.

3) *Brain Power*—Ultimately this is the resource upon which the success of any strategy depends. It is even more crucial for a minority. What we lack in quantity we must make up for in quality. Brain Power to liberate African peoples of the world must be carefully and

unemotionally selective. True, it must reject that aspect of white education which is clearly irrelevant, immoral, lacking in human values, committed to the preservation of the status quo and filled with convenient distortions and omissions of the truths of world history. True, it must seek the development of an educational content which includes the Black experience, elevates pride and dignity, and engenders a respect for us as a people—past, present and future. We must reject a self-serving materialistically-oriented education which has created and perpetuated the type of leadership which relies on military might as its major appeal for world allies and identifies as its successful and most honored citizens those who possess *things,* however immorally acquired.

But the effective Brain Power about which I am speaking also knows what not to reject: some of the cultural and the aesthetic—which makes us intelligent artisans; some of the art, the literature, the poetry, the drama that makes us cosmopolitan, aware and sensitive to all cultures; some of the behavioral sciences that make us not only personally aware, but also equally knowledgeable about the weaknesses of our oppressors, as well as the strengths of our forefathers; more than adequate knowledge of the helping professions (law, medicine, etc.) which have little color-component so that we can serve on more than equal terms our people who are so severely disadvantaged in these areas. And, finally, superior knowledge of the economic and political systems that for so long have entrapped and enslaved our people, if for no other reason than that those who would seek to reform or even to destroy that which is found destructive to the cause of our people must first know it, both its strengths and its weaknesses, and have some qualifications, if possible, to effect changes from within if external possibilities seem remote, as I suspect they are in the immediate future.

Brain Power, to the extent I have outlined it, will not be easy; to amass it in the degree needed will take time. But it is such an essential element in this whole struggle that for ourselves—and certainly for our children—it must become a primary obsession, an all-consuming effort . . . starting yesterday.

I have unprecedented confidence and faith in the intellectual capability and potential of our Black youth. I believe with all my heart that when and if given the opportunity they can compete with any and master whatever subject matter may be necessary to achieve power in a real sense, even as they become engrossed in those subjects which give us roots, pride and identity as a people. I confess here that during this period when some of the brightest white youth of the world are engaged in a search for their own self-identity, or for a more honest value system—a search which leads them into constructive, political efforts to elect better Congressmen, as well as into strange and bizarre experimentation with drugs, rock festivals and unusual styles of dress and behavior—our own Black youth might declare it a luxury to copy these their counterparts in the latter.

It is all too clear that without knowledge of the natural and social sciences, power becomes at best an aberration, not a fact. We, therefore, cannot afford the luxury of pursuing any path inconsistent with the intellectual offensive we have launched. The time for aberrations is past . . . the time for power—real power—has come.

I do not mean here to minimize the real value of Afro history—providing it is the real history of Africa and Afro-Americans and not restricted to the writings of current or ancient so-called revolutionaries, whose writings may titillate our emotions, but whose experiences and strategies may or may not have relevance for our time, our countries and against our current adversaries.

We all know, for example, that this is not by any means the first Congress of African People. A Pan-African Congress, including Black people from around the world, was first called in 1919 by Dr. W. E. B. Du Bois, representing the N.A.A.C.P., among others and held in Paris. Subsequent conferences have been held, focusing on the need for our unity as a people, but most important dealing rationally and unemotionally with realities and strategies for power, not only for the immediate relief of our people, but with those that would build a base on which future generations might expand. We can do nothing less. Any exposure to Afro-American history that does not include the writings of Frederick Douglass, W. E. B. Du Bois, John Hope Franklin, Benjamin Quarles, Charles S. Johnson or Lerone Bennett is a farce. Any study that excludes the lives and works of Alain Locke, Abe Harris, Robert Weaver, Sojourner Truth, Harriet Tubman, Nat Turner, Charles Drew, George Washington Carver, Mary McLeod Bethune, Booker T. Washington, Benjamin Banneker, Langston Hughes—just to name a few—is a sham.

And let me mention, also, that those who read such current books as *The Autobiography of Malcolm X*—or *Black Rage*—without reading well the last chapters, as well as the beginning and middle, are guilty of intellectual immaturity. True scholarship demands that we expose ourselves not just to excerpts and portions of our Black leaders' writings, or actions which support our own individual ideology, but that we view the whole of the person as he functioned and spoke in different situations during different periods of history.

Finally—let me address myself to a dimension of Power which for the Black citizen may well be the most immediately useful and effective. I cite this last but must emphasize that it may well be the most immediately essential because, unlike Economic and Intellectual

Power, this is something that practically every adult Black citizen has available to him *now.* In fact, the full, creative and astute use of Political Power could be a major determinant as to how soon and how much Economic and Intellectual Power we are able to acquire. This is a fact recognized equally by our oppressors in the society, and for this very reason the most vigorous efforts have been made to deny us this opportunity either through legal maneuvering, creating disunity and division within our ranks, and trying to discredit its importance among our youth—I might add, with some disturbing results.

We, as Black people in America, or in the United Nations, are in a unique position to use this instrument to effectively achieve power. Here, unlike Fire Power and Economic Power, our mere numbers represent a potential and a force to be reckoned with, whether in the United Nations or in the strategic urban areas of America.

But *Political Power* requires more than the right to vote, or even the exercise of that right. It requires major organization and planning before and after elections. In addition to a process for selecting candidates it requires identification and analysis of relevant issues and a method of sharing these with our voters. Finally, Political Power means getting out the vote. In all of this, financial resources are important, today more than ever.

My conclusion obviously, then, is that political action is for the Black today our most powerful immediate weapon. The extent of that effectiveness, however, is dependent on three other considerations: one, that we remain as a mass of people relatively independent in our party choice, either at the local, state or national level, to the extent of putting the cause of our people ahead of any party. In other words, we must never again permit our vote to be taken for granted.

Two, while we have made substantial gains in the last couple of years in electing Black citizens to public office, North and South, for the most part it has been under conditions where we represented from 35 to 90 percent of the population. This, obviously, occurs in relatively few voting districts in America. For this reason, as well as the very real financial and economic aspects involved in both election and administration, we must seek out and form coalitions with other varied interest groups. And, three, recognizing that politics is often referred to as the art of the possible, we as Black people have a responsibility to hold our leadership accountable. Accountability, however, is dependent upon support. That support must be predicated on our understanding of the nature of the political arena in which decisions are made. The stakes involved, the timing and the triggering effect of action, all have to be considered before we establish too quickly that there has been a "sell-out."

You will note that I have omitted moral and/or spiritual power.

This reflects only in part my admitted bias that the character of the white oppressive forces in world society rarely lends itself to moral appeals. My main reason for the omission, however, is that I feel there are many at this conference who can and will make the case far better than I. Personally, I believe an immoral society will eventually be destroyed, or will destroy itself—but I am particularly concerned here with interim strategy.

On segregation or separatism, I believe my views are well known. I believe that any time an educationally and economically disadvantaged group can be isolated it can always be, and without exception has been, subject to gross discrimination, exploitation and oppression. As for America, Black people have been here for more than four hundred years. We have contributed dearly in all the gains this land has made and suffered disproportionately in all its failures. We are already segregated for the most part, and those who are not can easily relocate themselves. I have frequently said and I say now that white Americans who engage in wishful thinking that we are going to take them off the hook and solve their problems by all of us collectively moving to separate states or leaving en masse for Africa should be told loudly and clearly, "Forget it; we are here to stay and in the process we are either going to make this country live up to its Judeo-Christian ethics and its democratic promise, or see it go down the drain of history as immoral and hypocritical, deserving of its fate."

Africa needs Black Americans, to be sure—as political and economic allies, mobilizing all of our strengths and resources in the pursuit of an American foreign policy (including economic and technical assistance) that will do for Africa what our tax dollars (both black and white) have done for Europe.

On community control and self-determination, we must make our objective clear. We seek through this method improved institutions, responsive and responsbile to the people they serve. As to the personnel who provide these services, our major criteria must be qualification and excellence, based on demonstrated results. The necessary resources, whether it be money or manpower—and we must be realistic—must come from people of all colors. Here we can learn as Black Americans, can learn from our African brothers who rarely reject foreign aid and technical assistance, whatever the source, if it meets a need which could not otherwise be met. In their program of Africanization, they never replace an alien for a native where technical strategic services are needed, until an equally trained and competent native is available. In other words, we, African people of the world, must distinguish nationalism from chauvinism. The former can be constructive, the latter most often self-defeating. If we assume any race has a monopoly on vice or virtue, then we will have made the same mistake as white society has made all these years. What we want from that society is its best, not its worst qualities.

My remarks this evening have been longer than I intended, and I have tried to be more substantive than rhetorical.

The reason for this is a simple and honest one. Our problems are too serious, the daily consequences too tragic to permit the luxury of deception or entertainment.

In the words of Frederick Douglass:

> Once again we hear the roar of the mighty waters . . . the steady and relentless drumming of the tides of change upon the shores of our nation's life. Beyond today's struggle, however, I believe there lies a tranquil sea upon which we may one day embark. Our vision must look forward toward it—the promise of a society of equality and excellence, of justice and of unity . . . undivided by distinctions of race, unshackled by issues of class, unbowed by fears of want.

Louis Farrakhan

National spokesman for Elijah Muhammad of the Nation of Islam. He has been in the Nation of Islam since the early 1950's and is presently Minister of Mosque No. 125 in Bronx, New York.

Asalaam Alaikum. In the name of Allah, who came in the person of Master Fard Muhammad, the great god who was to come, and has indeed come as the prophets predicted he would come, to seek and to save that which was lost; and we can find no other persons and no other people fitting that description of the lost brother, the lost sheep, than the Black man and the Black woman of America and the Western Hemisphere who have been lost from our native land and people for a little better than four hundred years. We have been found in a condition of mental and spiritual death; therefore, almighty God Allah has raised up in our midst the Honorable Elijah Muhammad to raise the Black man up from death, to give him mental life and put him on the road to self-independence again. And so I thank Allah for having met this great leader and this great teacher and this great guide in the personage of the most Honorable Elijah Muhammad.

To Brother Hayward Henry, to Brother Imamu Baraka, and to the great brothers who organized this great Congress of African People; to my beloved brothers and sisters from Africa, from the isles of the Caribbean, from Central and South America; to my beloved brothers and sisters from the plantation of America; we are indeed happy and honored by your invitation to us to attend this great conference.

I might say to you, my beloved Brothers and Sisters, it's a very hot evening; however, our enemies have made it hot for us a long, long time so we are used to heat. But though our enemies tonight may be in a cool, cool spot, when Black man and Black woman from America; when Black man and Black woman from Central and South America; from the Caribbean; from Africa, unite their hands in the bonds of brotherhood, it's a hot, hot day for the enemies of the Black man. My Brothers and Sisters, I feel very cool, and the message that I bring you from the Honorable Elijah Muhammad is a cool message; it's cool clear water to a Black man whose tongue has been parched and thirsty in the throes of hell and damnation for four hundred long years, it's a cool drink of water.

And so I am happy to be with you and I am honored to be here, to feel the spirit of my brothers and my sisters who don't want any more small, cheap talk of unity with an enemy before we unite among ourselves. We have not met at this great Congress of African People to discuss unity with white people; that is not our problem, today. Our problem—and the gravest problem facing Black people today—is the unity of all Black men the world over. And so it is on this basis that we come to you this evening. We don't come pompous and we don't come proud; we don't come to our brothers and sisters with a chip on our shoulders. We come humbly, as servants, for it's time that a Black man learn how to serve another Black man. It's time that those of us who would lead Black people understand that you cannot lead Black people from the top of the mountain; you got to come down into the valley. (All praises due to Allah.) We are here at this great congress not so much to confer but to exchange, or to listen to each other's ideas, as the time that we are living in is the Black man's time. This is the day and this is the time that the Black man *must* rule himself. I repeat, the Black man *must* rule himself! But, Brothers and Sisters, you cannot be left alone to do your own thing in ruling yourself, you're not independent in ruling yourself or guiding yourself, but a Black leadership must be fashioned for the Black man that's in tune with the needs of the Black man. I want you to pay very good attention.

The Honorable Elijah Muhammad says to us to tell you that we cannot use our old schooling of the white man to build us a school for tomorrow for the Black man. Those of you who are in the colleges and universities of America and the world—universities that have been set up by the English, by the French, by the Belgians, by the Dutch, by the Spanish, by the Portuguese, by the Germans, and by the white Americans—you must remember, my educated Black Brother, that the white man never set up an educational system to train a Black man how to lead a Black man in an independent way. There is not a Black leader, whether on the African continent, or in Central and South America, that has not been touched by the blinding touch of Satan, our open enemies. And therefore today, a Black man needs a new teaching, a new guide, for the Honorable Elijah Muhammad wants me to tell you that the wisdom of the white man's libraries, his textbooks and everything of his world will be destroyed in this final war with the Black man. I want you to listen: The Honorable Elijah Muhammad says all of his wisdom will be destroyed, his literature will be destroyed so that you and I will not fashion or try to teach and practice what he has practiced in his world. Therefore, the Black man needs a new teaching, he needs a new guide; the base that we are going to build on for the unity of Black men must be a new base, and the principles that we are going to act upon—they've got to be new principles.

I must talk to you in scripture language, as that is my mission from Muhammad; it is in scripture and in prophecy; and this is why the Honorable Elijah Muhammad and all that he has said to you and me over forty years has come true—all his predictions have come to pass because he is basing it on his wise insight into the prophets' sayings that have lain around in the corner, on our shelves, gathering dust—that we didn't understand. But Almighty God Allah has given us a man who does understand, and by his understanding we can be guided today. It is written in the scripture, "Behold, I make all things new." Who is talking here? Who is it that got to make all things new? This is a man that's dissatisfied with the world as it stands. The Honorable Elijah Muhammad says to us that the whole entire world of the white man is to be swept out of power. You see it coming today, he sees it coming, and this is why he pays good attention to Black people when Black people get together; he wants to know how wide awake you are to the knowledge of what is about to happen on our planet.

The Honorable Elijah Muhammad teaches us that the Black man has been out of power for six thousand years and now the Black man is being returned to power not by our effort, not by our great army, not by our great navies—for we have none at this moment (at this moment), but the Honorable Elijah Muhammad says that we are being returned to power by the act of the divine, supreme Being who is causing our enemies to kill each other off; and as our enemies begin to destroy each other this is beginning to produce now a rise in the Black man. But, as the Black man begins to rise he cannot rise into power holding on to the same thing that's dragging the enemy down into the ditch of hell. The Bible puts it this way: "If Satan casts out Satan, how then can his kingdom stand? A house divided against itself cannot stand." White people have delighted in dividing Black man against his brother; now, today, the same thing that they put on us, as the Bible puts it so beautifully, "As thou has done so shall it be done unto thee." (All praises due to Allah.)

Now in our rise, Brothers and Sisters, we cannot hold on to those things that our enemies would have us hold on to. We must understand the divisive tactics that are being used by our enemies to destroy the brightness of our rise. The Honorable Elijah Muhammad says to us that we should unite on the principles of the love of Black to build the foundation stone, or the cornerstone of a new world of the Black man. What do I mean? Muhammad asks you a question, "Are you here at this congress to try to salvage out of the white man's world something for us to build a world on?" That's a good question. Because, my Brothers and Sisters, Muhammad says if we are here for that purpose we shall never gain the unity that we desire. We are not here at this congress to salvage something from the junk pile of his world to build us a world on; for Muhammad says if you do this then you and I would be the same as he is, and we would rule our people according to his way of rule. Can we prove this? Yes. The Black man today is not willing to give up a white oppressor to receive a Black one in his place. Why is there so much talk of revolution in Africa? Why is there so much talk of revolution in the Caribbean? Why is there so much talk of revolution among Black people everywhere? It's because even though there's Black leadership in power, yet that Black leadership is trying to rule according to the way of the enemy and, therefore, they must be taken out of power. We have to have a new teaching. We got to have a new guide. The base upon which we build must be new. My beloved Brothers and Sisters you want a change: You want a change in Jamaica. You want a change in Trinidad. You want a change in Barbados. You want a change in Africa, a change in Asia, a change everywhere, but Brother, Muhammad says to us: Man makes the atmosphere. Man creates the environment in which he lives. Therefore, if you change a man's mind, that will change his environment. And if a Black man lives in hell, he has been put in hell by his enemy. Hellish thoughts are in his brain, the ideals of hell are rolling around in his head, the religion of hell he perpetuates, the education of hell he fosters, the politics of hell he asks you to vote for. No good, no good! Think it out. The first change that must take place, the first overthrow of government that must take place is the overthrow of the government of the mind. May I? Do I have a minute or two? Brothers and Sisters, it's written in the scripture (listen to this carefully) that when Elijah comes he will have to turn the hearts of the children back to their fathers and he would have to turn the hearts of the fathers back to the children. This is a very interesting scripture because if Elijah has to turn the hearts, the very turning there is an axis upon which a revolution takes place. Listen. Here is a child whose heart has to be turned back toward his own father. Who turned his heart against his father's? Why aren't their hearts united in one? An enemy came between the child and his own father. An enemy came between the Black man of America and his brothers in Africa and around the world and turned us against each other. (All praises due to Allah.)

But the book says Elijah would turn the heart. Why the heart? Why did the book say the heart? Let's stop and think about it a minute, shall we? The heart. The heart is the motor, it's the greatest pump known to man. It sits in the center of our chest. And with a masterful rhythm, that heart pumps the life fluid through the veins. Sixty tons of blood. Through sixty thousand miles of circulatory system. Every twenty-three hours, fifty-six minutes and forty-six seconds she pumps it on through. Called by scripture writers the seat of a man's emotions, it's the seat of a man's intellect; it's that point from which all of the issues of his life pour forth. If Elijah's got to turn his heart, is it talking about his physical heart? Muhammad says no, Brother, the heart is just a physical part that's the core of the physical being. But the core of a man's thinking is the heart of his mind. The heart of a man's mind is the seat upon which his thinking is built up, that's the government of his brain. Now if Elijah's got to turn their hearts, what happened to the Black man's heart that he today needs a heart transplant? What happened to the care of the Black man's mind that today he needs an operation performed?

The Honorable Elijah Muhammad says when they brought our fathers into the Western Hemisphere, brought us into slavery, they operated on us, Brothers and Sisters. They stripped us of our names—today we are called James and Johnson and Smith and Culpepper and O'Riley, Underhill and Overbrook and Understream. Ah! but you, my Brothers in the West Indies, he did the same to you, for the English white man called you McGillicutty—he gave you an Irish sounding name. And you, your French master in Guadeloupe and Martinique, he gave you a French-sounding name, so today as we are Jim Jones you are Françoise Jonese. (All praises due to Allah.) And to my Spanish-speaking Black Brothers, he called you César Romero. And to my Dutch-speaking Brother, he called you by a German name. But he divided us all up according to his European culture, and then he instilled into us his European hatreds and prejudices that came out of the Dark Ages of Europe. Now he's got a Spanish-speaking Black man against a French-speaking Black man against an English-speaking Black man and a Northern- and Southern-speaking American Black man. That's an enemy that divided us up, Brothers. Then he gave us his language, taught us in his schools—a few years ago, gave us his religion; he robbed us of the culture of our fathers, robbed us of the roots of our fathers. Then he robbed us of the minds of our fathers. And the Honorable Elijah Muhammad said since the Black man is the original man, he's not the last, he's the first man in the light of the sun. This is not hate, this is fact. You couldn't have a brown man, you couldn't have a yellow man, you couldn't have a red man, you couldn't have a white man if there was no Black man—he's the father. Muhammad said Black man is the father of it all. But look at this powerful Black man: After the enemy had destroyed our mind he put his mind in us. Think that over. Now when an enemy puts his mind in you then you become an enemy to yourself. Now listen, Brothers and Sisters, this is why you can look Black on the outside, you can grow your hair to the sky, you can put on a dashiki or whatever you care to wear, but I say to you as your humble brother, if the revolution of the mind takes place, or does not take place, you still the white man's nigger in a dressed-up way.

We haven't forgotten about the heart, now. If the heart is the seat of the emotions, how does the Black man feel? He doesn't feel like a Black man, he feels like his enemy. Therefore, when things happen to Black people he doesn't show the concern that he should have shown; but if anything happens to white people, something happens to America, he says our country, our stock market, our government, our flag, our this—what's the matter with you, Black man? You don't feel like a Black man. You can't even talk straight words because you're trying to please your master instead of pleasing your Black self and your Black kind.

Emotionally, the poor Black man feels like his enemy. What about intellectually? Don't you know when a man puts his learning in you, he puts his way in you? Intellect means to choose between. Any time a man is intelligent he has the ability to discriminate between what is good for him as opposed to that which is detrimental to himself. So when the white man puts his intellect in you, his mind in you, you can't choose what is good for you, invariably you always choose what is good for your master. Therefore, for four hundred years in America, no matter what we have done, it has always been to his good and to our detriment. Right? Wait, now let's look at it.

Every issue of the heart of life coming forth out of the seat of his government is from his enemy. Why are you a drunkard today, Black man? Because your enemy taught you to drink. He made the liquor, he sells the liquor; you buy it and get drunk off of it and call yourself having a good time! He has made a fool out of you. Wait a minute! Wait a minute! Listen! Why are you running after the Black woman —to destroy her morals? Why, Black man, do you want to put a Black woman on the block to sell her beautiful Black flesh for you? Why, Black man, will you allow prostitution to thrive in every city of America? Why do you walk by on the other side? Because every issue of life that comes forth out of you is your slave master's making. O my Brothers, my Brothers and my Sisters, cannot you see what has happened to us? The white people don't have to be near us, they could leave us alone; we would do the job now on each other because his mind is in us.

Now you have been to college; college hasn't changed your heart, changed your mind, changed your emotion, changed your intellect; it only fashioned it so it could be used better in his way. This is why whenever you try to start something you start it on his base, and you wonder why it breaks up in arguments, fighting, divisions all the time. Because you're using his mind. Oh, Brothers and Sisters, I wish I could just get over to you. Do you understand that the Black man needs a new heart, he needs a new mind, he needs new thinking, he needs a new government in his own brain; and that's the power of Elijah. The book said Elijah would turn his heart, Elijah would cause a revolution to take place in the government of the Black man's mind, and when that revolution takes place it's all over, it's all, all over. We need a new world to come out of us, but it can't come out of us until a new mind comes in.

And so, as I get near our conclusion, the Honorable Elijah Muhammad pleads with you: Don't try to carve something out of the junk pile of white people to build a future for yourself. We could make this meeting in Atlanta a great meeting, a meeting that would long be remembered if we act today on the principles of justice and equality for the Black man, and then carry those principles into practice among ourselves. And the fundamental principle, Muhammad says, is love of the Black man for his Black brother.

Now listen! Muhammad says to you and me—he gives us a picture —if you take bricks and try to make a solid wall with a bad mortar, those bricks cannot withstand the storm of nature because the mortar which you use to cement one brick to another brick is not a good mortar. What does Muhammad mean? When you come to this congress, Muhammad says you can't build a good brotherhood with a mixture of love and a mixture of hate, a mixture of love and a mixture of dislike. And do you know, Black Brother and Black Sister, that when we treat each other right, do justice by each other we actually produce pure love for each other. We cannot unite alone on the basis of Black skin; it must be on the basis of Black mind, and a Black mind that's full of love for Black brother. Listen, please. This mixture of love and hate, and love and dislike—arguing over who's gonna be the boss: "I wanna be the boss." "No, you be the boss." "I don't like your way of doing things." "I don't like the principles upon which you stand." Muhammad says we'll never build a nation like that. The white man didn't build his nation like that. He came over here to America and he got behind a leadership that he respected. George Washington was the first President of this country, but he was respected by his brothers as having more knowledge of how to lead them to independence over the Indian, and over the French, and the British. And so they united behind that leadership, and that leadership got them mastery over this country in the Western Hemisphere and mastery over those that once mastered them.

This is the way Black man must be. Each leader must look into his own heart—listen carefully, Brothers and Sisters—each leader must look into his own heart and answer this question to himself: "Am I qualified to lead Black people?" And come on up with the answer, and don't lie to yourself; you been lying long enough. Wait a minute! Wait a minute! Don't let the white man's television, his radios, his newspapers make you think that you are a leader. Think. Wait a minute. Wait a minute! Let's reason it out: White people are good at spoiling children. You know how children are: When you give children a lot of attention that they really don't deserve, they get spoiled. Do you know the white man is not a fool? Any Black man who jumps up, who is eloquent of speech, saying any wild crazy thing that tickles the fancy of an ignorant ear and a fool say, "Go 'head, baby, right on"; right on what? Then the white people plaster their face on the television, plaster their words in the news, then they are read about in magazines, and then when you meet the brother again, here he comes, he can hardly walk upright, he's strutting now, he's spoiled, now he got headlines and so he's not thinking for the good of his people, he's only thinking to make a headline to keep himself in the news; that is not a leader, that is an enemy to the Black man of America and the world. I want you to listen: The time is out for Black leaders to plan how they can get a march going to get their face in the newspaper. The time is out for Black people to play with the lives and the destiny of a nation. This is not a plaything! Any leader who wants to climb to fame on the innocent backs of Black people and on the ignorance of Black people must be prepared to take the consequences. When your leadership fails and runs your people into the hail of bullets that you are preparing for them with your unwise, ignorant mouth, Muhammad said to me to tell you: If you met here to talk about overthrowing the white man, with what? Wait a minute! Wait a minute! I want you to think now. Here's a man, well armed. He's so well armed, Muhammad said, he's like iron poured into iron. He is a man whose planes darken the sky. (I'm not telling you to be afraid of him because the time is out. We don't fear nothing but God Himself today. No one do we fear. This is not to make you afraid; this is to make you wise.) Here is a man who has a navy out in the Pacific; we've learned that he can keep a million and a half men at sea with his navy. He's got another fleet in the Mediterranean—the Eighth Fleet; the Sixth and Seventh Fleet, he's got them out in the Pacific. Do we have anything to match that, no? Well now, if we're going to meet together to talk about overthrowing a man that's so well armed like that, Muhammad said you're actually making a fool of yourself in this conference. It's easy to talk the big word (Wait a minute!) but to execute the big word after you speak it, then you make a fool of yourself. And you're dealing with a people that are cowardly: They'll put the mike in front of your face, "What you have to say about it?" "Well we're gonna get ya, that's all. We're gonna make it hot for you." And you got your girlfriend behind the door telling him, "Watch me how I tell him off, baby." And then in the middle of the night, two o'clock in the morning, when you and baby are sleep, here he comes with an enemy because you put the big word out, and when it came time to back up the big word you couldn't back it up. Muhammad said no man should talk ahead of his actual power to do. That's intelligent, isn't it? Don't say what you're going to do; and if you don't have the power to do, don't have the mouth to say.

So I guess it's time for me to conclude. The Honorable Elijah Muhammad says to you and me: If we are greedy over the leadership, we can destroy the fundamentals upon which we desire to build a Black brotherhood. I can't come before you, because you acclaim or applaud, and say, "Oh, boy, I'm a leader now." That's a game. I'm not playing a game. I love Black people. I love the baby that cries in the night. I love the unborn baby that's in my sister's womb. I can't play a game of leader with the lives of human beings, and neither can you.

Muhammad says to you, unite with him in his effort to put you on a road of independence. What do you mean, Muhammad? Muhammad says, "How you gonna be independent with your mouth in the white man's kitchen?" Listen, you talking revolution, here the Black man eats three meals a day—haven't you learned how to fast yet? Ninety million meals Black people eat in one day; 630 million meals a week, 760 million a year. All of these meals provided for us by white people. Now don't you know when a man got your breadbasket he got you? How you gonna be independent if you don't feed yourself? All of us wearing clothes—all of our clothes come from him, all of our shoes come from him; we're begging the white man to give us a job and if he won't give us a job we'll lay down and picket in the street—like children. Look at Muhammad. Muhammad is purchasing farm land to feed Black people; we have thousands of acres here in Georgia, many thousands now in Alabama, in Mississippi, and in several other states. What are you doing, Muhammad? "I'm trying to prepare meals for Black people that Black people can feed themselves." We have thousands of head of sheep, thousands of head of beef cattle. We just brought twenty tons of beef up from our Southern farm to our Chicago packing house. We have a lamb packing house and a beef packing house; lamb and beef processing plants, for what? We not showing off, we trying to show you, Black Brother and Sister, we can do what we will if we unite together behind the right kind of leadership. Muhammad got a plane in the sky, going down into the Caribbean bringing back produce from the Caribbean, putting it on the market here for you and me. We are now bargaining with the aviation companies for 707, 727, DC7, and DC9 jets, for what? To move our merchandise across the country at a faster rate of speed. We have a fleet of trucks bumbling over the highways of America now. Muhammad says, from California to New York, from the Great Lakes to the Caribbean, he got it all set up for Black man. He said this: That the way that Allah is guiding him, he has almost set up a nation and a government in one year.

What could he do if we united behind the man? You say, "Well, I don't want no religion." We're not going to argue religion, but we going to argue this: You don't want religion because you don't want to act right to you brother. Just listen. Now, if you want your brother's wife, naturally, you don't want Muhammad. If you want your brother's daughter, naturally, you don't want Muhammad. If you want to walk around with broken arms, naturally, you don't want Muhammad. When has a Black man even produced a freak? This is disgraceful! Now you want alliance with sissies. Let me tell you something. Black man, if you are caught up in that sick freakish bag, when you know the glory of being a man, how could you dare want to be a woman? And Sister, when you know the beauty of being a woman, the majesty of being a woman, when you know how honorable it is to be a woman—and a Black woman at that—when you know that every Black man of greatness that ever came forth came forth from the womb of a Black woman; when you understand you're a Black woman, how could you want to play man? Let me tell you something, Brother and Sister, that man that wants to be a woman or that woman that wants to be a man, no matter how much you play man, when it boils right down to it, you can't be any more than what nature made you. So, Brothers and Sisters, why not clean up and build our brotherhood on the fundamentals of love for each other? Why shouldn't we love each other as a brother, and do good to self? Why should you call your Black brother to arms, and yet he's a fool; why not make him wise first, when you put the gun in his hand, then he understands who his enemy is; but you arm him and then he kills his brother because he doesn't understand. You are doing all of this, trying to duck and dodge the leadership that is offered to you by the Honorable Elijah Muhammad. But, Brother, there is an old song that says, "Went to the rock to hide my face but even the rock is crying out." Um-um! you better get on to Elijah; that's the man that'll change your heart, that's the man that will change your mind. And when Black man comes into unity of Black man then the unity of Black man is the greatest weapon that we could produce the world over and when we fire the cannon of our unity, what enemy do you think could oppose us? There is none.

And, so, I close pleading with you, Brothers and Sisters, let's get behind a man who has proven that he is worthy of leadership and of men; though I speak with the tongues of angels, if I have not loved, my voice is as a sound of tinkling brass and a tinkling cymbal, and if I understand all mysteries and all knowledge and have faith that can move a mountain and I do not have love for my Black self and my kind—that's actually what the truth says—I am nothing. You know, Brothers, love is not proud. So when you go to strutting in these offices of leadership, remember you love Black man and strut around him. When they call off how many degrees you have, don't boast in what you got from a white man's institution. You say humbly, "Whatever I know I put it at the feet of my people." The more wise you become, the more humble you become; that's why all wise men are humble men, all great men are humble men, no great man ever walks proud with that loftlook. Do you love the Black man? If you love the Black man you won't play the game of leadership. If you love the Black man you will work night and day to develop programs for the good of the Black man; and if you have not developed that program and you look in the direction of Elijah Muhammad and he has that program already laid out, if you love Black man, you'll say, "Muhammad, how can I help you to implement that program?" We all can't be the head; this would be a miserable body of ours if all the organs wanted to be the head. That's in the Bible. Can you imagine the kidney talking, can you imagine the kidney saying, "Look here, I am down here working all the time and don't nobody see me. You know what, if I ever stop working, Jack, that heart would have a fit." And the liver says, "Wait a minute, I am pretty bad myself. I mean, I do a mighty work here in this body; I want more recognition. See me as I am, I'm the liver. Any resemblance to persons living or dead is not a coincidence." Then the heart says, "Man I do all this pumping all day long and the brain gets the credit. If I stop pumping how long will that brain think?" Now you'd have chaos wouldn't you? But here's one thing you've got to understand about this mighty structure, the human body; everything in this body works together for the common good of the whole. There is none greater, none least; all are important as long as they function where they should. Do you understand? So among us there is no greater, no lesser, no major, no minor, no high and low, there is Black man; and if Black man would live for Black man, who could stop Black man?

So, my Brothers from the Caribbean, please don't say, "That brother's from Jamaica, I am from Barbados, that one from Trinidad." Jamaica man this, Trinidadian that; that's our enemy talking. Black is not national; Black is universal. Though you are Black in Cuba, though you are Black in Guadeloupe, Black in Martinique, Black in Panama, Black in Costa Rica, Black in Ghana, Black in Guinea, Black in the islands of the Pacific, wherever you find a Black man, Black is not national, it is universal. For in the beginning darkness covered the earth. Think over the Book. Muhammad said before light came there was a universe of darkness. So we cannot be divided by national boundaries; our problems supersede national boundaries, languages, cultures. Are you Black, that's all we need to know; and if we are Black, let's stretch our hands across the waters, stretch our hands together and say, "From this day forward I will live my life for the Black man and when I can no longer live my life for the Black man, I will give my life for the Black man." And I say to you, as I sit down, the man who offered this message that I bring to you, the Honorable Elijah Muhammad, that is a man that I love with more passion than I have ever loved any human being because when I met this man I was naked mentally, naked spiritually, and naked morally and he clothed me. I was hungry for truth and this man fed me. I was weak and spineless and he gave me courage and stood me up as a man. I was disrespectful of the Black woman, but Elijah Muhammad showed me how to love her, to respect her, and protect her. How could I turn my back on this great and masterful teacher? I couldn't come before you and say I said it because I didn't say I said it—Elijah Muhammad told me what I am telling you. Some of you think it's a crime to repeat another man's name and give another man honor, but we been thieves too long, stealing each other's ideas, each other's inventions, each other's plans and putting our names on them. If you can say that Socrates said it and you don't feel bad, if you can say Plato said it and you don't feel bad, if you can play a number written by Charlie Parker and you don't feel bad saying Charlie wrote it, why should I feel bad when I quote my leader and teacher and say he said it? I love this man. I honor Muhammad, and I tell you don't you ever be deceived by eloquence; eloquence is no substitution for programs. My mouth speaks the words of Muhammad; but you got to learn to look by the speaker to the brain that's behind that speaker. I'm like a signpost on a road. If you're on your way to New York City and the sign says New York ten miles, you don't stop and hug the sign, you don't say, "I'm home," you just look at the sign, say, "Oh, I'm on the right road, let me keep on moving."

I pray to almighty God Allah that He will always give me this kind of mind to love my brothers and sisters more than life itself, that I may not deceive myself for them because you are a people who love oration and you don't care what is being said, or how, or the program behind it. Elijah Muhammad has the best program of any Black man in America, not because he's my leader, but because his works bear witness of him. So what can I say, if I love you; should not I say to you, come on, Black man, let's unite behind a man who can take us where we want to go.

May Allah bless you in all your efforts. I thank you so much for your wonderful attention. I pray that Allah will go with each and every one of the travelers back to the Caribbean, back to Africa, to Central and South America. But let us never forget what took place here at this African People's Congress—it's the beginning and not the end.

Asalaam Alaikum

Howard Fuller

President of Malcolm X Liberation University in Durham, North Carolina, and a member of Student Organization for Black Unity (SOBU). Fuller has been involved in the civil rights movement since the 1950's.

I would first like to read to you the message from Brother Stokely Carmichael, written August 17th in Conakry, Guinea.

> To the Brothers and Sisters at the Congress of African Peoples: I hope this little message finds you all in the best of health and Blackness. My wife and I are deeply honored at your invitation. We regret that we will be unable to attend. But we had previously committed ourselves to other engagements. I am very happy that the conference is taking a Pan-Africanist orientation. Personally I feel that this ideology is the ideology for our people. We must elevate our struggle to a higher level.
>
> Pan-Africanism is the highest political expression of Black Power. It includes all Black people and everyone knows all Black people are Africans. The ideology of Pan-Africanism must seek a land-base. Malcolm X says that all revolutions are fought over the question of land. As Africans we all know that Africa belongs to us. And until Africa is truly independent and unified, the African will not be free. We in the United States cannot afford to be tribalistic, we form an important part of the African nation as do our brothers in the Caribbean and our brothers on the continent.
>
> Black people MUST be unified. We have the historical duty to replace justice on this earth and to *crush* into oblivion the perpetuation of injustice and the disruption of world peace. We, the Africans, better than anyone, know the enemy of mankind. We know him with his imperialistic structures. We know him with his innate racism. We know him, we must destroy him. In order to do that we must be clear-thinking, dedicated, unified and willing to KILL. We must have a clear ideology—slogans arouse the people, ideology guides them. Our ideology must be crystal clear in our minds.
>
> I hope that the conference is successful. I hope that the dissention which is so rampant among our people will be swept away into an ocean of unity. Unity is paramount at this time. For the sake of our ancestors, for the sake of our unborn, for the sake of our suffering masses, scattered all over this world, may your congress inject a new feeling of unity among our people—which is essential to our world-

> wide Black revolution. And which this generation MUST bring about. My Brothers and Sisters, may the African gods be with you at this conference, for I am sure we shall conquer without a doubt. With an undying love for our people wherever we may be, Stokely & Miriam Carmichael.

Now, I would like to take up some of your time to talk about the things that we feel are very important for this conference, that we feel are very important for Black people wherever they may be. I do not have a hidden agenda, I do not have a particular program to push. I want to offer to you an analysis, an analysis for you to discuss, an analysis for you to see if it makes sense. I am going to talk about a number of concepts, and I would like to define these concepts from the beginning so that it is clear what I am talking about.

Nation. A nation is a group of people who have a common social, economic and political custom rooted in the same land. A nation first of all requires land, as land is the basis of all power. Revolution. Revolution is a swift and violent change in the political, economic and social structures of a people, with not only the result that they are no longer oppressed, but that their oppressors are no longer in a position to reinstate their oppressive structure.

Africans. Africans are those people all over the world whose political, economic and social customs are rooted in the continent of Africa and whose physical characteristics are Black. Ideologically it is those people who define themselves as Africans. Europeans. Europeans are those people, all over the world, whose political and social customs are rooted in the continent of Europe and whose physical characteristics are white, that is generally pale-skinned, straight hair, keen protruding noses, small lips and small buttocks, as they would say.

Now, if we are to understand Europeans and Africans, then we as an African people must understand that we are not Afro-Americans, that we are not Afro-Greeks, that we are not Afro-French, that we are not Afro-Jewish, that we are Africans. . . .

And if we begin to understand the nature of European settler colonies, then nobody will run around saying that I am not African, I was born in Brooklyn, or I was born in Atlanta, because we will understand that it is not where you were born, but it is where your ancestors come from. And so, Brothers and Sisters, what we must begin to understand is that Europeans have used the concept of settler colonies, that is they have taken land, they have changed cultures, and languages, they have distorted history and they have committed genocide; which means that Australia is a settler colony, that Mozambique is a settler colony, that Angola is a settler colony, that Zimbabwe is a settler colony (most of us don't know it as Zimbabwe, but as

Rhodesia, named after that cracker, Cecil Rhodes) this cracker, this cracker and all of his kind moved into Zimbabwe, said that you are no longer Zimbabweans, you are now Rhodesians, and they took our language, they distorted our history and they committed genocide against our people. . . .

Israel is a settler colony. There is no such place as Israel. It is Palestine, and so that all of you, all of you niggers who saw fit to sign that document saying that you support Israel, you are supporting nothing. We must understand that those Europeans who call themselves Jews moved into Palestine, took the land in 1948. This is what it's all about, and America is a settler colony. America is a settler colony. And any of us who have even a cursory understanding of history, understand that the only indigenous people to this land are those that Columbus called Indians because he thought that he was in India. So that while we're dealing on that level, then we will understand that we are Africans, Europeans are Europeans, not Americans, not Israeleans, not Afrikaners, they are Europeans, and it is these people that we must address ourselves to.

Now I hear a lot of people who talk about the question of what should we do with white people; should we not involve white people, should we not use white people? Should we not hold hands with white people, will we not overcome if all of us were standing side by side? Let me say this, at no conference of white people do white people ever take the time to discuss whether or not they should involve Black people. In the fifteenth century when Europeans moved on to the African continent, they took a clear hard-line position about what to do with African people. "We will enslave them or kill them. And all of those we could not enslave, we will kill; we won't talk about killing, we will kill," and what crackers did in the fifteenth century was to move us throughout this world, and it was a political decision based on whether or not we could be used. Brothers and Sisters, I submit to you that we are still the victims of this same European politics, that we are still the victims of crackers, and it doesn't make any difference what they call themselves; they can call themselves English, they can call themselves German, they can call themselves Italian, they can call themselves anything that they want, but when they get through calling themselves all of that, they are still crackers, they are still Europeans, and they still must be dealt with by Black people.

What we as a people must understand is that we are colonized people. That whether we are in Accra, or in New York, in London or in Georgetown, we are the victims of colonialism and neocolonialism. We are the victims because European politics dictates that this continues. So that, Brothers and Sisters, we must understand that we are in a position where white folks control every aspect of our lives.

They control the land, they control our minds, they control the production of goods and services, and they control the mechanisms of force and violence.

I would like to talk about these. We have said that land is the basis for everything. Land is the basis for everything. We do not control land. Now I know that some of y'all are going to tell me that you got a farm or some of y'all are going to tell me that in New York your daddy owns a great big house with a back yard, and that that's your land. Well, it is your land except for one thing, there's a little thing called eminent domain, which means that crackers have eminent domain over what you think is yours, and if and when crackers made a decision that they needed your house for a museum for Abraham Lincoln's daughter's toiletries, if that was the decision that was made, then you going to be gone, and what are you going to do? Are you going to get up your rusty gun that don't shoot? If you would, then we would have stopped a whole lot of urban renewal programs, but the reality, Brothers and Sisters, is that they control the land and not only do they control the land, but they control the air and they control the sea. They control most of the clothes that's on your back because a lot of y'all ain't paid for them yet, so if they tell you to leave the house and you get smart, he'll take the clothes and won't let you stand on his land and you can't get in his air, then where we going to be?

White folks control our minds. Lot of y'all going to say don't no white folks control my mind. Really? A whole lot of us are still saying that Black is beautiful, but we mean white folks. Whole lot of y'all still saying Black is beautiful because we still trying to convince ourselves that it is beautiful. Because the man has told us that we ain't what's happening. We are still divided up into house niggers and field niggers. We are still operating out of a Tarzan complex from our brothers on the continent. We claim to be Africans, yet many of us are scared to talk about Africa. We claim to be Africans, but yet we still think that Africa is a land inhabited by some long tall cracker called Tarzan. We still talking about country niggers and city niggers. Very interesting. Some of y'all came down to Atlanta and made the statement that I haven't been this far south before. You couldn't really be serious. You got the same rats, the same roaches, and the same crackers up in New York, so you couldn't be worse. . . .

They control the production of goods and services. White folks control the production of goods and services. Black people spent forty billion dollars last year in the United States, and don't control any of the factors of production. Don't control land, labor or capital. Some of you sisters who are wearing mini-skirts, you're not wearing them because you should be wearing them, because you look good necessarily; you're wearing them because crackers put them in *Bazaar*, put them in *Cosmopolitan*, put them in all those places, and it has nothing to do with how you look. It has to do with what kind of profit they can make. Now some of you sisters are either wearing African dresses, not because you're Africans but because the crackers reduced the hemlines down to midis, and now since they talk about midis, now you ready to be Africans. The reality is that the only reason he reduced it from maxi-mini to maxi-midi is because he got to make some more money because he decides what the market is going to be.

And the crackers control services; crackers say we need a poverty program, we had a poverty program. Crackers say we need model cities, we had model cities. We need human relations, we had human relations. Now some cracker in Virginia named Broyhill done put through a six-million-dollar mental health program because he done decided that niggers is crazy. So throughout the Black community—Youngstown, Ohio is a good example—they're building mental health centers, so that they can put a nigger in charge, three white girls, two paraprofessionals, and have us on the couch talking about the relationship between you and your mamma the first seven years of your life. They call this psychoanalysis, and I call it the dozens, because it don't deal with our oppression. Some of y'all are applauding, but you're applauding kind of light, 'cause you majored in psychology and because they getting ready to put you into the mental health center to deal with us. Think about it. Think about it.

They control the mechanism of force and violence, all the way from the city police on up. You know it's a very interesting thing, a lot of y'all are on campuses and you think that somehow that campus is going to protect you. Understand this. That the security police on that campus don't work for you, they work for the crackers. Because if they worked for you, if the National Guard ever set foot on your campus, they would shoot the National Guard, but they ain't going to do that, they going to shoot you, because they understand that if you beat them, they will bring in the city police. If you beat the city police, they will bring in the state police; if you beat the state police, they'll bring in the National Guard. If you beat the National Guard, they'll bring in the Regular Army. If you beat the Regular Army, they'll bring in NATO. If you beat NATO, they'll bring in SEATO. If you beat SEATO, they'll bring in Russia. Dig that, because Russians are white.

Now some of y'all think that you have reached a position where because you are in school, because you now wear a tie, because you are now what is known as a good nigger, that white folks won't kill you. Some of y'all think that you have some kind of badge that says

I am a good nigger. Let me tell you something, they will kill you. White folks will kill you, and when white folks go out to kill Black folks, they do not stop and ask, are you a good nigger or a bad nigger. All of you are niggers to crackers. And you know why that's important? Because some of y'all are going to leave here saying well, if I don't give no speeches, I'll be all right. I ain't going to wear my African clothes after I leave Atlanta, and I'll be all right. I ain't going to talk real bad, and I'll be all right. Looka here, those four girls in Birmingham were sitting in the white man's church learning about Jesus, and they killed them. William Penn had a doctor degree and they killed him. Those seven brothers down in Augusta that were shot in the back, they are dead. The two brothers on Jackson State campus are dead. The three brothers at South Carolina State are dead. So understand this, you don't have no protection. Your campus ain't no protection and unless you get something to work with, your house is no protection because the D.C. crime bill has dealt with that. Although they were doing it long before then.

So that, Brothers and Sisters, in spite of all of this, in spite of all of this historical reality, many of us still relate to the very ideas, accept the very values, pursue the same things which have contributed to the maintenance of African oppression, to the extent that many of us are still running around talking about the struggle to be equal. We talking about equality, equal housing, equal jobs, equal toilets, equal this and equal that. None of us have ever stopped to ask ourselves, what does it mean to be equal? Equal to what is the question, equality or freedom? Is the question integration or liberation? Is the question dependency or independency? And I would suggest to you, Brothers and Sisters, that the catechism of equality only addresses itself to the ever specific change in manifestations of our oppressions, and that we must begin to understand that it is not to be equal, but it is to be free.

Many of us are still, still, still allowing white folks to define consciousness. Very interesting thing that when a Black man gets up to talk about Black people, he is called a racist even by some of his own people, because we have come to think that when you talk about consciousness you are talking about white folks. We have not come to understand that when a white man talks about humanity, by definition he is talking about himself, because he has always defined us as things: things to pick cotton, things to shine shoes, things to abuse sexually, things to keep other things cool when other things get hot. So that until we begin to understand that we have to define our own humanity, we will never be free as a people. Many of us brothers and sisters have even gotten to the point where we allow crackers to decide what our program needs to be and what our problem is. Some long-haired cracker going to tell you that it's a class struggle, and you standing around singing yeah, it's a class struggle. That same long-haired cracker going to cut his hair, put on his pants, get him some shoes and go to his daddy's factory and come back and kick your behind and you still looking for the class struggle. . . .

Then crackers tell you don't talk about Africa. We can say, no we ain't going to talk about Africa, we can't get there, how we going to get there, where the planes at? . . . And Nixon sits back and laughs, because Nixon is talking about Africa. Nixon is talking about Africa because Nixon knows. Nixon knows that Africa is where it's at. Nixon knows that he's sitting on a decimated land, and that Africa has the kinds of things we need to survive. So that, Brothers and Sisters, what I'm saying is that as a people we must begin to develop an ideology that will deal with the realities of our existence, and that will help move us toward some kind of freedom and liberation that we must have.

I would like to define Pan-Africanism for you as I see it. Pan-Africanism tells us who we are, links us together around the world, and outlines our objectives as a people. In other words certain things are clear: that we are all African people, not red people, not yellow people, not brown people, but Black people. People of African descent. That number two, no matter where we are in the world, we are inseparably linked by our common heritage and our common oppression. Number three, we must govern ourselves in order to determine our own destiny and in order to determine our destiny, we must have a nation. Number four, we must develop an economic system which recognizes the underlying communalistic nature of African society. Our whole process of production and distribution of goods and services. So that, Brothers and Sisters, I am saying that nation-building is in fact what we must be about. As Brother Nkrumah stated, "It is far better to be free to govern or misgovern yourself than to be governed by anyone else."

So that, Brothers and Sisters, if we going to talk about nation time, if we going to talk about nation-building, then the first thing that we must understand is that we must have land, and that land cannot be seen as an abstraction, but rather as a harsh physical reality that must be seized, held and developed. And if we cannot seize, hold and develop it, then it does not in fact belong to us. And so that I have suggested, Brothers and Sisters, that our land base must be that which belongs to us and that is Africa. . . .

Richard Hatcher

First Black mayor of a major city. Since taking office, Mayor Hatcher has sought to improve the conditions of Black people in the steel town of Gary, Indiana.

Mr. Chairman, Brothers and Sisters:

It's a privilege to be here and to participate in this historic event. The underlying concept, I think, which guides all of us today and these last two days is the concept that we are all African people; the concept that we are working together to build a strong united African nation wherever we may be; the concept that we must work toward the unification of Africa; in other words, the concept of Pan-Africanism. "You cannot understand what is going on in Mississippi if you do not understand what is going on in the Congo. You cannot be interested in what is going on in Mississippi if you are not also interested in what is going on in the Congo. There're both the same —the same interests are at stake, the same ideas are drawn up, the same schemes are at work. Same stake; no difference whatsoever." Malcolm X said that and he also said that one can see the gigantic design to keep Africans here and Africans in Africa from getting together. And when you move from international to the national scene you can also see the effort to create division. But we, as Black people, must begin to look for that means whereby we can seize the kind of power that it will take for our survival. Someone once said that people should not stand and beg for that which they have the power to take. And so approximately four years ago when Stokely Carmichael shouted "Black Power" in that Mississippi school yard, he performed a mythic function that some poet must always perform at the proper moment in history. He gave voice, he gave a name to a development that was happening already in the life of Black America and which needed naming so that we could talk about it. And I say that he named it rather than created it because the movement toward Black Power has had a long and honorable past, and it has become the dominant theme of our emotions and our thoughts in the last few years. And that is only because like the proverbial snowball the increasing of the time and frustration has turned incipience into actuality and made of the snowball an avalanche.

This afternoon I would like to take those two words, Black and Power, and to talk about them from the vantage point of a man who has had some connection with both. Now, it is beyond dispute that I am Black. But I am too modest to add "and beautiful," though it is tempting. It is also a fact that for better than two and one-half years now, I've held the position that carries with it at least the modicum of power. It is a good time then, I think, for me to talk about what these two words mean to me.

My Blackness has been the dominant fact of life's experience as it is the dominant fact in the life of every Black man, not only here in America but all over the world. James Baldwin, with his usual brilliance, describes the condition in his famous essay, "Stranger in the Village," in which he discusses his own experience as the only Black man in a little Swiss village. And I quote:

> For this village, even though it were incomparably more remote and incredibly more primitive, is the West, the West onto which I have been strangely grafted. These people cannot be, from the standpoint of power, strangers anywhere in the world; they have made the modern world, in effect, even if they do not know it. The most illiterate among them is related, in a way that I am not, to Dante, to Shakespeare, to Michelangelo, Aeschylus, Da Vinci, Rembrandt and Racine; the cathederal at Chartres says something to them which it cannot say to me; as indeed would New York's Empire State Building, should anyone here ever see it. Out of their hymns and dances come Beethoven and Bach. Go back a few centuries and they are in their full glory—but I am in Africa, watching the conquerors arrive.

Now, because of the white man's rape of Africa and because of the implementing of slavery, because of long and barbarous history of segregation and discrimination, I find that I am a stranger in this, the American village. And because white Americans and white Europeans have developed the ideology of racism to justify the sociological and historical experiences that I mentioned, I am a stranger in this village. But from another point of view, because I am a man, because I've been reared on the words, though not the facts of Christianity and democracy, I am also an inhabitant, and in a strange sort of way, a citizen of the village. Now, much of the history of Black America is dominated precisely by that contradiction. We've been told one thing —"democracy," "freedom," "we hold these truths to be self-evident: That all men are created equal"—but we have lived quite another. The Ku Klux Klan, slavery, and white liberals are so concerned with Black people that they will tell them exactly what they ought to want, exactly what they ought to do, and exactly what they ought to become. Schools that don't teach us. Promises from the Supreme Court turn to ashes. So that is why we have been forced to fall back on our own resources. For you cannot be a stranger always. To be continuously a stranger is to pay a price that no people can endure forever.

So when Black America turns to what in Africa for a long time has been called "negritude," we have no apologies to make. From the time that I was a little child before I ever heard of Othello, or, for that matter, Shakespeare, I knew that I was Black. No wonder then that as a grown man I must turn to the words of Leopold Senghor, the Black African poet from Senegal, or to those of Langston Hughes, or Imamu Amiri Baraka, or Don Lee, or Gwendolyn Brooks. From the time that I was a little child, and before I ever heard of Beethoven or Bach, I knew that I was Black. And no wonder then that I must turn to Jimi Hendrix, Nina Simone, and Aretha Franklin, and that I recall with some anger the Black symphony conductor Dean Dixon who had to go abroad to practice his art. From the time that I was a child and before I ever heard of Paul Bunyan or George Washington I knew that I was Black, and no wonder then that as a grown man that I must turn to John Henry, Jomo Kenyatta and W. E. B. Du Bois, and I will stop being a stranger because I will recall that though a stranger in this village, I have lived here nonetheless; and that I have a history there and elsewhere, as in Africa, and that history will make me less the stranger. We assert what we are. We may wear a dashiki and we may look with favor on a natural. Being ourselves will make us less the stranger. We've tried being like the so-called natives and were not allowed to be like them, so we must turn to our own resources. So, my experience with the word Black is that of all Black people. Being Black has made me a stranger, being Black has dominated my life, and I cannot, nor would I wish to reject my Blackness and so I turn what the white world has attempted to make into a handicap precisely into its opposite. Black America is fortunate that our history, that our culture is more than rich enough so that we can find in Blackness an advantage, a source of pride, and a way to end our estrangement. But there's another side to this.

Even though I may find in negritude, and in Black culture, a way not to be so strange any longer, that is not enough—for my estrangement is also included in my powerlessness. I've not only been a stranger in the village but I've also been a stranger without power, and there are times in the history of this country when strangers have had sufficient power to keep themselves, at least, supplied with the necessities for a decent living. This has been true of many who came as strangers to the American shore—as after a generation or so, the Irish, the Italians, and so on—but it has not been true of Black Americans. We have been kept strangers, in part, at least, because our strangeness has provided white America with a means, a cheap means, for the hewing of wood and the drawing of water. Because

Black people have had no power, because the ideology of racism has prevented white Americans from thinking naturally they have been exploited and used and deprived of the minimum wherewithal for a decent life. That is why pride in being Black is not enough for our survival. That is why we've increasingly had to turn our attention to a means of wresting from the majority not only a new perceptive of our humanity but also a new place in this nation so that we can enforce our demands for the satisfaction of our needs. Now, we have tried many different ways of accomplishing this.

Power, I think, means, quite simply, a force strong enough so that you can get whatever it is that you need. Let me recall that in the last two decades or so we have tried all sorts of ways of achieving power. The Brown decision by the Supreme Court represented an effort to use power of the courts. We won that skirmish, but we have discovered almost seventeen years later that there was not enough strength in the power of the court to guarantee any fundamental change in the education of Black children. Legal power helped a little but it did not help enough.

Martin Luther King tried another form of power beginning with the Montgomery bus boycott of 1955. Dr. King tried with all of his skill and dedication, indeed he gave his life for it, to use nonviolent power of Black masses to achieve their needs. A very eloquent man, he said, writing in *Liberation:*

> There is more in socially organized masses on the march than there is in guns in the hands of a few desperate men. All history teaches us that like a turbulent motion beating great cliffs into fragments of rocks, the determined movement of people excessively demanding their rights always disintegrates the old order.

And this too is a form of Black Power though we didn't call it that at the time, but this form of power in and of itself we also found inadequate to meet our needs. Nine years after he had written those words, Dr. King had fallen to the assassin's bullet. Nine years after he had written those words, though segregation was a little less blunt in the South, though most of Black America was living in the horror of crowded, firetrapped, ghettos of the North and had not advanced two inches, we learned something else at this point taught by Malcolm X, Brother Baraka, Rap Brown and Eldridge Cleaver. We learned that when the stranger allies himself with the so-called native—a return to Baldwin's metaphor—it is very hard for the stranger to play anything other than a secondary role. In many struggles Black America carried on together with white people. We found, all too often, however, that well-meaning whites nevertheless conceived of us as strangers, assigned to us the role of strangers in our own struggle and that these white people knew what was good for us better than we did; they knew how we related to the American tradition better than we did, and they were always, willingly or not, the natives and we were always the strangers. To stop being strangers we had to find the road to power ourselves, and, whether or not one accepts other aspects of thoughts of Frantz Fanon, it is clear that the rising Black consciousness requires that we be led by our own, that we determine our own destiny, that we recognize our own needs and that white Americans have quite another task to perform, and that task is to work to cure the sickness of racism among their own people, to work on changes needed in the total society.

Efforts at achieving power in various forms combined with the rising tides of Black self-confidence bring us to the heart of the problem in America today—the heart of the problem to which this conference addresses itself. It is clear that pride in Blackness and all this implies—from a revival of Black history and other Afro-American studies to a new appreciation of our women, to being led on the road to better life by Black leaders—is an absolute necessity if we are to end our status as strangers. We have not yet, however, solved the riddle of the lever, or levers, that can provide the power we need to wrest a better way of life from the power structure within the total society. And we have a number of options, and I would like to discuss just a few of these including the one about which I am most knowledgeable. One option, of course, is to leave, to return, not only spiritually but physically, to lands of our African heritage. And no doubt some will choose this solution, but it cannot be a solution for most of us. There are physical problems as to where such a massive migration would go and cultural ones stemming from our distance from African cultures. But there are also other aspects: We own a good part of these United States, not legally but morally. Our sweat has gone to make the railroads run and to make cotton king; our brains helped to build Washington, D.C., and made heart transplant possible. Our talents helped to enrich the music, the stage, and the poetry of this nation. Our blood has been shed in too many wars, including the fiasco in which we are presently engaged, in Indochina. So we have a great investment in this nation, one that we ought not to be willing to give up; and our power ought to give us our rightful share in what we have wrought, and, therefore, I for one choose not to leave.

There is another approach: We could demand a piece of the nation for ourselves. We could demand five or six states as a territory for a Black nation. We can carve out the old turf in each city, the ghettos in each city as our own turf; and this has possibilities, and it has been explored by many thinkers both Black and white. W. H. Ferry wrote in the *Saturday Review* of June 15, of what Black town wants most white towns cannot confer:

> Black town wants independence and the authority to run its own affairs. It wants to recover its manhood, its self-love, and to develop its ability to conduct a self-reliant community. A successful plan for co-existence is not that of the new Jerusalem, it is that of a national community struggling with the untenable doctrines of integration. It is a vision of a "New federalism" that will give ten percent of our citizens the chance they seek to make whatever they want to make of themselves, their culture and their community.

And I do not reject this form of power either, on moral grounds, but I have not seen any evidence within this society that Black America can get such communities without first achieving the tremendous power necessary to force them into existence. Black towns are intriguing but they beg the question for we must, should we decide we want them, first find the power to get them.

And finally, I'd like to talk about political power. And I think that one of the great things that have come out of this conference is that Black people of every political persuasion have been represented here and are speaking from this rostrum. And I think we need not waste our time spending subtle word distinctions between "reform" and "revolution" or between "militant" and "moderate," or between working "in" or "out" of the system, since to live in this republic is to be hopelessly trapped in its machinations. What we need is not polemics but a viable politics for Black survival; that is, we need a political strategy which speaks to a condition and not to a theory. A strategy which can organize us so that we can at least neutralize those who are leaning on us: the racist police, the gouging merchants and landlords, the cynical employers, and all the other oppressors of the African that are here in America.

So I would like to talk about electoral politics. You may ask, How much Black self-determination can you get out of traditional politics? Not much, I would say very quickly, maybe an inch here, and an ounce there. But Black self-determination may never be absolute in America since it depends ultimately on who has the most economic, political and military muscle. So I have no illusions about the ultimate extent of my power as the Mayor of Gary, Indiana. Nevertheless, since our very survival is at stake, we are obliged to continue to search and scrape for every inch of power that we can get. And, therefore, I see electoral politics as a tool, an instrument that we would be foolish not to use on a massive scale to help better our lives. Now, the synthesis of protest and electoral politics, so lacking in the sixties, is emerging as the number one item on the Black agenda for the seventies. Mass political organizing is tailor-made for the more than 55 percent of all Blacks living in urban areas. Blacks are more than 59 percent of all people in Washington D.C.; in Newark, New Jersey; and in Gary, Indiana. Blacks are more than 40 percent of all people living in Baltimore, Maryland; Birmingham, Alabama; Detroit, Michigan; New Orleans, Louisana; and St. Louis, Missouri. And we are indeed more than 32 percent of the populations in nine of the nation's thirteen largest cities. And politically all of this means that because of our increasing number, we have the potential to influence decisions and the outcome of elections in major cities more powerfully than any other ethnic group in America. Now, assuming that the present urban pattern of Black immigration and white out-migration continues, we will be able to elect Black mayors in at least nineteen large- and medium-sized cities before the end of the seventies. And I would like to mention in some detail just a few of these cities. Right here in Atlanta, Georgia, for example, Black people are 49 percent of the population and almost 41 percent of the registered voters. This means that they have a better then average chance of capturing city hall in 1973, the next time around.

In Baltimore, Maryland, whites are beginning to accept the fact that 1971 is the year for a Black mayor according to Clarence Mitchell who himself may be a candidate. The chances of electing a Black mayor in Baltimore are good because Blacks are about 50 percent of the population and 45 percent of the registered voters.

In Chicago, which is now one-third Black, there should be a Black mayor no later than 1979. And by then the combination of white liberals and those disenchanted with the Democratic party organization, plus the very substantial Black voting population, will have the votes to win.

Now there are other cities. We cannot say a simple majority is enough; it is going to be necessary to organize and to register the voters in order to accomplish this—poor registration, in fact, is a painful problem in all of the cities that I have been talking about. Just think about Detroit, Michigan—just 3,500 more voters would have elected Dick Austin last year. Same thing is true in Houston, Texas. Curtis Graves last year became the first Black man to run for mayor of that city and he polled 32 percent of the vote and a switch of only five thousand voters would have forced a run-off between him and the incumbent mayor. I know that Curtis Graves and Richard Austin will be running again the next time around. There are also good prospects in Memphis, Tennessee, and Philadelphia, both of which are now one-third Black. In St. Louis the reapportionment of the city's twenty-eight wards in 1971 should increase the number dominated by Blacks from eight to thirteen. Blacks should be more than half of the population in St. Louis by 1975.

I do want to re-emphasize that more rhetoric will not elect Black mayors, that it will take organization and registration. You cannot simply bring an outside leader into a city and let him give a talk on registration, and then expect the great majority of unregistered voters to rush out and register. I know from experience that voter registration is also one of the keys to any serious effort at Black political empowerment. I do want to say one thing, quickly, that while this movement is developing toward Black political empowerment, the white has not—and I hope that you will listen to me—he has not been sitting still and simply allowing it to happen. There's always a funny thing when it comes our turn to have our slice of the pie, somebody always decides to change the rules. And what we see happening in the cities today is that the rules are being changed in several different ways. For example, we hear of a new thing called "metropolitan government" today more than we heard it before. And "metropolitan government" is just one more way to make sure that Black people in cities do not seize control and begin to exercise some say-so over their own destinies. What is taking place is a redefinition of political jurisdictions in order to develop the power that is necessary to continue to control Black people and to continue to keep them in colonies. There is another thing called dis-annexation which is the opposite of annexation, or adding on where there's a pocket in our community of Gary, Indiana. And so, they are going to separate themselves, and, in effect, create a new political jurisdiction and in that manner continue to exercise a control over their own lives and their own destinies.

And there are other things that are happening in cities. We see the flight to the suburbs. To me the flight to the suburbs is no more than an effort on the part of these whites who go not to seek better schools, not to seek cleaner air, but rather to redefine political jurisdiction and in that way continue to maintain political control over their lives. So we have to be very careful that as this trend of Black political empowerment continues, that others are very busy laying plans to snatch that power away. As a matter of fact, consolidation or metropolitan governments have already occurred in Nashville, Tennessee, which is about 43 percent Black; Miami, Florida, which is about 28 percent Black; Jacksonville, Florida, which is 47 percent Black; and Indianapolis, Indiana, which is 29 percent Black. So we find that this move is well under way in this country. It is very clear, I think, that the next stage, the next stage in the struggle for Black liberation in this country lies in the cities, that cities represent the beachhead of the struggle for Black liberation. And I hope that we will take advantage of the opportunity to organize those cities, to register people to vote, and to see to it on election day that they go out and that they cast their ballot. The time has come when Black people must stop electing public officials; they must begin to select public officials.

Now sometimes we talk a little about coalitions, and I think coalitions are important. But I do not feel very much hope about coalitions. The experiences of Black America with other segments of our society have most often been disappointing; perhaps they will be again. The poverty it seems that Black people are caught up in is such that it is not possible to develop really meaningful relationships with others. But I believe that Black Power for Black Americans can in part, at least, lie in political power.

In the essay that I've already quoted, and I would conclude with the following, in the essay by Baldwin, he said:

> No road whatever will lead Americans back to the simplicity of this European village where white men still have the luxury of looking upon me as a stranger. I am not, really, a stranger any longer for any American alive. One of the things that distinguishes Americans from other people is that no other people has ever been so deeply involved in the lives of Black men, and vice versa. . . . It is precisely this Black-white experience which may prove of indispensable value to us in the world we face today. This world is white no longer and it will never be white again.

Finally, one of the finest of our Black poets, Margaret Walker, ends her poem, "For My People," with a kind of incantation to the future —and let me cite it here in closing, for her vision is the vision of a Black woman who wrote these words more than a quarter of a century ago:

> Let a new earth rise. Let another world be born. Let a bloody peace be written in the sky. Let a second generation full of courage issue forth, let a people loving freedom come to growth, let a beauty full of healing and a strength of final clenching be the pulsing in our spirits and our blood. Let the martial songs be written, let the dirges disappear. Let a race of men now rise and take control!

"A race of men," Margaret Walker says, and I say right on, Sister.

Ambassador El Hajj Abdoulaye Touré

Representative to the United States from Guinea, one of the most progressive African nations.

Dear Brothers . . . I wish to apologize to you . . . to have to use another form of communication between us which is this language, French, I must use. . . . I would like to have love . . . to have addressed you in a language which would have been strictly African . . . but that is not your fault, it is not my fault, it is the fault of imperialism which has forced Black people to communicate with each other in alien tongues.

I would like to . . . to bring you brotherly greetings . . . from the people of Guinea . . . from the Democratic party of Guinea . . . and in one word, the greetings of the people of Africa to you . . .

It is a great honor to be invited to this congress . . . this congress which is held on a continent other than Africa, but which in spite of everything is inseparable to the African continent.

I would like to tell you that all of the Black people of Africa are thinking in this moment of their brothers and sisters on the American continent.

I would like to tell you and to reassure you that Mother Africa thinks about her brothers and sisters and sons and daughters in America, and that Mother Africa is in this struggle with you.

Your contribution for the total liberation of Africa, or the liberation of Black peoples everywhere is absolutely necessary.

I have seen on the program some titles, some workshops which are quite interesting and which show already bright promises, new prospectives for the future and for the evolution of Black people.

I would like . . . this evening to thank you . . . for the brotherly greeting and welcome . . . that organizers of this congress have given me . . . and all of you who are present here in this stadium . . . and to tell you and to repeat to you . . . that we are attaching to this congress much importance and much successful wishes.

And we wish that this congress will be a true congress of complete and total success.

Thank you, dear Brothers and Sisters.

Evelyn Kawanza

Member of and representative in the United States for the Zimbabwe Action Group, which is dedicated to the liberation of Zimbabwe from the white colonialists.

I feel very honored to be asked to come and speak to you here because when I first came to this country, I never thought I would ever have a chance to be among my own sisters and brothers as I am today. When I first came here, I came on a State Department scholarship; therefore, that meant I was so secluded from my own sisters and brothers that I never even knew that you loved me or I had anything to do with you. I remember one time when I was at school (I went to school in Connecticut), one sister was in my dorm and there were about ninety white kids in there and there were two Blacks—the two of us—but we never communicated at all until one day she came to me and said, "Evelyn, you must be very intelligent; how come you know how to wear stockings and you know how to dress in dresses; you just came a month ago? How can you learn so fast?" So I told this sister that when I came from Zimbabwe I was naked on the plane. I was wearing leaves around my side, and then when I got to Kennedy Airport, I found these white people there. They said this is the way you have to dress here. Here are the stockings, here is everything; you have to dress this way. And because of the way I answered, this sister understood me and from then on we were communicating, and the white kids were getting uptight about it. This is because they always tell us that, you know, these Black people here don't want you because they think they're superior, and they go to you and tell you these Africans don't want you; so that there is always a gap between us. So, I feel very, very happy to know that now, I just live among my own people, and I can spend months and months without seeing a white person. So, I am very happy to be able to see all of you here.

Now I am going to talk about my country, Zimbabwe, which the white man calls Rhodesia. I am sure, by now, all of you are acquainted about the situation. The situation in Zimbabwe is very hard at the moment. We have two liberation movements who are trying to fight for our struggle. One of them is called Zimbabwe African People's Union, and the second one is Zimbabwe African National Union.

Both of these liberation movements are based in Lusaka, and they are all doing what they can with the situation they are facing to wage guerrilla struggle in Rhodesia, which is a little different because in Rhodesia—in Zimbabwe—we don't have too many bushes so that they could hide behind them. It's a plain country; therefore, our brothers over there are having a little trouble.

What I will ask of you, Brothers and Sisters, is to do all you can to help us in our struggle. You can help us in different ways: The first one would be to try and get as much information as you can about the liberation movement in Zimbabwe. Since there are two of them, it means you have to read about them, and choose whichever one you feel is worth supporting, and this could be done by raising funds and then contacting these people and sending them the funds. The second thing that I think you could do is to form some kind of committee which you might call, maybe, Friends for Zimbabwe, or Committee for Zimbabwe, or something of that sort. This kind of committee would help to educate our own sisters here about Zimbabwe. So that when they hear about fund-raising for Zimbabwe they will know what it's all about. Because in New York when we are trying to have fund-raising things, you go to Harlem and you tell people come to this, come to this thing, they don't even know what you are talking about. So, I think it's very important that we should have an organization, or a committee, run by our sisters, and being helped by us in order to educate the community to know what we are fighting for, and this committee too would help in the raising of funds.

The third thing I would like to talk about is the political prisoners in Zimbabwe. As we are talking at the moment, there are people who have been in prison since 1964, without trial. They are either in detention or in restriction. They were just put there. They were never told what wrong they did but just they're Black, and they look to be revolutionaries in a way. So they are just sitting there and their families are suffering. School is very expensive in Zimbabwe, clothes are very expensive in Zimbabwe; some of them cannot even afford food. So, a few of us, a few of the Zimbabwe students in New York decided to form a Zimbabwe Relief Fund which would help in this kind of thing. The struggle should be fought right around. It's not just in the front of the military that the struggle is, we have to take care of the things outside the struggle.

Thank you very much.

Raymond Mbala

Member of the Revolutionary Government of Angola (GRAE) which is engaged in armed struggle to free Angola from the Portuguese imperialists.

Brothers and Sisters, it is a great pleasure for me, today, to address this unique congress. So, I thank you in the name of all African people, in the name of all Angolan people, in the name of all African Freedom Fighters, and in the name of the Angolan Revolutionary Government-in-exile.

As we know, we in Africa today are engaged in a great and a noble struggle against the forces of colonialist, imperialist, neocolonialist, and injustice. There is a mood of nationalism that swept through the continent of Africa. The freedom-loving people of Africa are united by their common sense of nationalism. We do not need to look around for a basis for unity as if there's a multiracial party. Our unity is already there. Our unity is in the color of our skin. Our unity is in our common suffering. If we look at the African nations that have achieved independence we see that a nationalist movement was, in each case, responsible. A multiracial party was not responsible. Our struggle today is your struggle, and it is part of the struggle going on in the world today for the survival of mankind. We support all efforts at securing the rights and the freedom of all Africans, wherever they are.

Most African states are independent today, but the great Southern Africa remains in bondage. Among these are Angola, Mozambique, Rhodesia, South Africa, South West Africa, and Portuguese Guinea Bissau. Colonial exploitation has always taken different forms, depending upon local geography, economy, and the social structure. In Africa, colonialism took three main forms. One, exploitation of manpower, two, exploitation of natural resources, and three, exploitation of the land and its agriculture. Today, the freedom struggle in Africa is directed toward achieving political freedom, but its main thrust is the complete liquidation of all these forms of exploitation. In Angola, we will close the doors, as surely as I stand here, to imperialist exploitation by Portugal and her allies on the Angolan soil.

Brothers and Sisters, colonialism as it was developed became an evil system of slavery and robbery, a ruthless raping of our land and our people by colonial powers. A majority of our people were plunged into the most dismal depths of poverty and human misery. Thousands, perhaps millions of our brothers and sisters were sold into slavery; their efforts to escape were crushed. No revolution ever, ever started without a reason. In Angola, we are fighting for freedom and self-determination. Our struggle is a struggle against a system of institutionalized oppression. We have waited and waited for a long time for the so-called free world to stand by us in this struggle; but we are still waiting; until now all we have seen are American guns, American grenades used to kill Africans in Angola. It is American money, through NATO—that is the "North American Terrorist Organization"—that allows the Portuguese fascist pigs to continue to resist independence. But we know that no nation, no matter how powerful, can continue forever to make African people suffer. The masses of people will always rise up to overthrow their oppressors and this is what our freedom struggle is all about in Angola.

Angola lies between the ex-French Congo Brazzaville and the ex-Belgian Congo Kinshasa to the north, and Southwest Africa on the South; to the east is Rhodesia, and the ocean is to the west. The population of Angola is around five million; nearly 99 percent of the people are Africans. Portuguese occupation dates back to the fifteenth century. The first so-called technicians from Europe were missionaries. They came teaching peace by using their great book called the Holy Holy Bible, but served imperialism and not the people. Portuguese fascists set up an ugly system in Angola. They separated the Angolan society into two classes. One class was called *assimulattos,* and the other class was called *indigenato.* The *assimulattos* were few in number; they were granted some education, and they became the elites. The *indigenato* was the class of the African masses, doomed to poverty and degradation. Every man, woman, and child over fourteen years must work for thirty days each year on the white-owned coffee plantations; they work without pay, and they must provide their own tools, even. In Angola, each person must carry his work cards, his tax receipts, and, if he's out of his own town, permission is required. Any incidents of so-called misconduct mean punishment by the Portuguese pigs. It is this situation that causes thousands upon thousands of our people to flee their villages each year, to walk on bare feet, for weeks, to the liberated areas of the country. It is this intolerable human condition that we fight against. We will oppose this regime with our last drop of blood—if that's what it takes.

Brothers and Sisters, we cannot afford to carry on any rivalry among ourselves, or battling among ourselves. We must turn all of our energies to fighting the common enemy—the oppressors of all African people.

Our revolution began nearly ten years ago. On March 1, 1961, at the farm in Angola called the Primavera, a Portuguese white farmer murdered several African workers simply because they asked for decent wages and working conditions. On the next day, sixty thousand Angolans rose up against their oppressors. The Portuguese retaliation against the united African people was savage: they sadistically killed defenseless women and children. Portuguese airplanes destroyed countless villages with napalm bombs in the slaughter of thousands of African men, women and children. We will not forget those people who have died. We pledge to them that we will continue our struggle until every Angolan is liberated.

There is no Portuguese army which can stop our Freedom Fighters. These brave commandos in the jungles in the forest have learned to defend themselves and the countryside. The Portuguese soldiers are afraid to leave the cities. They dare not venture into the countrysides, for they know the Freedom Fighters are in control. It is the Freedom Fighters who have the love and support of the masses of African people. The people know the Portuguese are the enemy. Recent reports from the battlefront areas in Angola tell of sure and steady victories that are being won by our Freedom Fighters. The Portuguese reaction is predictable. Already the Portuguese Government have come to their faithful friends, the United States of America, to ask for help. The United States Government must bear a great burden for killing African people in Africa. For without these United States weapons and support the Portuguese would be finished. Portugal is a third-rate and a poor country. It is being propped up by American dollars. And why is this so? Why does this country do this? One answer is that the United States wishes to maintain its military bases in the Portuguese territories.

Brothers and Sisters, as a representative of the Angolan Revolutionary Government-in-exile and the Angolan National Liberation Front, I would like to tell you briefly of the enormous task that faces our revolutionary movements. First, is the training of an army since 1961. More than forty thousand commando soldiers have been trained and equipped and sent back to carry on the struggle. The war goes on from three fronts: the northern front, the eastern front and the central front. We must face, in our struggle, tremendous obstacles: lack of education, lack of equipment, disease, lack of materials. But the army continues to grow; battles are being won. Portuguese equipment is being captured. Portuguese soldiers have been taken as prisoners. The enemy is afraid to venture out of the security of the cities. They fear the countrysides. But there is more to our movement than the Angolan National Liberation Army. There is also a major program of education and the technical training that goes on daily in the Republic of the Congo Kinshasa and the liberated areas. So far, hundreds of people have been sent to universities abroad to receive the necessary training to serve our people. The problems of fighting the war and educating our people are only the beginning. We must care for close to a million refugees actually living in the Republic of the Congo Kinshasa. These poor people walk weeks and weeks to escape the brutal Portuguese oppressions. Their feet are bare, their clothing is made from the bark of trees. These people come by thousands to refugee camps. They work for the revolution for only then will they return to their villages. There is some talk of Portuguese reforms in each colony. We reject strongly this idea. It is too late for reforms after five centuries. The die is cast. We must have freedom to shape our own destiny. We demand independence in the name of those thousands of people who have already died. However, we have never ceased to appeal to the Portuguese fascist government to find a fair solution to the Angolan struggle. We do this because we do not want to see any more innocent blood of African people.

Brothers and Sisters, some people see national liberation as a step in the march toward world Communism. Some direct their hostility toward Russia, some toward China; others admire Russia, others admire China. But our revolution is simply an effort to control our own destiny, and we can only control our own destiny by controlling the means of production. If some people must call that Communism, I don't care—that's what we want. To Portugal, Angola means coffee, diamond mines, gold, copper; it was sugar in Cuba and in Algeria it was oil. Our people will enjoy the fruits of their labor; they will be proud to call themselves Angolans and Africans.

Brothers and Sisters, we must know that Angola is of great importance to the entire Southern African political situation. Take a look at the map of Africa and you will see. Angola is on the very borders of Rhodesia and the white racist country of South West Africa. A free Angola will be a real threat to the white minority government to the south. A war of liberation cannot be fought from Cairo, from Dar es Salaam, from England, but the war must be fought from the forest, from the countryside, from the hills, from the jungles.

Brothers and Sisters, I ask your help today in our struggle, because our struggle is your struggle and it is our struggle. How can you help? Let me suggest these ways: First, find out what is happening in the African liberation struggle. This congress is an excellent way to do that. Go back into your communities and talk to brothers and sisters, tell them about the war going on in Angola.

Second, many of you may be represented in the Congress by our

African Congressmen and Congresswomen; urge them to fight continuously against financial support of Portugal through NATO—no more U.S. dollars to kill African people!

Third, support us by sending clothing and schoolbooks to be used by refugees, and support us with your dollars. The Angolan office in New York, which has the duty of informing the African people in this country of what is going on in Angola, had to close its doors more than a year ago for lack of money to pay the rent. So, I was forced, since then, to operate from where I sleep. Do I have a choice? The main role for the Angolan office which we have in New York is to supply information about latest events on the battlefronts. It also collects clothing for shipment to refugees. Right now, we have more than nine hundred thousand Angolan refugees in the Republic of the Congo.

Finally, refuse to buy any Portuguese products; refuse to buy products that are produced by the exploitation of African people in Angola. These include Gulf gasoline and oil, Gulf products, cork and cork products—a complete list is available from the Angolan office. Our latest records from Angola give us reason to believe that victory will come at last, the enemy is more and more desperate. As to the role of Pan-Africanism in the present struggle for liberation, I believe that it is very important because one cannot talk of African unity until all Africa is free. As long as some portion of the land, our motherland, is still under colonial domination, then African unity will remain meaningless expression. We must adopt a positive all-out, anti-colonialist and anti-imperialist, anti-neocolonialist and anti-injustice attack and this quickly for we cannot afford the luxury of delay. Time acts for the enemy no less than for ourselves.

The question of the use of violence in the liberation struggle is today past the debating stage, as witness the course of events in Angola, Mozambique, Zimbabwe, South West Africa, South Africa, and Guinea Bissau. Where the colonialists have without any provocation on the part of the African people resorted to practicing outlandish violence then the African people would be coerced to continue to take it all lying down and the independent African states would also be cowards if they failed to recognize where their duty lies in this matter. Africa demands that we keep on fighting until victory is won for entire Africa. Now is the time to fight; now is the time to win. Let us tell the colonialists and all those imperialists, Brothers and Sisters, that Africa is for Africans. It is not their business to categorize our attributes; that is for our African masses, wherever they are, to do so, and they will do it in a manner that will spell unity and not division.

To all of you, my dear Brothers and my dear Sisters, I would like to say, before I finish, that the African youth is the conscience of the people, and the role which we are called upon to play in the struggle for the liberation is very, very important. Since the youth makes up the living forces of the society, we have a role to play in the formation of our peoples. We all know that the races may sometimes bask on the assumption that one man has a right to determine the limit of freedom for another simply because he is physically different in appearance. Well, time is over to believe this because a man cannot change his color or his face; instead he has to be proud. Also, I think that Black nationalism should not depend on an emotional slogan and empty militant aggressiveness. Nationalism, Brothers and Sisters, must be expressed through economic, political and cultural institutions. Hence, nationalism should be expressed in social programs that aim to answer these institutions, to make them conform to the nationalist aspiration of the African people. We must be proud of our race because Black is beautiful. I am convinced that the African people of Africa, America, West Indies, Cuba, England, and so on are as good as any other race. Whatever others have done to ameliorate their problems and secure their daily happiness for their prosperity we also can do—did it! It is only for us, and only for us, to use the same key or solution that the others used: unity through nationalist leadership. Unity must be based on a doctrine and principles of confidence in our ability to meet the challenge of modern materialism.

Brothers and Sisters, as African people, let us remain faithful to this great common cause of Black liberation in Angola and throughout the world. For united we stand, divided we will always be exploited. All power to the African people. All power to the African people. All power to the African people. All power to the African people.

Thank you very much.

Roosevelt Douglas

Member of the Organization of Black People Union (OBPU), whose primary goal is the unity of all Black people in Canada and West Indies, and establishing alliances with Black people around the world. Roosevelt Douglas is also a member of the faculty at McGill University.

Good afternoon to my Brothers and Sisters:

. . . This is supposed to be a Congress of African People based on the political ideology of Pan-Africanism. Since we have been here, from Wednesday, there are many people who feel that we achieved our objective; there are some people who feel that we failed to achieve our objective; there are some people who feel that there are many Pan-African parasites; there are some people who feel that there are many Pan-African revolutionaries; my Brothers and Sisters, the success of this congress will depend on the level of work you intend to do when you go back to your respective communities.

I was particularly distressed with what many of the speakers said with regard to the development of Pan-Africanist thought. It was significant that many of our brothers stayed completely away from praising the work of the Honorable Marcus Garvey. My Brothers and Sisters, it is important that when we leave here today we understand what the chronological development of Pan-Africanist thought has meant to us since 1900, and why I speak about the Caribbean. It is important that you understand that the first Pan-African Congress held in London was organized by an African born in Trinidad, Henry Sylvester Williams. Many of you may not have heard of this brother, but it is important that you understand because Africans in the Caribbean have played a very significant role not only to the development of Pan-Africanist thought but to the liberation of African people wherever they live. There is no need for me to stress the history of African people; you all know what happened back in the sixteenth century in Africa. The Europeans came into Africa; they taught us to kneel down, we obeyed and we knelt down; they gave us the Bible, we took the Bible; they told us to look to the sky for Jesus and the angels, we looked to the sky for Jesus and the angels. While we were looking to the sky, they took our land, our gold, our bauxite, our diamonds, our uranium. But this was not sufficient; when they were finished taking all of this, they took us, put us in the slave ships, and sprinkled us all over the world—all over the Atlantic they sprinkled African people. Today there are 130 million African people in the Americas. Let us understand that there are only 35 million Africans in America. Therefore, we have to move to unite 130 million African people in the United States, in Latin America, and the Caribbean and this can only be done if we are serious about realizing that we can only depend on ourselves; we cannot depend on liberals, we cannot depend on crackers, we cannot depend on Marxists. It is important, therefore, that we understand that whereas we find ourselves in the grip of the struggle facing the United States, it is important that you understand that we are not only fighting against the United States, but we are fighting against Europe, we are fighting against NATO, and when the time comes and (if you don't believe me, you can ask the African students who have been to the Soviet Union) we will be fighting against the Soviet Union.

It is very important that we understand, further, what our history has been as far as Pan-Africanist thought is concerned since 1900. It is important because not only must we understand the chronological development of Pan-Africanism but we must relate the historical facts of our development to what is happening today. In the 1920's we had three Pan-African Conferences in New York, Philadelphia, and again in New York under Marcus Garvey. In 1900 we had the first Pan-Africanist Conference in London. What is important for us to understand is that if we are going, seriously, to unite African people, we must understand where we could hurt the enemy the most. When Garvey moved in the twenties he was able to mobilize millions of African people in the United States of America, Latin America and the Caribbean. We must understand why the Garvey Movement failed; we must understand what the crackers did to destroy the Garvey Movement; and we must understand the Negroes who were used to help destroy the Garvey Movement. Too often in the past we have refused to be honest with ourselves; we have refused to take stock of the mistakes we have made in the past. What I am saying is that every time we organize around a new political ideology there are certain elements that, first of all, oppose the ideology, then co-opt the ideology, then misuse our ideology. In the 1960's this is what happened to the Black Power Movement. We started calling for Black Power, certain people opposed Black Power, then they moved to co-opt Black Power, then they moved to destroy Black Power.

Today we are speaking about Pan-Africanism. There were certain people who opposed Pan-Africanism when Brother Stokely Carmichael introduced Pan-Africanism. Today many of them, still integrationist, still liberals—willing to support the Jews and the Zionists in Israel—turn and tell me and you, today, that they are Pan-Africanist.

They say that Pan-Africanism and Africa is the "in-thing" today and they want to be on the "in-thing." If these people are going to lead us, let us make an effort to leave this conference with a very clear understanding that Pan-Africanism means sacrifice, it means bloodshed, it means revolution, it means liberation. Brother Howard Fuller spoke two nights ago and he outlined to you what he meant by Pan-Africanism.

Let me tell you that our struggle in the Caribbean is based on Pan-Africanist ideology. Tomorrow morning I'll be going to court in Montreal facing twelve criminal charges and the possibilities of life imprisonment. This confrontation began two years ago when Black students at a white university in Canada launched a complaint against a professor who had insisted on failing Black students because he said that Black students and Black people were too damn stupid to be doctors. We moved against this and the professor was supported by the administration of the university. The administration of the university was then supported by the government of Canada. What is important for those students who are here is that you must understand that white universities are controlled by the very same people who control the economic resources of the Caribbean and of Africa. If you don't believe me, check out the back room of the members of the board of trusteeship or the board of governors at any major university and you will find Rockefeller, Brumsford, Ford and company. They control the government and they control the education.

This is what capitalism is about. And Lenin speaks about the high stage of capitalism that is imperialism; and Brother Kwame Nkrumah tells us that the high stage of imperialism is neocolonialism. Brother Nkrumah further tells us that in the 1970's the class war has transformed itself into a race war. So we must understand what Marxism and Karl Marx are about. We must understand that what Marx was saying was relevant insofar as Marx introduced a new method of thinking, a new method of social analysis. As far as communalism was concerned we were communalistic before Marx knew he was born. So Marx could not have taught communalism to African people. So Marx could not have taught brotherhood and love to African people. What Marx was saying was that in human society there is a dialectical development of thought; in other words, in simple language, human society changes, values change, institutions change, and what he was saying is that at every change in human society there will be what they call a unity and conflict of opposites. Using this system of analysis in the Europe of 1840, Marx realized that the capitalist in Europe would become richer while the working class became poorer and poorer; eventually there would be a confrontation at which point a revolutionary change would take place. What we must understand is that even when Marx spoke about a confrontation between the white working class and the white capitalist, what the confrontation was about was the control of the resources and human and physical wealth of Africa. In other words, what we are saying is that when Marx said that the European working class would be the most revolutionary class, and they would move to liberate the world, and move to introduce a socialist society, what he did not take into account was the fact that the people who were most oppressed in mid-1840 were the slaves in America, or slaves in the Caribbean, or the slaves in Africa; so, we were the ones who would have had to lead the revolution.

If this is the case, then we must understand that in the 1930's we made an alliance with the Communists and we got the shitty end of the stick. In the 1870's we made an alliance with the Progressive Movement and we got the shitty end of the stick. In 1970 can we make the same mistakes? In 1970, we must realize that this generation of Africans are the ones who will have to lead the revolution. We must understand that we have a responsibility. If we are to engage in genocidal activity then our young brothers and sisters coming after us could only be discouraged, and be discouraged to the point where they would believe that African revolution is impossible. We must provide an example. We must provide. . . . If we realize that we have a responsibility, and we are going out to fight our enemy, we must know how we are going to conduct this fight. The fight which we began in Canada—when we realized that we would be facing life imprisonment, and that we had no tangible support in Canada because there are only one hundred thousand Africans in Canada, from a population of twenty-five million crackers—we decided that if we were going to confront the board of governors at the university that control the wealth of the Caribbean and of Africa then, if we believe in Pan-Africanism, we have to expand the base of our struggle from Canada into the Caribbean where our brothers in Trinidad, in Jamaica, in Haiti, in Cuba, in the Dominican Republic, in Puerto Rico, in Guyana, in Surinam, would understand that when we fight against imperialists in Canada they must engage in a similar struggle in the Caribbean. It was on account of this understanding that the brothers in Trinidad came out in solidarity with their brothers in Canada. This eventually led to a confrontation between the masses of people in Trinidad and the government of Trinidad, a neocolonialist government. The government of Trinidad is controlled by Washington; the government of Malawi under Dr. Hasten Banda is controlled by Washington—and this, these so-called Black governments are prepared to sell the interests of Black people down the drain to white imperialists. This, my Brothers and Sisters, was the basis of the struggle in the Caribbean. When the struggle in Trinidad got to be a boiling point, the government of Trinidad called on the military of Trinidad, the army of Trinidad to move against the people of Trinidad and Tobago; the army of Trinidad and Tobago refused—they instead moved to defend the Black people of Trinidad against the puppet government. Today we must understand this as an example: While the brothers were in confrontation in Trinidad, two thousand troops were sent by Nixon to Trinidad to oppress the revolution in Trinidad. Of these two thousand troops, five hundred were Negroes. If the Black people who are trained in the U.S. Army were converted to Pan-Africanism, then when they're sent to oppress Black people in Africa, or in the Caribbean they will go willingly to those countries, but when they get there they will join the guerrillas in the hills. They will join the guerrillas in the hills and fight for the liberation of their people. The brothers from Trinidad, in the army, have sent a special representative to attend this congress. He was one of the people who was paid to move against his people; he refused. He is here now and I would like to introduce you to him. . . . So, my Brothers and Sisters, you understand that we have a responsibility. If we can learn from the drama of this brother, then we will be a few steps ahead.

The Bible teaches us that there should be no remission of sin without the shedding of blood. The white man has sinned against us; we are good and we got to shed his blood. We are no longer willing to wait for the life hereafter to liberate African people. We must be prepared to liberate our people in this life. Let us, therefore, understand that we must take home from this congress the very essential message that we cannot get help from anybody but ourselves; even the United Nations is a racist organization and we have got nothing from them. There are two areas of help which could come from the United Nations: one, liberation of African countries; two, economic development of African countries. Resolution 1514 passed in 1960 called for a central fund to use to develop Third World countries. The United States has been unwilling to give any money to this fund. But not only the United States, the Soviet Union has not given a black cent. This means that we must follow the unity which existed from the 1900's to the second Pan-African Conference, in the 1920's, to the fifth Pan-African Conference, in 1945, to the formation of the Casablanca group, the formation of the Brazzaville group, the formation of the Monrovian group, the formation, in 1963, of the Organization of African States, because by 1975 we need to really make the organization of all African people under one central government.

My Brothers and Sisters, at the moment three hundred brothers in Trinidad are facing charges of treason and a firing squad. This could come tomorrow, it could come in October, it could come in January. But this is an immediate problem and the brothers there have asked me to appeal to you to give a small donation which would go toward legal defense and toward buying necessary equipment for the struggle in Trinidad. . . . We know the struggle is going to be long, the struggle is going to be hard, the struggle is going to be difficult. But we were the first people on the face of this earth—the Black man was the first man on the face of this earth—and what we are saying is that we are not going to allow our gold, our bauxite, our uranium to be controlled by the crackers forever. We must understand that liberation is based not only on education and culture and politics but on military strength; therefore, we must pass a resolution before we leave: Call upon the Organization of African States to undertake a scientific project to build by 1975 several nuclear weapons for their defense. The most essential ingredient used to make nuclear weapons is uranium —75 percent comes from Africa. We are allowing the enemy to use our uranium to make nuclear weapons to use against us. We must make nuclear weapons for ourselves to defend our people wherever they may live.

My Brothers and Sisters, in closing, let me thank you for listening, for my voice has not been up to par. Let me further tell you that when I leave this conference and return to Montreal and then to the Caribbean I will be carrying a message: Our brothers and sisters in America stand in solidarity with us and realize the priority of the African continent. But before we can effectively liberate Africa we must go back home, clean up our own communities, control our own communities. Pan-Africanism must not be used as a form of escapism. We cannot allow ourselves to call ourselves African people, walk around with our Afros, dashikis, and our beards and not be ready to struggle. Let us get our minds together. We do not have so much time to waste. Genocide is right around the corner and our only guarantee against genocide is whether we are prepared to fight, to give our lives, and to kill for our people.

Thank you very much, my Brothers and Sisters.

Julian Bond

State legislator and civil rights leader. Out of the New South emerged Julian Bond, a Black Georgia State legislator. Bond was communications director of the Student Nonviolent Coordinating Committee from 1961 until 1965, when he won election to the Georgia House of Representatives from Atlanta's 11th District. Bond is attempting the difficult task of building a black power base in Georgia.

Brothers and Sisters, African People, Friends, and Enemies:

We have been meeting this weekend in what I consider an historic occasion. Historic because we have gathered this weekend in the section of the country from which most of us trace our immediate roots. It is historic because we have had a divergence of ideas, of ideologies, of opinions and expressions come before us. It is historic because we have done a Black thing here in the very heartland of the beast. And it is historic because our geographic location here in the southeastern part of racist America will hopefully lead us to an end of the kind of tribalization of class and geography and religion that all of us have fallen victim to. It is historic because by gathering here in congress, we reaffirm that we are first and foremost Black Nationalists. Black people reject the stupid notion of patriotism that has made us first in war, last in peace, and never in the hearts of our countrymen. And it is finally historic, and the location where we gather is historic, because some of the greatest figures of our past also walked and talked of Mother Africa on the same street where you walked. Martin Luther King went to school here. His widow and his little children live a few blocks away from here, subjected to vicious attacks by the little pervert who runs the F.B.I. . . . (Let me just interject that I used to call J. Edgar Hoover a sissy. But the Gay Liberation Front told me not to call him a sissy, so I won't call him a sissy, but he is a faggot and a punk.) Now even, even before Dr. King was born, Dr. W. E. B. Du Bois walked these streets. Dr. Du Bois lived in the house that now houses the Institute of the Black World on Chestnut Street. It was at this University [Atlanta] that he organized the first scientific, long-range study of Black people in this country from some of the very classrooms that you have been meeting in. Even before Dr. Du Bois, a Black man named Reverend Henry McNeil Turner, one of the earliest advocates of a return to Mother Africa helped to stir Black political power in this state and this region in the period of reconstruction following the American Civil War.

But despite all of the glorious figures you can conjure up from the past, despite the few shining examples, the very few shining examples of the present, examples of some minor political power, some affluence held by some Black people here, the Black people in this city, like Black people everywhere, live on the very edge of catastrophe—daily. We in this city know, as you know in your towns and your cities, that we existed all too often just for the pleasure of other people, just for their entertainment, or exist at all simply because we do not bother them enough for them to eliminate us. Some of these people like to compare their situation with ours, and like to explain that since they made it, why can't we. We all know the answers.

To be sure, we came to this country as they did, as immigrants. Unalike, however, we came as involuntary immigrants. They were not separated from their homeland at the point of a gun. They did not see child torn from mother, wife from husband. They did not have language and culture destroyed. They did not have a strange and alien religion forced upon them. They came here and discovered a system of mercantile capitalism that perfectly fitted their cash-box mentality. While we, a humanistic people, used to communalism and the extended family found instead our very right to form families was forbidden, and our labor, our skills and our intelligence were stolen to fatten other people's pocketbooks and to extend the crooked beak of the American Eagle into the affairs of other people around the globe. But we have survived, we endured, we struggled, we persisted, we even tried to overcome and now we are at an important point in our history. Important because for the last several years there has been intense debate about how we are to continue our struggle. Part of the difficulty arises, I believe, because we have struggled so hard in the past for gains and benefits that fitted other people's agendas and only marginally fitted into ours. For example, we struggled long and hard for the rights of working men in this country—as well we might. But as they grew more affluent and powerful they closed us out. The A.F.L.-C.I.O. are not our friends. We struggled against the illegal rape of Vietnam by this country—as well we might. But next to the Vietnamese people, we suffer from that war more than any other people on the globe. But the American Peace Movement has not returned that friendship in kind. We struggled for the more equitable distribution of goods and services—as well we might. But, as Brother Howard Fuller pointed out, our problem is not our class status. Even the friends of the environment now tell us that Black people have to wait for our chance for jobs and homes, until they have cleaned up the air and the water. Now the people who are in favor of good government tell us that our chance for political sovereignty has to wait because good government dictates a dilution of our votes.

But we are striving here at this congress for unity that will not stifle the natural desires of each of us in his own way to forward the movement of Black people, but will halt the kind of divisiveness that hinders us all. That kind of unity I would think would salute the candidacies of C. B. King and Dr. John Cashin, Black men running for governor in Georgia and Alabama. That kind of unity would salute Imamu Baraka who has demonstrated that the nationalistic ethic can wield strong political power in the most corrupt American city. That kind of unity would salute the brothers of the Black Topographical Center, as they attempt to warn us—and I'm afraid we are not listening to them—of the impending strangulation of our own communities. That kind of unity would suggest that it is a luxury for us to attempt to debate the relative revisionism of Ho Chi Minh. That kind of unity would suggest to us that the alleged security of the college campus is not the proper place from which to engage in social criticism of people who seldom see a book from year to year. That is the kind of unity that suggests that the very old dream which Black people have held since we first came to this country, the dream of uniting the boys on the block with the bourgeoisie, be made into a reality. Let me close with two selections from that great African, Dr. Du Bois. Two selections from his masterful mind, written thirty-seven years apart. The first written for the *Crisis* in 1921 and the second a part of his message to the All-African Peoples Conference in 1958. He begins:

> The growth of a body of public opinion among peoples of Negro descent broad enough to be called Pan-Africanism is a movement belonging almost entirely to the twentieth century. Seven hundred and fifty years before Christ, the Negroes, as rulers of Ethiopia and conquerors of Egypt, were practically supreme in the civilized world. But the character of the African continent was such that this supremacy brought no continental unity; rather the inhabitants of the narrow Nile Valley set their faces toward the Mediterranean and Asia more than Western Sudan, the Valley of the Congo and the Atlantic. From that time even in the rise of the Sudanese Kingdoms of the thirteenth, fourteenth and fifteenth centuries there was still no Pan-Africa and after the slave trade brought intense continental confusion.

Dr. Du Bois says, "As a boy I knew little of Africa save legends and some music in my family. The books which we studied in the public schools had almost no information about Africa, except for Egypt which we were told was not a Black country. I heard of a few great men of Negro blood but I built up in my mind a dream of what

Black people would do in the future, even though I was taught we had no past."

For four hundred years Europe and North America have built up their civilization and their comfort on thievery of colored labor and the lands and materials which rightfully belonged to the demands of the masses of men, but their yielding takes the form of sharing the loot, not of stopping the looting.

Here, then, my Brothers, you face your great decision. Will you—for temporary advantage, automobiles, refrigerators, Paris gowns—spend your income in paying interest on borrowed funds? This is the great dilemma which faces Africans today, one and all. We must give up individual rights for the needs of Mother Africa. We must give up tribal independence for the needs of the nation. Awake, awake, put on thy strength, O Zion. Reject the weakness of missionaries who teach neither love or brotherhood, but chiefly teach the virtues of private profit from capital stolen from your land and your labor. Africa, awake, put on the beautiful robes of Pan-African socialism. You have nothing to lose but your chains. You have a continent to regain. You have freedom and human dignity to attain.

Thank you.

Imamu Amiri Baraka

Poet, playwright, founder and Chairman of the Committee for Unified Newark, an organization dedicated to the liberation and unity of Black people; Program Chairman, Congress of African Peoples.

Habari Gani, Asalaam Alaikum, How are you doing?

I'm sorry a lot of our people are at home but I can dig it's been a long weekend. Everybody is ready to go back. I hope when we go back we don't forget to take something back with us in terms of some of the things that hopefully we've gotten together here in these four or five historic days. Congress of African People is a very historic kind of occasion if you can really think about it, really see it. It's very hard to think in America, especially Black people, because our nervous system is in the hands of our enemies. Very hard for a human being, a body, to think without a nervous system. But what the congress is trying to do is draw all the many different kinds of Black people together. All the different parts of the nervous system, the body, so that it understands again that it is a single body, like a man's body, and all the different African peoples all over this world are just part of that single African Nation, the African Nation which is rising again.

What we came out of the Political Workshop with was first of all the idea that what we wanted is a political party. A political party that would service the needs of Black people wherever they are. A political party that could deal internationally everywhere Black people were. What we are talking about is a national, international, nationalist, Pan-Africanist political party. A political party which will be the model for the nation becoming.

The problem is, usually, that the systems that we make to try to liberate us are usually not good models. Many times you know that Black people have these little organizations—they in the organization and the organization are supposed to be dedicated to steering Black people—but, meanwhile, everybody in the organization is living in exactly the opposite way necessary to free Black people. In other words, people are always saying one thing and doing another. Negroes are always talking Black, but living Negro. Like Sékou Touré says, "We're always talking new things but we always moving like old things." So what the congress is trying to do is find out what our new ideas are and then make us live by them. Commit us to live, be the best element of our ideas. It's very hard, because in America you are magnetized by America. You see, that is what Einstein was trying to tell you with his dimwitted relativity theory—several thousand years after Black people had said that—that bodies tend to magnetize things. So the more bodies you have the more things are magnetized toward those bodies. So if you have a whole lot of bodies that are practicing evil, then everything is magnetized toward evil. Can you understand that? So that in order to get away from the evil magnetism you have to begin practicing a more positive, a more *positive*, philosophy and ideology. And by the example that you create you will begin to magnetize Black people to you, in your various cities; in your various countries.

This political party we want to set up, that is set up, should be a model for the *nation becoming.* The Black political party must be an example of what we want the nation to be *now,* not in the future. We should not live as if we believe what the white boy says: that we would never be liberated. We must live on the one hand as if we were liberated people of a high value system; then more Black people will be magnetized to it and the larger our *nation becoming* will be.

A political party has to function in four areas. A lot of times Black people—because of the television and movies and radios and comic books, controlled by our enemies—believe that revolution is another thing. They believe it has to do with television fantasy or movies that's got something to do with "Up-Tight" or the "Lost Man" or that it has to do with some kind of instantaneous, overnight revolution where you emerge in flame and victory immediately. But that's not the case, Brothers and Sisters. There is no such thing as instant revolution. In the Russian Revolution or the Lenin revolution which was supposed to be an overnight revolution, the majority took control from the minority, captured the means of production. But in the United States of America the so-called minority mentality is the majority mentality. We are not the majority of people; we cannot overnight take power. We must build organizations in the four areas of political power. We must build people who are able to run for public office; we must build community organizations; we must make alliances and coalitions with people all around the world; and we must become skilled in the arts of disruption. We must have a political party that can do all four of those things, not just one unskillfully.

Many think that once they get a .22 rifle and go and shoot once a month that they are skillful enough to overtake and overthrow the United States Government which is the most powerful force on this planet. But that is not the case. Just being angry at white people will not overthrow them. I hope you understand that. Many of our brothers and sisters think that just because they are angry at the crackers, that the crackers will get frightened of them and die, they will dry up and blow away. There is no such thing as instant revolution. Free people are people who deserve to be free. You are slaves because you want to be slaves, because you deserve to be slaves! Can you understand that? You are slaves because you have not done anything that will enable you not to be slaves. You are not free people because you are not qualified to be free people. If you are qualified to be free, you would be free. That's hard to take, ain't it? If you had the skills, if you had the skills to overthrow the white man, you could overthrow the white man. If you were efficient enough, you could do it; if you were dedicated enough, you could do it; if you were disciplined and trained enough, you could do it; but you are none of these and most of you refuse to deal with the realities of becoming skilled and efficient enough to do it. It is not a little dream game where they give you a gift for being Black that you will be free. It is something that will have to be achieved through science and study and dedication and training. These are the things that we wanted to begin to talk about here at this congress; and even so, it's very difficult to get people to stay long enough—to get them to sit down in a chair long enough—to find out some information.

But the party that we want to see is a Black, a World African Political Party. A political party that will function in South Africa like it will function in Chicago, where you know that if you are in Surinam or Jamaica, or New York City this World African Party will be functioning to get power, to bring about self-determination for Black people. Our enemies work along these lines. Many of our brothers, yesterday for instance, in Political Liberation Workshop, wanted to come out and make a lot of condemnations of our enemies. Some of the brothers for instance wanted to come out and denounce super-Jew —come down on them—naming the Zionists as our enemies. But the problem is this. We are a people without an army, without a communication system, with no means of relaying what our brain has conceived to our arms and legs and our muscles. We are a body whose muscles do not even know they belong to the body that the head belongs to, and yet we want to neophyte on our enemies. You cannot achieve political power by talking bad to white people. You can only achieve political power by organizing well enough to take political power, and this is the point. That's a humbling thing, I know, that's humiliating sometimes to have to face that reality—that you are powerless. The nigger would rather talk like he has power, make those great Arab statements without Chinese power. He would rather neophyte, and say how bad he is; what the police ain't going to do and,

"We got these guns, hunky," and hunky come in and wipe them out. The nigger talking about a nation and can't even keep a storefront from being overrun by overweight policemen. Now let us face these realities: a nigger wants to put down the Zionist and the Zionists control the radio, the television, the movies, the education, the intellectual life of the United States, the morality of the United States—Judeo-Christian ethics. The minute you condemn them publicly, you die. They will declare a war on you forever.

The point would be getting strong enough to overthrow your enemies, not broadcasting your hatred for them. Also, there is no revolution without the people. All you leaders and vanguarders, all you niggers who think you going to single-handedly, super-duper nigger style bring freedom to all Black people—you can forget that, there is no such thing as that. Only the people can achieve national liberation. I say national liberation instead of revolution because a whole lot of long-haired white boys are singing about revolution, so I know that can't be the same thing I'm talking about. I'm talking about national liberation. There is no revolution without the people because it is the people themselves who are the only ones that have the power to make revolution. Only the nation itself has the power to change its life. No few bloods high on marijuana and white women are going to change the life style of Black people. There is no national liberation without the nation, without you belonging to a nation: a people with a specific way of life. You must see, as part of that nation, that you evolve to consciousness in that you become politically conscious enough to achieve liberation. If the people are too slow—like the nigger nationalist says—the people are backward because if you're supposed to be the smart, how come you haven't found a way to organize? If you're supposed to be super smart, how come you can't get them—if they so slow—organized into the direction they should go? You are the backward ones; not the people. It is the people that must make revolution, not the so-called vanguard.

Also, we say nationalism because, finally, what are we doing? Who are we trying to bring the power to? Who are we willing to die for? We are willing to die for our mothers and fathers and sisters and brothers, ourselves, our nation, our memory, our future, our past, not abstractions. It is nationalism. Once you become a nation then you can become international. What is so weird is that certain peoples always get niggers to fight harder for them than they fight for niggers. For instance, the radicals, the Jewish radicals have bloods willing to die to see Jews get political power (and that's not an anti-Semitic statement, I think it's a very congratulatory statement). I would like to get somebody to go out and do our dying for us, to run around getting slaughtered so that we could get famous, so that we could get to be free on the expense of some other people. But there is no other people dumb enough to do that for us. There are Jewish lawyers getting famous for losing cases for niggers. There are certain radical revolutionaries who are getting famous while our brothers are waiting in jail to be executed. You understand that? You can make alliances and coalitions with people of color, you can make alliances with people of color, Third World peoples, because they have the same destiny. But we say a political party that can move in four areas, that can move through public office in a Black community, should be nationalist or controlled by nationalists. If that is not the case, and you think you're a nationalist, you jivin'. If there's a nigger in your community running who is truly just a nigger, a tom, a white boy with a mask on, you are jiving. You are supposed to be the smart. Any candidate that runs in the Black community must face a nationalist candidate and the nationalist must soon become powerful enough to win. If you do not deal with that level of politics, by default, the white boy will take it over, as he always has, and his stooges. And Black people will respond to them because they can supply them with goods and services. No matter what our people say, when they get hungry they go where the food is. When they want a place to sleep, they go to the person who's giving out houses. When they need a job, they go to where the jobs are given out. No matter what they say, even the so-called revolutionaries do that.

You must control everything in the community that needs to be controlled. Anything of value: any kind of anti-poverty program, politicians, celebrities, anything that brings money, resources into your community, you should control it. You understand that? Anything of value in your community, you have to control it because if you don't control it, the white boy controls it. It's no need in you saying for instance that the anti-poverty program is jive, of course it's jive. It is designed by your enemy. Take it over, take it over, control it, control everything. The schools are jive. We know the schools are jive. Do you think you are going to keep Black people from sending their children to school? You can say, "This is the white man's education. You getting all these white symbols and they brainwashing you sisters and you shouldn't send your children to school," and she will say, "Yes, you right, Brother, you right, Brother," and tomorrow morning at eight-thirty they getting their faces washed and they're on their way to school. Now the point is: You must control the institutions that already exist in your community, through public office, community organization, coalitions and alliances. Make alliances with people of color in your community, Puerto Ricans. Negroes walk around saying Puerto Ricans, well, they think they're white. There is probably more niggers that think they are white than Puerto Ricans because there are more niggers. People could say that about us. But in your community where there's Mexicans, Puerto Ricans, Indians, you must make alliances with them as if you were a nation. Do not be brainwashed into thinking you just a slave or you will be a slave. Begin to function as if you were a nation—make alliances. You used to do it when you were in the gang. Make alliances with other groups. This extends your power.

In NewArk, we made an alliance with the Puerto Ricans, with the Young Lords—a Mutual Assistance Pact—because Anthony Imperiale attacked the Young Lords. A bomb was thrown into their headquarters and burned it out. So we made a statement that said, "An attack on the Puerto Rican community is an attack on the Black community. An attack on the Black community is an attack on the Puerto Rican community." In other words, if you attack the Puerto Ricans you attack us. Imperiale made a statement a couple of days later that he was going to the state attorney general to see what he could do about this "Pact" that we had made because it must be illegal. In other words, here's a man who makes his living murder-mouthing Black people. And once we declared our mutual assistance that we would meet anything at the level it was delivered—Black and Puerto Ricans together—then he wanted to know how come this Pact existed and wasn't it illegal. Because we had expanded our force and it wasn't just Black people that he had to be frightened of, but the Black people and the Puerto Rican people. And understand this, that if Negroes only want to be Negroes and to not evolve to become the African mind of Black men again, then it will be all the peoples around the world that will kill us when they kill the white boy. It will be you like a butler in the white boy's house when all the people come to burn down the house, the nigger still opening the door letting folks in so he can burn too. Either you will help burn it down or you will burn with it. This is a place where the so-called slaves can ride in Cadillacs; where the so-called revolutionaries can hang out with the enemy; where anybody who is supposed to represent anything has usually been bought and paid for by the time you even hear it. This is the most degenerate place on this earth, and either we will separate ourselves or minds first from this degeneracy, or we will go down with it. Either we will step away from this dying body or we will die with it. Either we will form alternatives to these dead institutions or we will die with these institutions.

The Negro don't have to be immortal. The dinosaurs didn't think they would be extinct either. The dinosaur used to be happy walking around eating off the tops of trees and then the climate changed and it wasn't no trees anymore. It was valleys and it was dry and the dinosaur was too stupid to get down lower and eat close to the earth and so he passed away and a new species came on the planet, that was better adapted. Now either we will be a species of people strong enough to transcend our enslavement or we will pass away with this epoch. Either we will be strong enough to survive into the next epoch or we pass away with this one.

This is not China, this is not nineteenth-century Russia, this is not Cuba, this is not Vietnam, this is not any of those kind of revolutions you can read about easily from the drugstore turntable of books. There is no literature really written on this revolution, on this struggle for national liberation. You cannot get it easily and talk about it at literary cocktail parties. This liberation has to be achieved through efforts and work. You must do enough work so that when the time comes when the bloodletting really comes down, that you are prepared to do it. In 1972, for instance, when they come back around the same cycle that went down in 1967. When it comes back around and the bloodletting comes back, what will you be prepraed to do? Negroes have sold white people wolf tickets for the last decade. All of the sixties everybody has sold the white boy wolf tickets, and now he believes that we mean to kill him; we have convinced him for ten years that we want to kill him and now he believes it. Now that he believes it and is getting ready to receive your terrible onslaught, with what are you going to attack him? You understand that? Where is our army? We are talking about going up against the armies of the United States, most of which are Niggers, your brothers. You haven't even convinced your brother not to be in the army, yet, of your enemy, and you are getting ready to attack him. Most Black people are involved with white mythology. They have pictures of Jesus Christ, Marilyn Monroe or the Beatles up on they walls. They are involved, whether with Beethoven or the Rolling Stones. They like Joe DiMaggio or Mozart. One of those scales—it's the same folks. They either trying to tell you about Marx and Lenin, one group of white boys, or George Washington, Thomas Jefferson, another group of white boys. They are all hooked up with white life.

Where is an army that would fight for the struggle and survival of the Black Nation? Niggers are talking about *now* revolutionaries; that they are not nationalists; they don't represent any nation; they don't represent any culture, they are cultureless; they drop from the sky and even if they did drop from the sky, that would be their culture—sky drops. We must not become the peasant army for the rising tide of Jewish political power. Napoleon had a concept of a peasant army. You hip to it? You can get a whole lot of peasants and talk to them about the international struggle and he would get them lined up with some pitchforks and some brooms and some stones, you see. And they would be facing the standup stomp German-Russian elite. And he would get all these farmers and peasants unarmed, unskilled, to run down in the way of the cavalry. And he would run groups of them down in front of the cavalry and they would fall out and be trying to kill the horses with the pitchforks. And they would be taking those muskets in they heads, and they would be screaming Napoleon's slogans, and Napoleon would be sitting on a hill with his cavalry. And he would wait until the peasants' army had taken the first wave, had disorganized the troops, had caused so much disruption, that the cavalry of the Germans couldn't function. And then he would come zooming down off of that mountain and would ease up and might become Governor of New York, might get on the Supreme Court, or might become a famous lawyer, as famous as William Kunstler.

But the point is this, our struggle must be a struggle that is organically connected to our lives. No one can pin a revolution button on you, an ideology, and say now, blood, you know about revolution, here's your copy of the "Red Book." It has to come out of the lives of the people themselves. I would rather make a coalition with Roy Wilkins or Whitney Young—with any of the most backwards upside-down Negroes in the world, because even they must be, in they jivist moment, committed to change. There are more Black people involved with Roy Wilkins than are involved with the Congress of African People. There are more niggers who think like Whitney Young than think like we do. We have to co-opt these people because they exist in our communities. You cannot merely say, "You're corny, nigger." You got to get him and embrace him and make him be with you. If white people have created some nigger stars and giant civil rights figures, we must love them and embrace them, we must unify with them in brotherhood. I hope you understand. Because it's like coming into this room. If there was Black people and white people in here and you come running in the room and you say, "All you Black folks," the white people got they foot on your neck—and they really would. They would all be standing up and they would have they feet on their necks. But what you have forgotten is that they have developed a relationship after these three hundred years and a lot of bloods *like* that. They feel more uncomfortable with you trying to take the foot off their necks than with the foot on their necks. You have to be able to deal with every area of the Black community. If you so bad and revolutionary that you have hostilized every element of the Black community then you are isolated from the Black community and they will shoot you at random, knowing that there will be no retaliation from the Black community. You must get in with the people; that is your only defense—the people, the community. You must get in with the N.A.A.C.P. and the Urban League and the nigger fraternities and sororities. You must surround yourself with them and function with them.

The nationalist must be the spine of the body of the Black nation. What the nation does the nationalist must make him do a little better, a little faster. If it's slow it's because we slow. You understand that? But the minute you put yourself away from the people (no matter how backward and corny you might think they are), then you are isolated, standing there by yourself—and you will get killed. You will get killed. We are not interested in suicide; it is not about suicide. The white boy is in the death syndrome, the death struggle. We want to live. We want a new life. We want a life that we remember vaguely, sometimes in the back of our heads, as a liberated African people. We do not want to die when white people die. I'm not interested in being killed when Richard Nixon is killed or being destroyed when Fifth Avenue goes up in flames. That's not my idea of what we are about.

So in NewArk what we are trying to do is create a sympathetic atmosphere in which to develop a strong organized understanding of what the struggle is. How we must win. How can we win? Everything of value in the Black community we must control. Whoever runs for public office must be a nationalist or be accountable to nationalists. Anybody that speaks using the Black community as his base must refer and deal with nationalism and Pan-Africanism. All our politicians must do as much for us and Africans all over the world as Javits does for the Jews. Have you ever seen a Jewish congressman jump and denounce Israel? How long do you think he will be a congressman? How long do you think Javits would be a senator if he jumped up and denounced Israel? But niggers can jump up and denounce Africa all day and all night and be elected to anything by Africans. Because you are unconscious like a piece of wood, like a vegetable trying to become a human being, like a human being trying to become something spiritual. That's the kind of evolution we going through, but it is slow. Some of us would rather be animals, some of us would rather be vegetables and some of us would rather be minerals.

I hope that everybody here has gotten something out of the congress. We mean to reconvene, sometime, probably in October. Some of the brothers are coming over to address the U.N. in October. So that in New York City we will probably have a reconvening of those committees of twenty-five in New York City—probably the middle or late October—to hear one of the outstanding philosophers from the African continent, one of the leaders of state, and also to go over our first work, the beginnings of our work. I hope some of you will not get so tripped out by tomorrow's re-emergence into the white world as to forget what we said and did while we were here. I know it's hard to be Black in a world controlled by white folks. Du Bois said we always have the double consciousness. We trying to be Black and meanwhile you got a white ghost hovering over your head that says if you don't do this you get killed, if you don't do this you won't get no money, if you don't do this nobody will think you're beautiful, if you don't do this nobody will think you're smart. That's the ghost, you tryin' to be Black and the ghost is telling you to be a ghost. We hope you won't submit.

I lost my voice, I don't think I'll be able to read the poem but I'm s'posed to read it.

In NewArk when we greet each other on the street we say, "What time is it?" We always say, "It's Nation time!" We say, "What's gonna happen?" We say, "The land is gonna change hands!" Say: "What time is it?" "Nation time," and what's gonna happen? "The land is gonna change hands." Now you think about that. Like Malcolm said, you want some land, look down at your feet. The African concept of who owns the land is who is standing on it. Who uses it owns the land. If somebody could sell you the concept of an absentee landlord, you're really a sucker—they could be on the moon and sell you the land! The land belongs to the people who are standing on it. And if there is enough of you standing on it you ought to claim it. The African Nation is wherever there are enough Africans to take it. The African Nation is wherever there are enough Africans who are willing to take it. You understand that? By *any* means, by *any* means, *any* way you can conceive to do it, *any* way you can conceive. Think about Malcolm, read that. Listen to that record again. I don't mean at a cocktail party, I mean by yourself. Listen to it. By *any* means. It's about land. If you're a revolutionary— WHAT? Black Nationalism. Listen to Malcolm what he said, it's about land. You want some land? What are you standing on? If there's enough of you standing on it, take it. That's what it's about. Nationalism is about land and Nation. A way of life, trying to free itself. So the next time somebody ask you what time it is you tell'em, "IT'S NATION TIME, Brother!"

IT'S NATION TIME

Time to get
together
time to be one strong fast black energy space
      one pulsating positive magnetism, rising
time to get up and
be
come
be
come, time to

be come
time to
get up be come
black genius rise in spirit muscle
sun man get up rise heart of universes to be
future of the world
the black man is the future of the world
be come
rise up
future of the black genius spirit reality
move
from crushed roach back
from dead snake head
from wig funeral in slowmotion
from dancing teeth and coward tip
from jibberbabber patme boss patme smmich
when the brothers strike niggers come out
come out niggers
when the brothers take over the school
help niggers
come out niggers
all niggers negroes must change up
come together in unity unify
for nation time
it's nation time.........
Boom
Booom
BOOOOM
Dadadadadadadadadadada
Boom
Boom
Boom
Boom
Dadadadadaad adadadad
Hey aheee (soft)
Hey ahheee (loud)
Boom
Boom
Boom
sing a get up time to nationfy
sing a miracle fire light
sing a airplane invisibility for the jesus niggers
come from the grave
for the jesus niggers dead in the cave, rose up,

passst jewjuice on shadow world
raise up christ nigger
Christ was black
Krishna was black Shango was black
Black jesus nigger come out and strike
come out and strike boom boom
Heyahheeee come out
strike close ford
close prudential burn the policies
tear glasses off dead statue puppets
they just imitating life
shango buddha black
hermes rasis black
moses krishna
black
When the brothers wanna stop animals
come out niggers come out
come out niggers niggers niggers come out
help us stop the devil
help us build a new world

Niggers come out, brothers are we
with you and your sons your daughters are ours
and we are the same, all the blackness from one black Allah
when the world is clear you'll be with us
come out niggers come out
come out niggers come out
It's nation time eye ime
chant with bells and drum
it's nation time
It's nation time, get up santa claus
get up Roy Wilkins
get up Diana Ross
Get up Jimmy Brown
It's nation time, build it
get up muffet dragger
get up rastus for real to be rasta farari
ras jua, get up nigger, get up nigger
come over here
take a bow
nigger
It's Nation
Time!

BOOK II: WORKSHOPS

Ideological Statement of the Congress of African Peoples

The congress itself represents African Nationalists of diverse description but all of the members of its Executive, Legislative, Coordinating and work councils agree that what the congress must provide is a functioning methodology for reducing the contradictions and artificial diversity of Pan-African Nationalist theory.

Basic to the concept that animates the congress is the idea that ultimately all valid concepts of Pan-African Nationalism will one day come together as a practical, achievable body of effective human accomplishment throughout the Black world. That is, one day we will have unity, or we will cease to exist; even in disunity. Thus it is imperative that we join our brothers wherever they are and move beyond merely rapping about *Black Power* to an understanding of what we finally want to achieve with *Black Power:*

A. Self-Determination: To govern ourselves rather than be governed by others. That means politically, economically and socially, whatever we see as necessary in terms of how we define necessary, we do as a free people. We will therefore build and develop alternative political, social and economic institutions locally, nationally and internationally, viewing each of these levels of activity as part of an organic process each complementing the other.

B. Self-Sufficiency: To provide all the basic necessities for sustenance and growth and survival of our people, i.e., food, shelter, clothing, etc., based on the principle of UJAMAA (cooperative economics).

C. Self-Respect: To build and develop a worldwide revolutionary culture and appropriate values, images, and forms that legitimize our thoughts and actions. Only when we have a revolutionary culture that affirms before the world our legitimacy can we respect ourselves.

D. Self-Defense: Acceptance of the common sense policy to struggle against those who struggle against us, and to make peace with those who make peace with us.

These *Four Ends of Black Power* we see not only as the priorities of

Africans on the American continent, or in the Western Hemisphere, but we recognize these four points as major priorities for Africans all over the world. By direct extension of this reasoning, we move to the position that finally all Black people are Africans, and that as Africans, we are bound together Racially, Historically, Culturally, Politically, and Emotionally.

A. Racially: To say Black is to say *African.* We are African and Black, and Black and African from the same biological roots.

B. Historically: Our history relates to Africa as white American's relates to Europe.

C. Culturally: Common generic attitude toward life, common creative motif and soul.

D. Politically: Garvey, Du Bois, Padmore, Nkrumah, Nyerere and others' concept of Africa as a unified power base to demand power and respect for Black people the world over, i.e., Pan-Africanism. Wherever African people are, we have a commonality based on common struggle.

E. Emotionally: Africans (i.e., Blacks) feel for Africans as a common people and identify with each other.

Basically when we speak of Pan-African Nationalism, we mean simply the knowledge that we are an African people, despite our slavery or colonization by Europeans or dispersal throughout the countries of the world. *Pan-Africanism is thus the global expression of Black Nationalism.* We believe our destiny as free people can only be realized as politically, economically, socially self-determining people conscious of the fact that what we will have brought to power is what Nkrumah and Sékou Touré have called "The African Personality," i.e., African Culture; *our way of life* as a free people. We recognize the central importance of the African Continent to Black struggles for National Liberation, however, we likewise recognize the necessity to build collective political and economic power in order to be a functional ally to African and Third World peoples. Although it is absolutely necessary to have a unified and independent Africa, we must simultaneously move to design viable institutional alternatives wherever we are in which a meaningful (non-romantic) Pan-Africanism can be practiced.

Thus, we have structured Work Councils which reflect major areas of Black (African) concern wherever we are struggling. Basically, the Work Councils are institution building mechanisms through which brothers and sisters gain insight and information on how to solve the problems of our people, i.e., the necessities of Nation Building. The Work Councils are thus the *programmatic* arm of the congress and are crucial to its operation.

I. Political Liberation—Its major role is to design, animate, and instrument, i.e., political party (and quasi political party structures), capable of systematically seizing power wherever possible—free of control from the existing political structure, although exploiting the latter for Black ends where possible. A further concern is how Black people in the colony (U.S.A.) relate to Black Liberation Struggles on the continent (Africa) and in the Islands or wherever those struggles are occurring.

2. Economic Autonomy—Black people must achieve economic self-determination. The concept of Ujamaa is our goal and the creation of mechanisms to maximize Black self-sufficiency, we must also develop ways of exchanging Black resources internationally in order to help Black people obtain economic control of their communities and countries. Of major importance is the creation of Black instruments for the funding of Black agencies in different countries.

3. Creativity and the Arts—The major role is to channel Black creative forms and images into instruments to heighten the consciousness of Black people and recreate the African personality. Emphasis is placed on a Black Value System conducive to our full growth and development into nationhood. We also work to ensure that African (Black) expressive forms can be employed in the other institutional areas of our struggle, i.e., politics, economics, education, religion.

4. Religious System—We must reassess our spiritual beliefs, values, and modes of worship, which must be related to our history as Africans. We must determine how specific religious systems enhance or retard the Black Liberation movement, because spirituality cannot be divorced from our daily life or from our struggle as a people. Therefore, it is important to seek out religious options and new religious forms growing out of the changing demands of Black revolution.

5. Education—Its major role is to construct appropriate definitions of "education" for Black people and how they relate to our protection, survival and liberation. How we develop self-learning processes to transmit Black values and nation-building skills is also of major importance. Movements such as "Community-Control," "Black Studies," "Liberation Schools," and "Independent Black Institutions" be evaluated and a method of interrelationship created. Educational forms of African people the world over are evaluated for their potential influences in any Black struggle. The Work Council seeks to establish a Black school system to remove the indoctrination of a colonized mentality and the legacy of imperialism which still lingers. Black educators and students will be brought together to devise ways in which schools and colleges in their countries can be made to deal effectively with Black needs.

6. History—To use African (Black) history as an interpretive (analytical) tool to understand the "political activity" of a people from

African freedom to American captivity and western colonization. To promote cooperation on an international scale among Black historians to communicate across the world our true history which will provide us with identity, purpose and direction, rectifying the inaccuracies and distortions about us and delineating the course of human events from a liberated Black perspective.

7. Law and Justice—Develop mechanisms to survive the oppressive "legal" system that exists, and determine how we can create an alternative system (and institutions) based on justice. [Relationship of Black lawyers to Black political activists is of central importance as well as the building of arbitration committees to negotiate conflict within the Black community.]

8. Black Technology—Brothers and sisters in the technical disciplines are being organized to formulate plans and programs to improve the technical capabilities of Black communities for any situation. The congress intends to assist in the development of the Pan-African technical potential through such mechanisms as an Institute of Black Technology.

9. Communications and Systems Analysis—Develop Black communications methods that utilize existing systems as well as design our own alternatives. New ways of controlling Black information in white media. Undertaken worldwide to perfect the generation and interpretation of Black events from a Black perspective. The congress will develop a Black communications system to express African Nationalist ideology. It will develop a cross-organizational information service to improve communications between Black people and Black organizations.

10. Social Organization—To evaluate and reinterpret fundamental roles and relationships among Black people, i.e., family and community in terms of Black Liberation. We will create institutions in which white definitions of Black social reality must be discarded and new definitions created out of our increased social awareness of our needs as a people.

11. Community Organization—The Work Council exchanges information and techniques of community organization and institution building at the local, national, and international level. Development of skills in fund raising, proposal writing, communications. Parapolitical and mass based organization are taught locally, regionally, nationally.

In each of these areas, these criteria, or aspects of the national (African) expression, we are enslaved, involved in (European) forms which themselves enslave us. In each of these areas we must create and apply alternative forms; it is the only solution to racism, which involves us in the oppressor's forms only insofar as we are then allowed to define ourselves as capable solely of being slaves. The slave master's institutions include us only as slaves. We must create forms, institutions, and values, which themselves are examples of the liberated African personality, and move to bring about the *Liberation* of all African peoples.

But in all of the areas through which men express their lives, those criteria for a culture, it is necessary that we find ways of making these areas relevant to our liberation, and the struggle to set up these institutions (forms), processes (organizations), is the actual struggle to liberate ourselves. In essence this is the purpose of the congress, to move politically toward creating those liberating institutions (with the benefit of such institutions already created and in operation in the Motherland). In order to create such institutions we must involve all Black persons and organizations capable of assisting us. Thus, the congress will move with the entire Black community and seek a unity based on *program* rather than *ideology*.

We also feel that one of the most detrimental characteristics of unsuccessful nationalism has been a tendency to "neophyte" i.e., to assume that we are the blackest souls on the planet, and to hostilize the rest of our community because we know that nobody is as conscious as we, who hold ourselves to be the most revolutionary, the most nationalistically conscious of our nation. We now understand that if we are the "most conscious" then that merely gives us the responsibility for bringing consciousness, for Mobilizing, Nationalizing and Organizing, our brothers and sisters. And not to hostilize, hence alienate them, isolating ourselves, thereby allowing our enemies to eliminate us.

We feel that it is necessary to organize the largest mass of Black people possible, world-wide, at any given time and to move in forms that will attract and politicize the largest number, and not always be talking solely to other nationalists. For this reason we feel the congress, for instance, should make an attempt to "appeal" to as wide a diversity of Black people as possible, so that Pan-African Nationalist ideology can sooner become truly the philosophy of the people.

Adopted by the delegates in attendance
at the first annual meeting of the Congress
of African Peoples, September 6, 1970,
Atlanta, Georgia.

POLITICAL LIBERATION

Coordinator's Statement

by Imamu Amiri Baraka

The Political Liberation Workshop must make moves toward the creation of a political institution that expresses and moves to fulfill the needs of Black people, wherever they are. At its most effective this institution is called a nation. But to develop this nation, an African World State, a preliminary organizing vehicle is critical. This is a political party.

There are four areas of political power.

1. Public Office (elected or appointed)
2. Community Organizations
3. Alliances and Coalitions
4. Disruption (actual or threatened)

It is necessary for this World African Party, as it finally will become through function (whatever it is "called") to be able to function in all four areas with equal effectiveness.

A political party must develop advocates skilled at dealing in all four areas. And it must be the energizing force as well as institutional receptacle for the movement called Nationalism and Pan-Africanism. A political party must set itself up to be a replica, except for the extent of its realized power, of the nation *becoming*. It must function as a Total Maintainer of the healthy life style that (would be) is our way of life as a liberated people.

Formally a party must be set up, in areas everywhere there are large concentrations of Black people, that can do the following.

1. Work on Voter Registration
   a. To create and increase power of the ballot within the community.
   b. Seize the incentive of campaigns as a means of mobilizing Africans.
2. Mobilize—bring about some awareness of the community to racism by uniting them around issues, etc.

3. Organize—at this phase Black people must now be shown things that suit their needs. Organization helps keep the community together, working for a common goal.

4. Politicize—raise the level of political sophistication by teaching them how to gain, maintain, and use power.

5. Run Candidate—who will be an adequate representative of the will of the people. Meets the five criteria for a Black politician. We believe that a Black politician must meet five criteria if he is to be relevant to the struggle for National Liberation.
   a. Accountability—to Black people
   b. Constantly expose the white system as corrupt and unworkable
   c. Raise controversial issues
   d. Manipulations to increase power
      1. coalitions
      2. alliances
   e. Support Nationalism, and Pan-Africanism

6. Make Alliances—in order to defeat concept of isolation—operational Unity.

7. Third World Relations—maintain communications with other people of color in struggle.

The National (finally World) African Party must represent in totality the Black man's needs. It must be an organic manifestation of the way of life of the African people. It must provide African people, wherever they are, with Identity, Purpose and Direction. It must also provide a value system, a way of living, that will ensure *predictability of behavior, ultimate authority,* and a *means of security.*

Each area of political power must be developed. Training and expansion should be the continuous activity of the party, involving the greatest numbers of Black people in the movement for National Liberation. In order for such a movement to succeed it will need:

1. An Ideology
2. An Organization
3. Resources
4. Communications. And it is the organization's—party's—responsibility to develop all of these four elements and move through discipline, training and operational unity from a community organization, or a diversity of scattered politically oriented community organizations to a national, then international, political party capable of raising Africans to political, economic, social self-determination, self-respect and self-defense.

The congress should be used as a formulator of the theoretical structure of such a party, but also as an initiating element and the actual beginnings of the party itself. Even though we are representatives of many different fragmented understandings of nationalist and quasi-nationalist, as well as varieties of Pan-Africanist, ideology. Still, the congress must begin to put the process of Operational Unity into motion, for Africans of any persuasion. That is, we must understand through achievement of practical projects that theoretical ideology must be subservient to the commonality of our experience, and by working together the gap between so-called ideologies will disappear and strong working relationships develop among Black people of seemingly widely divergent theoretical political ideologies.

Among three of the most common ideas relating to Nationalism and Pan-Africanism are what can be called:

1. Back to Africa (or Repatriation)
2. Separation (to another part of America)
3. Instant Revolution

We feel that Repatriation people must understand, and to a certain extent the Separation (meaning to remove to Africa or another part of the U.S.) people, that Black people, ca. 1970, ain't going anywhere. It is very difficult, as you well know, to get them to go up the street to a meeting. Garvey's thought is best interpreted as a movement to recreate the power of the African state, but finally, as a precursor to contemporary Pan-Africanism, along with brothers like Blyden, Padmore, Nkrumah and others.

To create Africa as a unified power base to demand respect for Black people the world over. This is Pan-Africanism, because wherever we are we have a commonality based on our common struggle.

But "Back to Africa" for certain, in all the ways we can reestablish contact, since we understand our connection Racially, Historically, Culturally, Politically, and Emotionally. But it is necessary to raise the level of our people's political consciousness, so that all of us are aware of our commonality, and readied to consciously wage a common struggle.

The South may be the great strategic battleground of the African in America perhaps; it has the food, and space, to allow a people to survive, against great odds, but whatever we would do with the people, with ourselves, actually, we must first organize. And if the struggle is raised, and of such a nature that we must all go into the South, or that we migrate constantly because of the mounting pressures that force people to that realization, then it will still be a raised level of political consciousness that permits that move.

In the meantime we must *separate the mind,* win the mind, wage the revolution to win the Black man's mind so we will begin to move *together* as a people conscious that we are a people, struggling for national liberation. Separation must come *mentally* before *any* physical movement can begin. Separation away from assimilation or brainwashing or subjugation by the mind of the white nation. And that separation from white control must be a prerequisite for the mental and emotional trip "Back to Africa," i.e., to realization that we are an African people (meaning Black of a common color culture and consciousness. And whether we call ourselves Arabs, Saudis, Sudanese, Ethiopians, Egyptians, Kamites, Hamitic, we have only said Black a number of different ways).

As Nationalists and Pan-Africanists we must understand that we must move to have self-determination, self-respect and self-defense wherever we exist in large numbers . . . whether it is Chicago or Johannesburg. And the process of "gaining, maintaining and using power" is basically connected whatever the local specificity method.

A political party is an organ of consciousness. It must bring consciousness to Black people in whatever context it is necessary. All the different ways men express their lives must be understood and shaped by the party, which is the nation becoming. Whether it is religion or history or economics, social organization, arts, or the national ethos, and of course politics, the community organization of significance and potential in the struggle for national liberation will be able to make ideological input in *all the areas of Black people's lives,* and hence give direction. A people's way of life gives them Identity, Purpose and Direction. Identity: who you are and therefore who your enemy is. Purpose: what is to be done in relationship to that identity, i.e., nation-building. Direction: how is it to be done, by any means necessary. A black-skinned man living a cracker way of life has, for all intents and purposes, the identity, purpose and direction of a cracker. The political party must have an ideology that provides the mass of Black people with alternatives to the Identity, Purpose and Direction of the white boy.

There is no revolution without the people. It is the organized community that is our only chance of self-defense or self-determination. The larger the community involvement the quicker change will come. No so-called vanguard organization can bring a revolution, only the people themselves can do this. An organization moving without the community, or alienating the community, will soon be isolated, and very soon eliminated.

The United States is not China nor nineteenth-century Russia, nor even Cuba or Vietnam. It is the most highly industrialized nation ever to exist, a place where the slaves ride in Cadillacs and worship their slave master's image, as God. American power over Africans around the world must be broken before the other colonial powers are completely broken. Also, it should never be forgotten that we are a different people, want a different nation, than our slavemasters. In the Lenin revolution, the masses, the majority, theoretically, overthrew the minority, almost overnight. In America the "minority," i.e., oppressors, are the majority, or think they benefit by oppression. (And what happened to the Asian masses because of the Russian Revolution? Or the Black masses because of the Cuban Revolution?)

We must think of our struggle as one for National Liberation just as colored people are fighting wars of *National Liberation,* all around the world. We are fighting alien colonialists and enslavers, we are not making "revolution" against our own people. It is important to understand this. We must not be co-opted by talk of instant revolution, into being the peasant army, the first slaughtered wave, for *another people's* rise to political power.

An organization, for world African Liberation, the developing prototype for the much-needed national/international political party must be an organic manifestation of that people's determination to struggle. It must have an ideology based on its own history and ethos, on its traditions and the immediate contemporary context in which it finds itself.

We are not the Chinese. Mao raised an army, a State within a State, then separated from the main and waged war on it until it capitulated. (But they were *all* Chinese!) But even today the Chinese are just emerging from the almost constantly continuing *Cultural Revolution,* which seeks to win the minds of the people, so that the overall development of the Chinese Nation can continue without being interrupted by externally and internally inspired coups such as toppled Kwame Nkrumah!

But the American situation offers only few usable parallels. We are controlled largely by the ideas of our oppressors. The political party must build *alternative* systems, values, institutions that will move us and raise us. How we build such alternative forms is what this congress is about.

It seems obvious that the only place the developing prototype vehicle-organization for the national-international African political party can exist healthily or with any relevance is in areas of most intense Black population, wherever in the world. In the U.S. the cities of major Black population must be the first areas of organization and Black intensely populated rural areas in the South.

The community organization is always the kernel for the political party. Though, because of a structure like the C.A.P. it is possible to set up offices to begin organizing on the level of a political party more directly.

The areas of political power should be the areas of organization:

Public Office (elected or appointed) . . . the local C.A.P. offices must be prepared to conduct voter registration. Money can be raised for voter registration from groups and national political parties interested in the Black vote, and other groups. The reason for voter registration drives is twofold, first obviously to try to move on local political power, and try to get hold of the goods and services that can accrue from even the smallest political office. These goods and services, and the monies available because of them become the energizing elements of a growing local party structure. This is very important because in the rush of fantasy revolutionary talk, it is not understood that whatever the level of the struggle, goods and services will be needed, and of course, finances.

The other obvious use of voter registration, is voter education, which becomes *financed projects of raising the African political consciousness.* Getting into the homes of Black people, every day, organizing from strictly local, to regional, to state, while the C.A.P. superstructure works to create the national and international cohesion and development.

But the local C.A.P. organization must not only conduct voter registration, actually voter education-drives, but also *run candidates,* in all elections. Again, it is a basic level of political power! Goods, services, finance . . . and two other important ingredients, the *gradual development of a sympathetic area in which to work,* and hopefully expand, and the "legitimate" areas of political (and gradually through an association with *actual,* rather than rhetorical) power.

When the most conscious Black activists do not move in "electoral" politics the area is left to stooges, thieves, and toms. They become the local power figures, and like it or not, have some allegiance from the community based on their ability to supply goods and services (e.g., jobs) and their association with legitimate areas of power. (When we say "legitimate" we mean in the association with symbols given legitimacy by white people, who we should not forget still control the symbolism and imagery in most Black areas, and of course the power which is the reason for the so-called "legitimacy" in the first place.) We must get beyond idle neophyte militancy to effective political organizing and build allegiance from our people by co-opting all so-called or seemingly legitimate political processes in the Black communities.

All political candidates must run against nationalists in the Black community, and finally nationalists, Pan-Africanists, must organize sufficiently to win. The Nationalist-Pan-Africanist political party must begin to represent some degree of *actual power,* not just frustrated rhetoric, and the local political area is one clear way in which to move. It is one level of political consciousness, and the African community's mind must be moved *from where it is* (i.e., you can talk about Black mayors to more Black people, with some credulity, than you can about nations, which is the problem). To where we believe it must finally get. But you must build where you are, and through such building, and continuous development through association and acquisition of some actual power, finally make talk of nation *legitimate.*

Community Organization is necessary even if the base of any so-called C.O. is the local Party office. This means that the C.A.P. office must offer a wide divergence of community programs, or at least see to their initiation—Health, Welfare, Education, Arts, in any of the areas that programs are needed in Black communities around the world. Free Health Care programs in the community move Black people into it who might never come into any thing "political." As such the C.O. is a clear area of political power. Also any kind of anti-poverty money must be controlled by the local Party office. All monies used against Black people must be diverted into the hands of the actual builders of the community, and the money used to expand the development of Nationalist-Pan-Africanist ideas. This means moving to control the local community organizations by merely mastering the numbers and nonsense (actually by being better organizers) that goes with so-called "democratic processes" in the election of community organization officials, etc.

In other words whatever funds or potential power available in the African community must be controlled by the Nationalist-Pan-Africanist political party.

Alliances and Coalitions are another area of political power. We can make alliances with all peoples of color, (and certainly our brothers) developing as we said a certain level of operational unity however diverse we might seem. But this whole area of political power must be approached formally and consistently as an important area of political organization. Alliances with other Black organizations, with Black student groups, professionals, church, community, business men, politicians, but also of Third World alliances, so that actually we will all be fighting the same battle at the same time to liberate ourselves, concentrating on our own areas but providing each other with a cross-fertilization of ideas and resources. The truly Pan-African international organization has yet to come into existence and this is precisely what world Africans need. An international Pan-Africanist party capable of dealing not only with the international problems of Africans by means of international alliances and international exchanges of information and resources, but also a party able to function on the smallest level, i.e., to win municipal election. Many times bloods want to deal internationally or Pan-Africanistically and cannot even win a local councilmanic election. To do the large you must learn by doing the small.

It is the need for all the smalls to be functioning, and hooked up to the large which brought us to Atlanta.

Needed:

1. Local Structure
2. Regional Structure
3. State Structure
4. National Structure C.A.P.
   a. C.A.P. centers set up according to population intensity with input from national C.A.P. coordinating council and political council of twenty-five. (Thirty-four top Black cities in U. S.* Black Belt, South.)
5. International Structure (W. Indies, Australasia, South and Central America, Continental Africa).

*U.S. Cities Ranked by Black Population (1960 census)

New York	1,087,931	Memphis	184,320	Norfolk	78,806
Chicago	812,637	NewArk	138,035	Columbus	77,140
Philadelphia	529,240	Birmingham	135,113	San Francisco	74,383
Detroit	482,223	Dallas	129,242	Buffalo	70,904
Washington	411,737	Cincinnati	108,754	Louisville	70,075
Los Angeles	334,916	Pittsburgh	100,692	Gary	69,123
Baltimore	325,589	Indianapolis	98,049	Mobile	65,619
Cleveland	250,818	Richmond	91,972	Miami	65,213
New Orleans	233,514	Oakland	83,681	Nashville	64,570
Houston	215,037	Kansas City, Mo.	83,146	Boston	63,165
St. Louis	214,377	Jacksonville	82,525	Milwaukee	62,458
Atlanta	186,464				

(all these figures are white-low)

Resource Papers

Resolutions of the Surinam Delegates

by Cyril Karg

Brothers and Sisters, although we knew at the very beginning when we heard of this convention of the Congress of African Peoples that the language barrier would be very difficult for us, a non-English speaking African nation, we still decided to attend the convention because of the importance of same to the Black people of the world. It is therefore, that we kindly ask you to bear with us if, in our presentation, we might not sound as clear as we would like to. However, we are here. We are going to talk to you, whether it be in English or whatever other language we know. Because our nation is still one of the few Black nations that has no independence and is from the outside being governed by the white man. The white man who never had the interest of the Black man at heart, but only tried to exploit him to the benefit of the white race. In order to do this he has killed, mutilated, dishonored and plundered the Black man and has often broken up the family life he once knew in Africa. Instead, thereof has made him, or at least tried to make him, into a corrupted group of people divided among themselves; so that today those who have gotten a bit of the spoils from the white man, or claim to be of lighter complexioned skin, do not consider themselves Black when imitating the white man in every way.

It is this group of people that today, 1970, is suppressing the independence of our nation. However, of all this I don't need to tell you because we know that you too have suffered under the same circumstances. What we are here to do is not to bring forward a complaint, but to warn the Black man that the whites by no means consider themselves beaten. They know, as we do, that the economic structure of the world is still theirs—since the Black man does not think it necessary to strive for a united Black economy.

They know, as we know, that communications, the strongest weapon in any fight, is still theirs—since the Black man has never bothered to create a worldwide Black communication system.

They know, as we do, that as long as the independent Black countries of the world are looking for their economic development from the white countries they can never wholeheartedly support a fight of the Black man against the white man. Because it is a known fact in the world that a beggar is not allowed to do anything else but kiss the hand of those that feed him.

It is against this, Black Brothers and Sisters, that we came here to warn you. While you in America, in Africa and in some other parts of the world are preparing for a fight to the finish with the white man, your Black brothers in still other parts of the world—like for instance, South America, Latin America and the West Indies—have to look up to the white man even for food and education of his children; and since they have to accept this, because you Black brothers and sisters who can afford to help them in the economic struggle do not do so, they are still a prey to the white man who, being the vulture that he is, will not let him go.

Therefore, we are here to beseech you to, as of today, start showing some more interest in your own cause and by helping your Black brothers and sisters in other parts of the world to get rid of that dishonorable so-called development aid given him by the white man. You, who can afford to do so, can invest in all the projects in our countries where the white man is investing today, and is making a huge profit of his investment. We prefer that in our country if there have to be foreign companies that this be Black capital and Black-owned companies. It is therefore, that we are inviting you, together with us, to start an Economic Development Plan for the underdeveloped Black nations by the economically stronger Blacks of the world. By doing so, you are not only investing your dollar in a sound business but you are, at the same time, weakening your enemy—the white man—at the places where it hurts him the most. Because every solid new Black republic is a threat to the cause of the white man. You know and I know that whenever you are tied up in a fight with the white man we who are independent of him are compelled to join you and form the threat *from the outside!* This is what the white man fears the most! And this is why I came here today to call on you on behalf of my people, the Black man of Surinam, to join us in our fight for economical and political independence.

Concluding, we are presenting hereunto you the following resolutions.

Resolution No. 1.

Considering that the Black people of the world are tired of being exploited, tired of the selfishness of the white man and are openly fighting against white brutality; considering that in order to win this fight, the Black people must strive toward a Black unity; considering that because of this, the Black people of the world have decided to hold this first Congress of African Peoples; considering that the Black man today will have to make the idea of unity into something more than a battle cry, we herewith present to you the following suggestions:

a. That during this session of the congress there will be decided upon to create a commission to draw plans on a world Black economical structure.
b. That this economical plan will include a study of how the Black man can participate in economical development projects in all Black countries of the world.
c. That the Black man himself take over the total economy of the world and lead it so that the Black peoples of the world will most benefit by this.

Resolution No. 2

Considering that the Black people of the world today have united in the struggle against the white terror; considering that the Black people of the world know that many countries who twenty-five years ago signed the charter of the United Nations to do away with colonialism are members of this world organization while they did not keep their promise they made twenty-five years ago, and still have colonial territories, we put forward the following suggestions to this convention:

a. All the white countries, among them the Netherlands, who made this promise and did not keep it should be accused in the United Nations—by the Black countries who are members of this organization—of breach of promise, and willfully withholding freedom from Black people who are eager for their freedom. As a sanction the Black people of the world today should start a boycott against Holland and the rest of the colonial powers who do not intend to respect this charter of the United Nations.
b. In case the United Nations decide not to accept this protest of Black nations that all the Black powers of the world immediately take steps to create an organization of Black United Nations of the World!

Introduction to Pan-Africanism: A Philosophy/Ideology for African-Americans

by Hannibal El-Mustafa Ahmed

I started this essay as a result of reading a speech by a friend. I responded to a section of the speech which in concept denied the fact that Black Americans are still an African people. My response was as follows: "On page 3, you said 'having been severed from his African base and denied access to the socialization processes of America, he [the Black American] is NEITHER AFRICAN NOR AMERICAN.'

"Although I understand our views and reasons for expounding this thesis, it is a very limited view and negative perspective of looking at a historical phenomenon. Let us briefly review our history. The white European went to Africa and brought some peoples to the Americas; these peoples were Black Africans. After the white Europeans stole and sold the Africans into slavery and made them live a life of misery in the Americas, the Black man still survived. This proves that in spite of the tragic and negative historical phenomena that the Africans experienced in the Americas, we are in fact still an African people.

"When the white Europeans put the Black Africans in slavery, they had to make the Africans think that they were nobodies. They could not call the Africans just Black because black is an adjective that modifies a noun; in this case the noun is man. Therefore, they did not call the Africans Black men because conscious fearless men will not allow themselves to be enslaved by other men. The white Europeans did not want the masses of the Africans to know where they were historically and culturally from, so they dared not let the masses of Africans know of Africa in a positive way and their great civilizations there. So they called the Africans Niggers and Negroes and taught them that their fortunate history began in 1619. From that time to the present, the African-Americans were definitely severed from our African home base and denied access to the socialization processes of white racist America. However, four hundred years is not much time compared to how long the Africans have been on the planet earth. We are the original peoples of the earth. We were the first people to build civilizations and all other people came after us, from us. The Black Africans have been on the earth since the earth was fit for living. Hence, looking at our history from this perspective, we can see that our experiences in the Americas took a relatively infinitesimal amount of time, and we can now view that historical development as a negative interrupted part of our journey on earth. As Malcolm once said, 'We are twenty-two million African-Americans—that's what we are —Africans who are in America. You're nothing but Africans. Nothing but Africans. In fact, you'd get further calling yourself African instead of Negro.'[1] And, in another instance where he was talking about how the Black Muslims progressed, he said, 'One of the things that made the Black Muslim movement grow was its emphasis upon things African. This was the secret to the growth of the Black Muslim movement. African blood, African origin, African culture, [and] African ties. And, you'd be surprised—we discovered that deep within the subconscious of the Black man in this country, he is still more African than he is American. He *thinks* that he's more American than African, because the [white] man is jiving him, and the [white] man is brainwashing him everyday. He's telling him, "You're an American, you're an American." '[2] Therefore, we were from Africa and now we are the Africans in the Americas. We, Africans in the United States of America, are natives of North America, hence our nationality is American.

"The Irish were in America a little over 130 years and they are still referred to as Irish-Americans and the Chinese were in the United States of America a little over 100 years, yet they too are still referred to as Chinese-Americans, and this has been the case with every last immigrant of whatsoever origin. Therefore, we too are African-Americans since our forebears were from Africa.

"We must promote the fact that we are Africans in the Americas. This immediately connects African-Americans with the Africans in the Fatherland, and this connection makes us aware that our condition in America parallels greatly with our brothers and sisters in Africa, and that we were and are both COLONIZED and NEOCOLONIZED by the Europeans; white Americans are Europeans." Generally when I say white Europeans, white Americans are included because they are really from Europe.

After making my observations, I asked myself whether I could prove my position and simultaneously propose a philosophy/ideology that will enable the African-Americans to see why referring to ourselves as the Africans in the Americas is so very important politically and philosophically. This essay is my attempt to do just that.

It must be understood that this essay is only an introduction to Pan-Africanism as a philosophy/ideology for African-Americans.

There are many statements made that are not supported and will be developed in a future book on the subject. This introduction is written basically for the aware segment of the Black community; therefore, certain terms like capitalism, imperialism, socialism, etc., are used based on the assumption that the terms are understood by the readers. It is also assumed that the readers are aware that African-American people constitute a sort of nation within America.

We know that the African-Americans are in a country which has proven to the world that you could have another racial group of people in your midst and miscegenation on a large scale does not have to occur. We also know that the reason for this is that the United States is a country which is controlled by white racists. The white society is racist and this white society did not allow African-American people to assimilate into it, no matter how hard African-American people tried. Hence, African-American people constitute a sort of nation within a nation. But, it is a captive and colonized nation that needs economic and psychic liberation from white racist America. To realize ourselves as a nation, African-American people must have total freedom, justice and equality. We must have economic and political freedom in America. We must be strong enough to demand justice from all people that we deal with. We must have equality of opportunity to build our nation. We must determine for ourselves our course of action, our economic system and our place in the world. But to do this, the masses of African-Americans must become aware that our only strength and salvation lies in Black unity, Black love for self and kind, Black self-determination and above all, African-American people must have a revolutionary philosophy/ideology or theories about how we must deal with our unique situation in America now, since this is our last struggle for survival as a people.

When I say that we must have a revolutionary philosophy/ideology, this does not mean that the African-American people take to the streets and begin to confront the establishment with sticks and rocks or throwing fire bombs at police officers and state troopers who are armed with Stoner-rifles and tanks, etc. I do not encourage our people to fight our enemies on the enemies' principles or terms; this would mean suicide for our people if I did.

When I speak of a revolutionary philosophy/ideology, I mean that the Africans in America must see our struggle within its proper historic perspective and accept the truth of what history reveals to us, especially in regard to our history in the United States of America. We must see the various philosophies we have had and where they have gotten us. And, when we agree that these philosophies have not gotten us our total liberation from white racist America, then we must develop a philosophy which will. The philosophy must deal with our present life style and illustrate and indicate how our life style ought to be and what our direction ought to be. A philosophy deals basically with giving men a way of looking at life and of accepting the various truths of life. In considering a philosophy, Malcolm X said we must have a philosophy that will enable us to go into some positive action. "If you have sit-down actions then that is because of your sit-down philosophy. Once you change your philosophy you change your thought pattern, and once you change your thought pattern it changes your behavior pattern; and once your behavior pattern changes, you can go into some positive action." He said as long as you keep that old sit-down philosophy, then you will have that sit-down action. Hence, it should be clear that we must have a revolutionary philosophy/ideology and that this is the most important thing that we must have to organize our people around. As Lenin said, there is no revolutionary movement without a revolutionary theory.

The concept of Pan-Africanism, e.g., the philosophy of the unification of Africa into one nation for the Africans at home and abroad, furnishes the African-Americans with a well developed foundation. Dr. Kwame Nkrumah noted in his pamphlet, *The Spectre of Black Power,* that "Pan-Africanism has its beginnings in the liberation struggle of African-Americans, expressing the aspirations of the Africans and people of African descent. From the first Pan-African Conference, held in London in 1900, until the fifth and last Pan-African Conference held in Manchester in 1945, African-Americans provided the main driving power of the movement. . . . The work of the early pioneers of Pan-Africanism such as H. Sylvester Williams, W. E. B. Du Bois, Marcus Garvey and George Padmore, none of whom were born in Africa, has become a treasured part of Africa's history."[3]

Marcus Garvey, the father of post-Civil War Black Nationalism, contributed indirectly to Pan-Africanism through his chauvinistic appeal to such people as Nkrumah, and who is sometimes spoken of as a Pan-Africanist, rejected all socialist movements as "inherently prejudiced against the Black race since they were dominated by whites. . . ." Du Bois dismissed Garvey's "back to Africa" movement as "bombastic, wasteful, illogical and almost illegal," and "harmful to the development of Pan-Africanism."[4] It should be pointed out that Garvey's analysis of white Communism was made at a time when extremely overt manifestations of white racism was apparent. It was also a period when the white Communists believed and promulgated that their way of life was the only correct way of life. Therefore, Garvey was extremely dedicated to preventing the Communists from gaining political control of the African-American people's struggle for their own ends. Garvey did not, however, make a careful analysis of economics and the social formulation of society as related to economics, and was therefore not able to understand the validity of the European's concept of socialism. Nevertheless, his "reaction to color prejudice and his search for a way to rise above it and lead [our] people back to Africa, spiritually if not physically, was the all-consuming passion of his existence. His glorious and romantic movement exhorted the [African] people of the world and fixed [our] eyes on the bright star of a future in which [we] could reclaim and rebuild [our] African homeland and heritage."[5] Hence, Garvey was definitely a Pan-Africanist in that he called for a unified "Africa for the Africans" at home and abroad.

Hence the streams of thought apparent in Pan-Africanism are 1) African unity, 2) socialism, and 3) Black nationalism. These are the reflections of the common experience of the movement's early spokesmen. Marcus Garvey, "W. E. B. Du Bois, George Padmore and the Africans active in the development of Pan-Africanism, despite their greatly different backgrounds, all shared the experience of alienation, of being marginal members of society. Du Bois and Padmore, the guiding spirits of the movement, initially sought a solution in democratic socialism."[6]

Pan-Africanism and African Unity

The philosophy of Pan-Africanism does not teach the Africans in America to just blindly migrate to Africa. It teaches us that Africa is in fact the very home of the Africans in the Americas, and that Africa was divided up in 1885 as a result of the signing of the Treaty of Berlin (February 26, 1885), e.g., when the major European powers (Britain, France and Germany) cut up parts of our Fatherland, Africa, for themselves. It teaches us that Africa must be one country again for Africans and people of African descent the world over. It teaches us that all Africans and African descendants must be conscious of the forces which are still in operation that are keeping our Fatherland, Africa, divided; and begin to work against those forces at home and abroad. As Malcolm X said, "You can't understand what is going on in Mississippi if you don't understand what is going on in the Congo. . . . They're both the same. The same interests are at work in the Congo that are at work in Mississippi. The same stakes —no difference whatsoever."[7] And, again Malcolm says in another quote that comes from a letter which he wrote from Accra, Ghana, on May 11, 1964: "Upon close study one can easily see a gigantic design to keep Africans here and the African-Americans from getting together. An African official told me, 'When one combines the number of people of African descent in South, Central and North America, they total well over eighty million.' One can easily understand the attempts to keep the Africans from ever uniting with the African-Americans.' Unity between Africans of the West and the Africans of the Fatherland will well change the course of history. . . . Just as the American Jew is in harmony politically, economically and culturally with world Jewry, it is time for all African-Americans to become an integral part of the world's Pan-Africanists, and even though we might remain in America physically while fighting for the benefits that the Constitution guarantees us, we must return to Africa philosophically and culturally, and develop a working unity in the framework of Pan-Africanism."[8]

Pan-Africanism teaches the African-Americans that, in order to enslave the African-Americans, the white slave masters had to completely sever our forebears' communication with the African continent and the African people. Therefore, in order to free ourselves from the oppression of the white oppressors then it is absolutely necessary for the African-Americans to establish communications with Africa and African people all over the planet earth and all work for the common cause of destroying the oppressors. In order to keep the African-American enslaved, the white slave masters had to limit the African-Americans' thinking to the shores of America to prevent us from identifying our problems with the problems of other oppressed peoples of African origin. This made us consider ourselves as an isolated minority without allies anywhere. Pan-Africanism changes the thinking of the African-American and liberates our minds by getting us to see that African people are in the Caribbean, South America, the Virgin Islands, Panama, Dominican Republic, and Bahamas, Haiti, Spain, England, Germany and in the Fatherland, Africa, thus enabling the African-Americans to see that we are in fact the majority with allies all over the planet earth. After enslaving the African-American, the white slave masters developed a racist educational system which justified the evil deeds that has been committed against the African-American people. Therefore, African-Americans must devise educational methods and procedures which will liberate the minds of ourselves and our children from the vicious lies and distortions that are fed to African-Americans to keep us mentally enslaved. It is most important that we understand our roots for "a people without knowledge of their history is like a tree without roots." In order to enslave a people and keep them subjugated, their rights to self-defense must be denied. They must be constantly terrorized, brutalized and murdered so as to make them fearful of revolting. Therefore, African-Americans must arm themselves and do whatever is necessary to build up a force to inflict political consequences upon white racist America whenever white racist America inflicts pain and sufferings on African-American people.

Pan-Africanism and Socialism

"Pan-Africanism recognizes much that is true in the Marxist interpretation of history, since it provides a rational explanation for a good deal that would otherwise be unintelligible. But it nevertheless refuses to accept the pretentious claims of doctrinaire Communism, that it alone has the solution to all the complex racial, tribal, and socioeconomic problems facing Africans [and African-Americans]. It also rejects the Communist intolerance of those who do not subscribe to its ever-changing party line even to the point of liquidating them as 'enemies of the people.' Democracy and brotherhood cannot be built upon intolerance and violence."[9]

Pan-Africanism teaches us that capitalism, colonialism, imperialism, and neocolonialism are the economic systems that white Europeans developed into the monsters that they are today. Pan-Africanism makes it clear that men's social relations are greatly determined by their economic system. Example: In a society which has rich and poor, you will always have people that desire to be rich or at least do anything to get some money. The key word is anything —from selling dope to dropping napalm bombs on innocent Southeast Asians. Crime, dope-selling and robbery all affect social relations. The question is, How can we have a harmonious society as long as people desiring money who would do anything to get it, are still around? The answer is that we cannot have a harmonious society as long as people of this sort are around. And, the reason that people of this kind are around is because the economic system that America has established is in fact the system of capitalism, imperialism, neocolonialism and racism, and is therefore the kind of system that causes antagonism among men. It produces a rich class of people and a poor class of people; a "have" class and a "have not" class.

Pan-Africanism and Islamic Black Nationalism

Now for us to accomplish what we must accomplish and go where we must go, Pan-Africanism teaches the African-Americans that we must build a power base in America before we can do anything. We must amass a base of wealth and we must develop a land base within America and develop the mechanism to secure that base. We must provide each other with food, shelter and clothing so that we can do for ourselves. We must organize ourselves into political parties, trade unions, cooperative societies and farmers' organizations in the support of our struggle for political freedom and economic advancement; we must gain control of our communities, politically, economically and socially. We must develop a socialist economic system that will work in our best collective interest and in the best collective interest of peoples struggling against the economic systems of capitalism, imperialism and neocolonialism, all over the planet earth. In short we must strengthen our nation in America. Remember that a nation consists of people with a common culture, common philosophical/ideological outlook, a geographical location that is called a country and a nation has a flag. The foundations of nationhood consist of people having in common:

1. *History*—The story of the beginning of recorded events which the said people lived through.
2. *Land*—A geographical location that the people can call home and country, thus enabling them to do for self and kind, and also to do trade with other countries of the earth, thus making them equal to all.
3. *Economic System*—The institution which provides the people's basic needs of life, i.e., food, shelter, and clothing, and enables the nation to trade with other nations of the world.
4. *Social System*—The institution where the knowledge of said society is taught; places such as schools, mosque, etc.
5. *Political System*—The institution that makes policy which directs the actions of the said people; policies such as constitution, laws, etc.
6. *Ethos*—That which distinguishes the said people from other people. Ethos such as the wearing of clothes, the eating of food and the moral values; in short, the customs of the people.
7. *Language*—A language that communicates; one that the majority of the people can understand.
8. *Names*—That which identifies said people with their geographical location as well as their history and ancestors. Plus the meaning of the name which said people must live by, such as Abd-Azim meaning servant of the Great which is Allah.
9. *The Right to Self-Determination*—The right of a people to determine their own way of life, customs, ethos, laws and in short, their own destiny.

By doing this the African-Americans can effectively aid ourselves and the Africans at home, especially those who are presently engaged in liberation struggles against the Western imperialist, colonialist, neocolonialist and racist.

What Must be Done to Become an African-American Pan-Africanist

An African-American Pan-Africanist must love our people and dedicate his life to our liberation from our oppression and from our own enslaved minds.

An African-American Pan-Africanist must take time to study both our people and our enemy so that he or she can clearly see and understand what must be done in order to gain real freedom for our people.

An African-American Pan-Africanist must study past revolutions, including the so-called American Revolution, and anything else of a political nature that can help him to understand how a successful revolution can be carried out. We then must understand why the Black revolution is different than any other and how the Black man's fight for the right to his own soul must be fought in a different way than any revolution in past or present history.

An African-American Pan-Africanist must decide his or her role, that is, skill or profession, in the revolution and master it so that he or she can make a perfect contribution to our righteous act, and thereby assure success and a better world.

The process of becoming an African-American Pan-Africanist is no fun. The first duty of an African-American Pan-Africanist is to revolutionize himself; to clean himself up of the decadence of white America.

Those of us who are enlightened, who clearly see that we can win our struggle against oppression if we study hard, discipline ourselves and struggle correctly, have a great burden to bear. We must perfect ourselves and make ourselves the examples for our people to follow. In order to be an African-American Pan-Africanist, all we have to do is decide this and accept the political, economic and social philosophy/ideology of Pan-Africanism, and be:

1. *Mentally in tune:* We must study the politics of the system that enslaves us so that we can better understand how to free ourselves. We must study about ourselves and our past so that we can better understand who we are. We must perfect our skills so that we can offer a better contribution to our peoples' struggle for freedom and peace.
2. *Physically in tune:* Our minds can function at their best only if we are physically healthy. When our bodies are tired or out of shape, so are our minds. Nation-building requires long hours of hard work; teaching, studying, building, planning, etc. Our struggle will be long and tedious. The physical strength to persevere and accept difficult tasks will be necessary for all of us.
3. *Spiritually in tune:* An important difference between the Black revolution and any other revolution is that the Black revolution is based on an understanding that the African-American destiny is to place things back in order with nature and the universe. Even though African-American people have many different spiritual beliefs, most of us do have some basis for understanding the universe. Islam as taught by the Honorable Elijah Muham-

mad provides African-Americans with a good, solid and positive spiritual base. This spiritual base will greatly help the African-Americans understand what we must do and why.

The African-Americans must align and unite with the Nation of Islam, especially since we want to survive. The Nation of Islam in America is the Natior made up of African-Americans who submit their will entirely to the will of Allah who came in the person of Master Fard Muhammad to Whom praises are due forever. Master Fard Muhammad left a messenger in this wilderness of North America whose name is Mr. Elijah Muhammad.

The Honorable Elijah Muhammad is the most beloved leader and teacher as well as the spiritual head of the Nation of Islam. African-Americans in the Nation are referred to as Black Muslims, meaning those Black people who submit to Allah alone. The Nation is founded on righteousness, peace, happiness in all walks of life, and love for "self and kind."

The Honorable Elijah Muhammad has taught the African-Americans that we are Muslims by nature, e.g., our essence is to be at peace with the universe and one in Allah, but living under the white Americans has caused us to go astray. He has taught us that we must fall away or separate from the white Americans because they are the real devils; other names are Iblis, Satan, Man of Sin, the Evil One, the Wicked One and Lucifer. Muhammad teaches that it is the white people who blind the people of color from the straight path to eternal peace and that it is they who have polluted the air and poisoned the land.

The Honorable Elijah Muhammad teaches that this country, America, is run on thirty-three degrees of knowledge. But that the Nation of Islam will run on 360 degrees of knowledge, because the knowledge of Allah is all-inclusive, it has no beginning nor ending and as long as we submit to Allah's will our Nation will never sink to the depths of corruption like the Western nations of the present era have done.

The Messenger teaches that once African-American people submit entirely to the will of Allah, we will immediately see the wickedness of white Americans. Also, that when we are members (spiritually or physically) of the Nation of Islam we will serve and worship Allah alone. "Allah is the Lord of all the worlds, the cherisher and sustainer of the universe" and the essence of African-Americans. How then can we put the white Americans and their unrighteous rulership before Allah?

The Honorable Elijah Muhammad is the Messenger of Allah. A messenger is sent to warn the people of the end of their time and what must be done to survive, and to separate the righteous from the unrighteous. Therefore, African-Americans who are conscious and really want our people to survive in America must support *our Messenger,* the Honorable Elijah Muhammad.

Here I would just like to clarify the term devil used by the Honorable Elijah Muhammad when referring to white Europeans; America is included. What some folks fail to realize about the teachings of Mr. Muhammad in regard to the white Europeans being a race of devils are two points. Point one is that devil or satan are words. When you look up the etymology of the word devil, you will find that it means the supreme spirit of evil; an evil spirit; malignant being, fiend in human form; accuser and slanderer. And, satan means adversary, plotter, and one who plots against. Therefore, devil or satan means one who consciously and willingly opposes the righteous and natural laws of the earth and the universe. I don't think that we can deny the facts that what the white Europeans did to the nonwhite people of the world, they did consciously. They were fully conscious when they systematically exterminated the American Indians, when they formulated their philosophy of racial superiority, when they placed the Africans in bondage, when they continued to perpetuate their system of capitalism, imperialism, neocolonialism and racism. They continue to perpetuate a system that they know works against the very laws that govern the earth. The laws of the earth are cooperation and unity. Example, it rains to the earth and the grass grows to feed men, and men take their animals and make clothes out of them, etc. Yet, the white European sets up an economic system that works according to the laws of competition, where white-owned and -controlled industries will do anything to monopolize the market for money. They will do anything from polluting the air we breathe to turning the water we drink into cesspools. The white Europeans are absolutely guilty of all these crimes and they were fully aware that they were going against the teachings of their own religion, Christianity.

And the second point is that everything in nature has a nature. For instance, you don't get upset and blame a lion for wanting to kill and eat, say a deer, because you know from your observations of the lions that it is in the lion's nature to want to do such things and the only way that you can put a stop to this is by making the lion other than its nature through the process of domestication. Everything in nature has a nature and its nature is illustrated in its actions and deeds. Man too is an animal in nature possessing a nature and regardless of his ability to be rational, his nature is manifested in his actions and deeds. When we look at the historical development of the white Europeans, especially after the fifteenth century, we can see that their actions and deeds have been that of vicious greedy beasts, ravishing the earth like madmen. Robbing, killing, murdering, raping and warring every place they have gone. They were conscious that they inflicted pain and suffering on the people that they conquered and colonized and made to slave and labor for their profit and benefit. Hence, it is clear that the white Europeans were and are the enemies or adversaries to the righteous laws of the earth and the universe and are therefore rightfully called the living race of devils.

Thus, understanding and accepting these facts and this point of view will give the African-Americans a philosophical outlook and context to work within. Once African-Americans work within this philosophical context, this will enable us to deal with any issue, be it welfare rights, rent strikes, political elections, education, anti-draft, slum conditions in our communities, or what have you, and we simultaneously have a theoretical base which we use to elevate our people's consciousness. We will then be mobilizing and organizing our people, not so much for the issue per se but for the greater cause of building our society to work in the best collective interest of the African-Americans and people in general. Hence, the national emancipation of the African-American people is an issue of no compromise. We don't compromise about whether we should stay in slavery or be free. For the African-Americans, total liberation from white racist America in America is a must. Then eventually we can physically go back home. When we go back home to Africa, we will be a totally revolutionized people without the decadence that we had been a part of in the U.S.A. We cannot be considering ourselves a nation then, but rather a state, to form a unit in the United States of Africa. As for America, it is as the Honorable Elijah Muhammad has said, "The destruction and fall of the world that we have known is now without a doubt in process. When we refer to the world, we are referring to the world of the white man, for the world of the Black man, the world of right has yet to come in. . . . The world of the Black man, by divine guidance is now merging in on the world of the white man [the capitalist]. This makes the destruction of the world of the white man imminent. Here in America, we can see nothing but the fall of America. It is no secret. It is obvious to those who can see. If we want to close our eyes and mind and claim that we do not see and understand then we will be fooling ourselves. Thus, refusal to see is foolhardy for regardless of how we may desire the old world to stand, we do not have the power to shove off the destruction of the white man."

Let us, the African-Americans, come together under the political, economic and social philosophy/ideology of Pan-Africanism. This philosophy/ideology will ultimately direct us to peace and paradise which will be in Africa.

REFERENCE NOTES

1 Malcolm X, *Malcolm X Speaks* (New York, Merrit Publishers, 1965), p. 36.
2 *Ibid.*, pp. 187–188.
3 Dr. Kwame Nkrumah, *The Spectre of Black Power* (London, Panaf, 1969), p. 5.
4 William H. Friedland and Carl G. Rosberg, Jr., eds., *African Socialism* (Stanford, Stanford University Press, 1967), p. 63.
5 Amy Jacques Garvey, *Garvey & Garveyism* (London and New York, Collier Books, 1970), Introduction by John Henrik Clarke, p. xiii.
6 *African Socialism, op. cit.*, p. 63.
7 Stokely Carmichael, "We Are All Africans," *The Black Scholar,* Vol. 1, No. 7 (May, 1970), p. 17.
8 Malcolm X, *op. cit.*, pp. 62–63.
9 George Padmore, *Pan-Africanism or Communism? The Coming Struggle for Africa* (London, Dobson, 1956), pp. 18–19. The "doctrinaire Communism" that George Padmore was referring to is that of Communist Russia.

Political Liberation

Philadelphia Council of the Congress of African Peoples

Black people in America are now talking about nation-building and having the freedom to decide our own future. One cannot talk about a Nation without talking about some form of organized structure or political party. A PARTY IS THE FIRST STEP TOWARD BUILDING A NATION. HISTORICAL CIRCUMSTANCES DICTATE THE NEED FOR FORMING A NATIONAL BLACK POLITICAL PARTY AT THIS TIME.

Chuck Stone points out in the December, 1969, issue of *Black Scholar* that of the 130 cities with populations of 100,000 or over, only two had Black mayors, and yet 39 percent of all Black people are concentrated in the ten largest cities. In the next ten years all ten could have Black leaders. In the South, the National Democratic Party of Alabama is showing what can be done when Black people unite and work together. Newark, where Kenneth Gibson was elected, is another example. NOW IS THE TIME FOR A BLACK POLITICAL PARTY.

Considering the differences in population ratios, the differences in the political structures that are in existence in given locations, it may well be that a formal Black political party is not a feasible alternative. However, we recommend that at least some sort of pseudo-party structure be planned through which the Black political agenda can be expressed. In other words, even when Black people are only 10 percent of the population, their politics should not be dependent upon white decision-making.

Ujamaa is an African Swahili word which emphasizes that we are an African people. Its literal meaning is family-hood, so it brings to the mind of our people the idea of total involvement of the family as we understand it. As we build on the rich past of our people then we will grow due to our own power. Our political party is a *Ujamaa* party.

Structure

All C.A.P. councils should evolve into one political party. People should be elected from each council to meet and plan on the type of political action that can be used in the next elections. A conference should be held at this convention to deal with the specifics of structure.

This party will serve as a clearinghouse for political communications and advise on the direction and distribution of this material. New breed Black politicians who hold office are invited to join in and help without giving up their party affiliation.

We should have close political ties with Black politicians and should support honest, able Black people who run for office as members of the two major parties.

We must devise strategies which give Black people the *sense of power* to create *power structures.* For this reason, the Black political party must be involved in community control of institutions such as health, welfare, housing, land, or any struggle deemed important by Black people.

Political Independence or Third Force

1. All Black people of voting age must register. We must find a way at this conference to begin to do this, teach our folks how to split a ballot at polling places.
2. Election of Black men and women for every public office.
3. In the ten cities (Chuck Stone, December *Black Scholar*) gain Black political control.
4. All Black students and workers should come together under the banner of the Black political party and begin to do political work in the community projecting a Black political party.
5. Immediate research should be done locally to determine the necessary steps for electing Black candidates.
6. We support the Republic of New Africa in its struggle to form a Nation on the American continent.
7. We support the Bill H.R. 8965 and the right of the African-American Repatriation Association to repatriate with their families and belongings back to the Motherland.
8. We demand that all Black political prisoners be set free.
9. We oppose the Vietnamese war and see no role Black youth can play in it. We demand the immediate withdrawal of all American forces from Vietnam.
10. We demand that the U.S. Government stop its oppressive fight against the Black Panther party and drop charges against its members and leaders.

11. We demand the right of community control over the police, health, education and any institution in a Black community.
12. Produce a newspaper and a handbook.
13. We support the efforts of Making a Nation (MAN) to mobilize and educate people around the question of genocide of nonwhite people around the world.

Foreign Relations

1. We support the activities of all African Liberation Movements.
2. We demand that the United States Government break relations with the Union of South Africa and other African countries where whites rule.
3. In regard to the stated policy of the United States Government on economic aid to Africa: We do not believe that economic aid to Africa should be in the form of private investment capital from United States industry. Aid to Africa should be subsidized through the tax dollars of African-Americans in the United States—our contribution toward the elimination of foreign equity on the African continent.
4. Introduce all African-Americans to their rich heritage, improve the communications between African-Americans and Africans.
5. Bring leaders of Liberation Movements to America to speak to African-Americans. C.A.P. should send members to Africa.

Survival

Political and economic survival is of the utmost importance. Therefore we see the following steps as necessary:

1. Each Black community must become a legal and political entity, free from control by the larger society.
2. Set up in every block some type of community house.
3. Find and develop resources.
4. Have people with skills organized and ready to work in communities.
5. Classes in political science, African history, economics, health—these classes should start as soon as possible.
6. Social affairs featuring African plays, fashion shows, jazz, and other events with political overtones.
7. Set up communal dining halls, sleeping quarters, and learning centers.
8. Have the total community working and studying, defining, redefining, and working for political power.

BLACK POLITICAL POWER FOR ALL BLACK PEOPLE
FIRST STEP TOWARD NATIONHOOD

The Liberation of African Prisoners of War on the American Mainland

by Hassan Olufu

Whenever a body of people exist who have suffered three hundred and fifty years of physical and spiritual slavery and cruel and unjustifiable treatment at the hands of another group with the free sanction of that group's government, the former are most assuredly affected more deeply than is possible to ascertain. There can be no measure of the products of three centuries of this unheralded oppression and arbitrary persecution of our people. No gauge can feel the exact toll of abortive alienation that Black people now feel as a result of the submergence of their very humanity by our oppressors!

In this year, 1970, we must and have realized that as Black people we can never assimilate ourselves into the white aesthetic, for no such thing exists. We have been repeatedly denied entrance into a meaningless value system and have become stupidly frustrated by this. Cessation of this blindness now caused us to analyze our environment in such a manner as to negate the conceivability of reconciliation between Black and white factions in this country, particularly in view of:

1. The illegal invasion and rape of the African continent by the imperialist Europeans of the Old and New Worlds, and the seizing of captive Black prisoners of war.
2. The subsequent transportation of these prisoners to the American mainland for no other purpose except the exceeding exploitation of their flesh to foster white economic interest.
3. The astronomical numbers of physical, moral, spiritual, intellectual and cultural crimes and hoaxes perpetrated against Black people during the time we have remained in this country. The total investment of Black blood that initially has and continues to contribute to the affluence and comfort and general well-being now unjustly enjoyed and viciously defended by white Americans.

We surmise the United States has endeavored to submerge these evils through the act of imposing citizenship upon Black prisoners of war for purely political reasons of expediency and that this citizenship, having been established without our consent, was at that time and is even now illegal. In fact, we are not American citizens but Black prisoners of war who continue to be unlawfully exposed to homicidal American mandates; and therefore:

To the extent of the massive and horrendous acts that have been committed against us, that these collective crimes are of such great political, economic, social, and moral and human consequences as to constitute an act of war on the part of the United States; we do, in lieu of immediate, inclusive recognition of Black self-determination, consider ourselves recipients of a declaration of war from this country's government, leaving Blacks with no other path than to create an atmosphere more conducive to the liberation of Black people through the extensive limitation of all transportation, communication and industrial operations in this country.

The People's Party for Liberation implores you to use all means within your power to bring about a speedy and peaceful victory for Black people through the enactment of the mandate for Black self-determination.

MANDATE FOR SELF-DETERMINATION

Brothers and Sisters:

(Workers, Homeowners, Students, Nationalists, etc.)

No oppressed people have ever achieved their rights by voluntary acts of benevolence on the part of their oppressors. It is futile, no, it is suicidal to wait in hope of such good results being initiated by our American enslavers since, at their hands, we have known nothing but death to our lives, to our pride, to our dignity and to our children.

Freedom, the right to breathe God's air and use God's land, is a right of birth. If you are alive you have the right to be free. Denial of a tenet so basic to man's existence can be accomplished by nothing less than an unfathomable injustice and inhumanity which the original Africans and their descendants could not begin to understand. It is no mistake that the people who have created and now control every facet of this war-ridden system are not people of color. Nor can their history of savagery be attributed to mere chance. Their very nature has and continues to motivate their immorality and lawlessness. They can commit no other acts except those of oppression and trickery of which we have been the recipients.

Black people, we have learned a very costly lesson; that the liberty of a people remains insecure when these people have not absolute control of their destinies. We must fight to secure our destinies as we must struggle for our liberation—with our whole selves, incurring whatever costs we may, for only in this can we hope to triumph.

To seek to secure and consolidate the political, economic and cultural future of a people is to advocate nationhood. Recognition as a nation is an unnegotiable need for Black people if they are to survive. Coexistence with the white man under one nationalistic framework (which he controls) is impossible for our people, for the reason that the elements of Black and white survival are so radically opposed to each other that adherence to one necessarily eliminates the possible fulfillment of the other.

We must ultimately extricate ourselves from the American system and consequently call for the adjustment of this system so that it will immediately accommodate itself to the following *intermediary* demands:

I. Distinguished Citizenship Acknowledgement

Whereas the African prisoners of war in America have suffered from large-scale persecution and inexcusable treatment on the sole basis of their race, we demand to be recognized as a unique racial and national group entitled to such special status including:

1. Exemption from regular taxation, which funds are currently being employed to finance illegal imperialistic enterprises throughout the world and are decidedly not in the best interests of ourselves or our Third World brothers.
2. Exemption from conscription laws which now utilize Black men as political and military pawns in urging them to participate in an immoral and foreign war when our only war, as our only enemy, runs loose in the American streets.
3. Right to trial by a Black or Third World jury who are our only true peers and comprise, therefore, the only just jury.
4. Exemption from more than tactical obedience to laws relevant to Black people since we have taken no part in devising the legal system from which these laws evolve and are therefore not legally bound by them.

II. Economic Development Act

That Black people have the right to channel all federal, state and local tax payments previously paid to the respective governments to a National Taxation Board (under the mandates of the National Congress outlined in Act II) and that these monies be utilized for the economic development of the federation, and the alleviation of appalling living conditions.

That all Black breadwinners who are barred from unions, underemployed and earning less than a sufficient living, all due to governmental sanction of institutionalized racism, unite and demand from the United States Government a yearly compensation for retroactive wages (under the jurisdiction of the council or federation).

1. That the council or federation be recognized to negotiate for any foreign assistances, aids, supplies or equipments
2. To be utilized to the economic development of Black people under the jurisdiction of the council or federation
3. Whose costs will be guaranteed by the United States.

III. Special Power Recognition

That the council or federation be recognized to send representatives to the United Nations and other international bodies to secure its own interests.

That the council or federation have complete jurisdiction over Black personnel in the United States armed services and Black persons in penal and mental institutions.

That the council or federation exercise joint use of all airports, all seaports, all roads and highways, including exemption from United States trade restrictions, tariffs, and commerce regulations; also, exemption from the Federal Communications Commission and public utility commissions and all other regulating commissions.

That these representatives be recognized to negotiate with the United States Government for land and reparation.

IV. Special Area Decree

That these demands be instituted and executed until such time as the negative effects of our *de facto* imprisonment in America can be removed through our removal from the American system. We call, in essence, for the creation of a physical site (on land reclaimed on this continent) in which Black people exercise total sovereignty of their lives, land and destinies.

African Leadership

by Ayuko Babu

African leaders have throughout the past and the recent present expressed their desire for African-Americans to aid them in the development of their countries. The latest public expression of this sentiment came during the summer of 1970 when Kenneth Kaunda of Zambia, speaking to a group of African-American students said, "We want African-Americans to come and help us build and develop." This sentiment has also been expressed in private conversation down through the years between Africans and African-Americans. The response for the most part has been on a personal basis. One example of this approach is best exemplified by George Padmore who devoted most of his adult life to the cause of Pan-Africanism. Another example of this approach can be seen in the work currently being undertaken by Bill Sutherland and Bob Moses, together with many lesser known brothers and sisters working throughout Africa.

I feel that this kind of individual work is important and must continue, but I feel that we must expand our effort from an individual basis to group efforts, concentrating these energies in a specific area where we can gain the most benefits from our energies. If this is accomplished we can: (1) strengthen our Pan-African bonds with our brothers and sisters in Africa; (2) strike a blow against economic domination of Africa by the U.S. and western European economic interests; (3) strike a blow against the settler colonies that still control our peoples' lives in areas such as South Africa and Rhodesia; (4) build pride and dignity among Africans all over the world by making a real substantial and meaningful contribution.

After having traveled in Africa during the summer of 1970 I feel that the three places best suited for this kind of organizational effort are Tanzania, Guinea and Zambia. The reason for this position is that all three of these countries have taken a clear position that they intend to be free, not only politically but also economically. All three of these countries are committed to the liberation of the settler colonies. All have placed their verbal commitment where it counts. They have given groups working for the liberation of the settler colonies and neocolonial states bases and training area in their respective countries. Also, these countries have taken a most active lead in encouraging Africans to build the Pan-African dream of a unified Africa, and an Africa where Africans from all over the world might find peace, happiness and power. Because of these positions these countries are under constant economic pressures from the world trading system which is controlled by the U.S. and western European economic interests. There are attempts at outright subversion by agents from areas of the settler colonies or from agents working in the service of the U.S. or western European political or economic interest groups, and last but not least the reactionary elements from within these governments who are more concerned with their class interest rather than being truly concerned about the development of the masses of brothers and sisters. A quick illustration of this point can be made by what this writer personally witnessed during the summer of 1970. In Tanzania there was a treason trial taking place (by the way, the trial was open to the public, and many visitors from other countries went to the trial and observed it); the trial involved several high-ranking military and political people who attempted to overthrow the Tanzanian Government and kill President Nyerere. It was rumored that the money came from either South Africa or economic interests in the Western world. One of the main witnesses against these traitors was a brother from one of the liberation groups fighting against racist South Africa, whose cooperation they had tried to obtain. While the trial was going on, one morning I awoke to read in the paper that the office of the National Liberation Front of Mozambique had been blown up and a brother on duty had lost an eye and arm in the blast. The next day we read the newspapers' account of a battle between Touré's army and a band of rebels who are attempting to overthrow Guinea. Example of economic pressures is the case of Zambia. They are forced to maintain economic relationships with South Africa if they wish to ship their copper to the sea. I learned from talking to a high ranking government offical in Dar es Salaam that Tanzania has had to struggle against price-fixing on its cotton, and was only able to win by borrowing money from a friendly country and getting into the bidding, thus raising the price of cotton higher. From these quick examples one can see clearly that these brothers are struggling daily for their birthright of *Self-Determination*. Before I go on I might add here that it is not only western European interests that attempt to undermine these countries, but Russia has been found to have interfered with Guinea. I understand that a high-ranking official from Russia was deported from Guinea for interfering. While I was in Guinea I saw a building put up by the Russians in the 1960's that had deteriorated so badly that it looked as if it was one hundred years old. It gave you the impression that it was done with a "don't give a damn" attitude about Africa; "it was put up to beat the U.S. and we will use Guinea for our playground as we fight our cold war."

I propose that we as an organization begin to help our brothers in their struggle against these forces. One of the most important ways that we can help is by assisting them in their regional development projects. The most important project getting under way is the proposed Tanzania and Zambia railroad. The significance of this railroad is that if it is completed it will free Zambia from its dependent role on South Africa. It will stimulate growth in underpopulated areas, it will build confidence in Africa and the world that Pan-Africanism is possible, and it will further strengthen the liberation fighters along the southern border.

Therefore I propose:

1. We African-Americans raise the sum of five million dollars in American money to be given to the Tanzania-Zambia railroad project and that the money will be earmarked in such a way they deem necessary within the general framework of developing and building the Tanzania-Zambia railroad, which will run from Lusada, Zambia, to Dar es Salaam, Tanzania, about 1,166 miles.
2. We should raise this money through a committee tentatively named The Pan-African Educational, Cultural and Development Committee. The committee should have a steering committee of ten people. The job of the steering committee would be to develop an action program by which this sum could be raised. I have drawn up a list of people who I think should be on the steering committee.
    1. Imamu Amiri Baraka
    2. Stokely Carmichael
    3. Huey P. Newton
    4. Jesse Jackson
    5. Julian Bond
    6. Bill Sutherland
    7. Bill Cosby
    8. Ralph Bunche
    9. Barbara Ann Teer
    10. Barry Gordy, Jr.

The money can be raised by tapping our national resource, which is Black art and artists. We could put together a "Soul Extravaganza" that will headline major stars which would tour the fifty major cities in the United States. If we can raise over ninety thousand dollars for Brother Joe Louis I am sure we can raise five million for Africa. The second part of this project is that we raise approximately four thousand green beret boots for the liberation forces in Mozambique and Angola which are to be given to them through the O.A.U. Liberation Commission. One last word—as I was flying back from Africa I read in the international newspaper put out by the *New York Times* and Washington *Post*, August 16, 1970, "Tel Aviv. Israel's Premier Golda Meir has urged Jewish leaders in the U.S. to raise one billion dollars for Israel in 1972, the state radio reported yesterday. Mrs. Meir emphasized the need to raise this amount, twice the sum expected to be collected in 1971, in a recent meeting with leaders of the fund-raising projects for Israel, the radio said. It added that American Jewish leaders had assured the Israel premier that there were good chances of large increases in contributions."

Right on . . .

Public Office: Appointed or Elected (Major Premise)

by John Cashin

I. Historical Definition of the Problem
   A. Slavery
   B. Civil War
   C. Franchise to Vote
      Reason: Northern whites used Blacks to vote white Southerners out of political power (economics)
      Result: (1) First Public Schools
              (2) Sewers
II. Compromise of 1876
   A. Black Codes
   B. Grandfather Clause
   C. Terrorism
   D. Disenfranchisement of Blacks
      Reason: 1. Withdrawal of Carpetbaggers
              2. Black people w/o arms
              3. Terrorism
              4. Economical Reprisals
III. How to Prevent the Mistakes of the Past
   A. Political Education
   B. Watchdogs (watchdog committee)
   C. Communications (against)
      1. No-knock law
      2. Preventive detention
      3. Black politicians must publicize issues that affect Blacks.
      4. Some type of national group that will assist Black politicians on issues that are relevant to Black people.
      5. Accountability
      6. Pressure groups
IV. (Premise) Itemize a *list of responsibility* with variations depending on the social, economical and political picture in various sections of the country.

V. Washington (District of Columbia)
   A. Appointed Officials
      1. Mayor
      2. Council
      3. Other cabinet positions
   B. Constitutional Amendment
      1. Home rule
      2. Legislature passing the House in re representation in Congress
VI. Legislative restrictions in setting up third parties. Bring in suggestions.
   Manual
VII. Qualifications (Manifesto for Black Candidates)
   A. Should move to restructure all institutions that have proven to be racist and operating against the interest of the community. Police Dept., Fire, Welfare, Health, Hospitals, etc.
   B. Appointed Official—put the pressure on the person that appointed him.
   C. Elected Official—recall him.
   D. Integrity
   E. Should work to implement the philosophy of self-determination.
   F. Honesty

An outline of recommendations for the three-hour session tomorrow. Suggestion—the Newark experience be put in writing to be utilized in other communities.

Feasibility of a Black Political Party
Nomination of persons on National Committee—members, officers, of the African Congress, *6 seats.*

Sub-Committee Report On Guidelines For Elected and Appointed Black Officials

Preamble: Black elected and appointed officials are today becoming more numerous as Black communities begin to discover that political gains can be achieved through Black unity.

In the face of these realities Black elected and appointed officials are generally not abreast of nationalistic trends of Black peoples in Black communities.

Whereas Black elected officials have a collective racial, historical, cultural, political, emotional heritage with all people of African origin; and

Whereas Black elected and appointed officials must understand that the collective destiny of African people of the world is dependent upon their mutual self-determination, self-sufficiency, self-respect and self-defense; and

Whereas this heritage mandates that Black elected officials must have a collective responsibility to support the liberation of oppressed African people of the world; and the question now arises as to what is expected from the elected and appointed officials in view of the political and social realities of the day.

We of the sub-committee on Public Office of the Political Liberation Workshop of the Congress of African Peoples do hereby set our hand to outline these expectations as itemized:

I. To change all present institutions such as Education, Police, Fire, Housing, Law Enforcement, Health and Welfare and all human resources to allow maximum representation and participation by Black people so that the needs of the Black community are met.

II. That they be knowledgeable of the history and culture of all oppressed people, the world over, such as mid-Eastern, African and Asian conflicts so as to be informed and better able to perceive the position of the Congress of African Peoples which is representative of the true concerns of the Black community.

III. That Black elected and appointed officials be politically aware and be able to communicate this awareness and sophistication to enable Black people to capitalize and maximize the electoral process.

IV. Black elected and appointed leaders must speak out against the current war in Vietnam and other wars of oppression against Black and Third World people that may be conceived in the future.

V. That Black elected and appointed officials be dedicated to the exposure and eradication of narcotics in the Black community. The inability of the white racist institutions to deal effectively with this problem either by design or default, has had the effect of committing genocide on Black people. Black officials must direct their efforts simultaneously in the areas of diplomatic initiative, law enforcement and treatment therapy.

VI. That Black elected and appointed officials be committed to make concentrated efforts to hire and appoint qualified Black people.

VII. That Black elected and appointed officials realize that it is not enough to take issue against recognized forms of organized crime but they must also take stands against the unequal administration of justice in the Black community.

VIII. That the Black elected and appointed officials realize that they have a responsibility to teach, translate and disseminate information that they acquire in performance of their duties. This accountability is mandated by the Black community.

IX. That Black elected and appointed officials take responsibility to train, educate, and totally involve young Black people in the political liberation in their respective communities.

X. That Black elected and appointed officials must be dedicated to fight repressive laws and acts such as "stop and frisk," "no-knock" and legal genocide such as the recent attempts by law enforcement agencies to exterminate segments of the Black community such as the Black Panthers.

Therefore Black elected and appointed officials must constantly be aware of these guidelines and work to implement and achieve these goals and objectives for their respective communities.

We, the sub-committee, further recommend that a task force be appointed to meet and develop a manual that would make specific technique, methodology, and strategy for implementation of these guidelines.

We, the sub-committee, further recommend that mechanics be established by this Congress to guarantee that there will be further and regular contact among members of this committee. This would insure exchange of ideas, and continuance of life and purposes for which this Congress was convened as well as guaranteeing implementation of our proposals.

The Pan-African Struggle in the Caribbean

by Roosevelt Douglas

Following the Pan-African Congress held in Manchester, England, in 1945 under the auspices of the International Africa Service Bureau, formed and organized by the late Black West Indian, George Padmore, a Declaration to the colonial worker, farmer and intellectual was made and read in part:

> All colonies must be freed from foreign imperialist control, whether political or economic. We say to the peoples of the colonies that they must fight for these ends by all the means at their disposal.
>
> The object of imperialist peoples is to exploit . . . Therefore the struggle for *political power* by colonial and subject peoples is the first step forward and the necessary prerequisite to complete social, economic and political emancipation.
>
> . . . Today there is only one road to effective action—the organization of the masses. And in that organization, the educated . . . must join.

Colonial and subject peoples of the world—unite.

Twenty-five years after this Declaration many continental African states led by Ghana under Kwame Nkrumah have made achievements—political, but not economic independence. But the continent is still in part in the grip of colonialism, as in Zimbabwe, so-called Portuguese Guinea and Angola, Southern and South West Africa, the Spanish Sahara and elsewhere, and almost wholly in the grip of white racist imperialism. In the Caribbean, particularly the English-speaking, there are four politically independent territories—those of Jamaica, Trinidad, Guyana and Barbados; while Grenada and the Grenadines, St. Vincent, St. Lucia, Dominica, Antigua, St. Kitts, Anguilla, Nevis, Montserrat, the Virgin Islands, the Bahamas, Bermuda, British Honduras, Aruba, Curaçao, Guadeloupe and Martinique all are still under colonial control. Our brothers and sisters in South America (80 million) are yet to be integrated into the present thrust of African Liberation.

In the United States, Canada, England, France, Holland, to name a few, we have our Black brethren under racist colonial and economic siege. What then is clear is that that Declaration of 1945 has still to be operationalized in its entirety, and it must be one of our primary purposes of this Congress of African Peoples to corroborate the Declaration and complement it with a call to the politically independent African and Caribbean territories to aid the liberation of their colonialized enslaved brothers and sisters and not by rhetoric but by *positive action.* We can say that the fight for liberation in the Caribbean and the human and economic development of the area was given a new lease of revolutionary life with the institution of a new stage of struggle against the insolent house slave leaders and government led by Eric Williams of Trinidad. The rest of the Caribbean will surely follow this path of struggle. Having been physically shackled by the chains of slavery and mentally enslaved by colonial education following emancipation, the Caribbean peoples are now breaking out of these prison-homes bequeathed to the Black Caribbean puppets of imperialism, who are attempting to substitute the pastiche of British parliamentarianism and their class conceptions of "Freedom" and "Democracy" for the basic needs of their people, viz., adequate food, clothing, shelter, education, and their independent self-activity, all of which can only be guaranteed to the people through full local control, not 51 percent control, and productive development of the natural resources of the area, that is, land, oil, bauxite, asphalt, lunasce, sugar, bananas, citrons, manganese, timber, cocoa, nutmegs and spices, arrowroot, cotton, the beaches and a creative people.

But having therefore assumed power with the conscious and deliberate aim of managing the foreign-dominated economics for the international white bourgeoisie, and collecting financial support and other dividends for doing so, the present Black political scabs in the Caribbean, especially Williams, Shearer, Duvalier and Barrow, thereby perform the functions of political superintendents, overseers, foremen and political policemen, and have no alternative but to carry out their class functions of attempting to manage the Black masses first and foremost since they have all signed agreements guaranteeing United States' investments against expropriation. Hence the internal witch-hunts, banning of books and people-floggings, opening of mail, race relations bills, public order acts, as now exist in Trinidad under Eric Williams, author of *Capitalism and Slavery* and *Preventive Detention,* also and threatened in Guyana, and all those totalitarian mores which are transforming these territories into isolated and insular ghettos from which tremendous mass political explosions will emanate.

But recognizing, however, that even struggles will assume rational proportions, and taking into account the law of uneven development, we of the Caribbean nevertheless recognize the necessity for internationalism, and hereby call on our international African brothers and sisters, especially our African-American comrades, who have a special responsibility to the Black workers to provide assistance in any and every way they can to help their struggling brothers in Trinidad and the whole Caribbean including the English-, French-, Spanish-, and Dutch-speaking Caribbean, their brothers in Zimbabwe, Guinea and Angola, northern Africa and elsewhere, while specially calling for the independent political liberation of the small islands of the Eastern Caribbean and asking the United Nations (General Assembly Resolution 1514–1960), we also call on the Organization of African States and African countries of Zambia, Tanzania, Guinea, Algeria, the United Arab Republic and the Peoples Republic of the Congo (Brazzaville) to take up this question of the undivided and unconditional political independence of the Eastern Caribbean, without which the area will never be truly united. Black people unite in support of the Black world and struggling humanity in the struggle against white imperialism, particularly United States imperialism, the main protagonist of racism, war and the cause of all undevelopment.

Pan-Africanism as a political ideology in 1970 can only be meaningful if it is expressed through the cooperative building of economic, political, cultural and military institutions—institutions that are voted in the social lives of our people and able to conform to nationalist aspirations. The ability of this workshop to make this contribution to the congress could very well help determine the future progess of our liberation struggle.

Yes—An Independent Black Nation in Our Time, in This Place!

by Imari Abubakari Obadele, I

During this past August on my way to Detroit from a meeting of the People's Center Council, the supreme legislative and governing body of the Republic of New Africa, just concluded in Jackson, Mississippi, I encountered an old acquaintance of mine while passing through Chicago. The man was one for whom I have great personal respect; he has fulfilled the promise of distinction which even those of us who were his contemporaries saw in him in the old days. Inevitably, before many words had passed between us, our conversation turned to the Republic, and my friend asked me—more patronizingly than, I am sure, he realized—"Imari, you don't really think they are going to let you set up a separate nation here?"

The question took me aback. I realize now that in the past intense weeks since we had moved the headquarters of the Republic into the Deep South (New Orleans) I had been dealing mostly with our own people, dedicated New Africans: persons who do not by any means think that *anybody* is going to *let* us set up a separate nation but who, by contrast, so completely believe that we will—through power—win a separate land mass in the five states of the South that our planning concentrates not so much on winning that land mass as on how we shall consolidate the revolution afterwards, how we shall build those new and better institutions which will in fact guarantee for our people a new and better life.

But the revolution *is* not yet won, and because successful Black people like my Chicago friend are those to whom we who are going to create "Israel" here must look for financial support, and for diplomatic (i.e., "political") support as we free the five states of the Deep South, it becomes not only important but crucial for us to make sure that he and others like him—none of whom may ever plan to come to "Israel"—understand what we are doing. They must come to understand that we are, indeed, talking about *here*—not somewhere else—and that we are talking about now. They must understand that we have a political theory that is viable and a political method that, we believe, will prove efficacious. So, for my Chicago friend and his brothers and sisters of Black American success, I offer these insights into the Republic and the work we are doing.

To begin with it is important to understand that we in the Republic of New Africa look upon ourselves in the same way that the brothers of Azania (South Africa) look upon themselves vis-à-vis the white South African. The Azanians are fighting to free their land from a white oppressor; we New Africans are doing precisely the same thing. Why land? you say. All the land in America belongs to whites, does it not? In Azania, besides, the Azanians are in the majority, are they not? In America, the whites are in the majority.

It is a matter of context.

Whites are in the majority in America taken as a whole, as presently constituted. Blacks are in the majority in central cities all over the U.S.; we are in the majority in the Black Belt area stretching hundreds of miles across the South. What we in New Africa have done is to delineate the land of the Black nation as the five states of the deepest South: Louisiana, Mississippi, Alabama, Georgia, and South Carolina —one-tenth of the United States (and we are, they say, one-tenth of the people in the United States). In Mississippi, of course, *they* count us as quite less than a majority, something around 40 percent; *we* estimate, with good justification, that we are in that state a numerical majority.

What is important is that the five states of the Deep South, with their contiguous, quarter million square miles, represent a settlement. We are saying, let us give up our claim to the Black areas of the many cities (reservations) across America—as *national territory*—and accept in return the contiguous, two-oceaned, five-stated land mass represented by Louisiana, Mississippi, Alabama, Georgia, and South Carolina, through which the Black Belt runs so fertilely, and where, in Louisiana with its total population of less than four million, more than a third Black, and in Mississippi, its population under three million, a half of it Black, we could easily establish numerical preponderance with fractional Black emigration from a handful of northern cities.

What we are saying, more importantly, is that our claim to this southern land mass as national territory arises from an observance of those criteria which civilized people have always held to be the test of *people's* claim to land, to national territory. These criteria say that a people may claim land as theirs if (1) they have lived on it traditionally, (2) they have worked and built upon it, and (3) they have fought to stay on it. This is the civilized rule of land possession, sanctioned by international practice, and it is quite clear that Black people in many northern cities, but especially in the Black Belt of the South, meet all these criteria.

We have lived upon the territory of the South for over three hundred years (and we have lived in New York, Philadelphia, and Baltimore—though our precise locations in these cities have shifted in time—for well over two hundred years). We have worked and built upon the land: indeed, the whole basis of white American wealth lay in the tricornered trade that involved Yankee ships bearing Black slaves from Africa to the West Indies and the United States South; then sugar, rice, cotton, and similar goods from there to the North and to England; then on to Africa again for another cargo of slaves —is clearly derived from the very essence of the Black man. We have built upon this land both under duress, for the oppressor, and out of love for ourselves, building our homes, our farms, our churches, our places of business and recreation, and always out of hardship. And we have fought to stay on the land—sometimes mistaking our affection for the land as an affection for the oppressor and his institutions. We have fought against night-riders and daytime courts and sheriffs and plantation stores, and against poor crops and hunger and disease and ignorance and fear: we have clung to the land.

So, as a people, we have met those civilized requirements of international law that make the land ours. We have (1) lived on the land traditionally; we have (2) built on and improved the land, and (3) we have fought to stay there.

The problem is that Black people have never subscribed to this rule of international law for ourselves. We have, instead, been overawed by another rule of international law, which says that if a people steal a land—as Europeans stole America—and hold it long enough, others will recognize that land as theirs. That is a bandit rule of law, which must—in a world where most of the people are people of color and virtually all of us are civilized—yield to the civilized rule of land possession: tradition, improvement, and tenacity.

What the Republic of New Africa is doing at this moment in the five states of the Deep South, and especially in Mississippi, our target state, is to organize a plebiscite. A plebiscite is an election whereby people in an area decide between two (or more) nationalities. Ideally the United Nations, as the international body closest to being an arbiter between nations and peoples, would conduct such a plebiscite. United States' power within that body, however, makes such an eventuality extremely unlikely. We, therefore, will conduct the plebiscite ourselves, in much the way that the Mississippi Freedom Democratic Party conducted a vote on its own during the winter of 1963 to demonstrate how Blacks all over the state would vote if permitted.

After the plebiscite, we will, of course, defend ourselves. But the work of organizing for the plebiscite is the technical framework within which the battle for liberation, for national sovereignty, is today being waged in the South.

Before I turn, finally, to the all-important question of how we shall defend ourselves—and do so successfully—I must stress that our work of organizing for the plebiscite revolves around three key elements.

1. First, our success is to be founded upon Black people understanding that there is no feasible way for us in the United States to solve the persistent problems that plague us as a people (unemployment and underemployment, poor health, bad housing, crippling education); that our only feasible solution is the establishment of a sovereign nation under enlightened philosophy.

2. Second, that the establishment of such a sovereign Black nation is feasible, first of all, because it is substantiated by international law. The land belongs to us as people and, also, we are not American citizens (I will deal with this below), and the question of our citizenship and status, therefore, still awaits settlement.

3. Third, that the establishment of a sovereign Black nation is feasible because we have developed a technique—involving an efficacious alignment of military, and diplomatic, and political-economic factors—for achieving liberation and sovereignty. (That method has been laid out in detail by me in two small books, *Revolution and Nation-building* and *War in America.*)

Because Black people in America remain the persistent victims of the same problems which have plagued us since the end of the Civil War, despite the efforts to solve these problems within the American system, despite the New Deal and Fair Deal and Good Deal, despite the poverty program and Martin Luther King, despite Julia, it is not difficult to establish with the majority of Blacks in America the community of belief that we cannot, as a feasible matter, solve these persistent problems as part of the American system. An honest analysis of our history in this country can lead to no other conclusion. Thus, our efforts in Mississippi center more forcefully on the other two matters: first, getting people to understand in their hearts as well as in their heads that the land does belong to us and that we are not citizens of the U.S. and are entitled to a bilateral settlement of our status, and, second, that our method for establishing sovereignty is, indeed, feasible.

The question of Black people in Mississippi coming to understand that the land there is ours is crucial. For, so long as we believe that the land belongs to someone else, to the white American to be precise, we believe also that we are some kind of ward or unwanted guest in the white American's house. In such status we are willing to suffer the householder's abuse in near silence. Once, however, we come to understand that the land is ours, that attitude changes, things are reversed, and the white American becomes the intruder. Only then are we ready to fight a people's war of defense for the land. And this readiness, certain to be put to test after the plebiscite, is the *sine qua non;* the absolute essential, for liberation and sovereignty. For only this attitude toward the land can carry us resolutely and victoriously through the war which white supremacy is virtually certain to force upon us.

Matched with the attitude toward the land is a necessity for an understanding of the fact that Black people are not citizens of the United States. In recent years it has become popular for young people and old Black nationalists to say glibly that we are not citizens. This fashionable pronouncement is usually based on a bitterness arising in reaction to the vile treatment which Blacks have historically suffered in America. It also, however, happens to be well rooted in a concept of international law. That concept requires that a state protect its citizens not only against deprivations by the state itself (as the United States did for Black people, forbidding, in the Fourteenth Amendment, any state from making or enforcing laws to harm Black people), but a state must protect its citizens from deprivations of other citizens as well.

It is clear that the United States never did this. The whole thrust of three decades of successful N.A.A.C.P. cases was to show that various forms of discrimination—white primary through segregated schools and parks were illegal not because white citizens acting as white citizens abridged the freedoms of Blacks but because, as U.S. law required, "state power" was somehow being used to effect the abridgement. Had the cases rested upon simple abridgement of rights by citizens, there could have been no success. The United States has provided for no such protection of Black people; her statutes and court decisions have, in fact, specifically restrained the United States from protecting the rights of Black people against abridgement by white citizens. Thus, if historically states have been seen to protect their citizens from deprivations of other citizens, and the United States does not do this for Black people (and, in fact, restrains itself from doing so), clearly Black people cannot be citizens.

More than this, however, is the fact that the Fourteenth Amendment to the U.S. Constitution, which purported to impose citizenship upon Black people, could not, in fact, do such a thing. The reason is relatively simple. The Thirteenth Amendment, which ended slavery, can be accepted as a genuine bill of manumission because it was effective, in terms of its operation upon the slave master, in actually ending slavery. But we think that the freedom of the Black man (like the freedom of any people) is a thing inherent in his humanity; slavery is incapable of being *rightfully* or *legally* imposed upon any people. Therefore, no people may *grant* freedom to another people but may only recognize that which each people's humanity has already established as an unconditional matter of right.

The Fourteenth Amendment is another story, because it attempted to impose citizenship on a free people, whose freedom had only two years earlier been recognized by the Thirteenth Amendment. The Fourteenth Amendment attempted to reach a group of free men, who had wrongfully and by force been taken from their original home and enslaved in America, and, instead of creating a means for the free men to make those choices which belong to free men in such circumstances, the Fourteenth Amendment made a single, unilateral choice for the free men: it "made" the free men citizens.

To do so the Amendment rested on what is known in international law as the rule of *jus soli,* which means, fundamentally, that a person born on the soil of a country acquires the citizenship of that country. The almost incredible effrontery of the Fourteenth Amendment, in so resting, lay in the fact that the presence of the Black man on this soil had nothing to do with any free choice of his to be here. And while the *individual*'s presence here might be an acceptable accident of birth, the presence of the Black man here, *as a people,* was the result of a purposeful and systematic kidnapping, transport, and enslavement of a people. In such circumstances it would clearly be a mockery of *any* system of law or practice to suggest that citizenship—implying obligations and duties as well as rights and privileges—could arise from mere presence.

Thus, after the Thirteenth Amendment, a great body of people, Black and wrongfully transported and enslaved, now stood as free, facing their former slave master. Not any other group or person could tell the slave what to do. The obligation facing the slave master was to repair the Black man for the wrongs inflicted upon him. The fights facing the Black man included the right to determine his future state relationships.

The choices, with regard to state affiliation, which lay before the freed Black man were these:

(1) Would he like to become a citizen of the U.S.?
(2) Would he like to go back to Africa?
(3) Would he like to go to another country?
(4) Would he like to set up a nation of his own?

What the Fourteenth Amendment purported to do—to exclude all these choices except one imposing upon the Black man a condition of special citizenship—could not be rightfully done. For the Black man was, indeed, free—free from the slave master's illegal act of enslavement. The insistence of the white man upon the validity of the Fourteenth Amendment, which denied to the freed Black man his rightful choices—meant only that the white man was insisting on a continuation of white control over fundamental Black decision-making. It meant, in other words, a continuation of slave status, if in a somewhat less odious form.

However, such a continuation of slavery could not be more legal or more right simply because it was less odious. It was quite as illegal and quite as lacking in right as the prior slavery.

The essential point is that since the Black man emerging from slavery was denied the four choices to which he was entitled, and denied these choices by whites possessed of the power to do so, the slavery of the Black man to the white man has continued though in a somewhat less odious form, and there has been no settlement of the question of state-status for the Black man. For, such a settlement could only evolve on the basis of bilateral agreements between the Black and white peoples, each of them free, and with the Black man enjoying his right—as a free man wrongfully transported and enslaved—to make a choice, freely, among the four options for his future that we have outlined above.

Black men could not have been rightfully enslaved. As free men wrongfully enslaved, with the wrong now admitted by the white enslaver, no law could shut out other options and IMPOSE upon this free Black man citizenship in the United States. And our status with respect to state affiliation and our future relations with the heirs of our fathers' white slave masters still remains to be settled.

The Republic of New Africa today frames the settlement. The options which we project are four, and logically derivative.

(1) Citizenship in our own sovereign Black nation, on a land mass that has become our traditional home with a significant reparations settlement, for those of us who want it;

(2) Citizenship in the United States, with a proportionate share in the reparations settlement, for those of us who want it;

(3) Return to Africa, with a proportionate share in the reparations settlement, for those of us who want it, or

(4) Em-patriation in another country, with a proportionate share in the reparations settlement, for those of us who can arrange it.

These are the terms. And we insist on settlement now.

It is one thing for the Black people to have a community of belief that we can find no feasible solution to our persistent problems by remaining in the American system and that, by contrast, a sovereign Black nation could solve these problems. It is one thing to have an understanding that the land is ours. And it is one thing to recognize that we are not U.S. citizens and that a settlement of our citizenship status remains to be made and to demand it be made now. It is another to succeed at creating that alignment of power relationships which will force the enemy to meet our terms—terms permitting sovereignty, terms permitting the evolvement of conditions (as, most recently in the Western Hemisphere, in Cuba) conducive to the creation of a better life in our own, self-determined mold.

How is the Republic undertaking to create this favorable alignment of power relationships? (Again, this is all laid out in somewhat greater detail in my books, *War in America* and *Revolution and Nation-building*.) But, essentially, what we are doing is attempting to, first, promulgate a correct political theory for establishment of the nation; second, stimulate internal domestic support (among Black people in America); third, generate positive diplomatic support among our foreign friends; fourth, create an effective overground defense force, and fifth, hope that the Black Underground Army in America will provide a telling "second-strike" capability against U.S. industrial power.

To repeat and elaborate:

We are saying, first, that we have labored into being a body of organized thought which provides us with a claim to land justified under international law; we have raised anew, in a compelling way, the questions of reparations and of the citizenship status of Black people, and we have chosen a method—the organization of the plebiscite and the call for negotiations—which show us earnestly seeking to settle all of the issues peacefully.

We are saying, second, that Black people, whether they care to come to the Republic or not, should help us in seeking its establishment much as many Jews in America, who have never planned to go to Israel, helped in its establishment. And we are calling for that help, for we have and will continue to have for some time a need for great quantitites of dollars and for the assistance of the political power which Black people wield through their congressmen in Washington and other posts in the U.S. Government in any action against us.

We are saying, third, that the correctness of our political position —our position on the land and our position with regard to an absence of American citizenship—provides the necessary basis for our friends abroad, principally in Africa and Asia but in Europe too, to speak out and act in behalf of us, much as they do for the Angolan freedom fighters or for the Vietnamese.

Fourth, we are saying that, white supremacy being what it is in America, we can count on United States forces—civilian armies like the Ku Klux Klan and Minutemen, and ultimately, the regular forces — to engage us in armed struggle before, during, and after the plebiscite, regardless of our peaceful professions, and so we are building a large, overground defensive force, of which the Black Legion was the first popular evidence, and we are undertaking to prepare the people in general for success in whatever war may be forced upon us. In a people's war, people who believe the land is theirs resist the enemy with all means at their disposal. They help to conceal and supply their own regular army. To hinder the enemy they destroy roads, bridges, and foodstuffs; they poison water and give out bad information.

Finally, we are saying that the white oppressor will be driven to a negotiated settlement and an end to the unjust war against us when the Black Underground Army in America—which the Republic neither directs nor controls nor is any more certain than any of you that it actually exists—brings American industrial capacity close enough to destruction to make it more feasible for them to negotiate a settlement than to continue the war.

In pursuit of these five strategies for liberation, citizens of the Republic may intrude into your lives in many ways. You will find us, of course, distributing literature and endlessly promoting a theoretical understanding of our struggle. You will find us seeking your signature on petitions designed to say to the Vietnamese and to the world that the war in Vietnam is a white man's war, that we Black people want and will observe a separate and immediate cease-fire with the Vietnamese and that we seek the release of Black prisoners of war in return.

You will find me coming to you in letter and publications, and sometimes in person, along with other officers and citizens asking your dollar-support for the establishment of the National Bank of the Republic of New Africa—a central bank, which all independent countries must have, which for New Africa will serve the same functions which the Federal Reserve Bank serves for the United States. We need to begin this now, even before liberation, because we have the immediate and costly need to lay the foundations for essential state-owned industries—especially the housing, electronics, and chemical industries. And we dare not wait.

I have, of course, truncated important arguments and statements. It is hardly possible in such space to give more than an outline, which we would hope you would find at least tentatively convincing.

Let me say that we are sure we shall win. We are concerned, now being sure we will win, with the kind of society we shall build after the war and after settlement. It must not, of course, be America all over again but in technicolor. It must be, truly, *New African*. And so, throughout America, in the cities where our consulates and government centers exist, the highest priority consists in the creation of New African schools, in which, soon, we hope to educate all the sons and daughters of color who yearn for a better life, and we expect that

that will be fully a third or more of all our people in every community. In these schools, too, we shall re-educate those millions who we hope soon will come to the promised land, acculturating them to a creed and a pattern of life that will assure that we shall not bring the ruins of Harlem to the virgin expanses of Mississippi, the heartland of New Africa.

Resolutions

by Imamu Amiri Baraka

The Political Liberation Workshop tried to move toward the creation of a Black political institution that will express and move to fulfill the needs of Black people, wherever they are. At its most effective this institution is called a Nation. But to develop this Nation, (an African World State) a preliminary organizing vehicle is needed: A BLACK POLITICAL PARTY. A local-international Nationalist-Pan-Africanist party (World African Party) capable of dealing not only with international problems of Africans by means of international alliances and international exchanges of information and resources, but also a party able to function on the smallest level, i.e., to win municipal elections.

Since politics is simply the gaining, maintaining and use of power, the Black political party must move to gain political power through four areas of political power: Public Office, Alliances and Coalitions, Community Organization, or Disruption. The workshop was broken down into these four areas of political power, and a report was made in each area, and resolutions in some:

Community Organization—Saidi Elimu
Coalitions and Alliances—Imari Obadele, RNA
Cyril Karg, Surinam
Veive Mbaeve, Namibia
Roosevelt Douglas, Dominica

Report of Sub-Committee on Community Organization:

The community organization body resolved that community organization is one area of political power. A community organization is an organization coming out of the community, which should be able to move in the other three areas of political power which are: Public Office, Alliances and Coalitions, and Disruptions. A community organization is set up to gain, maintain, and use power. Power means imposing your will, manifesting your thoughts into action. It was pointed out that it is essential to the control of anything worth anything in the community. Rather than call programs or organizations useless, we must take control of them and make them work for Black people.

The group moved further to adopt seven procedures necessary *for the formation of a political party, in areas wherever there are large concentrations of Black people,* that can do the following:

1. Work on Voter Registration
2. Mobilize
3. Organize
4. Politicize
5. Run Candidate
6. Make Alliances
7. Make Third World Relations

The delegates adopted four requirements for such a movement to succeed. First, it will require an *ideology.* An ideology gives identity, purpose and direction, meaning knowing who we are as a people and who our enemy is. It gives purpose in that it defines what we must do in relationship to our identity. We must strive collectively for the building and developing of our communities in order to restore our people to their traditional greatness. To say an ideology gives direction is to say it clearly shows us the way we must use for achieving our purpose. An ideology also must be a clearcut statement defining the organized process for carrying out our specific goals. Without this basic foundation we won't be able to advance from where we are to where we want to go.

Secondly, it needs an *organization* which is the prototype for the political party. An organization seeking to gain, maintain and use power. An organization makes your ideas valid and with it your ideas can be manifest into actions. It was noted that decision-making can be shared but leadership cannot. The administration of the organization must be based on commitment and efficiency. Members of the organization must have special skills and abilities, not merely be good talkers but people who get things done. In essence the community organization must be that which it wants to see for all Black people —the Nation becoming.

Thirdly, we need communications which is the distribution of information. There must be internal and external communications.

The fourth requirement for a movement to succeed is Resources. This entails financing what you plan to do. Sources are:

1. Community Control of all Community Resources
2. Anti-Poverty Programs
3. Organizations
4. Black Entertainers
5. Alliances and Coalitions
6. Individual Resources

It was stressed finally that in all these areas we must defend what we develop.

The final resolution was to do the following:

1. Organize Congress of African Peoples offices or use existing community organizations as C.A.P. oriented structures.
2. Use National C.A.P. input to help shape local C.A.P. structures.
3. Geographical areas to send C.A.P. delegates as well as general public to National-international Congress.
4. Local C.A.P. officials must be publicized as C.A.P. officers and represent area problems in four areas of political power.
5. Collaboration on national voter education drives.
6. Electoral candidates in different areas supported by National C.A.P. and paid und volunteer personnel C.A.P. can supply to area in question.

Report of Sub-Committee On Alliances & Coalitions
Philosophical In-Puts:

The purpose of consolidation of African peoples should be to acquire and share power, to defend and maintain our common interests, and to deny power to the forces of capitalism, imperialism, neocolonialism and racism.

The workshop chose the term consolidation as opposed to alliance or coalition for it is understood that as an African people we already ally and coalesce with our brothers and sisters, ideologically.

Thus, it is necessary to consolidate ourselves by solving our ideological, geographical and other differences. It is further understood that this cannot be achieved by rhetoric but only by meaningful and concrete programs and active participation of all Black people in the liberation struggle. We will support the total liberation of African peoples. In reference to ourselves, as an African people, we must consolidate our resources in terms of numbers, financial, technological, political, military and educational. We also recognize that non-European peoples in specific areas have acted in opposition to the liberation of African peoples. Thus, we will form alliances with those Third World peoples who show a willingness to support our goals and aims.

In reference to all other peoples, we will form coalitions based on specific issues to achieve results which will aid our goals of liberation.

Considering that the Black people of the world today have united in the struggle against the white terror; considering that the Black people of the world know that many countries which twenty-five years ago signed the charter of the United Nations to do away with colonialism are members of this world organization and still have colonial territories, the Congress of African Peoples urges that:

All the white countries (among them the Netherlands) who made this promise and did not keep it be accused in the United Nations—by the Black countries who are members of this organization—of breach of promise—of willfully withholding freedom from Black people who are eager for their freedom. As a sanction, the Black people of the world today are urged to start a boycott against Holland and the rest of the colonial powers who do not intend to respect this charter of the United Nations.

In case the United Nations decides not to accept this protest of Black nations that all the Black powers of the world immediately take steps to create an organization of Black United Nations of the world.

Be it resolved that the Congress of African Peoples, being unalterably opposed to the United States' war against the Vietnamese people, and being determined that Black people should no longer participate in this barbarous and unjust adventure, do urge Black troops in the United States military forces to cease immediately firing at the Vietnamese and do urge the soldiers of the Democratic Republic of Vietnam (the North Vietnamese) and the Provisional Revolutionary Government of South Vietnam to recognize this Black cease-fire, to reciprocate in it, and, as a further sign of accepting the cease-fire to begin to release Black prisoners of war to the Congress of African Peoples immediately and on an accelerated basis.

Be it resolved that the Congress of African Peoples form an "African Liberation Front" which would be a body to consolidate this body, the Congress of African Peoples, with the various national liberation fronts throughout Africa, the Caribbean, South and Central America as well as the U.S.A. In the case of the U.S.A. specifically the congress should establish a *Black National Liberation Front,* and set up a body to consolidate the Congress of African Peoples with all the various Black revolutionary movements in the U.S.A. including the League of Revolutionary Workers, the Black Panther party, and the Republic of New Africa.

Be it resolved that the Congress of African Peoples supports the right of persons of African descent who desire to repatriate to the independent African states to so repatriate.

Approved Resolutions

1. Be it resolved that the Congress of African Peoples send a telegram to the Summit meeting of the Organization of African Unity meeting in Addis Ababa in support of solidarity of the African world.
2. Be it resolved that the Congress of African Peoples send a telegram to the Non-Alignment Conference in Zambia with the expressed purpose of showing solidarity of the African world.

3. The Congress of African Peoples supports and will work to establish an "International Development Union of African People," including as a central feature the creation of a Black international development bank. The purposes of the Union shall include: A. Evaluation of national development projects brought before it by member-delegates and, B. The lending of monies or other resources to such member-delegates for those projects which it deems to be feasible. Member-delegates shall be those nations—and governments, liberation fronts, and parties, where Africans have not freed their land from white political domination—who apply for membership in the Union and meet the membership requirements hereinafter decided. The Union shall as a matter of principle include the nations of all African peoples and, as a matter of principle, will work with and through the Organization of African Unity and the African Development Bank, scrupulously avoiding duplication and conflict. The initial member-delegates of the Union will include one member-delegate from each government—or front, or party, where the land of a nation is not free—represented in the congress and one member-delegate from the Congress of African Peoples for each African nation so represented. Funds for the development bank will be solicited from Black, private individuals and groups.
4. The Congress of African Peoples recognizes the Republic of New Africa as an African nation in the Western Hemisphere whose land is subjugated and supports the right and effort of the Republic of New Africa to organize a peaceful plebiscite among the people living in the subjugated national territory. The Congress of African Peoples explicitly opposes and condemns any efforts of the United States or its political subdivisions to interfere with the peaceful organization of the plebiscite or the peaceful carrying out of its results.
5. Considering that the Black people of the world are today tied in a struggle of life and death against the white oppressor, and considering that in this war the weapon "communications" between the Black people practically does not exist, and considering that in the Black countries communications is still governed by the white press that publicizes only that which it sees fit for the white man to know, the Congress of African Peoples directs the Communications Workshop to start its own Black press service to serve the cause of the Black people and to get correct and true information to all of the Black people of the world, so that they too can join in the fight against white oppression.
6. Be it resolved that we, the Congress of African Peoples, raise a substantial amount of dollars in American money to be given to

the Tanzania-Zambia railroad project, and that the money will be earmarked in such a way that the two countries may use the money as they deem necessary within the general framework of developing and building the Tanzania-Zambian Railroad, which will run from Lusaka, Zambia, to Dar es Salaam, Tanzania, about 1,166 miles.

7. Be it resolved that we, the Congress of African Peoples, raise a substantial number of combat boots for the liberation forces fighting in Africa. These boots should be given through the Organization of African Unity's Liberation Committee.
8. Inasmuch as the sovereignty of a nation-state rests with its political and economic autonomy, the Congress of African Peoples denounces unequivocally the present political and economic rape of all African nation-states by European, American and any other external interests.
9. The Congress of African Peoples hereby supports the Cairo United Front in its struggles for a decent life for Black people and against the oppression and assaults by the white power structure and urges all African peoples to demand that Black office-holders use their power to end the intimidation and assault of Black people in Congress.

Report of Sub-Committee on Disruption:

Subject Matter: Disruption (Actual or Threatened)

Definition: Positive methods of stopping the operation of persons or institutions that oppress Black people (e.g., boycotts, sit-ins)

Purpose: With reference to the following facts:

1. There exist at the present time disruptive methods as a means of effective political, social and economical change. It is resolved that this workshop is to develop ways in which Blacks can elevate these existing forms of disruption.

   Areas: Resolutions in areas to be dealt with *openly*

   Economics
   Political
   Institutional
   Economics

We also resolve that the following be adopted by the congress:

1. That methods become complete. Boycott of Xmas buying during the December-January period (1970-71).
2. Declaration of war on organized crime in the Black community.
3. That methods be developed through research whereby Blacks can effectively withold payment of income tax.
4. That methods be developed to bring about the withdrawal of Black monies from white commercial institutions.

Political: Methods suggested—Exposure of the present corrupt political system on local, national and international levels: by organizing positive concrete alternatives to present political system, i.e., Newark Mayoral election; Fayette, Mississippi, elections.

Institutions: i.e., schools, churches, media.

Methods Suggested:

1. Infiltration at operational and decision-making level.
2. Mass demonstrations
3. Reparations
4. Coercion

In conclusion

1. Delegates of this congress should return to local communities and identify those resources that may be used for positive disruptive purposes.
2. As community organizations develop, consideration should be given to include a standing committee to deal specifically with strategy and tactics.

SOCIAL ORGANIZATION

Coordinator's Statement

by Bibi Amina Baraka

I. The natural characteristics of the Black woman, that is excluding all influence of Western training.
   A. Will bring us back to natural role of complementary, completing and making perfect that which is imperfect.
   B. As Maulana points out, "What makes a woman appealing is femininity and she can't be feminine without being submissive."
      1. Defining submissiveness in the role of the Black woman we are talking about submitting to your natural roles, that is understand that it will take work and study in areas that deal specifically in things that women are responsible for. Such as Maulana teaches inspiration, education and social development of the nation.
         a. *Inspiration* deals with attitudes. Attitudes toward man, your house, children and the work that has to be done in the National Liberation of your people.
         b. *Education* deals with the work and study of what Maulana points out as the Seven Criteria of a Culture: Mythology, History, Social Organization, Political Organization, Economic Organization, Creative Motif, and Ethos and understanding that study is a constant development while work is a sustainer of life.
         c. *Social Development of the Nation* almost becomes impossible without the understanding of the African personality. Social Development itself deals in the defining of the roles and the responsibility that goes along with those roles. In order that the social order that we develop benefit the innate personality of Blacks rather than our oppressors, it becomes paramount that we study the cultures and concepts of people and have a strong moral value system (*Kawaida*) as a guide to balance our results, i.e., tradition and reason. As Maulana points out, "Our

culture must take what is traditional and apply it to the concrete needs of Black people in America."

2. Nutrition
    a. Cooking classes
    b. Learning about foods and their functions
    c. Make up menus and recipes
    d. How to shop
    e. Hygiene
3. Nationalist ideology and philosophy
    a. Leaders and Heroes
    b. Visiting lecturers to reinforce ideology

II. Education
  A. Teachers' workshop for Children's Liberation School
  B. Children's Liberation School
  C. Child care classes
  D. Group study of seven criteria
    1. Mythology
    2. History
    3. Social Organization
    4. Political Organization
    5. Economic Organization
    6. Creative Motif
    7. Ethos

Each project should begin with the history of each area. The results of these projects and programs should be the foundations for setting up permanent Black institutions.

Resource Papers

The Black Family

by Akiba ya Elimu

The Black family is a very important area of social organization because it is the smallest example of how the rest of the nation works. As Imamu Baraka points out in one of his poems—the nation is like ourselves, whatever we are doing is what the nation is doing or not doing. The family unit is the basis of all nations and the understanding of the roles of those who make the house unified is essential.

We understand that it is and has been traditional that the man is the head of the house. He is the leader of the house/nation because his knowledge of the world is broader, his awareness is greater, his understanding is fuller and his application of this information is wiser. The accepting of the Black man's leadership has involved the understanding of the African personality which has no superior or inferior, only a complement. The man has any right that does not destroy the collective needs of his family. After all, it is only reasonable that the man be the head of the house because he is able to defend and protect the development of his home.

In understanding the levels of unity, you yourself have to be unified first. You cannot conquer the world if you have not conquered yourself. In getting yourself together physically, mentally and spiritually, the other aspect of yourself has to be unified which is your house. There is no house without a man and his wife. They are the basis of the nation. As Maulana Ron Karenga points out, "A good example is the best teacher." In teaching the community, nation and eventually the world of unity—our homes have to be complete in their example. The roles of the men and women have to be complementary. The roles are important in that they in turn define the responsibilities to the home, community, and to the nation. In defining the man's role as the leader, his responsibilities to his house are also defined as being necessary to provide emotional, physical, and economical security.

In a process of dehumanization resulting with our present condition of slavery, one of the various steps has been that of destroying the family. Black men and women were separated, given conflicting roles, and the creation of various myths assured our nation to be disunified.

One of the most harmful myths was created by a German named Bachkofen in which he imagined and imposed the idea of the Black matriarchy. The Black woman's role was defined in such an intentional manner so as to emasculate our men and give them a limited responsibility, to guarantee broken Black homes. Since this myth exists in the enslaved minds of Black people and therefore affects our attitude and actions, it becomes extremely necessary to define the Black woman's role as specifically as to reemerge the nation.

The necessity of the acceptance of our roles, therefore our responsibilities, is essential in making the Black family whole again. To understand the importance of this custom and concept, we must keep in mind an African proverb: "The destruction of a nation begins in the homes of its people." But also remember another African proverb: "We are Black, beautiful people. TOGETHER WE WILL WIN."

Marriage Ceremony

by Kasisi Washao

We have come to witness the sacred ceremony of marriage. We have come to bring the highest form of spiritual unity in the universe to this man and this woman. Let us also understand that in this union is the smallest example of how the nation works. The family is all the tiny components we are talking about that make up the complex body called nation. Black people should start with their family, because talking nationalism without first taking care of the home is like running down the beach trying to collect sand instead of collecting it where you are. A marriage can be defined in what it gives and first it gives a chance for Black people to give, to give of themselves to each other, to their communities and to their nation.

We as Black people must realize that equality is a false concept and what we are talking about is being complementary to one another. What the man lacks his woman makes up, what she lacks he makes up. Black people talked about being complementary since the sun first shone on the African soil. By complementary we mean to complete or make perfect that which is incomplete or imperfect. It is by tradition and reason that we may say this tradition is our foundation, reason is the movement so that we must adjust our African past to meet our new African destinies.

The family is then just like an organ and the woman's function must be to inspire her man, to educate the children, and participate in social development. The man must then provide security—first emotionally, so the woman may feel secure in her love; then economic security to be free from finance hassles and scenes, and give physical security from people and problems that threaten her. In essence we say the marriage must be beautiful and in Africa beauty is said to be "that which promises happiness." So may the beauty of your relationship promise you both happiness and may that beauty reflect on a smaller scale the nation becoming and as it is said so let it be done for now and for always for as long as the sun shines and the water flows.

Let us see the Marriage Ceremony.

An African Marriage Ceremony

Couples to be married line up facing each other with the men in one row and the women in the other. All look at the leader-priest who stands at the head of the rows and in the center.

Opening:

We are here to participate in and witness the sacred ceremony of marriage which has been since the time of the first born, a means of establishing a house. That is to say, to start a home and a family. For it is by this that the community endures.

Saidi, you are and shall be the head of the house. You must always provide emotional, economic and physical security for your wife and children. You must lead, but not be a burden, be strong and loving, considerate and creative, respectful, faithful and understanding.

Muminina, you are blessed to have a man who will love you, fulfill your needs and protect you. Be humble and loving, appreciative, and resourceful, faithful, respectful and understanding: so that you can provide continuous inspiration for your husband, culture education for your children und participate in the social development of your nation.

Saidi and *Muminina,* you must be as one in your thought, belief, and action. And though you, *Saidi,* are to lead, and you, *Muminina,* are to follow, there is no superior or inferior one. You are both complementary. That which completes and fulfills and perfects the whole.

Without you, *Saidi*, there is no house and without you, *Muminina,* there is no house.

We must remember that it is never the great things that destroy a house. It is always the small things. So let each of you guard against the small things and together you can defend your house against the great things.

Likewise, it is never the great things that build a house, it is always the small things. So let each of you take care of the small things and together you can enjoy the great things. And when age has come and turned the color of your hair and fervor has lessened and your need for each other has increased, think of how much you have done together and how far you have come: not where you are now or where you shall go or what you should do afterwards. For if you've created something of value, you will live forever. We promise nothing unreal: but where there is love, faith, work and endurance . . . a house of happiness.

A house of happiness can be built which lasts forever. For it is by love that we begin to build our house, by faith that it is sustained, by work that it is strengthened and reinforced, and by endurance that it brings us real and lasting happiness.

Now you must promise each other always to love, have faith, work and endure. For it is this commitment to each other that is the basis for the commitment to the community.

Saidi (the groom's name is called by leader-priest) (Bibi) Nine Kuahidi! (He promises the bride in Swahili) (MTU) Nina Kuahidi! (Bride promises Groom in Swahili)

(Stepback)

For as Long as you honor this commitment,
so shall your house be one of happiness.
For us long as you keep this commitment, so
shall your every need be answered.
For you there shall be no longing, for you
shall be fulfillment to each other.
For you there shall be no harm, for you
shall be a shield to each other.
For you there shall be no falling, for you
shall be a support to each other.
For you there shall be no sorrow, for you
shall be comfort to each other.
For you there shall be no loneliness, for
you shall be company to each other.
For you there shall be no hassle, for you
shall be peace to each other.
For you there shall be no searching, for
you shall be an end to each other.

As *Saidi* and *Muminina* are aware of their responsibilities to each other, to their children, and to the community, and sincerely want to establish their house, so let us all accept it.

(The groom and bride take one step toward each other. He takes her hand and they turn and face leader-priest together. Leader-priest then passes the groom the unity cup. He accepts it, faces his bride and drinks. She then claps her hands two times and the groom passes the unity cup to the bride. She drinks and passes it back to him.)

Leader-priest: And as we have all accepted it, so let it be done, for now and all times, for as long as the sun shines and the water flows.

Kwanza

I. Meaning

Kwanza is a word meaning "First" or in this case it signifies the *First Fruits.* Celebration of harvesting the first crops or first fruits is traditional in Africa. At this time of year our people in Africa came together to make joyful noises, give thanks and enjoy the blessing of living and acting together for the community. Everyone brought what he grew or made to contribute to the *Karamu* (feast) that took place in the celebration. Songs were sung, dances danced, food was eaten and drinks were drunk, in a word—life was lived in sheer enjoyment.

II. Symbols of Kwanza

A. *Mkeka (Mikeka)*—The *Mkeka* is a straw mat on which all the other items are placed. It is a traditional item and therefore symbolizes tradition as the foundation on which all else rests.

B. *Kinara (Vinara)*—The *Kinara* is a candle-holder which holds seven candles, and represents the original stalk from which we all sprang. For it is traditionally said that the First-Born was like a stalk of corn which produces corn which in turn becomes stalks which reproduce in the same manner so that there is no ending to us.

C. *Mshumaa (Mishumaa)*—The seven candles represent the Seven Principles (Nguzo Saba) on which the First-Born set up our society in order that our people might get the maximum from it. They are Umoja (Unity); Kujichagulia (Self-Determination); Ujima (Collective Work and Responsibility); Ujamaa (Cooperative Economics); Nia (Purpose); Kuumba (Creativity); and Imani (Faith).

D. *Muhindi (Mihindi)*—The ear of corn represents the offspring or produce (the children) of the stalk (the father of the house). It signifies the ability or potential of the offspring, themselves, to become stalks, i.e., parents, and thus produce their offspring—a process which goes on indefinitely and insures the immortality of the Nation. To illustrate this, we use as many ears of corn as we have children which again signifies the number of potential stalks, i.e., parents. Every House has at least one ear of corn, for there is always the potential even if it has not yet been realized.

E. *Zawadi*—The presents represent: 1) the fruits of the labor of the parents, and 2) the rewards of the seeds sown by the children. For parents must commit their children to goodness which to us is beauty. We must commit them to good acts, good thoughts, good grades, etc., for the coming year and reward them according to how well they live up to their commitments. Goodness, again, is beauty and beauty is that which promises happiness to the family and community. For all acts, thoughts and values are invalid, if they do not in some way benefit the community.

III. Dates and Procedures

A. The dates are December 26 thru January 1.

B. Procedures—On each day of the week of Kwanza, when asked,

"Habari gani," the answer will not be "Njema," but one of the Seven Principles—depending upon whether or not it is the first, second, on to the seventh day, i.e., on the fifth day if someone asks "Habari gani," the answer would be *Nia,* which is the fifth principle.

Approximately a week before the 26th, decorations should be put up and/or arranged. First, we should use a red, black and green color scheme. These are the colors of our organization, US. Red, for the blood of our people which is not shed in vain; black is for their faces, and green is symbolic of our youth, Simba Wachanga (the Young Lions) and their permanent role in our future. Items such as crepe paper, napkins, tablecloths, dishes, and pictures are just a few things which can be used in colors. Secondly, the main table should have as its centerpiece a straw basket of mixed tropical fruits and vegetables. Thirdly, either the floor or a low table should be used to place the *mkeka* and the other items. After the *mkeka* has been spread out, place the *kinara* in the center. Then place the ear(s) of *muhindi* (mi) around or on the sides of it. Place the *zawadi* on the *mkeka* in any arrangement which is artistic. The *zawadi* can be placed whenever they are available. Finally, the *mishumaa* should all be placed at the far right of everything else so that they might be available for daily lighting. Each day one of the *mishumaa* should be placed in the *kinara.* And at dinner, it should be brought to the table, lit and explained in terms of the principle it represents. The children should explain it as far as possible, since it is for them that this is done. Therefore, on the first day one *mishumaa* should be lit, and on the second day two *mishumaa* should be lit and so on until the seventh day on which all are lit. Each night the *kinara* should be replaced on the *mkeka* after dinner and the *mishumaa* should be blown out until the following night.

Finally, on the day of Kwanza, the seventh day, January 1, the *zawadi* should be opened. Moreover, it is important that a large dinner be prepared that day, and that at the table the last Principle is explained and discussed and that the children's commitments for the coming year be heard. It would be good to play African Music all that day if records or tapes are available. *Please note* that the children should do as much in preparation and celebration of the holiday as they are able to do, i.e., decorate, cook, place items, etc.

IV. Karamu (The Feast)

The night of the feast is especially for grownups. It is a part of the Kwanza celebration and takes place on the 31st of December. It was traditionally an all-night set and can well be now for all those who have made adequate baby-sitting arrangements (smile seriously).

Karamu consists of the seven main things that feasts usually consist of: food, drink, music, dance, conversation, laughter, and ceremony. All the things mentioned are provided by the different Houses that make up our community, i.e., the families. The women get together and decide what is needed and the men come up with the necessary money and/or material. They prepare everything by the Third Principle, Ujima, (Collective Work and Responsibility). Also, everything is done in the traditional manner—foods in the African style, and eaten without European utensils; we bring out pillows and we sit on the floor, dance African dances, listen to African Music, tell African stories, make our traditional *tambiko* (sacrifice offering) and drink from the *kikombe* (the unity cup), drinking from which we shall each say "Harambee!!!"

After the African part of Karamu we move to a position of Afro-American expressions and gig all night long.

The decorations for Karamu should be the same as for the rest of *Kwanza.* It should be at the largest house among the brothers and should be donated for the set. A long low table should be used to place the food on a style similar to the American buffet style. Again, the color scheme and the centerpiece should be used, as well as the other symbols which the House should already have.

This is in brief our holiday which we have decided upon tradition and reason as is our custom. To us it is a sign of self-determination and self-respect. And it is one of the legacies that we leave our children, so that they will not turn to each other and say "our fathers have left us nothing." And finally, we do it because we are creative, and we enjoy creating images and the foundations upon which these images rest. For it is the wisdom of our fathers that no matter how well an image is made, it must stand on something. Surely, by things like this, we provide that something of value.

Resolutions

by Bibi Amina Baraka

The Social Organization Workshop of the Congress of African Peoples has evaluated and reinterpreted fundamental roles and relationships among African people, i.e., family and community, in terms of Black liberation.

We concluded that we must maintain unity in the family, community and race. That is necessary for us to build and maintain our communities together and to make our brothers' and sisters' problems our problems, and to solve them together.

To ensure follow-up and implementation of our findings it is necessary to establish and maintain the following:

1. Establish liberation centers for our children so that single women with children may work, but most important, to educate our children toward manhood, womanhood, nationhood, and a value system.
2. Establish a session with a cross-section of men and women to thrash out problems in Black woman and Black man relationship.
3. Set up regional and/or local groups to check on community work.
4. Develop a true sisterhood by establishing workshops in that direction in your local areas. We will keep close contact with each other by establishing a national organization with regional chapters.
5. We must adopt a Black value system which would define our lives in terms of the African personality and which offers a total alternative to the now established European system.
6. We must train for the purpose of revolution, i.e., medical skills, weaponry, and warfare, etc.
7. We must by any means necessary move to infiltrate and co-op *ALL* the existing social institutions for the purpose of gaining, maintaining, and the using of power correctly. We will at the same time move to create alternative social institutions which are based on a Black ideology.

In order to carry out the above we realize that we must deal on all levels with priorities on the following institutions because of their crucial effect on the lives of African people:

1. Adoption Agencies
2. Welfare and Health Centers
3. Day Care Centers

We will move constantly while at the same time maintaining discipline so that our goals will be reached. We will not compromise with what our needs are and we must be strong in our faith so that we will not be corrupted.

Our two representatives to the National Coordinating Committee are: Akiba ya Elimu
Emily Moore

CREATIVITY

Coordinator's Statement

by Larry Neal

Habari gani, Brothers and Sisters. I have been assigned the important task of coordinating the workshops on creativity and culture for the Congress of African Peoples. And let me say; I am deeply and humbly honored to have an opportunity to participate in what amounts to the shaping of ideas and values that go to the heart of question of liberation for people of African descent living in the United States. I hope that I am worthy of the task assigned me. So let us begin:

Creativity is the soul of the Nation. It influences and shapes the mind and direction of the struggle for National self-determination. It is concerned with the individual and collective ethos of the people. Without it, the whole of whatever we want to be cannot be realized. For when we speak of creativity, of art we are, in fact, speaking about the spiritual manifestations of the people, of their will to survive beyond the merely physical. We are speaking of ways of thinking, ways of styling the struggle, and ways of insuring that the victories gained in the area of politics and economics, will not be lost in the battle for the Soul.

It is the assumption of the creativity and artistic workshops that people of African descent living in the West *do, in fact, have a culture.* It is assumed that there are concrete manifestations of this culture apparent throughout the entire Western world wherever Black people are. It is African in modality, but it has been transmuted by the African peoples' contact with the enslaving West. Therefore, we are no longer talking about African culture in the "pure sense." To be perfectly honest with you, there is no such thing as an African culture in this Western Hemisphere in the "pure sense." Therefore, we are confronted with the reality of cultural hybrids. There is no use spending a lot of time escaping this reality. Because, even in its hybrid state African culture in the West represents the *main creative force at work* in today's world. Consequently, we are essentially talking about a Neo-African culture, "new" African culture; colonialism and imperialism have irrevocably altered the traditional cultures of the African peoples. But even in its alteration, tradition *is a commanding force* that must be dealt with. It must be evaluated, and the good of it retained, while rejecting its weaker aspects. So what we got to do is to take this "new" African culture and use it as an instrument for National self-determination. We have to confront the culture as it is, and transform it, by understanding what it consists of, to a higher stage of *conscious* and committed social development. That is the essential destiny of the Black man in the Third World.

In other words, our own culture (the culture of Black America) is the essential starting point for whatever we do. I know that this amounts to a mild form of tribalism, but it just bes that way. The key to psychic liberation is rooted in the most *immediate* manifestation of our National spirit. To be specific, we must begin to discuss and organize the arts around those aspects of our group culture that most readily reveal themselves to us. It is only after we have taken this first step, this most immediate step that we can begin to extend our world view, as dispersed Africans, into the larger Third World of Africa, Asia, and Latin America. In the language of the block, I mean you got to *bring* something before you get something. If you are convinced that we have nothing to give to our brothers and sisters in Africa and the Third World, then you have lost before you get started. We have a powerful African culture here in the Americas.

But it is an exploited culture. It is controlled by the demonic ideologies of the West, everything from capitalism to Marxism. We are addressing ourselves here to Black institutions that can direct this culture toward National self-determination and spiritual fulfillment. Black institutions will not only strengthen us here, but will also form the basis of artistic and cultural unity with Africa and the Third World. We, in the arts, are in the unique position of making Pan-Africanism the living reality dreamed by many of our ancestors (Delaney, Blyden, Garvey, Padmore, Malcolm, Du Bois).

Therefore, as coordinating chairman of the Creativity and Arts Workshops, I have structured all discussions to take place around the building of Black institutions whose essential purpose is to meet the spiritual and artistic needs of the Black Nation, and whose function resides in being totally *committed* to the growth of Black self-consciousness. In our workshops, I would like to stress a great deal of discussion on concrete operational ideas, and not on *rhetoric* and vilification of individuals and organizations that may have differing attitudes about what must be done. Therefore, I will take executive powers to squash the following lines of thought:

1. "Blacker-than-thou-attitudes." This represents a dead-end dialogue. We are all Black with varying degrees of consciousness.

And the most relevant ideas will win out when tested against the realities of the socio-political world.

2. Endless discussions about the nature of Black Art. Save this line of thought for a symposium on the theory of Black Art. (We will try to have at least one of these.)
3. Non-productive criticism of famous Black artists. Instead, we want productive ideas for bringing the so-called Black elite of the cultural world around to those ideas of ours that are proven to be valid when tested against concrete realities.
4. Lack of respect for all individuals in the congress who are engaged in discussing the problems of cultural revolution.
5. Arguments that attempt to rigidly define the range of artistic inquiry. Let the art flower. The strongest, most committed manifestations will survive.

What we are looking for in our workshops are the following:

1. How can Black institutions be built? How can they survive? How can they be internationalized?
2. How do we arrive at operational unity with our diversity of ideas?
3. From people who are now operating Black artistic institutions, we want to know how you do it. How did you do it? What kinds of economic ideas can be brought to bear on the discussion?
4. We want to develop an operational set of guidelines that can be made available to all Black institutions; or persons who want to set up such institutions.
5. We want a communication system (national and international) among these various organizations, for the purpose of developing and training skilled brothers and sisters in the arts.
6. We want to know in concrete terms how the artistic wing of the nation can support the political wing and vice versa.
7. We want a moral code of behavior based on mutual respect among our various institutions. In concrete terms, we want to discuss the previous barriers to unity.
8. We want definite *follow-up* ideas; and we want a sincere *commitment* for ongoing structure.
9. Lastly, we want *honesty,* criticism that is based on a positive desire to help and not on ego-tripping.
10. O.K., now go on with your bad selves. And long live Black Art!

Resource Papers

Creativity

by Cheo Katibu

Kuumba—To do always as much as we can in the way we can in order to leave our community more beautiful and beneficial than when we inherited it.

Specific input re: Theater New Lafayette is donating to Congress of African Peoples.

1. Should be co-op for groups around the country who would contribute money; in return they would be guaranteed time to perform. There should be enough money for administration and maintenance.
2. Special input should be made to foundations by people like Woodie King, and Macbeth.
3. Would involve Black Arts groups, music groups, big-time performers to perform and contribute money, (Sidney Poitier, Stevie Wonder, Spirit House Movers, etc.) The Spirit House (function), we volunteer to help, and offer programs and money.
4. A functional committee should be formed.
   1. Need to know cost to run it.
   2. Need to know how much we have to pay administration.
   3. Need to know cost of advertising.
   4. Need to know the number of seats in the theater.
   5. How much can we make as a profit.

Purpose—To create a cross-fertilization. To draw people that dig James Brown and people that dig Black Art, i.e., separations that exist in Black music, etc., are the same separations that exist socially and politically. And by doing this it will really make this proposed institution truly a reality (collective, functional, and committed), in terms of expressing our Creative Motif, which is really a dominant theme or attitude which expresses itself in music, literature, technology and determines emphasis on culture. Ours must be revolutionary concepts (change) based on tradition and reason, i.e., foundation and movement. From a foundation we move and create new values from that movement.

Creativity Workshop

Free Southern Theatre

Objectives

1. Establish an instrument for the documentation and communication of the Black Arts movement.
2. Produce the first document for general distribution.

We feel this is important in order to:

A. Connect Black people with each other
B. Provide a firm instrument for future reference
C. Cut out some of the stealing of Black Arts (exploitation)
D. Help get us out of the trick of spiraling slavery

Session 1

Purpose of the workshop
Presentation of what is included in the document
Consideration of other ideas
Work assignments

Session 2

Planning
Presentation of proposals
Discussion
Work assignments
Description of programs

Session 3

Implementation
Presentation of programs
Collection of materials
Definition of continuing responsibilities

Needs

1. Information
2. Method of collection and compiling information
3. Distribution system
4. People committed to doing the work
5. Means of production

A Proposal for a semiannual journal to document the development of the cultural arts of people of African descent: to be an instrument for the communication of these important processes.

Objectives

1. To establish an instrument for the documentation of and communication about the efforts of Black people to define and operate cultural arts programs and institutions.
2. To produce a basic model for the document we propose during the time allowed for this workshop.

Method of operation

1. Develop an outline of important information that groups must provide in order to satisfy the needs of the journal. The information might be organized so as to answer the following questions:
   - A. What are the specific problems that the group is addressing itself to?
   - B. What is the character of the areas or communities that group is operating in?
   - C. What is the purpose of the program?
   - D. What is the range of the program and how old is it?
   - E. What important changes have occurred in the program since its beginning and why?
   - F. What kind of things have succeeded and what has failed? Why?
   - G. What does it cost to operate the program?
   - H. How are these funds raised?
   - I. What is the structure of the organization?
   - J. Other . . .
2. Develop a method for the collection and compilation of data. The following method might be feasible:
   - A. Divide African people into manageable areas and rotate the editorial responsibility from issue to issue. And as the editorial responsibility shifts so does the focus of the journal.
     - (1) African People on the African Continent
       - a. West Africa
       - b. North Africa
       - c. East Africa
       - d. South Africa
     - (2) African People in the Americas
       - a. U.S.A.
       - b. Northeast
       - c. Midwest

d. West
e. the South Island Republics
f. Central and South America
(3) African People in Europe
(4) African People in Asia

B. A basic editorial board should be developed that is broadly representative of the above areas. This group should meet at some time prior to each publication.
Initially, plans should be made for at least three issues.
C. Publication and distribution should both be handled by the same agency.
D. People committed to doing the work
(1) the *first* editor—must have a secretary and space to assign for work to be done in
(2) people in each area to assist in the collection of data
(3) people willing to sell the book in each area upon its completion

Money and Finances

Ultimately, it would of course be better if the project could afford to support its own full-time staff.

At the present time a basic budget should be projected around the following needs:

Printing and distribution, typing and stenographic services, telephone and mailing, travel.

I. We need to get together. Everyone concedes that point quite readily. The real question is how do we get together *and* what it is we want to get together. If nothing else this journal will make it possible for Black people everywhere to become aware of each other's existence. It will connect us just by being a focal point for the documentation of the work of Black people. It will increase our self-knowledge and destroy myths that are passed from Black man to Black man by our oppressors.

II. We need more reference material. If we are to really study ourselves we will have to get down to work and look long and hard at the actions of Black folk, their accomplishments, their failures, everything they have done. Certain knowledge that we have must be made available to future generations of Black people.

III. We need to know what is ours and who we are; otherwise the gross theft/exploitation of the work of Black people will continue unabated. This happens, often simply because we don't know any better. Too many of us are unaware of what Brother Baraka calls the "straws that our oppressors are sticking in our heads to suck out our life juices." We must begin blowing the whistle on those who steal from us. In some cases we must "shoot um fo they run."

IV. We must stop making the same mistakes our brothers and sisters made before us. If we are to break this trick of spiraling slavery it will be necessary to know how our energies were enchained and thwarted in the past. Just as we should make note of every success, it is important that we consider our failures, especially very common/extremely extraordinary failures. The failures that seemingly repeat themselves endlessly and the failure of a seemingly foolproof operation; we must study these situations and learn from them.

Dynamite Voices: Black Poets of the 1970's

by Don L. Lee

> The Black writer, like the Black artist generally, has wasted much time and talent denying a propensity every rule of human dignity demands that he possess, seeking an identity that can only do violence to his sense of self. Black Americans are, for all practical purposes, colonized in their native land, and it can be argued that those who would submit to subjection without struggle deserve to be enslaved.
>
> HOYT W. FULLER

> . . . the Black writer can never accept elitism, or a barrier which separates him from other Black men. Whether he wills it or not, unless he is very lucky or very white, he is not an individual but part of a group and his fate is mirrored in that of the group's. He is no sophisticated minstrel entertaining the sons and daughters of America's academic establishment, but rather a Black artist whose every walking moment is a preparation for war, whose every word is an utterance of defiance, whose every action is calculated to move man towards revolution, and whose every thought centers about the coming conflict.
>
> ADDISON GAYLE, JR.

Explanation: insights, hindsights—going-ons

It's time to freshen the air, to declare a direction; time to take *time* to look at our own critically, in the hope of moving past the surface of confusion. We must assess our contradictions and try to move from them so as to develop an atmosphere of political consistency. To be functional in a positive manner sixteen hours a day is not a sacrifice; it is, as Ralph Featherstone has said, "a commitment."

The Black man who writes is a new definition. We've always had writers who happened to be Black, but the sixties brought a new and universal definition to the Black man who chose words as a part of his life style. Life style is essentially what the new writers are about, a quest to legitimize and define their own place in space. To some, of course, this was a venture into the unknown, a feeling that there was no place else to go, and to others this new definition was a reassertion of that which they had believed and felt all along; they were not in a position, however, to drop hammers and be heard.

We'll deal with the poets, the seers who saw and spoke. We heard them, quietly screaming to a Black world that needed a new music. Their voices, many, hit us sometimes unclear and insensitive, sometimes overloud and frightening, often raw and uninhibited but in most cases sincere and selfless, inflicting mental anguish in many of us. The latter part of the sixties is when the echo repeated itself the loudest. The poetry was being read on street corners and in alleys, used in liberation schools and incorporated into the Black theater. Welfare mothers manned picket lines with the words of Gwendolyn Brooks and Mari Evans; Black students (university, high school, etc.) demanded that the Black poets' works be included into the lily-white rhetoric and literature courses. The works of LeRoi Jones (Imamu Amiri Baraka) and Sonia Sanchez actually preceded the Black studies programs and were being echoed through the Black communities like the music of the Dells and Otis Redding. For the first time in the history of the Black man in this country, Black poetry was being recorded, incorporated in dance and acted to at a mass level. This was the case from the *Black House* in Los Angeles to the *Afro-Arts Theater* in Chicago, to the *Concept East Theater* in Detroit, to the *New Lafayette* and *National Black Theater* in Harlem, to *Spirit House* in NewArk, to the *Free Southern Theatre* in New Orleans. Public poetry readings by Nikki Giovanni and Carolyn Rodgers evolved as noticeable competition for the idiot-box programs like "Julia" and "Room 222." The *Last Poets* became the first to record an album that would be listed on the best-selling lists and would be sold out of record stores in less than a week after it was issued, all without extensive publicity.

The grapevine or Black vine emerged as the prime source of publicity. Black bookstores appeared in many of the large Black areas and the new Black publishing houses supplied them with the newest of the new and the oldest of the new. Black poetry books were coming off the presses and being sold in the thousands weekly—one poet produced books whose sales reached the phenomenal number of one hundred thousand copies. With the call for Black universities and Black studies programs, the poets were in the unique position to supply the various schools with the *new* knowledge that was to become the most exploited field in the late sixties and early seventies. The major publishing houses which had traditionally overlooked and discouraged the Black poet/writer began to saturate the market with "reprints" of out-of-print materials, while pulling as many of the young Black poets/writers as their little green bait would attract. The new poetry was like the new music to the popular publishing houses, i.e., not understood or taken seriously, but highly profitable. Thus, the latter part of the sixties and the beginning of the decade of the seventies ushered in the *new Black poets.*

Our objective is not to be objective. We tend to agree with Imamu Baraka, "There is no objective anything . . . least of all poetry. It is all connected to meaning . . . *the criticism* now is *the absence* of *what shd be.* The critics themselves will be the builders. And not of pat sets reflecting 'intellectual activity,' but of the reality now which will be Black and pointing toward the necessary reality." Our mission is not to say who *is* or who *isn't* a poet or to pass on who's good, who's better, or who's unmentionable and should try another profession. We cannot and will not try to define that which is definitely *Black* or vice versa. We plan to take one man's point of view (mine) and try to clear up some of the misinterpretations, to show contradictions and inconsistencies, and, above all, to give alternatives and direction to that body of Black poetry which exists. Hopefully, in undertaking such a task my efforts will help legitimize the Black music-lines which are, as far as I'm concerned, already legitimate but unnoticed.

Black Critic

The best critics are creative writers, especially published writers who are confident of their own worth—which as critics puts them above the common *hatchet men;* Gore Vidal calls them *literary gangsters.* The "frustrated writer" is out to build a literary reputation at the expense of others. The competent critic is not a "frustrated writer"; he is a writer who chooses criticism as an extension of his craft. He is also one who goes into criticism with the same honesty and fairness that should be a part of his other creative works.

The Black critic is first a Black man, who happens to write; just as the poet, he has the same, if not more, responsibility to his community to perform his function to the best of his ability. He understands the main dilemma of the Black writer: "Is he a *writer* who happens to be *Black* or is he a *Black* man who happens to *write?*" The argument is not a new one. Arna Bontemps speaks of it in connection with some of the post-Harlem Renaissance poets: "But in those days a good many of the group went to the Dark Tower to weep because they felt an injustice in the critics' insistence upon calling them Negro poets instead of just poets. That attitude was particularly displeasing to Countee Cullen." This was the type of disillusion that not only would plague the poets but was definitely felt in the other art forms that Black people ventured into. As with Countee Cullen, another well-known poet of the post-Harlem Renaissance period, Robert Hayden, refused to acknowledge that he was a "Negro" or Black poet. Bontemps relates it this way: "One get the impression that Hayden is bothered by this Negro thing. He would like to be considered simply as a poet." Which is almost like *any* Black man in the world saying to the worldrunners that he would like to be considered a man, not a Black man. Nonsense! The mere fact that a request of that type is put forth denies the chance of one's being considered anything else. So the point is to stop asking those who can't grant the wish in the first place, and to deal positively with the situation (Addison Gayle calls it the *Black Situation*).

Claude McKay, whom Wallace Thurman has referred to as "the only Negro poet who ever wrote revolutionary or protest poetry," was able, like Gwendolyn Brooks, Frank Marshall Davis, Margaret Walker, Melvin B. Tolson, Langston Hughes and Sterling Brown, to deal with the dilemma so that it did not affect his work to the point of *color distortion,* i.e., being one thing and trying to write as another, what Fanon calls black skins, white masks.

We must understand that this will be the decade of the Black critic. It will be his responsibility not only to define and clarify, but also to give meaningful direction and guidance to the young, oncoming writers. To perform that function the critic must, if possible, remain detached from his material so that he can fairly filter the music from the noise. So we reiterate that good criticism calls for detachment and fairness, not pseudo-objectivity.

Objectivity at its best is a myth and a very subtle game played on Black people. We are a very *subjective* people. All people are. In the final analysis, all one can really try to be is *fair.* One immediately obliterates the whole concept of objectivity when he takes into account the different variables that helped shape our lives. How can one be "objective" about, say, good housing if he has never lived in such; or about hunger if one has been *truly* hungry. How can you be objective about Black music if it has played an important part in *your* general survival; or about Christianity even though it was forced on you; or about the war if you don't have any power over foreign affairs; or about anything, for that matter, if it involves the human predicament. Objectivity, in matters of importance, such as in the arts, cannot truly exist; true art is as much a part of the culture as is the critic who judges it. So from the get-go the critic is at a disadvantage because he can't disassociate himself fully from that which he is to "objectively" criticize. Some Black critics, however, having been schooled in academia, tried to criticize Black literature from a different, conventional perspective—and failed. James T. Stewart relates the reason for such failure in this way: "His assumptions were based on white models and on a self-conscious 'objectivity.' This is the plight of the 'Negro' man of letters, the intellectual who needs to demonstrate a so-called academic impartiality to the white establishment."

We must understand that white critics write for white people; they are *supposed* to; they owe their allegiance and livelihood to white people. The Black critic is in a very precarious position at this time in history; we agree with Albert Murray (and that's unusual) when he said that "being Black is not enough to make anybody an authority on U.S. Negroes." Being Black *is not enough,* but is, at this time, a necessary prerequisite.

It has become increasingly clear that one starts with the roots and then defines the type of tree. That is to say, *any* writer was first Black, white, yellow or red before he became a writer. Like the tree, the to-be-writer acquired certain characteristics notable in particular lineage, such as language, religion, diet, education, daily life style. So, up to a certain point the to-be-writer was just another Black, white, yellow or red manchild, right? This is universal: naturally development into manhood is partially predetermined—which is to say that because of the different cultural patterns of Black, white, yellow and red men, there exist normal differences and variety in each of the four mentioned; and each type will look at the world the way he/she has been taught to view it. The core of my argument is that I, as a Black man/critic, cannot possibly accurately judge or assess, let's say, Chinese literature. And, if we look at the reasons why unemotionally, I'm sure you would agree: First, I can't speak the Chinese language (which means I can't read the literature in the original); second, I never lived among the Chinese people—so I know very little about their daily life style; third, my only knowledge of Chinese religion comes from what I read—which puts me at the disadvantage of accepting someone else's interpretation, which is always dangerous; fourth, my knowledge of Chinese music is terribly limited; fifth, my knowledge of Chinese folklore and dance is negligible; and finally, I've never been to China, so would be unfamiliar with many of the references used in the literature.

Have I made myself clear? The critic is first and foremost a Black man, red man, yellow man, or white man who writes. And as a critic, he must stem from the same roots that produced him. How else can his style and content presently be understood? Which brings us to whites who study from the outside looking in, maintaining that they can learn as much about the tree from distant observation as from intimacy, or that they can interpret by anatomically dissecting the organism (keep in mind that even in dissection one has to touch that which one dissects).

With a tree, they may be successful in some of their findings. But in dealing with humans, one has to almost become a part of the humans he wishes to understand. When looking from the outside, one almost has to use the tools of the anthropologist—has to live, sleep, eat, suffer, laugh and die among the people about whom one is trying to gain some insight. *No* white critic has done this. Sure, Robert Bone may have had some in-depth conversations with Sterling Brown, but that doesn't give him the tools that are necessary to pass judgment on the entirety of Black literature. William Styron may have let James Baldwin spend some time on his farm, but obviously knowing and listening to Baldwin, as perceptive as Baldwin is, doesn't give Styron the sensitivity necessary for recording the adventures of one of our greatest Black heroes, Nat Turner. David Littlejohn may have taken a few courses in Black literature and sat in on some of the Black writers' conferences, but obviously for him all of that was a prerequisite for a bad, pretentious book that Hoyt Fuller rightly maintains should be avoided "like the plague." Edward Margolies lives in the heart of the literary capital; that's where he should stay, and leave the native sons alone. Irving Howe and Richard Gilman had best stay with Jewish and WASP literature respectively, and leave their natural opposites alone; their ignorance is showing in whiteface.

The argument intensifies as the "Negro" apologists say the reason Bone, Styron, Littlejohn, Margolies and others tried to write about the Black writer is that there were no *Black critics* willing to do it. Well, we can look at that statement from two points of view. There have always been Black critics, e.g., James Weldon Johnson, William Stanley Braithwaite, Benjamin Griffith Brawley, Sterling A. Brown, Alain Locke, and Nick Aaron Ford, just to mention a few of the earliest. The problem, however, was not that there weren't any competent Black critics; the problem was getting into print. Some of our contemporary "Black" critics found it not beneficial to make a life out of the study of Black literature—still leaving out Africa, the West Indies, and many of the Asian countries. World literature to them meant, naturally, that which was white and Western. But there's still time for them to come back; James A. Emanuel pulls their coats when he says that "the pages of *CLA Journal,* to select but one representative, Negro-managed scholarly publication, are regularly filled with excellent Negro commentary on the works of white authors. If more of such professionally trained Negro critics were to turn their energies to the explication of literature by authors of their race, the enrichment in the feeling and knowledge of both Black and white readers would be imponderable."

The Black critic—as a Black man first and writer second—illustrates a profound understanding of his responsibility to himself and to his community. He is what he reflects or projects. If he moves throughout the world quoting the qualities of John Donne and F. Scott Fitzgerald, that's where he's at; if he marvels at the achievements of William Dean Howells and François Rabelais, that's probably where he wants to be, and to try to move him from that point may be an exercise in futility. The Black critic, like that Black creative writer, is a part of a people and should not isolate himself into some pseudo-literary wishing land. The Black critic/writer must understand that writing is, after all is said and done, a *vocation* like that of a teacher, doctor, historian, etc., and becomes a way of life only when established within a concept and identity compatible with the inner workings of the self. That is to say, some of us Blacks may think we are white, but that concept comes under daily question and contradiction, and is forever inflicting pain on the inner self. We are Black men who happen to write, not *writers* who happen to be Black. If the latter were true, Richard Wright, Ted Joans, William Gardner Smith and Chester Himes would not have left this country; Ralph Ellison would have published another novel by now; Sam Greenlee wouldn't have had to go to England to get his book published; John A. Williams would be as secure and rich as Norman Mailer; *Black World* wouldn't exist; and Frank Yerby, after a long record of denials of his "Negroness," wouldn't have published *Speak Now.*

What the Black critic must bring to us is an extensive knowledge of world literature, along with a specialized awareness of his own literature. He must understand that a "mature literature has a history behind it," and that that which is being written today is largely indebted to the mature Black literature that came before. Thus, if looked at from the proper perspective, the whole of Black literature can provide reliable criteria for the new critic to use. The competent Black critic will have a love for and an intimate experience with the literature on which he is passing judgment. This will give him a basic philosophy for such judgment. As Stephen Coburn Pepper puts it, "It follows that good criticism is criticism based on a good philosophy. For a good philosophy is simply the best disposition of all evidence available."

We agree with T.S. Eliot in "The Frontiers of Criticism" where he states, "Every generation must provide its own literary criticism, each generation brings to the contemplation of art its own categories of appreciation, makes its own demands upon art, and has its own uses for art." The poet/writer will take the language of others and of his own generation and extend and revitalize it. The poet/writer as critic is at his best when he uses his own poetic talents—for as a poet/writer he is uniquely capable of knowing and understanding the potential of other poet/writers. What the critic does in many cases is make people more aware of what they already feel but can't articulate. The Black critic understands that today's poets have revitalized and enriched the language, and in doing so have opened up new avenues of communication among the world's people.

The Black critic, like the Black poet, must start giving some leadership, some direction. We agree with Darwin T. Turner where he states, "Despite fifty years of criticism of Afro-American literature, criteria for that criticism have not been established. Consequently, some readers judge literature by Afro-Americans according to its moral value, a few for its aesthetic value, most by its social value, and too many according to their response to the personalities of the Black authors." This narrow-mindedness must end and substantial criteria must come into existence. We can see innovative movement by looking at the statement of purpose of *The Writers' Workshop* of the *Organization of Black American Culture* (OBAC) under the direction of Hoyt Fuller. That purpose includes the following:

1. The encouragement of the highest quality of literary expression reflecting the Black experience.
2. The establishment and definition of the standards by which that creative writing which reflects the Black experience is to be judged and evaluated.
3. The encouragement of the growth and development of Black critics who are fully qualified to judge and evaluate Black literature on its own terms while at the same time cognizant of the traditional values and standards of Western literature and fully able to articulate the essential differences between the two literatures.

We're sure that other writers in different parts of the States have traveled or are beginning to travel in similar directions.

We must pull in the brothers and sisters that are academically involved, people like Darwin T. Turner, James A. Emanuel, Addison Gayle, Jr., Richard Long, Catherine Hurst, Stephen Henderson, George Kent, Helen Johnson, Sarah Webster Fabio, W. Edward Farrison, Richard Barksdale and Dudley Randall. We must optimistically encourage the young to continue to seek innovative change and standards; let them know that we hear them and are listening to them, because without Carolyn Rodgers, Mary Helen Washington, Johari Amini, David Llorens, Carolyn Gerald, Larry Neal, Toni Cade, Clayton Riley and others the controversy over criteria and a Black aesthetic might not ever have existed.

Lastly, a word of caution to our new and established critics. You cannot be concerned continuously with the intellectual diplomacy such as that of the white critic who before placing his stamp of approval on some studies must first check indexes to see if his name is listed as a reference, thereby perpetuating a closed literary system dangerous to Black people. The Black critic must learn to use language for the benefit of Black people. For rhetoric can be a dangerous communicative device if it is not correctly used, especially in the world of letters. Black critics who do not have a tradition of social rhetoric must now become masters of an alien language, that is, if Black people are to survive. And survival is what we are about. Not individually, but as a people. To quote Addison Gayle, Jr., "The dedication must be to race"; you see, the wolves, ours and theirs, are waiting for us to fail. We have a surprise for them.

Black Writing

We see the sixties as a movement beyond the shadowiness of the Harlem Renaissance and the restrictiveness of the Negritude Movement. The poets of the sixties and seventies move beyond mere rage and "Black is beautiful" to bring together a new set of values, emotions, historical perspectives and futuristic direction—a transformation from the life style of the *sayer* to that of the *doer*.

Black writing as we view it today is the result of centuries of slavery and forced alienation from Africa and the self. We've been exiles in a strange land where our whole life style repeatedly faces contradiction after contradiction. Black writing to the African-American is the antithesis of a decadent culture that over the centuries has systematically neglected and dehumanized us with the fury and passion of an unfeeling computer.

Literature produced by black hands is not necessarily Black writing. What has to be embodied in Black writing, first and foremost, is the consciousness that reflects the true Black experience, the true African-American experience—related in a style indicative of that experience. Which means that new forms as well as adaptations of forms now in use will have to come into existence. Black consciousness, in any case, can be a conscious or an unconscious effort in Black writing; if one is Black, it's very difficult to write otherwise. We must understand that there will be a pervasive presence of everything and anything that is indigenous to the African-American people.

Black art is a functional art; it is what the Africans call a collective art. It is committed to humanism; it commits the community, not just individuals. As someone has said, Black art commits the Black man to a future which then becomes present for him, an integral part of himself. The Black writer/artist works out of a concrete situation, his geography, his history as well. He uses the materials that are at hand and the everyday things which make up the texture of his life. He rejects the anecdotal, for this does not commit because it is without significance. Black art, like African art, is *perishable*. This too is why it is functional. For example, a Black poem is written not to be read and put aside, but to actually become a part of the giver and receiver. It must perform some function: move the emotions, become a part of the dance, or simply make one act. Although the work itself is perishable, the *style* and *spirit* of the creation is maintained and is used and reused to produce new works. Here we can see clearly that art for art's sake is something out of a European dream, and does not exist, in most cases, in reference to the Black poet.

Most Black art is social: art for *people's* sake. That is, the people will help shape the art, and although the work may not be here forever, through the active participation of the people, its full meaning will be realized. Black art is total being: it cannot be separated from Black life. As Dr. S. Okechukwu Mezu puts it:

> Poetry is . . . a part of human life and does not have to be written and in fact for a long time African poetry was mainly oral and unwritten. In the African village, traveling bards sang songs and recited poetry to the accompaniment of musical instruments. These bards told stories and anecdotes. Some of these recitals were serious and historical, bringing into light the events of war and peace with occasional commentary on the reigns of various chiefs and strong men of the village. Others were lyrical, while a few were coarse and bawdy. But most of them were roundelays and quite often people joined in the narration.

Publishing

There is a heavy concentration of poets on the East Coast. The East Coast (namely New York), since it is the literary capital of the world, affords some of the Black poets a better choice of publishing houses than that offered by other areas of the country. We find that most of the major Black anthologies published in the latter part of the sixties and in the early seventies were heavily saturated with East Coast poets. With Black people's new attitudes, new feeling everywhere, it would seem that Black writers would leave white publishing houses in search of Black publishers (in part, Imamu Baraka and Gwendolyn Brooks have done this).

The Black writer, after taking into account all the sociological, historical and psychological avenues he has had to travel, still is saturated with contradictions and insecurities. As in other art forms the writer is still all too dependent upon his enemy to publish him. For instance, one of the main reasons the Black musician remained/is so powerless is that he has had no control over his own contributions. There are no Black record companies (Motown included) and there are no Black distributors. It is easy to understand that if one doesn't grow his own food, there is an acute chance that he might starve. If he doesn't starve, most certainly he is dependent on someone else to feed him, and in most cases he finds that he owes his allegiance to those who lessen his hunger pains. Consequently, there exist among Black musicians many creative prostitutes.

One way of looking at the publishing scene is like looking at some of our most vocal militants—talking Black and sleeping white: or, in the writer's case, writing Black and publishing white. We can rationalize for days the many reasons for this, but we have to question the validity of the writer's work when we see him legitimizing his Blackness in the pages of *Evergreen Review* rather than *Black World* (formerly *Negro Digest*), in the *Nickel Review* rather than *Freedomways*; in *Commentary* rather than *Liberator*, in *Poetry* magazine rather than the *Journal of Black Poetry*. In essence, by his publishing in the white market what he is doing is not only raising serious doubts about the audiences he is trying to reach but lending support and legitimacy to white organs as if they are vehicles Black people should support and read.

Actually, what it all comes down to is that there exists among many Black writers (poets, novelists, essayists, etc.) a deep-rooted sense of insecurity. I truly believe that many of today's Black writers really don't feel that they can write unless some white boy publishes them or says that "here we have a writer." It seems that some of our most vocal "Black" writers do not have the confidence or the inner strength to say no to white publishers. Yet, some of these very writers feel that they can give direction to other Black writers and Black people, not realizing that they themselves are living a life of the greatest contradictions.

It is clear that *unless*, unless the Black writer moves to help Black publishers, unless he moves to make the Black medium his first source of publication, he will fall into the same destructive trap that has engulfed talented Black musicians. And the Black pride we speak of, as most whites wished and predicted, will become a thing of the past like that "Blackness" of the Harlem Renaissance and the Negritude Movement.

This is for real. A writer is what he reflects, and if we can read his work only in the pages of *Mademoiselle, The New York Times, Poetry* magazine, or the *New Yorker*, we have reason to question his identification, to assume that he is a white poet in blackface trying to write Black. After all, very few Black people read the *Massachusetts Review*; most have never heard of it. The Black poets of the seventies in most cases are dedicated to building their own medium of communication. If they are not committed to this, they are quite obviously jiving, and should be told so—*out loud*.

The fact of the matter is that we cannot continue to live illusions, for to do so is only a prologue to death. Some Black poets (or poets who happen to be Black) continuously reinforce the European concept of the job of the poet, that the poet should be indirectly concerned about his people because "his direct duties are to his language, first to preserve and second to extend and improve."

The family is the foundation of any nation and if we're talking about nation-building, the writer/poet must become a part of the family. We must build and support the institutions that are *working* for *us*—that's important. We need a commitment to nationhood if we're to survive.

Resolutions

by Larry Neal

Creativity is the soul of the nation. It influences and shapes the mind and direction of the struggle for national self-determination. It is concerned with the collective ethos of the people. Without it, the whole of whatever we want to be cannot be realized. For when we speak of creativity, we are, in fact speaking about the spiritual manifestations of the people, of their will to survive beyond the merely physical. We are speaking of ways of thinking, ways of styling the struggle, and ways of insuring that the victories gained in areas of politics, economics, education, religion, etc., will not be lost in the battle for the soul. We therefore must be concerned with establishing our own cultural institutions devoted to cultural analysis and cultural education.

Contrary to popular belief, an institution is not merely brick and mortar. It may be thought of as a set pattern of social action and interaction. It concerns a value system. It concerns the manner in which people should relate to one another. One of the most positive examples of institution-building is the Congress of African Peoples itself. This is an institution committed to the creation, recreation and circulation of the positive ideals of nation building.

Art for art's sake is an invalid concept; art reflects the value system from which it comes. It is the charge of the artist to create, preserve, promote and perpetuate these values through art. Art must speak to and inspire Black people.

INSTITUTION-BUILDING PROPOSAL

We the members of the committee for institution-building understand the necessity of building and stabilizing Black institutions that are relevant and elevate the ongoing struggle for self-liberation. We propose to initiate through the C.A.P. a major effort to build new institutions and make relevant and consequently stabilize existing ones. It is further understood that these institutions must be founded and sustained using the principles of self-determination, eventually self-sufficiency and self-respect at all times.

The Committee for Black Institution-Building recommends the following schedule for local members of the Congress of African Peoples and the national creative workshop of the Congress of African Peoples.

Schedule of activities for local members of
the Congress of African Peoples

A. Get a legal charter prepared and submitted within two weeks after the adjournment of the congress.
B. Upon receipt of a charter (estimated time November 5, 1970), immediately apply for a tax-exempt status.*
   Note: The percentage you are granted determines the percentage of income a donor can give. Apply for the highest percentage initially, since applications for changes in percentage are not easily obtained.*
C. Upon receipt of the tax exemption (estimated ninety days), local members should notify the congress of their tax-exempt status.
   Note: Miss Elma Lewis of the National Center of Afro-American Artists stated the center would assist *all* creative member organizations upon receipt of tax exemptions. The notification should be done by letter and should include the conceptual view of operations and the needs of the local member's organization.

Duties of the congress with regard to building and
sustaining creative institutions

A. Creation of a component to deal with the problem of funding for member organization.
   1. The congress should have on file a proposal from each member organization.
   2. The congress should have on file all foundations, companies and individuals who *can* contribute to cultural groups.
   3. In an effort to concentrate larger amounts of monies, the congress should attempt to obtain bulk grants for all member groups. This could be done by the congress submitting the proposal in the name of *all* member groups. Upon receipt of funds the congress would act as the distributing agency.
B. The congress should establish an international pool of groups and personalities immediately. A list can be started by members

*Costs vary from $25 to $100 according to the state.

of the congress having international contacts. This list should be made available to all members of the congress.

C. The Congress of African Peoples should immediately begin to collect all available data (slides, poems, short stories, etc.), to begin the establishment of a cultural repository. This could be done by each member group submitting a copy of its works to the congress. Within sub-groups (regional and other) a repository should be set up for the same purpose. This should be coordinated with the existing Atlanta University effort. Also, members should submit the works of non-members who are desirous of cooperating with the venture.

D. Sub-groups of the national congress should be established regionally to carry out the area program. This should be done upon issuance of the list of members.

E. An endowment should be established for the purpose of putting congress monies into investments. Each member should be taxed 10 percent of his income reporting on a monthly basis. The exact use of the endowment should be determined by the creative council; some suggestions are needed about how to purchase equipment, buildings and how to hire essential personnel. Since an endowment is not money received from a foundation, it can be used for outright purchases.

F. A tour bureau should be established for the purpose of coordinating and expanding the range of touring members. This could be achieved initially by the present touring groups submitting schedules to the congress for study. This effort would permit the exchange of sub-groups and personalities between members of the congress without undue strain on either member.

In summary, the Institution-Building Committee of the Creativity Workshop of the Congress of African Peoples took under consideration the twin problems of institution-building and stabilizing. The suggestions made should by no means be considered complete, but rather a step in the right Black direction.

THEATER:

1. The New Lafayette Theater Workshop's facilities were donated to the Creativity Workshop of the Congress of African Peoples, which should be used collectively, functionally and committedly for:

   A. Co-opting groups around the country who would contribute money and in return guarantee time to perform, insuring enough money for administration and maintenance.

   B. This would involve Black Arts groups, music groups, big-time performers to perform and contribute money. The Spirit House Movers volunteer to help and offer programs and money.

C. The Congress of African Peoples' theater should be used as a model for setting up new theaters.

D. The building should be a physical statement of National Liberation.

2. Theater groups should submit a list of their personnel and materials available to their regional representatives so that we can pool our resources and skills. Theater groups are requested to allow slots within their yearly schedule for visiting groups to perform. This will insure collective and operational unity within theater movement.

3. The Negro Ensemble Company has donated its theater from June 13 through September 1 to the Creativity Workshop of the Congress of African Peoples, which should be used for cooperative economics mainly to build and maintain the C.A.P. Theater and to profit together from it.

4. It was proposed that a semiannual journal would come out of and be supported by the Creativity Workshop, which would be involved with the arts. It would:

A. Rotate editorially.

B. Aid in strengthening publications already existing, i.e., *Cricket, Journal of Black Poetry.*

C. Committee would operate with Poor Peoples Corp. in Jackson, Mississippi, which would house an office for operations, and Free Southern Theatre would be the copy office.

5. It was proposed that a clearing house organization and periodical be implemented through the Pan-African Artists' Alliance, an established organization for exposure and sales, and that a permanent council of Black literature and press within the Congress of African Peoples be established. This council will involve itself in:

A. A periodic bulletin listing of all books produced by Black companies which will be published by them.

B. It was proposed that a list of books be selected to be included in a special Christmas newsletter. This newsletter will be a part of the abovementioned campaign to advertise, promote, and sell books for raising the level of Black consciousness.

C. A C.A.P. negotiating committee should be established to induce Negro publishers to place aware Black editors on their editorial boards and protect presently employed journalists from arbitrary dismissal by their Negro press employers.

D. A Creativity Chest Fund will be established with cash donations coming from (1) affluent writers, (2) fund-raising activities. The creativity section of C.A.P. should initiate and carry out the work involved in making this proposal work.

E. There should be a Congress of African Peoples' library and Research Center for all Black publications, papers on the movement, works of Black artists, etc.

Revolutionary art must be collective, functional, and committing, i.e., from whole people to a whole people, it must speak to and inspire Black people, it must commit you to revolution (change).

MUSIC:

1. A Black Music Center should be set up to collect and gather information on, and knowledge of, the various musical concepts of Black music.
2. Black musicologists are to be trained to produce a creative cadre of qualified persons who would be able to synthesize, conceptualize, and actually describe our music from a correct perspective, i.e., a Black frame of reference (cultural ideology).
3. Formation of a National Black Music Orchestra. The purpose of this orchestral unit would be to contain, develop, and preserve all of the elements of our musical forms, African traditional music, folk, blues, bebop, new music, etc. It would seek to collect all of the music, so as to break down the differences that now divide us. It would propose by its very form and feeling an alternative to bars and nightclubs.
4. The maintenance and distribution of a Black Music Journal—i.e., strengthening of *Cricket*.
5. Establish a recording studio and a publishing firm. Also, this institute would maintain the following: a worldwide library on the music of peoples of African descent; a legal counseling service, and services for economic and business consultation.

Within the next three months, we will be preparing, submitting, and publicizing proposals among various influential persons and institutions for funding, grants, loans, concerts, and fund-raising banquets.

Special Proposal Passed by Creativity Workshop

The Creativity Workshop agreed to set up an apparatus for the purpose of having a Pan-African Festival of the World African Arts, during the year 1971; preferably it would be held in Africa. This idea was proposed by artist Dana Chandler and passed unanimously by our workshop.

VISUAL ARTS PROPOSAL

1. *The Problem*
   A. Institutions and individuals are not taking advantage of knowledge now available for dealing with individual and institutional problems, due to inadequate channels of communication. Some of the things neglected and/or omitted are:
      1. processes which acquaint African peoples with African art, artists and institutions.
      2. the promotion of a concept of nationhood through unity, developed by a communications/information/resource exchange.
      3. a vehicle whereby African peoples and African arts can be brought together.
      4. helping individuals and institutions to get around problems by helping them to profit from each other's mistakes and successes.
      5. overcoming the "Ebony Fashion Fair" syndrome that high-priced Black visual art has created. We emphasize that this statement is not intended to isolate *Ebony,* but is being used as a symbolic, rather than a specific qualitative reference.

   B. PAAA
      Our discussions led us to the idea of a clearing-house type organization and a periodical to meet the problems mentioned in an expeditious manner.
      The Pan-African Artists' Alliance (PAAA) is the nonprofit organization instituted to meet this need.
2. *Implementation*
   A. A catalog of work, and a sales system, for exposure and sale of work by the PAAA.
      1. Proceeds from items in the catalog will pay for the first publication costs of our periodical.
      2. Subsequent finances will be acquired from sustainer/supporter membership fees and from individuals and groups such as: African peoples, Black student unions, art departments at high schools and colleges, art clubs, libraries and Black businesses, whether small or large.
      3. These individuals and organizations would be required to pay an annual membership fee which entitles them to:
         a. access to PAAA art works and audio-visual material
         b. PAAA journal,
            articles on African artists, traveling shows, historical information, socio-aesthetic dialogue, reviews and criticism, consulting service on printing and reproduc-

tions, techniques and educational resources. In addition, funds will come from donated works, from artists not in attendance at the congress, and through the sale of work consigned to PAAA. These procedures will eliminate the need for public advertising in the journal.

c. As of today, PAAA has sustainer/support committments from Howard University, The National Center of Afro-American Artists (Boston), Pride, Inc., Atlanta University Center, Wayne County Community College (Detroit), Anton Studios (New York), Eugene E. White Gallery (San Francisco), and Arthur Britt (Savannah). Tentative committments have come from the Nairobi Cultural Center and the Mid-Block Art Gallery (New Jersey).

3. *Task Assignments*

The following *ad hoc* assignments have been made:

A. PAAA's mailing address is: Pan-African Artists' Alliance
c/o Jeff Donaldson, Chairman
Art Department
Howard University
Washington, D.C. 20001

B. The *ad hoc* council will consist of: Jeff Donaldson, Barry Gaither, Terry Hamilton, Floyd Coleman, Harold Neal and Eugene White. The council will maintain close communications and administrate the above program until a permanent mechanism is established, at our second meeting, which is to be held in Boston, January 22, 23, 24, 1971.

4. *The Time Schedule*

Bank account established:	September 10, 1970
Sustainer/support invitations extended	September 20, 1970
Initial sustainer/support fees due	October 5, 1970
Catalog—"Images of Independence"	November 5, 1970
Sales of works	December–February, 1971
Publication—PAAA Review, Vol. 1, Issue No. 1.	March 15, 1971

BLACK TECHNOLOGY

Resource Papers

Toward Black Technology

by Saidi Jengaji

Due to the necessity of defining one's subject matter before beginning to develop and expand it into new areas, I deem it fitting to analyze the concept of Black Technology to see whether technology is capable of being developed and whether or not it will satisfy our needs of survival in a modern world.

Webster defines a technology as a systematic method of producing some desired outcome. The operative key here is the word "systematic." It connotes *regularity* and *organization, principle* and *design,* as opposed to impromptu disorganized procedures. So we are talking about devising systematic, designed, principled, organized, regular methods by which Blacks can obtain *any* goal we may determine as having priority.

But of course, a successful methodology has great value as *knowledge,* and in fact knowledge is the basis of technology. I want to emphasize this point because many times we equate the use of capital goods with technology, whereas the two are quite distinct concepts. Capital goods are simply *implements* embodying a knowledge of how to combine smaller implements into a larger unity that can produce a desired good. This embodiment of knowledge in artifacts is a necessary aspect of advanced technology, but only one aspect. Non-implement systems also constitute technologies, and indeed because Blacks have very little access to raw materials of which large implements are fashioned, our technologies tend to be non-implement systems that rely heavily on another aspect of technology, arrangement or organization of people with small, readily available artifacts. It is important to understand that these arrangements constitute technologies fully as much as do knowledge-embodying capital implements.

When speaking of a Black technology, we must recognize that although capital-intensive technologies are most productive in the white economy, in the resource-poor Black community, labor-intensive technologies can produce relatively higher gains in the short run. When we attempt to develop technologies, therefore, we are interested in maximizing the efficiency of currently used Black technologies, while at the same time planning for the gradual infusion of more capital-intensive systems into the Black community.

The Source of New Technology

We know of only two ways by which new methods, arrangements and artifacts are discovered for use. The first is by accident, upon which Blacks in the American diaspora have depended too greatly and for too long a time. This preponderance of accidental technological innovations in the Black community can be viewed as "fall-out," or external economic effects of more structured innovative methods practiced by the white economy. It is seen to result from the exclusion of Blacks from technical positions within the aerospace, electronic-electrical equipment, chemical and machinery industries, where the second method of discovery is predominant.

This second method is the so-called scientific method, the research and development method. Use of this method is concentrated in the industries named above. (About 85 percent of research and development personnel were employed in those industries in 1957. Richard R. Nelson, *Technology, Economic Growth and Public Policy,* table III-t page 50.)

The effect of exclusion of Black workers from technical positions in firms inhibits the diffusion of technical knowledge to the Black community as a whole. Relatively few plant managers of design engineers resign from white firms to form their own companies because they know they will not be able to attract supporting personnel. Whites generally decline to work for Blacks, and few Blacks have the requisite skills and training for the positions.

The importance of training can be seen by examining the process by which new technology is adopted. There are two large phases involved. The first is screening. In this phase the existing stock of knowledge is sifted, and preliminary proposals for new artifacts arrangements, or combinations are developed. Ideas in these proposals are refined until a workable model can be built or structured. Once this workable model has been built, the next step is to test it in detail, weighing all its component systems to determine their strength and durability and testing the entire product to determine if it is marketable, i.e., acceptable to consumers who will be its ultimate users. This step is where money becomes a constraint; the innovator must test the model under many conditions, so that labor and material costs become extremely high. As a consequence individual inventors, particularly Black, have great difficulty in getting the public to accept their ideas.

Once an idea has proved both technically feasible and potentially marketable, the second phase has been reached. This is the adoptive phase. The rate of adoption of new ideas, products and methods has an S-shaped profile, indicating that acceptance is initially slow, then accelerates, then decreases. Such a curve may be explained by observing that any new idea or product either substitutes for or complements some existing idea or product. The assumption is that substitution is more common. As a result, demand for existing products and public acceptance of old ideas, declining *disequilibrium* in product markets and factor markets, when demand for the new product has reached the level of demand for the old thing it replaced, the new thing has been fully adopted by the consumer.

But production and marketing the new product strains money markets, as demand for loanable funds to meet the high product demand is generated. Thus there is also disequilibrium on the supply side. Only when enough funds have been attracted by a rise in interest rates can market equilibrium be reached again, for the increase in interest rates according to economy theories of the accelerator-multiplier, causes demand to decline.

Keepers of Western Technological Traditions

Most observers divide institutions involved in research and development into three specified categories: Federal Government, industry, and universities; and a catch-all category, other nonprofit institutions. The government finances 65.5 percent of R. and D., industry finances 31.9 percent, universities finance 1.6 percent, and other nonprofit sources finance 1.1 percent (Nelson, *op. cit.*, p. 45).

However, when looking at who performs R. and D., a slightly different picture is obtained. The government performs 14.2 percent, industry 73.7 percent, universities 9.5 percent, and other nonprofit sources 2.6 percent of R. and D. work (*Ibid.*). It is evident from these figures that R. and D. plays a very substantial role in cementing the anti-democratic structure of the military-industrial-university complex.

The government is in effect subsidizing the profits of individual companies, for R. and D. activities are characteristically undertaken by a firm with the objective of "improving (its) own products and processes" (*Ibid.*, p. 46). That is to say that the net effect of the government-industry-university alliance as related to R. and D. is to increase concentration and income inequality.

Labor-Using Technological Change in the Construction Industry: Factor Supplies in Central Brooklyn Housing Construction, Housekeeping During the Revolution

1. The operative constraint on housing construction in ghetto areas

of large cities is financial. Financing is necessary to pay the costs of the factors of production, land, labor, human capital, and physical capital.

2. Because much of the existing housing stock in the central city is dilapidated, it must be destroyed, leaving vacant land. In the central Brooklyn area, about 25,000 units were destroyed or scheduled to be destroyed in 1969 alone. (Central Brooklyn Model Cities Needs Analysis, 1969)

This means that the stock of usable land is in surplus and therefore is not a constraint even though ownership of this land is vested in absentee landlords. Labor unemployment hovers around 33 percent in Central Brooklyn Model Cities area (Model Cities Needs Analysis), so that labor is also in surplus and is therefore not a constraint. There were 87,000 unemployed workers in 1969 (*Ibid.,* E.D. p. 7).

Human capital in construction is embodied in the training and experience of skilled carpenters, plasterers, plumbers, electricians, masons, etc. These are already trained craftsmen. The number of such craftsmen available is considerable largely because of past and present discrimination by white craft unions that deny Black craftsmen the right to work.

In 1969, there were 32,000 such craftsmen, unemployed in Central Brooklyn Model Cities area (*Ibid.,* E.D.) at their profession. Thus the supply of human capital available is also in surplus and is not a constraint. Capital in construction is embodied in the machines and materials necessary to construct a building. These include bulldozers and cranes, steel, bricks and cement which are all in short supply in the ghetto. Thus, capital is a constraint, as initially stated.

Scientific Technology in Black Community Development

by Benjamin Scott

In Western nations a sense of nationalism has been fostered among the people based on imperialistic programs of expansion of influence and dominance of weaker nations. Implementing the programs called for systematic support of technological development by the governments to enhance military and economic power with little systematic support of technology for improving communities or the individual lives of the people. These matters have been left in a haphazard way to the "private sector" in capitalistic countries and to petty bureaucrats in socialistic countries.

Black technological development is to be used also to enhance nationalistic sentiment, but around anti-imperialist programs of the various African nations and other Afro communities. This requires a reordering of priorities, a retraining of Black technologists ideologically and a coordinated plan for development among the African and Afro nations.

A Pan-African Academy of Science and Technology is proposed as a workshop subject. Its purpose is conceived to be to plan the overall rapid development of a political-technological complex among the African and Afro nations.

This is a very tall order for the hoped-for Black technological establishment. The elegant logic of an imperialist strategy has produced educational philosophies in tune with the strategy. As technique is transmitted to the student, philosophy about how the technique should be used in the national interest seeps into his mind from the atmosphere of the university, its contrasts and involvement with the national government and the international economic establishment. Now comes the Black movement denouncing imperialism and requiring technological development according to a new act of priorities. Moreover, it comes without resources and vulnerable to attack with a demand that technological effort contribute substantially to the political goals. Coming, as we do, from an educational system supported by government to provide technologists for imperialistic national policies, it is hard to be sure of where to start, hard to trust one's analysis of what is needed as being ideologically sound. It is especially hard for the physical scientist, since the priorities of the new nationalism are still being set.

The technology of liberation will deal with the same basic materials as the technology of imperialism—of that we can be sure. The pile of stuff is the same: oil, petrochemicals, aluminum, plastics, paper, cloth, fertilizer, steel, copper, ceramics, etc. What engineers make from the pile depends on the ideology. If an African nation wants steel to be worked into farm machinery and construction machinery, then engineers will produce that kind of machinery, of course. But there is more, depending on whether it is a Pan-African venture or not. If steel machinery is to be produced for world markets in open competition with Japan, Scandinavia, Germany, and the U.S.A., the kind and the quality will be different and responding to different stimuli. If the national ideology will be shaped to accommodate whatever means are necessary to guarantee that success. If, however, the production of farm machinery and construction machinery by an African nation is under Pan-African sponsorship for primarily the Pan-African market, its success will be measured by the comparative productivity of the African farmers who use its machinery, and secondarily by how well it sells in the world market.

Black technology in support of anti-imperialistic nationalism must, it seems to me, to be either based on complete self-sufficiency within each nation with as little international trading as possible, or on a Pan-African trading. Which nation shall have which specialty is a nice political question, but it can be easily answered scientifically and that is the first step that should be undertaken.

A Pan-African Academy of Science and Technology to plan an overall rapid development of a political-technological complex among the African people would be a good institution for the times. Member nations would contribute to support it and its recommendations would be implemented through capital funds from all nations. As early as possible the Academy would begin retraining technologists in the new thrust.

The political problems of implementation are of course great, but certainly the establishment of the Academy itself should not pose many problems.

In this way Black technology can make substantive political contribution to Pan-Africanism while carrying out its primary purpose of developing economic power and fostering improved living conditions. And indeed unless technology is Pan-African, it will willy-nilly become a part of each African state's need to promote its own national interest regardless of the interest of Africa as a whole. Black technology harnessed to individual states will eventually be used for imperialistic nationalism, and the first to suffer from it will be other African peoples.

From these considerations I therefore present as a workshop project the designing of an outline for a Pan-African Academy of Science and Technology, dedicated to strengthening non-imperialistic nationalism in each participating state through a collective Pan-African technological economy.

The direct support for development of technology by government is the cornerstone of nationalistic power. Historically in Western nations where nationalism has been so intense, the use of tax money for support of science has been in proportion to the importance of aggression in the philosophy of the nation. The direct support in the main part has been for military technology with fall-out support to medical and basic scientific technology. The use of the technology for community development has been left to the private sector in capitalistic countries and to minor bureaus and departments in socialist ones. Lip service is given to the idea of support of research for the improvement of life but the habit of justifying the use of taxes in terms of "national security and national interests" has curtailed the implementation. Except in support of agriculture and life science research in the last decade or so, support of technology purely for improvement is nonexistent or nearly so.

Support for technological development flows logically out of the strategy planned for developing nationalistic sentiment and programs. If these programs are primarily imperialistic the strategy will dictate that military technology dominate, followed logically by transport technology, communications technology, business, medical, food production, etc., in perfect order of importance to the national goals of dominance and control in areas remote from the homeland. Housing, recreation, pollution control, etc., will quite logically be at the bottom of the list.

Presumably, if the strategy for increasing nationalistic sentiment is based on pluralism and collectivism and anti-imperialism, the order of priorities for technology will be drastically rearranged with most of the things at the bottom of the list now at the top and vice versa. Black technological development will be in the direction of those things which strengthen Blacks, economically, politically, physiologically, psychologically, and which promote the value system of the developing new nationalism.

A Black Perspective of the Health Crisis

by Hubert Hemsley, M.D.

The role of the Black professional in emerging health programs is to assure that quality health care as a basic right to all Americans becomes an actuality—rather than empty rhetoric.

In our middle-class role and our intellectual assimilation with the status quo, we, the most fortunate of Blacks must break out of our psychological straitjackets and become mindful of the great obligation we owe our less privileged brothers, still confined by poverty, racism and rigid institutions, hell-bent on *antes muerto que mudado* (death rather than change).

We have a challenge that should consume our every waking hour with never-ending dedication. We have been allowed to share in the American Dream, but only by helping bring full justice, equality and good health to all Americans can we fully realize our destiny as Black men and women.

In order to attack the manifold problems in existing health services, we must identify the problem areas as best we can:

1. Poverty, racism
2. Inefficient methods of organization and delivery of health services
3. Dual standards of medical care
4. Inaccessibility of medical care
5. Shortage of doctors and ancillary medical personnel
6. Increasing costs of medical care
7. Inability to relate to community needs.

The old concepts of charity medical facilities and services must perish if dual standards of medical care are to be abolished! Instead, there must be a mixture of private and public services, all directed toward treating the entire patient and oriented toward the fundamental needs of the community it serves. The *major* emphasis must be placed on service to the patient and the community with teaching and research to enhance the medical environment rather than rob a person of his dignity in the pursuit of esoteric goals.

No matter how well intended, the success or failure of any health program will be largely governed by the way in which it fits the modes, thoughts and actions of the recipient population. *Only* if this basic concept is recognized NOW will the health industry be able to avoid the turmoil and chaos that confront the field of public education today.

Thus, health workers, like other agents of social change, need to understand the nature of social and cultural patterns; what purposes they serve, why they persist and how they change. In their planning and in their approach, health experts need to be particularly aware of four gaps which often impede the utilization of programs' aims: (1) The Cultural Gap (2) The Status Gap (3) The Urban Adjustment Gap and (4) The Research Gap.

1. *THE CULTURAL GAP*

There often exist differences between the culture of the beneficiary population and that of the health team, so that goals, priorities, health concepts, etc., are viewed in entirely different perspectives. This gap is certainly in existence in Los Angeles today, where the poor and angry masses are crying out for needed medical facilities which are humanistic, comprehensive and accessible, but have thus far received only the traditional crisis-oriented ameliorative programs which have failed so abysmally in the past.

Any public health approach which fails to understand the culture it serves can never successfully implement programs which depend on human motivation, and well might meet with resistance in every area.

2. *THE STATUS GAP*

In any social system there are gradations of classes and social statuses. In America, this gap exists between physicians (who, for the most part, are white, middle-class, Anglo-Saxon Protestants) and other health personnel as well as between physicians and patients.

When you consider the fact that minority physicians have been restricted in medical school opportunities, residency training and hospital staffing, and thus far from meaningful participation in emerging health programs, the dilemma grows!

It is incongruous that public health officials with billions of government tax dollars can effectively stimulate young minority group persons into health professions when they do not treat the existing minority group physicians and health workers equally! As a result, "health" is a hierachy of command, where mistrust, envy and hypocrisy characterize the relationship between the team and the clientele.

3. *THE URBAN ADJUSTMENT GAP*

The migration of minority groups into urban areas breeds conditions of crowding, poor health and sanitation, maladjustment, unemployment (social revolution), and violence against themselves (alcoholism, drug addiction, etc.).

4. *THE RESEARCH GAP*

Emphasis on the *human* aspects of community development and health care is almost nonexistent!

It is axiomatic that in order to achieve good health for a person or a community, poverty and racism must be eliminated! Any approach to the solution of health problems which does not attempt to eliminate them is piecemeal and doomed in its inception.

Poverty, racism, and institutional rigidity have combined to produce disastrous effects on the health of poor and minority people in America.

The association between poverty and health is illustrated by data from New York and Chicago, which indicates that poverty areas had higher infant and maternal mortality rates, less prenatal care and a higher incidence of prematurity.

"Poverty is the third leading cause of death in New York City. Comparisons of wealthy and poor areas concerning deaths caused by disease showed that there were 13,000 preventable deaths which were attributable to poverty."

Of the estimated 183 million persons in the civilian noninstitutional population during the period from July 1962 to June 1963, approximately 23 million (12 percent) were living in families with incomes of $2,000. About 18 percent of the population had family incomes of $2,000 to $3,999, 34 percent were in the $4,000 to $6,999 bracket and 31 percent had incomes of $7,000 or more. (The remaining 5 percent includes persons with unknown amount of income.)

The 23 million persons living in families with less than $2,000 annual income were rather evenly distributed among the age groups, with roughly one-fourth in each of the age groups: under 15, 15 to 44, 45 to 64 and 65 years and over.

In 1964, there were 22.6 million nonwhites in the United States. This comprised 11.8 percent of the total resident population; Negroes accounted for 91 percent of the nonwhite population.

Of total households in 1960, 12 percent of the white households and 57 percent of nonwhite households had a 1959 family income of less than $3,000. At the other end of the income scale 43 percent of white households and only 15 percent of nonwhite households had a family income of $7,000 or more.

Life expectancy for the nonwhite population in 1965 was approximately 10 percent shorter than for the white population (64.1 years and 71.0 years respectively).

In 1963 the number of maternal deaths per 100,000 live births was 24.2 for the white population and 98.1 for the nonwhite; 16.7 neonatal (under 28 days) deaths per 1,000 live births for the white population and 26.1 for the nonwhite; 5.5 post-neonatal (28 days through 11 months) deaths for the white population and 15.4 for nonwhite.

The incidence of infant mortality among the less educated and unskilled is more than four times the mortality of upper-class infants; 40 to 50 deaths per 1,000 versus 10 per 1,000. The incidence of prematurity, mental retardation, cerebral palsy, deafness and blindness is also correspondingly high.

Millions of Americans are not able to secure the medical care necessary to prolong their lives or the lives of their children. More than 66 percent of the children from low-income families have never been to a dentist and *prenatal care is nonexistent for half* of the nation's pregnant women who have their babies in public hospitals. A study on one month's admissions to the obstetrical ward of the Los Angeles County U.S.C. Medical Center revealed that 26 percent of medically indigent mothers received no prenatal care.

The nation's infant mortality rate has been declining at an ever slowing pace since the early fifties. In 1955, the U.S. rate was 24.8 deaths per 1,000 live births, ranking the country eighteenth in the field of maternal and child care. In addition to the general unavailability of care to the poor, their living conditions, poor nutrition, and multiparity are also major factors contributing to the high incidence of infant mortality among the indigent.

Studies of obstetrical care and social patterns in Boston indicate a negative correlation between social class, need, and professional care. Those women, young, unmarried, *most in need of* professional obstetrical care were usually treated by *less experienced, discontinuous hospital residents,* while white married suburbanities had 97.5 percent of the attention of board-certified obstetricians. Unmarried Negro teenagers had only .03 percent of the specialists' attention. Unmarried white women and married Negro women also had low percentages of obstetrical care: 1 percent and 1.2 percent respectively. Since low birth weight is significantly related to maternal age the unmarried mothers whose average age is under twenty years should have received the most care, but did not. The identical situation exists in Los Angeles today.

The incidence of birth injuries among North American Negroes was reviewed over a ten-year period at two hospitals which account for 60 percent of all deliveries of Negro children in the District of Columbia. Among these children representing an economic cross section of the Negro community, the *incidence of birth injuries was 5 per 1,000 live births.* Significant difference occurred in the hospital with the larger number of mothers from the lower socioeconomic group. The incidence was twice as high as at the middle- and upper-class hospital. As a control, two New York hospitals were studied, one in New York City, the other outside of the city. The city hospital had

2 birth injuries per 1,000 live births whereas New York State had approximately 7. The higher rate in the District of Columbia study of Negro infants was at a municipal hospital, while the lower rates which correspond with the New York City hospital was at a Federal hospital. There is a *distinct* correlation between socioeconomic class and the incidence of birth injuries although not a definite racial correlation.

"The infant mortality rate of most countries is a function of that nation's per capita gross national product, (G.N.P.) and the number of hospital beds per 10,000 people. The G.N.P. indicates the income and standard of living for the masses of people while the number of hospital beds indicates the scope of the community's concern for individual health. The U.S. has the world's highest per capita G.N.P. but also has a high infant mortality rate of twenty-seven deaths per 1,000 live births. Eight other nations, some with G.N.P. only half of America's have lower mortality rates. The position of the Negro and *other deprived social classes explains this paradox.*"

The average obstetrical service of our teaching hospitals characterized by long waits on hard benches for frenzied impersonal services provided by a kaleidoscope of different interns and residents "passing through the O.B. Service." The subsequent results, of little or no adequate *quality* prenatal care, a high incidence of deliveries out of sepsis, prematurity and other obstetrical problems of varying magnitude are the logical consequences.

Approximately 5 to 10 percent of the intern and residency programs throughout the United States are filled each year, and because of the tendency for specialization (straight internships excluding O.B.) and the rigor of the O.B. Service, it is usually avoided by many interns. In recent years this gap has been filled by graduates of foreign medical schools who have been serving in ever increasing numbers in charity hospitals. These foreign medical school graduates account for about 25 percent of all physicians in training programs in the United States. Each year the United States imports the equivalent output of about 26 United States medical schools or 2,135 physicians.

During the thirty-one years from 1935 to 1965 inclusive, a total of 49,753 physicians were examined by state boards on the basis of credentials obtained in countries other than the United States and Canada. Of these on the average 40.4 percent have failed the examination during this period. Indeed in 1966–1967 the number of foreign medical graduates entering this country outnumbered graduates of United States schools 8,540 to 7,743.

The following questions must be answered:

1. How will the medical care to be rendered differ from the services received in the past?

2. Who will provide the actual medical care? Specifically: interns, residents, attending staff, private practioners, etc?
3. Will there be outpatient dispensary clinics in the typical charity hospital tradition? If not, how will they differ?
4. What is clinical research? Who will do it? Upon whom? How will it be conducted?
5. What steps are being taken to get the full involvement of the local health professionals and community people?

The major emphasis of all health programs must be placed on the *Service* to the patient and community! The Community Ambulatory Care Center must serve as the focal point for all personal and environmental health services and must collaborate with other health agencies in planning and action. For this to become a reality, a true partnership must be formed so that the vested interests of the various health professionals, public and private agencies are subjugated to the overriding interest of the community! Service must be available, accessible and acceptable!

"The relative failure of charity medicine (because much good has been accomplished) can be understood in the light of the fact that the American Medical Association has always sought to be relieved of the burden of providing care for the indigent and view their services as charity or utilize the indigent clinical patients for self-aggrandizement and research.

"Instead of providing comprehensive health care for the entire family, a potpourri of clinics proliferate where each specialty picks out an organ system and ignores the others. In this system the highest priority is to teach interns *and residents, secondarily to conduct research and ultimately to provide patient care. As a result, there is* no *single physician or health team responsible for the total care of the family unit.*"

Medicine, like a number of our institutions, stands at the crossroads. We the citizens of Watts-Willowbrook-Compton can as modern Booker T. Washingtons accept the paternalistic hand that will surely keep us locked into medical, social and economic apartheid, or *we can demand a new system*—new institutions that will clearly benefit the citizens of our Black communities and not an absentee health hierarchy who will become the new experts on ghetto medicine!

In areas of highest health need and where no first-class ambulatory services are available, seed money for construction should be supplied by the county or federal agencies to new professional groups, health cooperatives, nonprofit community cooperatives or existing groups in cooperation with paramedical workers.

Comprehensive medical centers owned by health cooperatives or community building corporations in which the doctors, consumers, paramedical workers, and interested community groups own stock would provide the needed medical facilities in urban areas.

The health cooperatives or building corporations will own the land, building, fixed equipment and lease it to the medical group. The medical group, in turn contracts with a prepayment plan for health services. The role of interested agencies is to give the building corporation low-interest loans and expertise in planning to help organize prepayment insurance plans, and the medical group structure. The medical groups, ideally, should comprise all specialties and structure their facilities to the unique needs of the community with an eye to long-range goals rather than the rigid confines of budgets. As I envision this concept, each comprehensive center will become involved with the area medical school in postgraduate training of both physicians and ancillary medical personnel and replace the antiquated outpatient department with all of its inherent deficiencies with the more personalized care of the medical team within the immediate community, responsive to the total needs of the family and the local situation.

This would eventually free the government from the *awesome bureaucratic task of constantly asking for higher budget appropriations; for these centers would quickly become self-sufficient and indeed pay taxes rather* than add to our mounting deficit.

To the Black physician and community resident it would mean, not only would he *own* a share in a health facility of his choosing, but he would have a meaningful voice in decision-making, planning and implementation.

The Importance of Technology to Black People

by Malaika Jalia

Brothers and Sisters, before reading this paper I would like you to conduct a simple experiment. I am not trying to be facetious; I am merely trying to make a point.

Take any small object such as a pencil or coin and hold it above a table. Look at the object with scorn, and demand it not to fall if you let it go. Tell the object that it is a fascist, racist object if it falls. Call it a pig, or say anything else to make this object remain in mid-air, if you should let it go. Release the object. If the object remains in mid-air then you have out-talked the Universal Law of Gravitation. Please report your findings to all revolutionary centers, because you have discovered a valuable new tool for oppressed people. For example when napalm is dropped on brothers in Mozambique they can "talk" the napalm right back into the sky. If the object falls, please read the rest of this paper.

This paper is concerned with one of the many problems that face Black people: the lack of technical expertise. Just as our ancestors in Africa with spears were no match for Europeans with muskets, a functionally illiterate or technically illiterate people are no match for the technically proficient oppressor of today. To say that ours is a technical environment is an understatement. One must control his environment if he is to survive and prevail.

Why are we as a people not encouraged to become proficient in technology? Why (especially since the new Black awareness) are we encouraged to "do our own thing"—to open clothing stores, to open liquor stores, to have Black fashion shows, to dance, to paint, to sing, to tell jokes, to perform in *The Great White Hope*, to "tell it like it is" to groups of liberals, etc? Black people are encouraged to do these types of things, because our oppressor does not want us to become proficient in the technology that he uses to keep us down.

During the period of colonization the European did not show his African captive how to produce and employ muskets, cannons, and sailing ships because the only way that the European was able to maintain his position of superiority was to maintain a technological edge. He no longer uses muskets, cannons or sailing ships; he has developed many sophisticated technical disciplines to maintain his plantation called earth. The following are some of those disciplines:

The civil engineer is responsible for the design and construction of buildings, bridges, dams, roads, irrigation projects, and other civil works. This is the oldest branch of engineering, and it has the most areas of specialty.

The structural engineer is concerned with the technical (the architect is concerned with aesthetic design) aspect of frames of buildings, silos, and water tanks.

The hydraulic engineer is concerned with the flow of water as in the case of irrigation and drainage projects.

The surveyor collects data for maps and lays out buildings, bridges and roads. He can be seen looking through an optical instrument supported on tripods called a theodolite.

The sanitation engineer is responsible for providing clean water and for disposing of all types of waste.

The transportation engineer is concerned with the design of freeways and for the coordination of all modes of travel, i.e., railway, air, etc.

Heating, air-conditioning and plumbing for building as well as engines of cars, missiles, airplanes, ships and trains are associated with the field of mechanical engineering. The mechanical engineer also designs and supervises the production of a variety of machines used in factories that produce machines.

Electrical engineering is one of the fastest growing disciplines. Wiring for buildings and street lamps as well as circuits for televisions, radios, computers, missiles and eavesdropping devices are included in this field. The electrical engineer and the mechanical engineer play a prominent role in developing modern weapons such as the "super" helicopter now being used in Vietnam.

Many new products used in peace and war are produced from complicated chemical processes developed by chemical engineers. Synthetic materials such as rayon, nylon, plastics, polymers and cosmetics are examples, as well as napalm, high explosives and poison gases.

Modern technology requires many new types of metals for buildings, bridges, boats and also for rockets, bullets and electrical wires. The metallurgist develops these metals.

The great sailing ship has been replaced by very sophisticated tankers, battleships, aircraft carriers and submarines. Naval architects design and supervise the construction of these vessels.

Aeronautical engineers design airplanes. They are responsible for designing a safe and efficient aircraft. Many tests have to be performed to ensure its performance. One such test is the wind tunnel.

The foundation of all technical disciplines is mathematics and physics. Only after mastering these two disciplines can an engineer perform in the modern technical society.

The modern white man is also very careful not to share his technical expertise with the people that he is oppressing. He has devised many tricks to keep us in the dark about technology. Observe that most of the brothers from Africa who attend college in Europe or the United States study nontechnical subjects. When these brothers return to Africa they are unable to make a real contribution to developing their country (i.e., provide clean water, heal sick babies, build hospitals): they are only qualified to cloud the political picture or spread the lies and decadence they learned from the West. It is no accident that those Europeans in Africa take great pains not to let the Black folks learn the theory of mining copper, drilling oil, mining gold or building dams.

In the United States there is a similar trend. Most of the Black people who go to college study nontechnical subjects. The white man is so slick that he's even encouraging us to go into brand new nontechnical disciplines like "urban studies" and "Black studies." He's even allowing us decision-making roles in these new academic disciplines of self-defeat. He wants us to come to his college and "tell it like it is"; that way we volunteer more information to him so that he can exploit our people more efficiently. While he is showing the nigger into liberal arts and letting him have that all-Black dorm the white man is involved in an intense effort to make engineering more appealing, and he is recruiting more white youths into technology.

What about the Black people who do pursue technical fields? The white man's solution to this problem is classic. He takes advantage of the old myth that a good engineer must not get involved in social or political issues: he hides behind his slide rule, and he concentrates only on solving specific technical problems. For the brothers that do not fall for this line he has other measures. He may shoot one of his women on them or give them a token amount of power, or give them a little more money, or swell their heads by making them the "First Negro to . . ." Black men have made great contributions to technology. The masses of Black people have not benefited much from them because these men were separated from the masses and were always encouraged to produce for the good of America or to "benefit all mankind," in both cases the white man.

It is important that Black people master technology but even more important that we master it within the correct ideological framework. There are many brothers and sisters who are using their technical creativity to develop new methods of warfare for the white man to use on Black people throughout the world. It is doubly tragic because these technically trained brothers are selling their people down the river for ten thousand dollars per year and fringe benefits. These are the brothers that appear in employment advertisements for large corporations like DuPont and Lockheed. These people aren't evil; they're just misled.

The United States has the greatest military machine in the history of the world. The people of Vietnam have been able to battle this great machine to a standstill because they have learned to do more than shoot guns and make fire bombs. They have learned to build bridges in twenty-four hours, to intercept intelligence communications, to move large numbers of men and equipment swiftly and to perform many other tasks which require technical expertise.

In this country the Movement has been a haven for many insecure Black men. These are the men who claim to be revolutionaries, who are unafraid of policemen but are scared stiff of mathematics. If one feels that he lacks the talent and stamina of simply going to classes and learning something useful, then what makes him think that he has the talent and stamina to endure a revolution? These men have only demonstrated their talent and stamina to talk bad.

This paper is not intended to demean the importance of the cultural and ideological aspects of the revolution, but unless we become proficient in technology we will find that Black folks will end up with the culture and ideology and the white man will still have all of the power. In this technological age simply "picking up the gun" is suicide, just as "picking up the spear" was suicide for our ancestors.

Technology is our creative means which devises the way out of our predicament (that of being a powerless nation). Black technology is that instrument through which we will survive. We must express our traditional selves in forms that are reasonable for 1970.

Black technology must be spiritually orientated because it must raise man's consciousness. Each technological achievement must answer positively to the questions: What does it contribute to Black peoples' self-determination? Is it created to build and sustain our Black nation?

We must remember that we do not want a Black America. That is to say, we cannot be committed to Western ideas, Western forms, Western limitations or we will be copies of Westerners. We are actively engaged in the total process of building, developing a technology designed for our own selves. Machines reflect the culture of their makers. Our machines must reflect our African personality. We must be free from all Western forms and develop our own technology, from our own ideology—a Black ideology: one of progressive perfection. All that we create or develop has to come from a totally Black framework. This way, coming from us, it will work for us.

For instance, a Black architect would create a complex that had schools built for the number of children living in a particular area. The school would be where the students and teachers lived.

The grocery stores and shopping centers would be where the mothers could get to them without having to travel long distances. The houses would reflect the ethos of the people living in them. The community would be bright, colorful, and functional. Health centers would be there, community worship centers would be there, all centrally located. Health centers would deal in nutrition and hygiene and other healthful systems of life perpetuation. Birth control centers—No! We are to be concerned with creativity, not destruction. We instead would develop a means, a methodology of using the earth to feed the masses of people. Storage housing for unused foods—No!

Those who have technological skills must teach technological skills to others of the Third World. Doctors must train nurses, now. Doctors must also find out what they are treating, what causes it, and then tell the mothers not to feed it to their children. Find out what is healthful and use that to maintain a healthy nation.

We must explore the possibilities of linking up psychology and sociology with physics and medicine, so that our mind, body, and spirit are in tune with each other and benefiting from the natural forces of this planet. We must not have separate scientific studies; mind, body, spirit complete a total Black unit.

Finally we have to hook up Black teachers with Black students no matter where they may live, educational alliances with all people of color for the restoration of Black people to their ancestral greatness.

A. We must accept and move from a Black ideology: one of nation-building.
B. We must study the relationship of each scientific field and create a study out of this developed for our needs.
C. Set up Black Technician Referral Center: function—a referral center for people that need technological assistance in building or repairing anything.
D. A Black Technological Recruitment Staff: function—to give seminars at schools on the importance of having Black technicians and what Black technicians are needed in our community development.
E. A Black Technological Training Staff: function—to make a commitment of giving available time to develop potential Black technicians in the Black community.

Resolutions

The Black Technology

by Ken Cave

Historical Perspective of Black Technology

Western technology has developed in a climate of complete disregard of human values. In spite of lip service to the contrary, in the U.S.A. for example the departments of the national government concerned with basics such as food production, health, education, housing and welfare are among the youngest. And in the areas of delivery of health services and systematic control of environmental side effects, national programs are still struggling to be born in the most technically advanced nation in man's history.

Inevitably, this attitude of lowest priority for human values has affected the training process of Western technologists. And since all Black technologists have been programmed to compartmentalize our intellect and to separate the human factors out of our problem-solving and research, pollution, overcrowding and alienation of human personalities have been blocked from our catalog of responsibilities to the same alarming degree.

In addition, however, because of the racist tradition of the U.S.A., the work of the Black technologist has been subverted and used to bolster oppression of Blacks. The Black inventor of the sugar-refining process produced a strong incentive for keeping slaves. For example, the Black inventor of the shoe lasting machinery gave impetus to the northern industrial capacity and increased its need for the products of slaves. Even today Black technologists are employed in chemical production of napalm and nuclear weapons which have only been used against nonwhites. Efforts at social reform by providing jobs for ghetto dwellers have resulted in the grotesque picture of Blacks, and production of tents and war material for use against Asians.

Overall there has been in addition a conspiracy to limit the production of Black technologists, resulting in denying to the Blacks of the U.S.A. the major benefits of the technological society. The high infant mortality and early average age at death among Blacks is traceable directly to the conspiracy to limit Black medical technologists to only token workers. The generally dilapidated state of Black housing is the result of the dearth of Black technologists in construction, a dearth due entirely to conspiracy.

The Proposed Solution

A. The creation of a new system subordinating technology to human values is required. The new system should be built on the best of the traditional and modern African values as the model most likely to succeed as an anti-imperialistic technology in competition to survive in the milieu of an imperialistic world.

We recognize the need to relate the new system in each African or Afro-American nation for the following reasons:

1. For building pride and enthusiasm among technologists.
2. To afford strength to the building of nationalistic sentiment in member nations.
3. To consolidate resources for more efficient use.
4. To foster increasing cooperation and interdependence and self-determination of Pan-African nations on economic and technical matters.

B. The overall planning for implementation should rest in a Pan-African Institute of Technology. The Institute should provide for retraining of Black technologists in the new human value system and to provide for the continuing training of political leaders and other personnel of the member nations, in the basic technical aspects of science and engineering.

The control of the Institute should rest with a board comprised of members selected by each participating nation. The member should be of ministerial status.

Each nation should contract to contribute the services of top rank scientists and technologists, experts in the following areas:

1. Health services delivery
2. Physical science and engineering technology
3. Biological science technology
4. Social science technology
5. Systems and resources analysis
6. Financial and industrial technology

In the area of health and housing, the Institute will collate the manpower resources available in each country with its needs. It will develop plans for the sharing of technological manpower among the nations as needed. And to plan the accelerated production of technologists in the most needful nations first.

In the area of heavy industry the Institute will make recommendations concerning the best and most efficient distribution of the various components of the Pan-African industrial complex among the member nations. These recommendations will be based on the technical analysis of the most efficient use of mineral and other resources and the most beneficial human aspects among the Pan-African nations.

Finally, the Institute shall plan research establishments for the areas above with recommendations for their implementation. These institutions will be designed to foster the birth of the new scientific approach which we conceive as Black technology.

I. Implementation

1. SOCIAL TECHNOLOGY

Priority 1. Health *(Physical & Mental)*
All health must be related to the Black life style. This means an all-encompassing approach to viewing health in a total Black perspective.

Priority 2. *Home (Total Environment)*
The Black family shall be the controlling unit of the Black nation. This also involves the element of decision and choice. Emanating from the family are all facets of Black life and the family shall be the forceful vehicle for establishing, sustaining, maintaining and continuing the Black nation.

Priority 3. *Knowledge of resources*
Comprehensive community resources, resources, health, education, communication, legal, political.

Priority 4. *Channels for obtaining money*
1. Volitionary taxes
2. Finance our own projects
3. Lottery
4. Proposal grants to Black nation
5. Donations to Black nation

Priority 5. *Psychological revitalization*
1. Cultural Institution
2. Basic readings that Blacks need to know
   a. Young brothers and sisters
   b. Students of science
   c. Scholar/Theoretician
   d. Lay readers

Qualifications:

Must be depictive of total Black input into the whole world. Publications must be on all levels of sophistication.

Attitude re-evaluation

a. Transitional members of Black nation
b. Negative positions of the Black nation
c. Acceptance of Black nation

The Black institute is in charge in specific areas of priorities, and in the general area of providing overall accountability to the Black nation. In the specific areas these are serious responsibilities. In general areas this is a supreme responsibility as accountability is the lifeline of the Black nation.

II. Skills Bank

The skills bank division of the technology workshop was given the task of providing the guidelines for the development of a central resource file and referral system which would be available to Black people throughout the world who are in need of trained technicians and other specialists.

There are two ways proposed to deal with the problems involved in the setting up and maintaining of such a bank over time. One is discovering and recording in a central data bank the Black technical, human and educational resources which already exist and which could be drawn upon immediately. Such resources would include individuals, programs, accessible equipment, financial resources, and space.

Within six months a complete directory of resources will be prepared and ready to be used by those in need of technical assistance.

In order to provide for the continual expansion and replenishing of the recruitment and development of new technicians as well as in the retraining of others who are already skilled to fit them into the framework of nation-building, we will develop training programs and curriculum materials to be used in the formation of a Black technology institute which would operate both independently and also in conjunction with other already existing educational institutions. The formation of the institute and the development of materials is a long-range goal and one which could not begin to be implemented until after the first phase, that of identifying and obtaining the commitment of resource people and materials, has already been accomplished.

From the directory of resources we shall bring together a core group of committed technicians who will work on implementing the second and long-range phase, which is the expansion and replenishment of the skills bank.

We shall employ a number of intermediate methods through which the resources of the skills bank could be expended until the Institute of Black Technology is functioning on a full-time basis. This will be done primarily through the use in specific and limited ways of already existing educational institutions and resource people who are not necessarily committed to Pan-Africanism or the goals of nation-building.

III. Information Science and Communications

The advent of cybernetics has produced a new dimension in information gathering and communication. Now tremendous amounts of data can be recorded, stored and subsequently retrieved at more than rapid rates. Along with its benefits, the use of cybernetics has created the monstrous invasion-of-privacy dilemma. Although this congress should be aware of the dangers of cybernetics, we should be primarily concerned with the beneficial services it can provide the Black community in NATION-BUILDING.

Areas of Concern for Black Technology Communications Sub-Group:

1. Black technological communication with both Black technologists, Black adults and Black youths. This is designed to alleviate the lack of skilled technicians and to solve present day technological problems facing the BLACK COMMUNITY.
2. Use of Black technology in the solution of health and housing problems in their relation to communication. This involves the transmission of information on new and old advances in technology and the dispatching of skilled technicians to solve the technical problems of health and housing.
3. Use of Black technology to better facilitate the organizational structure of the information network of the CONGRESS and the resulting organizations and programs of the CONGRESS.

Possible Solutions and Timetable for Implementation:

1. The establishment of a "Black Technology" journal to be coordinated with the Communication and System Analysis Commission. The first two editions will be produced semiannually and thereafter it will be a quarterly edition. The first edition will include the articles presented at the first CONGRESS and be produced in six to nine months. The first edition will also contain a call for papers for the next journal.
2. We intend to use the current Black people in technology (accessible through the Institute of Black Technology) to promote and supervise seminars and counseling for Black students in the advantages of Black technology to NATION-BUILDING. These representatives will be responsible to:
   a. contact the local schools and counselors;
   b. hold seminars, exhibitions and displays on jobs, job opportunities and training requirements and availability in Black technology;
   c. report back to the communication center any pertinent data concerning their efforts.

   This will be implemented by early December, 1970, since it will be a loose-knit configuration whereby the individual technologist will make all arrangements on the local level. The communications center will only handle regional assignment of Black technicians. Immediately all CONGRESS members are asked to perform the above responsibilities in their local areas.

Working through the Communication Commission, we will provide continuous tips, techniques and articles on inexpensive technological improvements of homes. These may include nontoxic paints and uses of various types of building materials—their cost, durability and applicability. Immediately we can provide for the dissemination and awareness of various governmental and private publications on home rehabilitation. As a long-range goal we could produce our own handbook and dispatch skilled technicians in various house-building and maintenance fields to aid in the rehabilitation.

To aid in NATION-BUILDING the use of the computer technology will be a most valuable asset in providing services to all aspects of the total effort of NATION-BUILDING. The following areas of services are all feasible:

1. General file of all participants of the first CONGRESS which may have the following keys for retrieval:
   a. Area of expertise
   b. Degree of expertise
   c. Area of residence (preferable dividing each state into districts to simplify the coding but to increase accessibility)
   d. Community organization affiliation
   e. Government affiliation
2. Use this file to create a complete mailing list for the CONGRESS.
3. Maintenance of a file on all supporting activists and non-activist groups. Not particularly by member but by activities.
4. Maintenance of a file on all groups which we classify as dangerous to the success of the CONGRESS and thus to all Black people.

Note: The last two suggestions are a must if NATION TIME is to become a reality. Knowledge readily and easily accessible about our adversaries and cohorts is a must.

IV. Health Service Delivery Technology

It was the concern of the Health Economic Sub-Group that health institutions in this country function in a form of "health colonialism" which is directly responsible for the existing health crisis in the Black community.

Health services are dependent upon economic and manpower resources and while these are available in the Black community, they are not utilized to the maximum benefit of the Pan-African nation because of the racist nature of the health care delivery system. The first step in the liberation is to provide for institutional means to direct the existing financial and manpower resources. This could be essentially done by the formation of two institutions: (1) Health Repayment Plan and (2) Health Cooperative.

In order to appreciate the magnitude of the problem and the financial ramifications certain facts must be known. Sixty-three billion dollars per year or $250 per person a year is spent for health services. It is our contention that if new Black control institutions could be derived at a proportionate share, these health dollars now being spent could be channeled through the community, i.e., twelve million Blacks times $250 per year.

(A method to accomplish this is already existing in the white community which could be adopted and modified to the extent that it does not serve an elitest group but could effectively change the present economic health complex. A prepayment system based on the principle of capitation [number of dollars per person per month] would be the vehicle by which this could be done.)

We recommend that a prototype or model should be established within the next year to demonstrate the feasibility and relevance of these institutional approaches to the health care crisis. A site must be chosen within the Pan-African community to assure success. The criteria are as follows:

1. Demonstrative need of health services (Health, Housing, Misc.)
2. Resources
   a. Manpower
   b. Economic
   c. Social Technology

Further details of the implementation of this will follow.

RELIGION

Coordinator's Statement

The Introduction of African Origins of the Major "Western Religions"

by Dr. Yosef ben-Jochannan

Introduction

> No positive religion that has moved man has been able to start with a tabula rasa, and express itself as if religion were beginning for the first time, in form, if not in substance. The new system must be in contact all along the line with the older ideas and practices which it finds in possession. A new scheme of faith can find a hearing only by appealing to religious instincts and susceptibilities that already exist; and it cannot reach these without taking account of the traditional forms in which all religious feeling is embodied, and without speaking a language which men accustomed to these old forms can understand. . . .

The above is the manner in which Robertson Smith began his classic study entitled *Religion of the Semites.* But Mr. Smith's words could be extended to include, that . . . *no major religion of today is exclusive of moral and philosophic concepts of any of the peoples with whom it had contact in its earliest development.* This would, of course, give credit to those African and Asian predecessors who were the ones that really began the religions which are today called *Judaism* (Hebrewism), *Christianity* and *Islam* (Mohammedism, formerly Mohametism).

If what has been said so far could become common knowledge, the general public would have no difficulty in recognizing that much of what they read in their Torah (Jewish Holy Book or Five Books of Moses), Christian Holy Bible (any version—Roman Catholic or Protestant and Christian Scientist) and Moslem (Muslim) Koran or Quran, would be conceded to be of African origin, as well as Asian, and adopted later by Europeans and European-Americans before they arrived in the Americas, the New World. But as long as racism remains the basis upon which these religions are taught, rejection of the indigenous African and Asian peoples' contribution to them shall continue to be camouflaged into the authorship of those who did least to start them, but most to continue them as their own exclusive domain.

To say at this time that Moses, of the Hebrew (Jewish) religion and peoples, was an indigenous African (Black or Negro), would create a catastrophic consternation among theological racists and bring down all sorts of anti-Semitic charges by the same people who equally as strenuously would admit that *Moses was born in Egypt,* at the same instance, forgetting that Egypt is in Africa. This would not stop them from saying that *Moses was found floating down the Nile River in a bulrush basket,* conveniently forgetting that the Nile River's source begins in Uganda; also that there are two Niles, the White and the Blue; and that the White Nile is more than four thousand miles long, flowing northward through Sudan (Nubia) and Egypt (Sais) and finally emptying into the Mediterranean (Egyptian) Sea. They seem to forget that the Blue Nile's main source of water comes from the Ethiopian Highlands —at Lake Tana; and that the other source of the Nile—the Atbara River, also starts in the Ethiopian Highlands and flows into Sudan—where it joins both the Blue and White Niles.

The TEN COMMANDMENTS spoken of in each of the so-called WESTERN RELIGIONS' moral code of ethics are based upon extensions of philosophical developments by the indigenous Africans—the so-called *Negroes* and *Bantus*—of the Nile Valley civilizations from pre-recorded history. The laws that say THOU SHALT NOT KILL, and THOU SHALT NOT STEAL, etc., were used in Egypt (Sais) and Ethiopia (Kush or Cush) thousands of years before the birth of Moses of the Hebrew (Jewish) Torah. Yet these two laws, including all of the other ten that made up so-called Western Religions' basic moral codes, are still being taught as if the first time they ever came to the knowledge of mankind was when they were allegedly *given to Moses on Mount Sinai.* At least, this is the manner in which they are presently taught in Europe, the Americas and wherever European and European-American religious and economic controls are in evidence.

It will be shown that the statements so far may hold true with regard to the almost successful attempts to make all philosophical concepts in the major religions cited as beginning with the usually mentioned *Greek Philosophy* and *Greek Philosophers.* In this sense the Greeks are treated as if they were in no way whatsoever influenced or taught by the Egyptians, Ethiopians, and other indigenous Africans along the Nile Valley—whence the philosophical concepts, now called *Greek Philosophy,* were originated—thousands of years before the creation of the Greek nation. In this regard, Professor G. G. M. James, in his book entitled *Stolen Legacy,* states on the title page:

> "The Greeks were not the authors of Greek Philosophy, but the people of North Africa, commonly called the Egyptians."

Strange as it may seem, the ancient Egyptians are being called *Caucasian* by most European and European-American *educators,* purposefully ignoring Herodotus' description of them in his book, *The Histories*—Book II.

Count Constantine Francis Chasseboeuf DeVolney, who personally visited Egypt in 1789 from his native France (Europe), wrote in his book, *Ruins of Empires,* published in 1802, the following:

> The earth, under these holy lands, produces only thorns and briers. Man soweth in anguish, and reapeth tears and cares. War, famine, pestilence, assail him by turns. And yet, are not these the children of the prophets? The Mussulman, Christian, Jew, are they not the elect children of God, loaded with favors and miracles? Why, then do these privileged races no longer enjoy the same advantages? Why have those blessings been banished hence, and transferred for so many ages to other nations and different climes?

Count Volney's questions could be asked of the Africans who are today being called *Negroes, Bantus, Hottentots, Bushmen, Pygmies,* and a host of other degrading terms, whose ancestors were responsible for the development of the religions mentioned herein; starting with the worship of the Sun God, Ra, then passing on to the Gods, *Jehovah, Jesus Christ* and *Allah.*

> How much longer are we to remain outside of the religions we originated in our "Mysteries" in Egypt and other High Cultures along the Nile?

The answer in this case would be simple. At least, the peoples of Africa can still point to such religious works as recorded in the *Book of the Dead* (translated from its original hieroglyph by Sir E. A. Wallis-Budge); *Facing Mount Kenya* by Jomo Kenyatta; the edited works in Janheinz Jahn's *Muntu.* Of course there are countless others that show the variety of depth in the philosophical concepts of African traditional religions—Judaism, Christianity and Islam, presently being analyzed.

In the *Book of the Dead,* the origin of *Heaven* and *Hell* are clearly seen to be nothing more than places, poor ones at that, of the indigenous Africans of Egypt's NETHER WORLD and MYSTERIES developed along the Nile Valley, all of which stemmed from civilizations that preceded the birth of the first Haribu (Hebrew or Jew)—Abraham (Avram or Abram) centuries before the creation of the first Hebrew nation—Palestine. Therefore, in this work, the God Ra is shown to be the "... *jealous God...*" who wants "... *no other Gods before me* . . ." This, the Hebrew copied in Egypt and changed in the following manner:

> Thou shalt have no Gods before me, sayeth Yvah.

In the case of the Reverend Placide Temples' book, *Bantu Philosophy,* this Roman Catholic priest failed miserably to dispel the confusion in his own mind to prove that there are basic philosophical concepts in traditional African religions on an equal level of spiritual consciousness to Judaism, Christianity or Islam, yet he continued to show how much better Christianity (his own religion) is than any of the so-called *Bantu* religions and *Bantu* thoughts he examined.

Janheinz Jahn, who claims no special religious affiliation or preference in his work, attempted to show many basic philosophical elements in a few traditional African religions which are comparable to the three religions called *Western Religions.* In his book, *Muntu:* The New African Culture, pages 29–30, as translated by Marjorie Green, Grove Press, Inc., New York, 1961, from its original work in German entitled—*Muntus,* published by Eugene Diederichs Verlag, Dusseldorf, Germany, 1958—Mr. Jahn gives the following account on Voodoo:

> I. OLD ACCOUNTS OF THE CULT
>
> Voodoo! Word of dark vowels and heavily rolling consonants! Voodoo! Mysterious nocturnal sound of drums in the Haitian mountains of abominations they have read about! Voodoo, idolatry, sorcery; Voodoo, epitome of all impiety, all depravity and terror, witches' Sabbath of the infernal powers and ineradicable heresy! What is it all about?
>
> Some people have tried to derive the word from the dance of the Golden Calf *(veau d'or),* and it has also been related to the heretical side of the Waldensians (Vaudois) who were reputed to practice witchcraft. In fact, the whole practice of witchcraft in the Middle Ages was called *vaudoisie.*
>
> The word is written in many different ways: Vaudou, Vaudoux, Vodoo, etc., but it comes from Dahomey in West Africa, where it means "genius, protective spirit"; in the Fon language it is "Voduh" and in Ewe "Vudu." The name of the cult, like the cult itself, is of West African origin, for the Haitians for the most part come from there. The reason why it was the religious conceptions of Dahomey in particular that came to prevail in Haiti is apparent from a London report of 1789 which tells us that ten to twelve thousand slaves were exported yearly from the Kingdome of Dahomey. The English exported only seven to eight hundred of these, the Portuguese about three thousand and the French the remainder, in other words more than six to eight thousand a year, who were shipped to the French Antilles, above all the Saint Dominique, as the principal French colony of Haiti was then called.

The earliest indication of the survival of African cults in Haiti we owe to an anonymous French report, which says: "The slaves are strictly forbidden to practice the dance which in Surinam is called 'Water-Mama' and in our colonies *'Mae d'Agua'* (Water Mother). They, therefore, make a great secret of it, and all we know is that it highly inflames their imaginations. They make immense efforts to do evil things. The leader of the plot falls into such transports that he loses consciousness."

Moreau de Saint-Mary, an enlightened scholar, lawyer, and politician who was born in Martinique and practised law for nine years in Haiti before playing an important part in the French revolution, employed the leisure hours of the North-American exile forced on him through his quarrel with Robespierre in describing in detail the geographical, social, and political conditions in Haiti.

In his work of several volumes this relative of the Empress Josephine describes, among other things, a Voodoo ceremony. "According to the Arada Negroes, Voodoo means a great supernatural being, a snake that knows the past and the present, and through the medium of the high priestess and of a Negress, foretells the future. These two are called King and Queen, Master and Mistress, or Papa and Mama."

The meeting takes place, he says, only secretly and at night, far from profane eyes. The initiated put on sandals and wrap themselves in red cloths. The King and Queen wear girdles. A chest, through the boards of which one can see the snake, serves as an altar. The faithful present their wishes, then the Queen leaps upon the chest, falls at once into a trance, begins to prophesy and gives her commands. Sacrificial gifts are brought; the King and Queen receive them. The receipts are used to meet the expenses of the community and to assist needy members. Then follows an oath similar to that at the opening of the meeting and "as fearful as the first," an oath of secrecy and obedience.

Jahn's details of a "Voodoo ceremony" on pages 42 and 43 of his book show very clearly the common relationship between traditional concepts in Judaism, Christianity, Islam and Voodooism which most twentieth-century moderns do not know exist. He continues on:

In the Voodoo ceremony the first loa to be invoked is Legba. He is the lord of roads, and streets, the Hermes of the Voodoo, Olympus, the protector of crossroads and doors, the protector of the herd. His wife, Ayizan, is the Goddess of the markets and the highest goddess of the Arada Olympus. Legba's symbol, his veve, is the cross—a cross which has, however, only its form, not its meaning, in common with the Christian cross. The vertical board means the deep and the heights, the streets of the loas, the invisible ones. The foot of this vertical world-axis is rooted in the waters of the deep. Here on the "island under the sea" is Guinea, Africa, the legendary home; here the loas have their permanent places, from which they hasten straight

> upward to the living. Every vertical, above all every *stee,* and especially the *poteau-mitan* in the *hounfort,* symbolizes the "tree of the Gods" which unites the damp earth, from which all things spring, with heaven. The horizontal bar of the cross signifies the earthly and the human world. Only at the crossroad, where the human and divine axes meet, does contact with divinities take place. And this crossroad is guarded by Legba. In Dahomey and Nigeria he is the interpreter of the gods who translates the requests and prayers of men into their language. In Haiti he has the function of opening the barrier that separates men from the loas. He is invoked in the *vanvalou*—rhythm and dance.

The music and songs of the dance are very similar in purpose to that of the so-called *storefront churches* of Harlem. Thus the following from Jahn's description above.

Aitibo LegbaLuvri laye pu nwe
Papa Legba, luvri baye pu mwe
Luvri baye pu m'kapab ratre
A tu bon Legba ouvre la barrière pour moi
Ouvre la barrière pour me faire capable
de rentre

There are many more stanzas to this song; however, the reason for not showing the entire song, is due to the fact that the main purpose of noting it was not to learn the entire song, only to get an insight into the projection of man and his God as seen in the Voodoo ceremonial dance and song.

On the island of Cuba, not too far from Haiti, Voodooism becomes *Maniquismo*—a name which carries in the mind of most European-Americans the synonymous meanings of *black magic, satanism, idolatry, heathen superstition,* etc. Fernand Ortiz, one of the foremost writers on this subject known to European-Americans, disclaimed any religious origin whatsoever for *Maniquismo* in his book, *La Africania de la Musica Folklorica de Cuba,* La Habana, 1950. Ortiz called it "A secret society, a kind of a free masonry, to which only the initiate, who has sworn his allegiance, may belong."

Ortiz, who is of Roman Catholic Christian origin, overlooked the fact that Christianity is still a *secret society* in many lands today; and that it too was once so labeled everywhere. It was, and still is, a religion to which only the "initiates," who have sworn their allegiance, may belong. But Ortiz's position is typically what happens when "unbiased analysis" of another person's religion is given.

If one is to take Ortiz's premise as the criterion for what is a *religion* and what is a *secret society,* then the baptism (christening) and confirmation rites of the Christian initiations must be omitted, equally circumcision of the Jews and Moslems, also, the exclusion of women from direct worship with their men in Orthodox Judaism and Islam. Or, are these not *secret rites?* Are they not special requirements in which only "sworn" members also may rightfully indulge?

The opinions and expressions already shown are but a mere sampling of how religious personalities see each other; religion, not only how they see each other in religious roles; but how they also deny the existence of each other's God. Of course the indigenous Africans, the so-called Negroes, niggers, etc., and their descendants are not even entitled to have the respect of being capable of creating a religion with common philosophical idealism, much less having a God which does not secure the endorsement of those European and European-American judges who are in charge of the department of certification of fitness and qualification of religions and Gods. Since there are no African or African-Americans allowed on the "Board of God certifiers," due to their inferior color and race, the traditional African religions must then remain "secret societies," while the certifiers' religions—Judaism, Christianity, sometimes Islam, receive "the good God and religious seal of approval"; all others are damned to the pagan depth of inferiority, and only can they expect to see God if they abandon their pagan God and heathen religion for one of the approved religions, preferably Christianity.

The Africans and their descendants (Black people) everywhere need not defend their traditional religious philosophies and philosophers upon the approval of European and European-American standards; neither shall this work even try to so do. Why? Because within the three most accepted religions in Europe and the Americas—Judaism, Christianity and Islam, often called Western religions—Africans have been the founders of said religions and their teachings along with the Asians hundreds of years, in some cases thousands of years, before they were known to the peoples of Europe. The fact that within the last three to four hundred years the role of the indigenous Africans in these major religions has been carefully and purposefully denied, suppressed, and in most cases, omitted, will not stop the truth about their indigenous African origins from coming to the surface. In light of all that has been so far stated, further revelation of the general and specific role certain Africans had in the founding of all three religions—Judaism, Christianity and Islam—is being retold; all in the objective of setting the record straight, or revealing the truth.

Hopefully, from this work, knowledge about some of the major indigenous African contributors and their descendants in the founding and development of Judaism, Christianity (an extension of Judaism) and Islam (an extension of Judeo-Christianity) would spread to those who do not now know that the religion they practice and the

God they worship are as much African (Black) as they are Asian (yellow and brown) and/or European (white).

Since Christianity, the European-American version of it, is the major religion in the Americas—the Caribbean included—it is the center of focus to which this work must mainly address itself; moreover, because the vast majority of African peoples and their descendants—both in the Western Hemisphere and Africa—are critically conditioned and/or affected by it.

Islam, the major contender with European and European-American oriented Christianity for the minds of the African and African-American people, will of necessity receive particular consideration with regard to its foundation—which is so intensely African (Ethiopian in particular) in structure.

Judaism, which today has very little or no real influence on any large segment of the African peoples anywhere, due primarily to the inhuman pressures brought upon the indigenous Hebrews of Africa by Christian and Islamic missionaries in their conversion crusades, will nevertheless be carefully examined with regard to its previous control and influence on many indigenous African societies; also its indigenous African origins will be highlighted.

As the clamor for "violent" or "nonviolent" action challenges the moral fiber of this Anglo-Saxon Greek-centric-oriented United States of America, many noted religious "prophets" within the major Black communities asserted themselves as "spiritual leaders," all of whom believed they had received some sort of a calling from a Caucasianized "God." The most noted of these are listed in the order in which they appeared on the national or international scene, thus, Father (Peace) Divine, Rabbi Wentworth Mathews, Prophet "Sweet Daddy" Grace, Prophet Elijah Muhammad, and the Reverend Dr. Martin Luther King, Jr. To these must be added the name of the Honorable Marcus Moziah Garvey. He was not a minister of the gospel; yet it was he who brought a different dimension to African-American Christianity which no other Black man in this area of the world has ever attempted.

The men above, all of African origin, have produced an immeasurable impact on that which is labeled today Judeo-Christian civilization and white-power-structure (government)—names which are used synonymously with the United States of America.

In the case of Father Divine, he gave Jesus Christ much more of a humanistic posture than any of his contemporaries. On the other hand, the Prophet Elijah Muhammad, reportedly of a former Baptist preacher background, debunked European-American style Christianity and Judaism as currently practiced. Not only has the Prophet removed his followers from what he called, "The hypocrisy of the white devil's religion . . ." but he also modernized the Moslem Koran (Qu'ran) "to suit the needs of the Asiatic Black peoples . . ." according to the message being given to the "dead Negroes" his followers desire to save. This is a basic tenet in the Nation of Islam—the correct name for the so-called Black Muslim.

The Honorable Marcus Garvey, late President-General of the Universal Negro Improvement Association, Inc. (U.N.I.A.) started a new Christian philosophy, and made Jesus Christ appear Black for the people who worshiped him throughout the Harlems of the Western world. Garvey took his image from the Jesus Christ depicted in the Ethiopian Koptic (Coptic) Church—the oldest Christian church and nation in existence.

This work's ultimate goal is to show the definite links between Ju Ju, Voodoo, and other exclusively indigenous traditional African religions with Judaism, Christianity and Islam, among other religions more commonly known to the European-Americans, and of course, to those of other ethnic groupings. It will also show that when Ju Ju and Voodoo, as well as other traditionally African religions, meet the conversion efforts of either three so-called Western religions—Judaism, Christianity and Islam—the latter three must accommodate the first two by adopting many aspects of the basic tenets in order to keep the new converts. For this reason, and many others not being mentioned here, it is virtually impossible to find an African convert in Africa who has surrendered all of his or her traditional culture and religious practices—especially customs associated with ancestral worship and oracles—for European-style Judaism and Christianity or Asian Mohametism (Islam). Because of the same reason most African-American forms of Judaism, Christianity and Islam take on concepts and emotional outlets not common among their European-American religious contemporaries of the three so-called Western religions. However, no attempt whatsoever will be made to prove whether Abraham, Moses, Jesus Christ, Mohamet, Bilal or Oledamre, and any other Gods and prophets were Black, white, yellow, brown, red or technicolor; except in cases where they already have been made to appear Caucasianized, and in fact, are known to be African or African origin. This work shall not attempt to convey any special political, cultural, economic, moral or religious message; nor shall it refrain from any area heretofore considered to be controversial and anti-established order by certain ethnic, religious or political groupings. If this work were to receive the endorsement of everyone, then it is certain that it has said nothing meaningful, by virtue of the subject matter alone.

AFRICAN ORIGINS OF THE MAJOR RELIGIONS ADOPTED BY THE WESTERN WORLD shall seek out and report truth as it is discovered in the pages of recorded history; also through personal knowledge and contact by the author—this is all it is intended to accomplish.

Scholarly excellence is the goal this work attempts to achieve. Thus, it is written on a level somewhere between the college sophomore and the generally articulate reading public, which is the primary academic prerequisite for this course of study.

For the reasons already stated there are very few footnotes on the pages of the text. The major notes are given at the rear of the book in sections entitled: Notes for Chapter No. 1 Shango, etc. This method of documentation affords the reader a free flow of the information without having to be immediately distracted by footnotes in which the average reader may or may not be interested. By the same token, the necessary notes and documentations are still available to the much more inquiring student or general reader who may desire to become involved in further research, or just to verify the author's sources of information and references. At specific points in the work, however, it became necessary to insert in brackets certain documentary or related notes and evidence as part of the integral whole of the free-flowing information, all of which dealt with recorded events; otherwise the quality and uniqueness of this work would not have been maintained.

Lastly, another major objective of this work is to make the past relate to the living present by means of the materials presented. The old (past) should be relevant to the contemporary (present) in order that the new (future) can be best planned, approached, and subsequently obtained; if this be not the reason for works such as this but instead only its historic chronological findings, then this would have been a waste of good time and academic research.

The role of the Africans (sometimes called Negroes, Bantus, Pygmies, Hottentots, Bushmen, Niggers and a host of other such degrading terminologies) and their descendants in the field of religion, as in all other areas of human endeavors, is too often ignored, and in too many cases, completely denied. Because of this existing condition it is necessary, if for no other reason, to bring to the forefront, once more, a few of the African (Black) personalities that preceded the Reverend Dr. Martin Luther King, Jr., in trying to put religion into religious congregations and institutions. It is also necessary to show many of them as the people who were most responsible for the origination of the philosophical concepts by which European-Americans and African-Americans are guided as moral codes, all of which today is called Western religion and Western philosophy.

The events of the death of Minister El Hajj Malik Shabazz (Malcolm (X) Little) and the Reverend Dr. Martin Luther King, Jr., caused certain delay in the completion of this work which was more than three years in preparation. Those who knew of this work in its earliest stages will notice that Chapter V has been revised to meet the above events; and by doing so, the entire manuscript has had to be rewritten in many places. This new dimension has enhanced the current value of the material content. However, it will be noted that none of the personalities mentioned in this work is rated over any of the others. If this were done, the purpose for which this work is created would have suffered beyond repair. In closing, and with respect to the major contributions of all of the Africans and people of African origin mentioned herein, the following African saying is given:

> . . . An offspring without a spirit past is a
> being without an ancestral tie. . . .

Resource Paper

Religion

by Sababa Akili

This undoubtedly should be considered a very profound piece of literature.

All *religions,* i.e., spiritual beliefs expressed through acts of worship, reverence, and discipline, are based on mythology. *Mythology* is the answer to the origin of things, which enhances and reinforces a people's positive self-concept and in turn gives them a chosen people concept; for example, Zulu (people of heaven), Olmec (sun people).

Mythology is the first criterion for a culture. *Culture* gives a people *identity, purpose,* and *direction* or in other words, who we are as opposed to who our enemies are, what we must do in relation to who we are, and how we must go about doing it (by any means necessary). So we must as Black people have a Mythology that says we are the chosen people, or the winners; therefore our God must be *Historical,* that is to say been with us for a length of time; *Beneficial,* he must benefit us psychologically and or physically in terms of motivation and enhancing our position; and he must also be *Like Us* which means that he must resemble us and feel for us.

It is necessary to define as we go along so that everyone can understand what we are saying. In other words, we should use *Self-Determination* to arrive at our definition.

Spritual values or beliefs promote human life and development. You can have many beliefs, i.e., attachments, but you don't have faith in everything, or in other words faith is the foundation, a firm foundation or base for different beliefs. Love is the highest form of spiritual values. *Values* give people some predictability of behavior. For example, many Blacks have gone into business and failed because they couldn't predict the behavior of their brothers. *Values* are an ultimate authority; in other words, they serve as a gauge to minimize conflict between us. Values finally give security which serve as a shield to protect us against problems and people that may threaten us. Black people *need* a Black value system as opposed to the present Euro-

American value system that we have been worshipping for the past 450 years.

In dealing with religion we must make a distinction between living and existing. Living implies a conscious form, while existing involves a mere presence. Blackness involves Color, Culture and Consciousness; to be Black we must be living rather than merely existing.

God is a man with *Knowledge, Understanding* and *Wisdom.* God is one who moves in *power* and *force* or one who is able to change things, involve, influence, control, build and destroy. Personal gods serve the house while collective gods serve the nation.

We as a people have always recognized more than one god; therefore we practice:

Monotheism—we recognize one god as oneness in the universe

Polytheism—we recognize many gods; each man as the god of his own house

Pantheism—we recognize the spirit running through everything in the universe—in the beginning there was only energy and matter.

The spiritual death is the worst death; we must be interested in life. Spookism is a degenerate form of spiritualism; it engenders fear and perpetuates ignorance, therefore one dies mentally. The Christian mind was the only one that created a hell, the Christian is our worst enemy. Quiet as it's kept, it was the Christian who enslaved us. Quiet as it's kept, it's the Christian who burns us. Quiet as it's kept, it's a Christian that beats us down on the street, and quiet as it's kept, when the thing goes down, it will be a Christian that's shooting us down. You have to face the fact, it's the Christian who is doing all this. There must be something wrong with Christianity.

The Black value system must be developed by Blacks. It is the basis for things that we do. We can't hold Blacks together without giving them values.

We propose the *Black Value System* written by Imamu Amiri Baraka as a profound source of reference.

Resolutions

by the Reverend James Cone and the Reverend Bill Land

As Malcolm X said, "All revolutions are based on land." Our future is that of an African people. It is "infantile optimism," and "lack of serious study for a Black nation to exist anywhere without recognizing Africa." We should prepare our people to relate to the physical base of our new nation. Thus, a mechanism should and must be established to politically support the liberation and the development of the African continent.

Introduction

The members of the Religious Systems Workshop have agreed that since this is "nation-building time," we need religious systems and institutions which will give us the spiritual insight to build our nation. We have seen that there has been no successful nation that did not have a religious or moral code as its foundation.

We want a "revolutionary" theology not a "plantation" theology. A theology that teaches us no matter what we call ourselves (Baptist, Muslim, Hebrew, etc.), that we are Black first, and all those other things next.

We want a theology which will teach us how to function in the area of politics, economics, structure, revolutionary preaching, sacraments and rituals, diet and fasting.

We want a religious system that is separate and apart from those things which are traditional "Western." In short, we want religious systems which will give to the Black man freedom, justice and equality.

An outline of, and complete papers of eight sub-groups of our workshop are herewith presented.

We shall call a meeting within three months to set into motion ways and means to implement all of our resolutions.

Revolutionary Preaching

What do we mean by "revolutionary preaching"? Revolutionary

praying and preaching will address itself to what might happen or what we want to happen within the course of the immediate years and realizing the probability of our actually becoming a separated people, actively engaged in guerrilla warfare. Actually experiencing bloody revolution stage by stage, cycle by cycle, keeping in mind those who are now children and even the not yet born.

In short, revolutionary preachers will not let Black people be caught by surprise or unprepared. Revolutionary preaching challenges one to commitment unto death for the cause of the Black Nation and its people; forces one to revolutionize himself and everything he touches; seeks to establish and reorganize a spiritual foundation of the Black Nation.

Where do you find revolutionary preaching material? Any area where oppressed people are found.

As revolutionary preachers, we will start our scriptive development, that is, develop sermons from the present-day Bible with an extension to twentieth-century Spiritual-Political leaders like Brother Malcolm, Dr. King, etc. All of these scriptures taken from the Bible will be reinterpreted as it relates to the Black struggle, starting with the gospel according to the gospel of our Spiritual-Political leaders, and any other Black person who has something to say that is relevant to the liberation and freedom of Black people and Africa.

Ecumenical Religious

A program to relate the various Black religions to the course of the Black struggle.

Set as a national goal for love of our Black brotherhood—Golden Rule.

Protect, love and honor all Black women immediately. Vehicle for success.

1. Establish a working communication between all national Black religions and National Black Organization.
2. Set a congress (Congress of African Peoples) in each of these organizations.
3. Have a meeting at least twice a month in each local area.

Economic

We recommend to the Congress of African Peoples that they delegate the Religious and Economic Continuing Committees of twenty-five to deal with the economics of the church jointly.

Food, Diet and Fasting

Slavery in the United States was unlike any institution of slavery that has been on the face of the earth. History shows us that when slaves were held by all other people, they fed and clothed the slaves in like manner as they fed and clothed themselves. However, in the United States, slave masters gave slaves only that which they themselves discarded—this garbage was used by a wise Black woman to make palatable meals (hog guts, etc.).

It is recommended that you read the following books:

Up from Slavery
People That Walk in Darkness
Africa's Gift to America
Coming of Arabic (Black) Peoples to U.S.
How to Eat to Live

Birds eat bird food, dogs eat dog food, fish eat fish food, slaves eat slave food.

Your stomach is *your* fuel tank. You wouldn't think of pouring just any old thing into the fuel tank of your car. We are very careful what we "feed" our automobile—and totally careless and indifferent about how we feed ourselves and our children!

If you tried to oil a fine watch with axle grease you wouldn't expect it to keep time, and when you put all kinds of foul things into your stomach which the Great Architect who designed your human mechanism never intended, you foul up your body and bring on sickness, disease, aches and pains, a dulled and clogged-up mind.

Now some believe that God did not intend any animal flesh to be eaten. God's revelation on that point is, however—and many have argued it both ways—God has revealed that certain animal meats are to be eaten as food now, in this age.

When the first written revelation of God came to man through Moses, God instructed man as to which kinds of animals man ought not to eat (Leviticus 11 and Deuteronomy 14).

It is necessary to recognize that God is the author of all law. There are laws of physics and chemistry, law of gravity, spiritual law: working in our bodies, regulating our health.

The animals whose flesh was properly digested and nourished the human body were so made in the original creation. No change was ever made in the structure of men's bodies at the time of the flood or at Jesus' death or at any other time. Neither did God make some sudden change in the structure of animal flesh, so that what was once unfit food will now digest properly and supply the body's need.

God is not some unfair monster who imposes foolish hardships on his people. Whatever God instructs us is for our own good. Swine flesh (pork, ham, bacon, sausage, etc.) is simply not for human consumption.* The same is true with oysters, lobsters, clams, crabs, shrimp, crawfish, dogs, snakes, rats, and skunks.

*U.S. Government booklet on *20 Parasites Found in Pork.*

The only seafood fit for food are fish having both fins and scales. Halibut has both and is clean. Catfish is a skin fish—unclean. There are many common, easily accessible substitutes for swine flesh (corned beef, pastrami, breakfast beef, beef sausage, tongue, ox tails, etc.). You never get a choice of rare-medium-well done with pork. They know if you don't kill those germs they will kill you.

What about Peter's vision? The purpose of this vision was not to change God's laws on food and health, but to show Peter "that I should not call any MAN common or unclean" (Acts 10:28). Why? Because the Jews had been taught to regard Gentiles like unclean animals. The voice from heaven in the vision spoke unto Peter three times because three Gentile men—two servants and a soldier (Vs. 7) —were at that moment on their way to see him! Peter went with them to see Cornelius. This is when Peter understood the vision. He confessed in Verse 28 "God hath shewed me that I should not call any man common or unclean."

Now Peter understood. Why don't all "popular" preachers understand? Maybe it's because they are afraid of finding their congregations and losing their salaries.

Common sense tells us that God did not intend for us to eat every creature. But we are just unwilling to let our creator tell us which meats will give us lasting health and strength. Some people still want to argue with God! One test they will use is found in 1 Timothy. 4:1–5. Read it carefully.

Notice that these "doctrines of devils" include commanding to abstain from meats which God hath created to receive with thanksgiving of them which believe and know the truth. "What is the truth?" John 17:17 says "the word is truth," the scriptures themselves reveal the "truth" concerning which meats are good for food. A prophecy for the future as written in Isaiah 66:17 says "They that eat swines' flesh the abomination, the mice shall be consumed together—in the wrath of God—saith the Lord."

God condemns also the eating of animal fat or blood (Leviticus 3:17; 7:23–27). Butter, olive oil, and some vegetable oils and shortenings are all right, but animal fat should be cut off before eating meat. Cheap hamburger is not good because it is mixed with much fat. Your doctor tells you about cholesterol. What is commonly called ground round is preferable. Lard should not be used. These things will wreck any stomach in time.

FASTING—the process of cleansing and purging the body of impurities and sharpening or conditioning the mind to understand the natural phenomenon of nature. Fasting also gives one an insight, the futility of the use of drugs.

Fasting gives the mind the ability to master its own destiny without the use of artificial stimuli. In the practical sense fasting is the best method of weight control. Fasting has been an integral part of all of the world's major religions since time immemorial. These are a number of ways to fast. As revolutionaries, we must be able to discipline ourselves to the extent that we can control mind over matter—FAST!

Remember that in open confrontation, it is probable that we will be cut off for days from all sources of food. Anyone who cannot endure three, four or five days without eating will cause a lot of grief and turmoil in the ranks.

Revolutionary Religious Ethics

1. Historical definitions of the problems.
   a. No moral codes relevant to our (Black) basic nature.
   b. Lack of cooperation and coordination amongst men of the "cloth."
   c. Lack of revolutionary spirit amongst men of the "cloth." Such as: David, Moses, Jesus, Mohammed, Buddha, Krishna, etc.
2. Support data and experience.
   a. There has never been a successful nation that did not have a religious or moral code of ethics as its root.
   b. *Black Theology* does not exist in W.A.S.P. America (White, Anglo-Saxon, Protestant).
3. We prefer the terminology, positive solutions over possible solutions, in an effort to assure the congress of the immediacy and urgency of the situation.

The African Peoples Congress must undertake as its primary goal the establishment of a sound philosophical religious base, coming from all religious backgrounds which can only be done by a Black seminar of Black clergy nationally and internationally. This seminar must take the responsibility of developing, establishing and implementing a sound moral code of ethics that all people of the African Peoples Congress can and must be subordinate to.

The Constitution of this body (African Peoples Congress) must embody the concepts of these projections and standards as they will relate to the total nation we profess to be building.

We request the officials of this body to undertake immediately to set a date that this national and international seminar must take place, preferably January–February, 1971, the place to be designated by the officers of this congress.

4. Institutions and Timetables
   a. Should be instituted by existing bodies and/or committee. (African Peoples Congress)
5. Resolutions on Specific Issues
   a. Whereas the Committee is firmly convinced there is a lack of

knowledge in the Sunday School Bible class in all phases of religion, there must be an innovated study instituted immediately.

b. We suggest commentary to engender philosophy of sound religious principle.

Sacraments and Rituals

What have we accomplished? A tool that can be used in the future. The spirit of Blackness will bring all the positive elements together. Remember it is the spirit of an action that determines whether it is negative or positive. "The life that we live" dignity being unifications through an act. Does it inspire us to be active in the Nation?

Seven Principles of Sacraments:

1. It is complementary to the person involved to bring all persons closer to the perfection and completion of Nationhoood.
2. It is only important because it *related to the Nation.*
3. It must be symbolic of *Divine Black Unity.*
4. Persons involved must realize responsibilities to each other which is symbolic to their responsibilities to all African people.
5. It is the willingness to sacrifice our own self-gratification toward the preservation of unity in the family, community and to the Nation of African people.
6. Our right to perform these ceremonies is legitimized by our concept of Nationhood.
7. Our place in history makes it necessary to perform our ceremony in this way, at this time.

Sample of Ritual of Marriage:

We have come to witness the sacred ceremony of marriage. We have come to bring the highest form of spiritual unity in the universe to this man and this woman. Let us also understand that in this union is the smallest example of how the Nation works. The family is all the tiny components we are talking about which makes up the complex body called Nation. Black people should start with their family because talking Nationalism without first taking care of home is like running down the beach trying to collect sand instead of collecting it where you are. A marriage can be defined in what it gives and first it gives a chance for Black people to give, to give of themselves to each other, to their communities and to their Nation.

We, as Black people, must realize that equality is a false concept and what we are talking about is being complementary to one another. What the man lacks, his woman makes up. What she lacks, he makes up. Black people talked about being complementary since the sun first shone on the African soil. By complementary we mean to complete or make perfect that which is incomplete or imperfect. It is by tradition and reason that we may say this tradition is our foundation; reason is the movement so that we must adjust our African past to meet our new African destinies.

The family is then just like an organ and the woman's function must be to inspire her man, to educate the children and to participate in social development. The man must then provide security—first emotionally so that the woman may feel secure in her love; economic security to be free from financial hassles and scenes, and lastly to give physical security, from people and problems that threaten her. In essence, we say, the marriage must be beautiful and in Africa beauty is said to be "that which promises happiness." So may the beauty of your relationship promise you both happiness and may that beauty reflect on a smaller scale the Nation becoming and as it is said, "so let it be done for now and for always for as long as the sun shines and the water flows." (Kasisi Washao—September, 1970.)

Religious Education

Areas of Religious Education As It Now Exists

1. Summer Camps; 2. Sunday School; 3. Adult; 4. Youth Education; 5. Worship and Materials for Worship; 6. Pastoral Training; 7. Leadership Training; 8. Communicant—Confirmation; 9. Boy and Girl Scouts; 10. Vacation Church Schools; 11. Conferences and Retreats; 12. Muslim Education System (Model for development of education system).

Problems

1. Few religious education programs geared toward liberation struggle.
2. Religious materials prepared by people with white orientation.
3. Teachers are not trained adequately.
4. Few promote concepts of Nationhood.
5. No Black monies are utilized for religious education.
6. Religious materials reach very few Black people.
7. Religious education consumes only a small part (one day at most) of total education.
8. Dull and has no positive image.
9. Does not speak to social development (total concept of involvement).
10. Religious education is private as opposed to communal.
11. Other-worldly oriented.
12. Inadequate definitions.
13. Lack of understanding and interpretation of other religions.
14. Black ministers are not prepared to properly analyze scriptures.
15. No training for lay people to become involved.
16. Exclusiveness oriented.

Needs of Religious Education

1. Religious education, as it now exists, must be destroyed and replaced by something positive.
2. It must be functional and geared toward the liberation of African people.
3. Materials must be developed on many levels designed to:
   a. Expose the exploitation that's going on
   b. Motivate
   c. Educate
4. Must be geared toward attacking problems in this world as opposed to waiting to get on the other side of Jordan.
5. Interpretation of scripture to fit our historical position in the world.
6. Blacks teaching "alien religion" must be confronted.
7. Develop a curriculum for new religious training which should include:
   a. History of African people
   b. History of religion
   c. Community organization skills
   d. History of the Black church in America
   e. Black theology
   f. Rituals and sacraments
8. Religious education must become broad-based, that is, geared toward becoming a way of life.
9. Seminary training must be developed, that is open-ended (exchange programs with Nation of Islam).
10. Each local church must become a religious education center on a seven-day-per-week basis.
11. Emphasize pre-school education.

Recommendations

1. Allow clubs and gangs to use church structure while organizing them into movement vehicles.
2. Establishment of religious training programs, immediately, for all African people.
3. The theme of the congress should become a theme of unity in all educational matters and materials.
4. Council of Religious Education to be composed of representatives from NCBC, Nation of Islam and all other religious bodies for the purpose of composition, interpretation and distribution of educational materials. This information should be used in all Black churches.
5. There must be a total separation from the traditional interpretation of religion and Western religious principles with the goal of creating a total education system for African people based

on justice principles geared toward building, developing and defending a nation (freedom, justice, and equality).

6. Dialogue must be set up between all levels of our people.
7. Chapters of the Congress of African Peoples should be established in each local area for the implementation of workshop recommendations utilizing the physical facilities of each *religious body*, i.e., churches, mosques, and their constituents.
8. That a request be sent to the Honorable Elijah Muhammad for a weekly full-page column in *Muhammad Speaks* for the purpose of disseminating educational information on the Congress of African Peoples on a regular basis, along with other independent Black media.

Local Church Involvement

Definition of Role:

To define and determine the real needs of the people.

Provide the necessary rationale for taking care of these needs.

Illuminate the mode and direction of action.

Major problems impending community involvement, plantation theology:

1. Resentment to Blackface saints
2. General old-time conservatism
3. Socio-political separation
4. Sunday involvement
5. Social alienation
6. Selling of favors by pastors
7. The involvement of brother

Necessary Components for Solution:

General: Build a political base within the local church;
Alliances and coalition with the church structure;
In the beginning you must be successful, choose your issues carefully;
Good discipline, keep commitments, be on time;
Constant and dynamic.

Leadership Development and Re-orientation:

Congress of African Peoples must undertake developed program seminars based on principle of Black Nationalism.

African Religions and Modern Western Religions:

1. Historical definition of problem
2. Mythology (religion), History, Social Organization, Economic Organization, Political Organization, Creative Motif, Ethos.
3. Purpose of Religion
4. Historical feature of African Religion
5. Religious systems (detriment, attributes)

Black Church Involvement:

All Black churches should become involved and totally committed to our common goal, regardless of our religious practices. Our first battle is to win the minds of our people, to help build the Nation.

Definition of Role:

—To define and determine the real needs of the recipients.

—Provide the necessary rationale for taking care of these needs.

—Illuminate the mode and direction of action.

Major Problems Impeding Community Involvement:

Leadership:

—Leadership devotion and re-orientation

—Congress of African Peoples must undertake a development program, seminars, lecture services for pastors—based on the principle of Black Nationalism must reorganize church structure toward functional groups. This differs from place to place.

Points to follow. Reason or Rationale:

1. Transfer of power within church.
2. Programmatic advancement.
3. For establishment of new perspective statement.

General:

The preacher goes with the congregation.

Programs to involve the people.

African and Modern Western Religions

Introduction: What is the problem?

Over five hundred years ago, the Europeans violently entered Mother Africa and stole one group of Africans from the land and colonized them externally. Simultaneously, the Europeans stole the land from the other group of Africans and colonized them internally; consequently the African way of life (culture) was partially, but seriously, severed. Thus, the functional mythology or the religious systems were scientifically severed from further socialization.

The end result is that the Europeans were able to superimpose an alien culture. The following processes of cultural development were interrupted:

1. *Mythology* (religion): An answer to the origin of things which relates you to this origin. It also provides the "Chosen People" concept which is necessary for a good self-concept.
2. *History:* A continuation of mythology in more human terms. It is a record of images, issues and events that reinforce a good self-concept.
3. *Social Organization:* A means of socializing through the teaching of roles and concomitant responsibilities—family structure/social groups.

4. *Economic Organization:* Ways and means of providing goods and services. Communalism as opposed to capitalism. *Ujamaa!*
5. *Political Organization:* System of obtaining, maintaining and using power.
6. *Creative Motif:* A dominant theme or attitude which expresses itself in art, music literature, technology, etc.
7. *Ethos:* The dominant characteristic of a group based on the other six areas and their emphasis. Bloods are only known for 100-yard dashes and records.

Purpose of a Religious System

Purpose of a religious institution is to unify Black people toward their liberation from human servitude, providing them with self-determination, collective work and responsibility, cooperative economics, purpose, creativity, and faith.

Seven Functions of Religion

1. Humanizing of things: Minimize mystery and fear, i.e., lightning, thunder and flood.
2. Simplification to unifying principles: How the world began, God, people become ill, sin, ugly acts.
3. Construction for the convenience of living: Ethical systems, Seven Principles, Seven-Fold Path of Blackness, Ten Commandments of Judaism, the attitudes of Christianity.
4. Provision of a system of values that defies revision: A source of certainty in a world so full of uncertainties, Nirvana can be reached by living the right life; heaven can be seen through love and faith and a nation can be built by creativity, and brotherhood, etc.
5. Reaffirmation and consolidation of related values: Thou shalt not kill relates to birth control, UMOJA relates to anti-individualism.
6. Provision of social control beyond brute force: To control the need to confine the physical body.
7. Provision of answers for children: What do we come from? Why are there races? How did the sun get up there?

Present religious institutions should give support to the feelings of Black Nationalism through their teachings or provide economic support. A religious institution must seek to change the definition, interpretation, and references connected with our brief Negro experience and institute one of meaning. For example: As Negroes, we believe that God was undefinable and unexplainable, but we are taught that there are three characteristics of a God—knowledge, understanding and wisdom—and that our God must be historical, beneficial and like us, i.e., *Look* like us and *Love* us.

Historical Features of African Religion

The historical features of African religions after European colonization include the following:

1. *Destruction of Communication:* Blacks speaking the same language were separated (fear of rebellion). To destroy language is to destroy the mind.
2. *Mixed Tribes:* Blacks were already fighting in Africa and the mixture of tribes during slavery further added to disunity.
3. *Black Fights:* Were held for the entertainment of whites. Brothers still engage in Black fights in order to please the white boy.
4. *Division of Labor:* Field, house, and yard Niggers.
5. *Destruction of Culture:* Blacks were denied the seven criteria for a culture.
6. *Indoctrination:* Blacks were made to feel inferior and uncivilized. The devil justified his acts religiously, by saying it was his obligation to civilize.
7. *Destruction of the Family:* Family roles were reversed and destroyed. Was most damaging, for the family is the smallest unit of cultural transmission.

African religions before European invasion were basically the opposite of negative influences of European colonization stated above. If a religious system does not accomplish the aforementioned purpose, it retards. If a religious system does accomplish the aforementioned purpose, it enhances.

Evaluate and Assess Religious Systems Now in Terms of Purpose

1. Historical and slave Christianity. (For information regarding the authenticity of historical Christianity, see the Resource Paper for the Congress of African Peoples prepared by the Reverend Albert B. Cleage, Jr., and the Reverend William L. Land. The same paper may be consulted for European misuse of Christianity.)

2. Islam: Because of variant expressions of the Islamic faith it was not possible to give a definition of this religion that would be agreeable to all. According to the Islamic teaching, the basic principles of Islam are 1) Faith, 2) Prayer, 3) Charity, 4) Fasting, 5) Hajj.

Five Principles—The Honorable Elijah Muhammad, Messenger of ALLAH

1. Belief in Allah and his Holy Apostle, the Honorable Elijah Muhammad.
2. Belief in the Divine Revelation and the Hereafter.

3. Belief in Prayer, at least five times a day.
4. Belief in giving to the poor, charity in its broadest sense.
5. Belief in fasting, especially during the Holy Month of Ramadan.

Other views of Islam will be pursued by this workshop in the ongoing continuation of this work.

Kawaida

A total value system—both Religion and Ideology founded by Maulana Ron Karenga to suit the needs of Afro-Americans, and to answer the needs and problems of Afro-Americans so as to get the maximum benefit out of life.

Some important principles of the Kawaida faith include Unity (UMOJA), respect for elders (*Saidi*), rejection of the God in the sky and *high* moral standards. Note: Due to lack of time, this section of the topic will be pursued in greater detail in the future work of this workshop.

It is obvious that Black people need new spiritual forms in order to achieve political, social, economic and spiritual liberation. The appearance of the Kawaida faith and reinterpretations of existing forms of Christianity and other religions are evidence of that fact. It is hopeful the religious system workshop of the Congress of African Peoples will pursue various possibilities in that direction. An aspect of the new spiritual forms must include elements of Black Nationalism and Pan-Africanism so that Black people all over the world will realize that their liberation involves all people of color.

Submitted as Definitions: Derived at through self-determination, in other words, defining and speaking for ourselves.

RELIGION The system of spiritual expression which may be evidenced by acts of worship, reverence and discipline.

SPIRITUALISM Is an intense emotional appreciation for highest values of man which are positive to human life and development; that is to say, those values which most promote human development.

SPOOKISM Is an intense emotional attachment to intangible things which are identified with the supernatural which engender fear and perpetuate ignorance.

MYTHOLOGY Is a body of knowledge that deals with myths of the origins of things. It gives the relationship between man and the supreme force/being which gives the chosen people concept. Which gives the highest values of man by which he can preserve and promote human life.

MYTHS Beliefs or legends dealing with the relations of the gods to man and the supreme force, which answers the origin of things.

MONOTHEISM We recognize one god as oneness in the universe.

POLYTHEISM We recognize many gods, each man as the god of his own house.

PANTHEISM We recognize the spirit running through everything in the universe—in the beginning there was only energy and matter.

LIVING Implies a conscious form.

GOD Is one who moves in power and force or one who is able to change things, involve, influence, control, build and destroy. One who has knowledge, understanding and wisdom.

HISTORY A continuation of mythology in more human terms. It is a record of images, issues and events that reinforce a good self-concept.

Nguzo Saba (Seven Principles)

UNITY To strive for and maintain unity in the family, community, nation and race.

SELF-DETERMINATION To define ourselves, name ourselves, and speak of ourselves, instead of being defined and spoken for by others.

COLLECTIVE WORK AND RESPONSIBILITY To build and maintain our community together and to make our brothers' and sisters' problems our problems and to solve them together.

COOPERATIVE ECONOMICS To build and maintain our own stores, shops and other businesses and to profit together from them. This must include the concept of land and bread.

PURPOSE To make as our collective vocation the building and developing of our community in order to restore our people to their traditional greatness.

CREATIVITY To do always as much as we can, in the way we can, in order to leave our community more beautiful and beneficial than when we inherited it.

FAITH To believe with all our heart in our parents, our teachers, our leaders, our people and the righteousness and victory of our struggle.

Suggested Reading Materials

Message to the Black Man by Elijah Muhammad
Black Value System by Imamu Amiri Baraka
Africa's Gift to America by J. A. Rodgers
How to Eat to Live by Elijah Muhammad
Up from Slavery by Booker T. Washington

EDUCATION

Coordinator's Statement

Principal Concerns: Education and Black Students

by Preston Wilcox

Introduction

We are a nation of people of African origin engaged in a worldwide effort to cast away the bonds of oppression and colonization. We have been victimized by racism, classism, sexism, colonialism, and capitalism—all of which are forms of social organization designed to convince their victims to acquire the skills to victimize others. We are divided because we view racism, classism, sexism, colonialism, and capitalism as separate and discrete tools of oppression when their effective impact is the same. We allow this to happen because we have been conditioned to apply Westernized analytical tools in order to understand our own situation. If Westernized approaches are scientifically colonialistic, then we have allowed ourselves to become Africans who fulfull such prophecies. We have been essentially educated to live up to Western dreams which are organized to frustrate that very realization for Pan-Africans. The American Dream is unachievable and perhaps undesirable for authentic Pan-Africans. To believe that dream is to accept the responsibility for preventing other Pan-Africans from surviving *on their own* terms.

Authentic Pan-Africans have no need to victimize other Pan-Africans or to incorporate Western values. Rather, they are concerned about how to build within themselves and to embed it deeply in the ability to refuse to participate in their own oppression and to mute those forces organized to destroy them. The education of Pan-Africans, then, must concern itself with the reality that Pan-Africans exist as nations within hostile nations and within a hostile world. Whether one resides within a world colony or the American colony or in Accra or in Harlem, his ultimate survival *on his own terms* depends on his ability to *not* be controlled, manipulated, co-opted, or oppressed by the white shadow that has systematically exploited him.

Another part of this question relates to the tendency of far too many Blacks having to depend on white solutions for Black problems, not realizing that the self-interest of whites is *their* primary interest.

Our problem has been that our self-interest has often been viewed as being synonymous with their self-interest; a policy that has guaranteed the maintenance of white racism, hereafter defined as the ingrained tendency of white people to look out for each other.

To be meaningful, the education of Pan-Africans, then, must educate Pan-Africans *to look out for each other; to refuse to participate in their own oppression* whether in class, sex, racial, political or economic terms; *and to define the terms on which they will relate to others.* Our accountability should be to each other; we should refuse to victimize each other; we must define our own values; and our own concept of the family, our communities, and our nation.

All this must take place by doing it, not merely by describing it. Education is an act; it is not a resolution. It is an event, not a description of it. It is the struggle, not the preparation for it. It combines thinking, feeling, and acting into a single whole. It is a human act. It respects the learner and frees the teacher to learn. It is a people-building, family-building, community-building and a nation-building act—or else it is indoctrination, brainwashing, domination and Westernization. It places the major responsibility for learning on the learner himself. It vests the teacher with the skill to foster liberation but not the skill to control. It is a human loving act between two people whose common destinies are bound together. The learner has a need to learn. The teacher has a need to teach; neither has the need to compete over the possession of knowledge. Their task is to figure out how to cooperate in the use of that knowledge on behalf of the collective liberation of Black people.

Education is a political act as are *all* acts. Since the theme of this gathering is "It's Nation Time, Labor For A Nation," we have convened here to discern together *how* we can create those educational institutions which will further those aims. We will not attempt to tackle the total problem. We will just tackle those that we are capable of tackling. We ask not for a single solution or a multiplicity of solutions, but the involvement of an increasing number of brothers and sisters in the problem-solving process. We are not here to list resolution; we are here to make *resolutions to act.* We are here to discover those issues about which we can act together. Collective actions around common educational issues is our first message. The second message is how do we use education for the task of nation-building.

This workshop sees its responsibility in two areas:

1. To pull together into workable units those who call themselves educators in the interest of developing those instruments and institutions which will further the Pan-Africanization of the formal educational process; to develop new educational institutions and to humanize those that serve the Black world.

2. To provide an educational service to the Pan-African world; to fill those gaps in knowledge and technique which, if filled, will further the nation-building process.

The ideology of the Congress of African Peoples has been proposed by the National Coordinating Committee. Copies of it are enclosed in your registration kits. To that degree, then, this is a directed conference as against being open-ended. All programs must flow from that ideological position; a position that asserts essentially that the only people who serve to gain from the liberation and survival of Pan-Africans on their own terms are Pan-Africans themselves. The other world has chosen to survive *despite us* or *without us.* If the Pan-Africans' world and the other world survive *with* each other, it will be because Pan-Africans want it that way.

The ideological statement reads as follows as it relates to education:

> Of principal concern to the workshop will be appropriate definitions of "Education" for Black people and how such definitions relate to our protection, survival and liberation. How we develop self-learning processes to transmit Black values, and nation-building will be given major consideration. Issues such as Community Control, Black Studies, Liberation Schools, Independent Institutions will be evaluated in light of new information and new experiences. Educational forms of African people the world over will be evaluated for their potential influences in any Black struggle. A Black school system must be established to remove the indoctrination of a colonized mentality and the legacy of imperialism which still lingers. Black educators and students have the responsibility of devising ways in which schools and colleges in their countries can be made to deal effectively with Black needs.

The action imperatives presented herein are not mine. They represent the hopes and aspirations of a growing number of Black teachers, students, parents, administrators, and community residents. The ideas herein are drawn from the efforts and experiences of at least twenty-eight affiliates of the National Association for African American Education, from forty-seven cities in which the school community control movement is being cultivated, from the experiences of over sixty-two independent Black educational institutions and those of the National Association of Black Students and the Student Organization for Black Unity. Materials from these organizations have been reviewed—and some of them will make their reports here. What follows is my synthesis of these ideas; my understanding of what is necessary and possible based on the available manpower and financial resources. You are challenged to listen carefully and to join in and help to create the institutions so proposed. The proposals are listed on the following pages.

I. Black Studies Program Consortium

A. That the Black Studies Programs on white campuses form a single Black Studies Consortium to be named after a distinguished Black scholar such as W.E.B. Du Bois or Carter G. Woodson to serve as an accrediting agent for all Black Studies programs; to develop and own all test instruments, to insure that federal, state and local funds designed to serve minorities are controlled by the respective Black Studies Programs and to develop their own criteria for admissions, evaluation and graduation. This consortium would assign specific research, development and fund-raising responsibilities to the Black Studies Programs who affiliate with it.

II. Black Student Unions on White Campuses

That Black student unions on white campuses organize to ensure

A. that Black students study on white campuses as members of the Black community. Course credit and technical support should be provided to enable them to study and work within the Black community with the consumers of white oppressors to find solutions for such political problems as drug addiction, deteriorated housing, unemployment, economic exploitation, inadequate housing services and the like. A secondary purpose of this thrust is to develop employment opportunities within the Black community for Black graduates.

B. to distinguish between alliances and coalitions with white students. The former is a permanent arrangement, the latter is a temporary crisis orientation. Brother Imamu Sukumu will discuss this further. It is clear that Black student unions must begin to define the problems as they see them and to lead themselves.

C. to develop a humanized body of knowledge about the Black experience; to reorganize the library cataloging system and to insist that the libraries be stocked with authentic Pan-African literature; to develop relevant courses and to engage in systematic and depths research about the Pan-African experience. This can be achieved by systematic study of the white agenda as a tool to understanding its impact on the Black experience.

III. Black Teachers and Administrators in Public Schools

A. That Black teachers and administrators withdraw immediately from the NEA and the AFT and assume a guidance role in the formation of *community unions* involving parents, students, teachers, and administrators on a graduated dues-paying basis within the Black community. These community unions should function as community educational corporations designed to influence all other public services that impinge upon learning such as public assistance, health, unemployment, housing, drug addiction, police services, etc. They should become instruments for assuming control over all community services; a vehicle for tapping federal, state, local and philanthropic appropriations, for training teachers and community interns and for guarding the sanctity of the Pan-African experience. Importantly, it destroys the participant-consumer cleavage in that everyone becomes a participant and a consumer. It can become a base for cooperative economic development, effective partisan political actions and for communalized community development. The saving in union dues paid to white-controlled unions would be phenomenal. This plan is developed for those communities and for programs wherein administrators and teachers are selected by the students.

B. That an effort be undertaken to Pan-Africanize the curriculum by making the problems of the community the core of the curriculum and by humanizing the educational process by removing chains off doors, not making kids raise their hands to get permission to go to the bathroom, and by ending suspensions, expulsions and corporal punishment. No Pan-African teacher should permit himself or herself to be used to abuse any Pan-African child or allow himself to be used as an advocate against the interests of the host community. Despite the source of the teachers' income, they are called upon to psychologically identify with the Pan-African community. See "I Ain't Playin' No More," a film on the Morgan Community School, Washington, D.C.

IV. Community Control of Schools

A. That an effort be made to control all schools located around or serving a predominantly Black student body. This control is expressed through the selection and evaluation of all staff, the control of funds, setting of educational policy, the incorporation of a concern for all of the students' problems and those of their families into the agenda of the school, the construction of buildings and the development of new job opportunities for local residents. A national network should be developed for this purpose. See the Twenty-Point Position Statement from Harlem's I.S. 201

V. Independent Black Educational Institutions

That a parallel school system be developed incorporating schools of all levels into a national Pan-African school system that

A. gets the Black community involved in its own self-education

B. develops curriculum materials for schools serving the Black community
C. trains teachers for service in both systems
D. produces a new kind of Pan-African from the ground up
E. moves toward the establishment of a national Pan-African university with ties to our brother institutions elsewhere in the world.

Interestingly enough, employees of such systems are freer to concentrate on Pan-African affairs. It is "illegal" to do so in many white-dominated schools.

Brother Frank Satterwhite of the California AAAE and Nairobi College will present his own ideas on the subject.

VI. Black Colleges as Employment Vehicles

That an effort be made to use Negro colleges as bases for the development of employment opportunities for Black brothers and sisters by introducing commercial and industrial enterprises onto their campuses with work-study arrangements for students and job training for real jobs for non-students. Recall that when Brother Booker T. Washington made his famous Atlanta Exposition speech he was really saying to Black people, "Serve the people."

For too many of us heard only what he said to white people. The Atlanta University Center is a good starting point. Brother Jason Benning will have more to say on this issue.

VII. Early Childhood Development: Materials Development

That an effort be made to make a major effort to develop the spirit, mind and aspirations of our young people. A systematic effort must be made at the cradle end of the march to the grave to insure that our young people are provided the fullest opportunity to perceive this world the way it really is and to obtain the skills to survive meaningfully within it. Our expectation is that a major effort will be made to develop and transmit information as to how to educate our young people to become full and productive members of their families, communities and nation. They must be educated for life through scholarship and not for scholarship alone.

Sister Furaha of the NewArk's African Free School, Brother John Churchville of Philadelphia's Freedom Library Day School and Sister Lonneta Gaines of Atlanta Learning House will discuss this further.

VIII. A Federal Funding Apparatus

That an information service be developed to keep Black communities fully informed of the funds available for educational purposes. This service would involve a network operating at the national, state, regional and local levels and should draw upon the support of Black elected officials and national Black organizations and caucuses. A third level of concern would involve local communities in developing the organizing and mobilizing skills to prevent appropriations which are designed to further degrade them. Sister Jackie McCord will have more to say about this.

IX. Language of Humanism Directory

That a team of scholars be organized to develop a Black Directory or Dictionary which uncovers the racism of Western terminology and replaces it with a humanistic language including the languages of our origins. We have debated integration issues when if we understood it for what it is—domination—we would not expect such an educational process to accredit the Black experience. Similarly, part of our frustrations emanate because we render ourselves invisible when we seek to become white. Not only is it not possible; it does not address itself to our basic problems.

Lloyd Yarbura will have more to say about this.

X. Alternate Issues

That those issues which are not addressed above and for which there are the possibilities for action, an opportunity be provided during this conference to encourage the formulation of action plans.

This statement has deliberately omitted references to African history since the workshop on history is handling that subject. Further, it has not sought to assign specific responsibilities to existing organizations since the challenge being offered is to get our brothers and sisters to commit themselves on their own in helping us build a nation.

It may be that we will not be able to design and implement an institution for all of the areas indicated above. But let us hope that whatever we come out with will mean that we will operate differently on the morning of September 8, 1970, than we did when this conference began. POWER TO THE CORRECT PEOPLE!

Resource Information

The following mailing lists are available through AFRAM Associates, Inc. 103 East 125th Street, Harlem, New York 10035; 212-876-9255. Congress members can obtain labels of such lists for the cost of having them run off onto the label.

a) Black Studies Programs (170)
b) Community Control Schools and Advocates (125)
c) Independent Black Educational Institutions (62)
d) National Black Organizations and Caucuses (120)

e) National Black Publications and Journals (43)
f) The National Black Press (100)
g) Black Education Organizations (28)
h) Black Educators (700)
i) Black School Board Members (500)

Resource Materials

Black Power Conference Reports (Philadelphia, August 30–September 1, 1970, and Bermuda, July 13, 1970). New York: AFRAM Associates, Inc., 1970, 71 pp. $3.00 + .50 postage.

Significant Educational Statements: A Bibliography. New York: AFRAM Associates, Inc., August, 1970.

Congress on Africa, Atlanta, December 13–15, 1895 (Africa and the American Negro Series). Atlanta: Franklin Printing and Publishing Company, 1896.

Resource Papers

Education

by Acklyn Lynch

During the past three years Black self-assertion challenged the educational system as young Black students demanded that proper focus be given to the historical and cultural contributions of Afro-Americans to the American social order. They also questioned the relevance of the education which they were receiving as it related to their commitment to work in and for the Black community. At first, these demands were rejected either from the point of view that Black Americans did not make significant contributions to American cultural and intellectual life, or that the students were making chauvinistic claims that were non-scientific in principle and immoral in persuasion. This assertion led to serious confrontations in both Negro and white centers of higher learning, for Black students were aware of the contradictions of libertarian democracy and egalitarian education contained in the principles of the 1954 Supreme Court decision, and its proper implementation in white America.

The liberal integration posture had collapsed before their eyes, for Black students clearly recognized that integration as defined by white America meant the acceptance of the dominant ethic along with acquiescence to the authority and power of the existing social and political institutions. It did not mean a full participation as equals in the destiny of their community. Integration had its referent in white culture and its legal authority as established by the white power structure. Integration did not provide identity nor did it give emotional security to the Black student. For him, integration was a world of uncertainty, of shifting sand, depending on the exigencies of the polity and its interpretation of libertarian democracy. Integration meant white control of integrated Negroes. Integration meant assimilation into an American synthesis. The student realized that integration was an intellectual accommodation, not a political reality, because it did not provide for full participation in the arena of power.

Faced with this stark reality, the Black student in 1967–68 was prepared to challenge the educational system and dramatize the malaise of educational institutions in contemporary America. This was the logical extension of the cry for Black Power, for where would this power reside but in the creative energies of Black youth who will be the leaders of tomorrow. Consequently, there arose a crisis in American education, as Black students were prepared to go on the firing line and confront trustees, presidents, administrators and faculty. They were determined to close down the universities (both Negro and white) in order to reform the educational process and change its direction, to introduce Black studies or Afro-American studies into the curriculum, to employ more Black faculty members and administrators in these universities and colleges, to obtain separate living accommodations, to increase proportionately the number of Black students entering these schools, and to make the substantive work more relevant to the needs of the Black community. This confrontation between Black students and white America (the second in the decade of the sixties) was both violent and nonviolent. It represented the logical extension of the earlier sit-in movements organized by colleges students, the voter registration drives in the South and the urban riots from Watts to Harlem. The confrontation began in the San Francisco Bay area and swept across the nation, for Black students had struck at the nerve center and perhaps the Achilles' heel of the American socialization process. The American educational system has been historically racist in design and political posture, for it is a mere reflection of the larger social order, and Black students didn't have to read the Kerner Commission Report in order to understand this objective reality.

During the 1968–70 academic years debates were held in academic circles about the validity of Black studies programs. Howard, Fisk, Atlanta, Yale, Harvard, and Berkeley among other universities held conferences, retreats and other "rap" sessions on the topics:

a) Is the special study of the Black experience intellectually valid?
b) Is it educationally responsible?
c) Is it socially constructive for both Black and whites?

These "traumatic" questions were of great concern to American educators. Arguments presented by establishment Negroes, progressive Blacks, conservative and liberal whites, as each faction projected its political (*sick* intellectual) interests. W. Arthur Lewis on one side of the fence, Vincent Harding on the other. Martin Kilsen, Jr., on one side, Nathan Hare on the other. And, as we might expect, establishment types like McGeorge Bundy, C. Vann Woodward and S. I. Hayakawa joined the debates. Today, we know the results of these discussions.

While the verbal battle raged and the confrontation became more intensive, the white liberal establishment sanctioned either Black studies or Afro-American studies and gave direction to these programs. History repeated itself, for Blacks found themselves in the same "trick bag" as in the student movement of the early sixties and the more recent struggle for community control of public schools. The liberal establishment persuaded the conservative elements on campus that it would be "cool" to allow and even encourage Afro-American studies provided that it reflected cultural pluralism or as long as its political teeth had been pulled out and provided that the programs were controlled by Negro scholars dependent for their legitimacy on the generosity of the white establishment. Consequently, Black students from Howard to Fisk and from Yale to U.C.L.A. were given Afro-American studies programs in their respective schools.

Because these programs were watered-down versions of the original demands, they were given second-class rating in the university status structure. As a result, the programs were not respected either by Black or white professors. Students were encouraged to take a few courses in Afro-American studies, or to design a joint major with Afro-American studies and another more practical discipline in the social or natural sciences in order to make certain that they could be gainfully employed upon graduation. The popular arguments were:

a) Where can one get a job with a B.A. degree in Afro-American studies?

b) What use will Black studies be to anyone after graduation?

No one respected the programs. Few persons took them seriously. They became curious enclaves in the academic world, designed to assuage militant overzealousness. The expectation surfaced that they would fade away as Black students awakened to the realities of "making it" in the American social order. Courses in Black studies were generally treated as "sop" courses, in which the noncompetitive Black student could obtain easy grades and get rid of his frustrations and neuroses. These programs were hastily designed, poorly organized, improperly staffed, and inadequately financed. In fact, many of them were doomed to failure even before the first lecture was given. The serious students who fought for these programs soon recognized that they were caught in a "squeeze-play" for they were getting white studies with Black labels.

The drama had unfolded. The students had been duped. Their frustrations had not been minimized. The educational process had not improved the qualitative dimensions of their lives. The political hopes had been betrayed once again, and many Black students became victims of narcotics which had been pumped into Black colleges, Black studies programs and Black communities. Seriousness went out of the window and some of our best young minds turned to drugs as a withdrawal vehicle.

It has now become necessary to examine this phase of the Black struggle very carefully and to suggest ways of correcting the political errors of the recent past. Malcolm X University, The Center for Black Education in Washington, D. C., Nairobi College and several newly formed independent institutions have already recognized the dilemma. The people involved in the establishment of these independent learning centers have been guided by a firm political commitment, a precise educational goal, and a consistent philosophical posture; and in so doing they have moved beyond the Afro-American studies mirage. However, since these centers cannot absorb the totality of the present Black student population, we must seriously offer direction and leadership to those Black students who are still involved in existing Black studies programs. We must provide Black students with a value system, a consistent and substantive life style, and a political direction.

This paper will attempt to make a few suggestions to Black students who are trapped in these programs in either Black or white institutions. The suggestions are based upon the experience of independent centers in the past year, especially the Center for Black Education in Washington, D. C.

The paper will project a Carter Woodson Institute of Black Education as a model for Black students, faculty and administrators, who are concerned about the future of our struggle for freedom and independence, to examine and criticize. The paper deals with the foundations on which the Institute could be established and offers direction consistent with our commitment to the future.

The Carter Woodson Institute of Black Education

The Carter Woodson Institute of Black Education will be dedicated to the educational preparation of African peoples, wherever they might be. It must recognize the need for preparing African peoples spiritually, philosophically and technically for the progressive leap forward which we must take in the years ahead. This preparation must be undertaken from a Pan-Africanist perspective, which defines all Black people as African people and negates their tribalization by geographical demarcations on the basis of colonialist spheres of influence. In the diaspora we are people of African origin and our legitimate concern must be our unification and liberation.

The challenge of our age demands the need for the Carter Woodson Institute of Black Education. The Institute will advise and prepare scientists, technocrats, engineers, analysts, teachers, administrators, artists and leaders whose continuing concern will be dedication to the enrichment of the flow of life in the Black community. All Black people involved in the Institute will be considered workers who will be expected to develop functional technical skills, a positive attitude to collective work and a disciplined posture to creative thought and analysis. Workers still demonstrate an unswerving commitment to the elimination of the critical problems of hunger, disease, poverty, illiteracy and drug addiction which affect Black people.

Basic to the tenets of the Institute is the realization that African peoples are faced with common crises, whether they are on the African continent, in the Western Hemisphere, or scattered throughout the world. Historically, all African people have experienced economic exploitation, political oppression and cultural alienation. Our future will depend upon our ability to harness our creative energies to clearly defined objectives as we attempt to eradicate the causes of our oppression and to build a new African social order. Our *goal* is the liberation of African peoples. Our *aim* is the unification of African peoples. Our *dedication* is the rebuilding of the African continent in the interest of political, economic and social goals constructive to the future of African peoples.

Consequently, the Carter Woodson Institute will move in a new direction and develop a new synthesis. It will not be concerned with teaching Afro-American History, Afro-American Literature, Urban Sociology, the Psychology of the Ghetto or Race Relations in Urban America. The Institute's main thrusts will be:

1) the harnessing of our human resources for self-determination and nation-building. Emphasis here will be on:

a) attitude
b) analysis
c) commitment
d) action
e) creativity
f) problem-solving
g) administration
h) leadership
i) technical and scientific training

2) The development and projection of courses that will highlight the similarities of the historical problems of African peoples, and the need for common solutions in the African world while taking into serious consideration the realities of implementation on a local level. For example, the Institute will examine the political significance of the artistic expressions of Black people in the decade of the sixties. Such a course will include artistic achievements both on the Continent and in the Americas. The course might be narrowly focused in time and in subject matter but its perspective will reflect the totality of the creative genius of the African world. In the same manner we might examine the organization and development of agricultural or housing

cooperatives in northeastern Brazil, Martinique, Mississippi or Mozambique. The Institute will design courses which will examine structural engineering problems in Black communities. It will develop courses in architecture consistent with the sweep of our cultural heritage, the rhythm of our life style and the economy of our resources. Although concrete problems will be analyzed in the classrooms, it will be recognized that conclusions have heuristic applicability in other parts of the African world.

The Institute will be concerned with developing the architects of independence and the engineers of growth and development in the nation-building process. We will encourage students to study the natural sciences, applied technology, public administration, social engineering, systems design, armaments technology, military science, agronomy, medicine and public health, trade and finance, transportation, delivery systems, geopolitics, communications, education, architecture and art, but they will be infused with a fixed responsibility to the future. Thus, the Institute will be actively engaged in redesigning curriculum for Black students and will concentrate upon the areas in which shortages of developmental skills presently exist.

When we use the term "nation-building," we are not referring to the traditional concept of a nation as defined by geographical demarcations, territorial rights, legal structures, a national flag, or a national anthem. We are not talking of nations like Luxembourg, Albania, Portugal or Taiwan (Formosa). We are referring to a broader concept of nation-building. We are talking of a union of African peoples, wherever they might be, based upon a recognition of the unique cultural heritage which defines our existence and provides our identity. This heritage has been shared by historical experiences of colonization, oppression and exploitation. We refer to the creative genius of Black peoples which has been nurtured by the retention of Africanisms as demonstrated in the rhythm of our life styles. This genius has been informed by our intuitive sensibilities. We must effectively energize this kinetic and spiritual bond in order to unify and liberate our people. When we speak of nation-building we are also referring to our determination to control, produce, develop and defend the resources on the land occupied by Black people and to utilize those resources for our own interest. In other words we must organize ourselves to protect that which we have created for our sustenance and enjoyment in order to enrich the flow of life. The Black nation and the Black community exist wherever Black people are living. We must build that nation and that community. The assertion of our identity, the expression of our creative genius, and the development and fullest utilization of our resources (natural, human and capital) must be harnessed to meet the objective of shaping and controlling our own destiny. This new focus on our destiny in the spirit of *Ujamaa* and brotherhood will provide the foundation for self-determination and liberation.

The Carter Woodson Institute will eliminate paternalistic attitudes born of guilt and condescension which historically separated Blacks in the university from those in the community. We will not encourage missionaries or "do-gooders" who wish to go out and help the community out of the generosity of a privileged station in life. We are the community and we have our duties and responsibilities to its progress. In addition, the Institute will not encourage urbanologists, whose sole purpose is to study and exploit Black communities for the sake of Research in order to become the GRAND PREFECTS of tomorrow. However, the Institute must not become a re-entry vehicle for Black students and professionals who wish to be involved superficially in a Black thing in order that they might appear to be cool, hip and relevant. The ultimate justification for participation in the Institute must be hard work and concrete results which relate to meeting the ongoing needs of the Black community. The Institute will not encourage a token, second-class, pacification Afro-American studies program which will allow Black students to groove and get "high" on Blackness while studying Afro-American History, Afro-American Literature, and other bogus courses in the social sciences. The Carter Woodson Institute must be fully aware that each system makes concessions that anticipate the next stage. Therefore, we will attempt to avoid the pitfalls of the political trap which has been neatly devised for us.

In the Institute, there will be no distinction between the community, the students, the administrators, the staff, and the faculty. We are all members of the Black community or community of African peoples; we face common problems and share common aspirations with regard to the ordering of the present and the future. We will not accept the aforementioned labels, i.e., students, faculty, staff, etc., because we recognize that the divisions inherent in such labels are counterproductive to our liberation. The unification and liberation of Black people demand workers and planners and not chiefs and chieftains. All participants in the Institute will be considered as workers, whose creative energies are geared to the progress of our people. Designated lines of responsibility will inculcate a correct attitude toward work, dedication to service and respect for human dignity. We shall respect each other as brothers and sisters and rewards will be based not upon rhetoric, but upon leadership, commitment, discipline, responsibility, tolerance, and productivity.

The ethic of work and the attitude of seriousness which will permeate the Institute's life will compel workers to concentrate on the acquisition of problem-solving abilities, the development of quantitative reasoning skills, the nurturing of our creative energies and artistic talents, and the heightening of our political sensitivities and analysis.

The Carter Woodson Institute will be concerned that its workers develop a consistent and substantive life style. We consider drug addiction one of the most dangerous problems confronting Black people today. Drugs have and continue to systematically destroy the creative potential and productivity of our people. In recent years, Black youth has been deliberately narcoticized in order to stymie the progress we have made in the identity revolution. Drug addiction has been used to immobilize our young people by placing them in a sedentary, illusory world. We must take the position that no one who is involved in drug addiction should be allowed to work in the Institute or participate in any of its activities. Any persons who are known to be under the influence of any type of narcotics on the Institute's premises will be suspended immediately. We must purge ourselves of this defect if we are serious about nation-building. The Institute will help in this expurgation by working closely with programs and with addicts themselves for the elimination of this social disease.

All workers in the Institute who are earning salaries will be required to give an agreed-upon percentage of their salary to a building fund, so that we can prepare to organize an independent school as quickly as possible. All workers in the Institute must teach and take classes. This will make everyone a teacher and a student in addition to other specific line responsibilities. Short reading periods of about one hour's duration will be scheduled every day and each worker will be required to participate in one of these reading periods unless he is out of town. The essentiality of this kind of mandatory discipline requires no explanation.

We shall avoid debates, arguments and schisms between "intellectuals" and "activists," "Greeks" and "non-Greeks," "revolutionaries" and "bourgeoisie," "revolutionary nationalists" and "cultural nationalists," "those who are ready (so-called)" and "those who are not ready," "those who are very Black" and "those who are not Black enough." Name-calling and ridiculous time-consuming arguments will not be encouraged in the Institute. We will be about WORK and all Black people associated with the Institute will be WORKERS.

Brothers will respect sisters in the Institute and sisters will respect brothers. Brothers will not mistreat and disrespect sisters, and sisters will not be engaged in deballing Black men. There will be mutual respect and responsibility, with Black men demonstrating masculine virtues of strength, self-assertiveness and self-confidence, while Black women will project their femininity consistent with the charm and beauty of African womanhood. In the Institute we must establish and maintain a hierarchy of values which every worker will respect and project. All visitors to the Institute will be cordially received. A distinct warmth will radiate from our welcome. African people must always be happy in our midst. All workers must develop a sense of service expressed in the way that we meet the needs of others. The Institute will not become a place where folks can "hang-out" and "do nothing." There will be no "shucking and jiving" around the Institute for we will be seriously engaged in work. However, we shall enjoy our work in the spirit of African communalism.

Every worker in the Institute will have the responsibility for conducting a project or carrying out an assignment in a project. Each project leader will have autonomy in the operation since that worker will be close to the concrete situation. Emphasis here will be on creative responsibility. The project leader will communicate his progress to the project coordinators who will be responsible for several ongoing projects. The coordinators will examine and determine priorities as they are consistent with the direction and philosophy of the Institute. There will be several governing boards designed around special administrative areas, i.e., Finance, Discipline, Review, Program Planning and Evaluation, Public Relations and Executive. These boards will be composed of workers, who are nominated to them on the basis of expertise, history of work, and demonstrated responsibility. There will be a Director of the Institute who will carry out administrative responsibilities and provide the directional leadership consistent with the philosophy of the Institute.

The Institute must quickly become a viable independent institution that will survive us. We must build models, systems and institutions that we can pass on to those who succeed us. We must work toward phasing ourselves out of a job, so that others may come along and bring creative freshness to that job situation. Leaders must not be involved in building islands of power that we monopolize for our own grandeur. In fact, we have no power in the traditional political sense, except the energy that we give off through our disciplined life as we become new men of the African world. We must not become addicted to the physical plant, to our pay checks, or to job security, for if these things were removed, we will become paralyzed and cop out. What we are working for and what we believe in must reflect our essential reality, for it is more important than where we work or for whom we work.

In the Institute we shall discourage petty arguments and jealousies about lines of responsibility or authority. We need authority and leadership, and this can only come from performance, conviction and expertise. Prestige at the Institute will come only from hard work and hard times. We must be prepared for this sacrifice. On the third

Saturday of every month the Institute will have its Village Meeting, in which we shall analyze our progress and plan our future. We shall make errors in the early stages of building and we shall have contradictions. This monthly review will enable us to build slowly and systematically. We must have revolutionary patience in the building process. We must always strive to effectively minimize our contradictions.

What will the Institute be qualified to do:

a) to provide philosophical, spiritual, political and technical direction to African workers
b) to engage in research and scholarship in African thought
c) to open up new areas of creative work for Black people
d) to design, plan and operate programs that will attempt to eradicate the social ills that destroy Black people
e) to strengthen our cultural heritage as we unleash our creative energies
f) to move workers to the level that we break out of the vicious circle of dependency in order that we can move to the fullest assertion of independence and self-reliance. We must cut the umbilical cord which ties us subjugatingly to our oppressor. We must assert our Africanity and construct the highway to nationhood.

The Carter Woodson Institute is determined to terminate the miseducation of Black people. We recognize that the immediate needs of Black people include food, medicine, clothing, housing, employment, education and the elimination of drug addiction from our communities. We shall design programs that will specifically deal with these basic issues and we shall devote our energies to tackling them. In addition, we shall attempt to eliminate our dependency complex as we strive for self-determination and liberation. Freedom and independence are difficult roads to travel but as we journey on the highways of the present, we shall achieve our goals of the future. A liberated people, a liberated man, a liberated mind remains a fundamental necessity. Workers at the Institute must undertake this challenge. We must build a nation of Black people that will provide a new synthesis to the family of nations.

Concluding Remarks

The writer has put these ideas into the marketplace with the hope that there will be critical responses. It is necessary always to deal with the relationship of life styles to a political direction. Unfortunately, as pragmatists, we are very prone to be concerned with programs rather than principles. We believe that if we introduce new programs and we patch up hostilities, then we can ease a critical situation. But history will show us that this leads to political disaster, a betrayal of ideals, unprincipled conduct and opportunism. Therefore, it is necessary to establish a firm political and moral basis for our actions and decisions. The model presented in this paper deals with fundamental guidelines for the redirection of emphasis on existing programs. The purpose of the model is an attempt to give workers a focus on their destiny as they are directed to nation-building skills consistent with a political vision of the unification and liberation of African peoples.

Social Services in Black Universities

by Acklyn Lynch

The Division of Social Sciences in Black colleges and universities must decide whether the traditional approach to the study of Social Sciences disciplines can meet the growing needs of Black peoples who face the historic challenge of nation-building. This traditional approach emphasizes a linear division between disciplines such as Sociology, Psychology, History, Economics and Government. In addition, the approach has provided a supportive function to the power elite and the captains of industry as Social Science educators justify the ordering of American society based on a caste/class system. Their writings and lectures have given credence and legitimacy to the capitalist superstructure and the ethic of individualism and materialism.

For decades Black colleges and universities have been influenced by this political direction, since they have always been financially, spiritually and intellectually dependent on the generosity of affluent philanthropists, foundations or state and federal funds. Consequently, the Social Science Divisions in these institutions of higher learning have been dominated by white professors, and Black students are trained to give credence to a body of knowledge that exploits and manipulates Black people. Black students are not prepared to break out of the vicious circle of dependency nor can they free themselves up for the discovery of social truths, in order that they might become the architects of a new social order.

It has also been recognized that the Social Science graduates from Black universities and colleges have not be able to deal directly with the problems affecting Black peoples, for the disciplines to which they are exposed have very little relevance to the Black community. The graduates have few opportunities to analyze and examine critically the problems of Black peoples from a Pan-Africanist and international perspective. Rather they have been locked into a parochial approach to problem-solving, and generally they are only involved in describing social phenomena. They are never directed toward new forms and new systems that are essential in providing a philosophical basis for

Black life. Finally, they are neither afforded the opportunity to develop their creative potential nor the correct political stance which the Black scholar must adopt as he attempts to build an independent Black community.

In the decade of the seventies, it has therefore become necessary to question the future of the Division of Social Sciences based on traditional departmental arrangements. I would like to recommend for serious consideration a School of Social Engineering which will fuse the theoretical, applied and planning aspects of human engineering. Emphasis will be placed on people and communities with the students being exposed to a thorough understanding of the cultural forces and the political objectives of the Black communities which they will eventually serve. Students entering this program will receive a Bachelor of Science degree in Social Engineering, after completing a body of work designed in four areas, viz., Social Thought, Applied Sciences, Human Engineering and Systems Design. The student will concentrate on one major system. He will know how to design, plan and administer a system consistent with the needs of his community and with nation-building. The student will also have some appreciation for the relationship of the system of his major concentration with that of other systems.

The School of Social Engineering will be divided into four institutes and students will take courses in each of the four institute concentrations:

THE INSTITUTE OF SOCIAL THOUGHT

- Political philosophy
- Moral philosophy
- Economic theory
- Legal thought
- History

THE INSTITUTE OF APPLIED SCIENCES

- Mathematics
- Statistics
- Computer Science and Technology
- Applied Economics
- Accounting
- Budgeting, Forecasting and Cost Analysis
- Management
- Public Administration
- Psychological Aspects of Learning Process
- Applied Sociology
- Applied Psychology
- Market Analysis
- Political Behavior (Behaviorial Analysis)

THE INSTITUTE OF HUMAN ENGINEERING

Culture and Consciousness
Artistic Achievements of African Peoples
Art and Politics
Sociology of Religion
Social Organization
Leadership
Personnel and Public Relations
Psychology of Oppression
Cooperatives
Learning Incentives, Motivation
Love, Power and Justice
Family Relations
Family Institution
Child Development
Communicative Skills
Languages
Education for Nation-building
Environmental Science
Art in Architecture

THE INSTITUTE OF SYSTEMS DESIGN

Education
Health and Medicine
Communications—Telephone, Telegraph, Radio, Newspapers, TV, etc.
Visual Arts—Fine Arts, Museums, etc.
Postal
Housing—Architecture, Environmental Science
Energy—Electrification, Power, Nuclear
Transportation—Roads, land bridges, railway, bus, freight, marine, air freight, airports
Port Authority—Harbors, wharfs, docks
Irrigation
Food
Water—marine, rivers, ports, streams, dams
Land development—agricultural
National service—military systems
Corrective Institutions
Fire brigade systems
Public administration and law
Building Political Structures
a) local
b) regional
c) international

Community Organization
Banking Systems
Distribution, Retailing, Merchandising
Manpower Development (Labor)
Population Training and Skills

Concern will be for preparing students who will have the ability to design and operate systems consistent with the needs of their community. Students will be involved in theoretical and practical approaches to problem-solving. They will develop analytical skills which are fundamental in designing and planning, but they will also strengthen their intuitive sensibilities, so that they might appreciate the human aspects of growth and development.

Students must take courses in the four core areas with major emphasis in one of the system areas. Each student will present a major paper in his senior year as one condition for graduation. This paper will be presented to a Board of Conveners, equally composed of students, faculty, staff and community people, all of whom will determine whether the design project is consistent with and useful to the future needs of the community.

In the School of Social Engineering, there will be organized several committees comprised of students, staff, faculty and community people who will be responsible for designing and developing a work project. This work project must be completed within one year and community people will be trained to carry on its operation. These work projects might involve the building of a health center, the organizing of laundry services on a cooperative basis, organizing a library, operating an independent school, the establishing of a museum, a shopping center, a radio station, etc. Every year there should be about six on-going projects in the school to which students, faculty, staff and community people will be assigned. Progress reports on these projects must be made to the communities involved at announced dates.

The School of Social Engineering will be expected to publish a weekly newsletter and a quarterly journal. The newsletter will inform the community of events, projects, studies, lectures, seminars and other operational matters of the school. The journal will present scholarly articles in areas of pertinent research. The journal will explore new frontiers of social thought as it attempts to deal with the serious analysis which Black people must conduct in order to come to grips with independence and nationhood. The journal will encourage new areas of research and creative thought as Black people examine critically their historical problems. Both the newsletter and the journal will be published at minimum cost, and will educate the community to its progress.

The School of Social Engineering will carry out active recruitment in Black communities and especially in area schools. This recruitment program will be organized to create an interest in Social Engineering as distinct from traditional Social Science disciplines. It will emphasize the role of planners, administrators and of nation-builders who will complement the work of the scientist and the technocrat. The systems manager will be able to translate in human terms the impact of new scientific breakthroughs and he will also be able to establish and recommend priorities in the building process. The excitement of the systems manager and the manner in which he can optimize his creative potential will be highlighted in the interviewing stage. At all times, recruiters will point up the exploratory aspects of the school's work and the psychic benefits gained from developing one's fullest creative potential. Creativity involves openness to experience. Concern in the program will always be for optimum use of available resources and maximum use of time.

The School's educational objective will be shaping the moral character of the student systems manager with regard to commitment and integrity. The student's attitude will be crucial in the development of his personality. Here, emphasis will be on the student's attitude to other people, to his work, to discipline, tolerance, responsibility and productivity. These character traits will be constantly encouraged and fostered. Our concern will be to eliminate the hustler's mentality which encourages exploitation and corruption of all parties involved.

The School will develop a cooperative ethic that will be demonstrated in the day-to-day activities of administrators, faculty, staff, students and visitors. We should be courteous to each other and there should be developed a concept of service to the community with respect for individual choice. Disputes will be settled and arbitrated by an elected school council comprised equally of students, staff, faculty, and community people.

The School will always be concerned with the developing of technical skills which are necessary for nation-building and the enrichment of community life. Each graduating student should master the technological aspects of a system so that he could design, administer and manage the system of his choice, while possessing a thorough knowledge of its relationship to other systems. Classes should be held in the community or on project sites in addition to the classroom. Guest speakers should be invited to speak in an organized schedule on areas of pertinent consideration.

The School must provide an example for others by its commitment to the future, its involvement in the present, and its careful analysis of the past. The School should be willing to challenge and promote new ideas. It should take a leadership position in the community, the city and the nation. It should take a stand on issues as they pertain to the educational process, and its position should be known publically to the community. The School should be activist oriented and leadership oriented. It should produce courageous and disciplined leaders with independent, creative ideas, open minds and a collective consciousness.

African Free School

by Mama Furaha

For the past two and a half years I have been teaching children from ages four to fourteen in African Free School, Newark, New Jersey.

African Free School was founded three years ago as an answer to the realization that there is a *need* for Black children to be taught a cultural foundation, i.e., a way of life.

In order for our children to continue to build and make the Black nation eternal, they must be equipped with the knowledge and understanding of:

Customs and Concepts
History
Swahili
Art
Reading
Math
Health

these subjects of the African Free School which are explained more in depth in the attached Methodology of Instruction and sample Lesson Plan.

Methodology of Instruction

History; geography; reading, including phonetics and speech; language arts, including penmanship, literature, spelling, and grammatical construction, e.g., sentence structure, paragraph composition; will be taught concurrently using history as the actual curriculum subject.

History text will be mimeographed pages compiled periodically from both current events and recorded history. European history will be taught as it relates to African history. Literature will be introduced as a part of history; for example, Langston Hughes will be taught as a literary figure as well as an historical image.

Spelling lessons will be taken from the daily texts. Reading, writing and grammatical construction will be taught not by fundamental rules but by actual practice. Oral instruction and student response will be emphasized because people write the way they talk.

Swahili will be taught as a second language, but in relationship to English; while building their English vocabulary, the children will be increasing their Swahili as well.

Hieroglyphics, which are parts of the first language, will be introduced in art class as a third language. While learning art forms, which are actually the expression of the feeling of a people, a language will be learned as well. This concept again relates to history.

Science, health and safety will be taught in physical education class through a program we have developed called *Simba Wachanga* (Young Lions). The children will exercise as well as learn the effects of different foods on the person, that is mentally, and spiritually, as well as physically. Speech is incorporated in this learning situation in that students will be giving oral recitations on matters pertaining to nutrition and science.

The prime method of teaching in African Free School is the teaching of subjects in unison, not as separate, individual subject matter. Students learn the relationship of each subject to another and how the subjects are relevant in their lives.

Lesson Plan

I. History
 A. Reference—Afro-American History Highlight—Henry E. Dabbs
 B. Subject—Rosa Parks
  1. Who
   a. biography
   b. experiences relevant to actual event
  2. What
   description of event
  3. When
   a. date & historical contexts
   b. related events in history
  4. Where & Why
   a. place
   b. relationship of this event to total outlook of U.S.A.
 C. Summary
  1. Effect on both Black & white people of this event
  2. Visual Aids
   a. photos of Black people in Southern states—working
   b. photos of white people in Southern states
II. Geography
 A. Subject—Montgomery, Alabama

1. location—on map to rest of U.S.A.
2. climate
3. crops
4. economics

B. Visual Aids—Maps

III. Reading & Phonetics

A. Text—paragraphs taken from history lesson.
(Selection will depend on age level of children.)

B. Phonetics taught by rhymes made from history lesson.

C. Example
A Black woman who was quite a human.
Refused to sit in the back of the bus
and caused quite a big fuss.

IV. Speech

A. Subject—history lesson

B. Daily recitation

V. Penmanship—students will write theme on what they would have done if they had been Rosa Parks

VI. Spelling—list will be compiled from lesson

A. Example

1. Black
2. woman
3. Rosa
4. Parks
5. bus
6. ride
7. sit
8. the
9. back
10. tired

VII. Grammatical Construction—Sentences and paragraphs made from spelling words.

VIII. Literature

A. Subject—Margaret Walker

B. Text—poems & writings
explanation of her works in terms of historical reference.

IX. Physical Education

A. Exercise

B. Subject—Nutrition

1. example; light breakfast
   a. juice
   b. toast
   c. piece of fruit
2. Breakfast effect on person
   a. mentally—psychological effects of food consumption
   b. physically—chemical analysis

X. Science

A. Subject—fruit bacteria

B. How fruit carries germs

C. Oral recitations on nutrition & science and their relevance to the children's development

XI. Swahili

A. Subject - Rosa Parks

B. Vocabulary

1. *Weusi* (Black)
2. *Mwanamke* (Woman)
3. *Ye Ye Nani* (Her Name)
4. *Waridi* (Rose)
5. *Ua* (Flower)
6. *Sisi* (Us)
7. *Nguzo Saba* (Seven Principles)

Aims and Objectives of the Black Education Program: A Position Paper

by Staff, Center for Black Education

The necessity for a Black Education Program and its eventual recognition as THE educational process for Black People has aptly been stated by one of our Black giants of the twentieth century, Dr. Du Bois.

> After the Egyptian and Indian, the Greek and Roman, the Teuton and Mongolian, the Negro is a sort of seventh son, born with a veil, and gifted with second-sight in this American World—a world which yields him no true self-consciousness, but only lets him see himself through the revelation of the other world. It is a peculiar sensation: this double consciousness, this sense of always looking at one's self through the eyes of others, of measuring one's soul by the tape of a world that looks on in amused contempt and pity. One even feels his twoness—an American, Negro; two souls, two thoughts, two unreconciled strivings, two warring ideals in one dark body, whose dogged strength alone keeps it from being torn asunder.

Black education must take these forces into consideration and seek to make these forces reality. These forces are revolution and nation-building. Education which does not seek to achieve these goals is irrelevant to Black people. Although these forces fuse, they also have separate characteristics. Revolution is the process of struggle toward the objective: nation. Revolution must give definition to the nation. Revolution must call for and act to end white supremacy, colonialism, and oppression embodied in Western ideas and individuals which affect and infect the existence of Black people. The process of nationhood must conceptualize and structure the projections and possibilities of future Black existence. The nation must be defined in terms of human materials and historical-cultural resources of the people.

The Black Education Program has as its purpose the sustenance and revitalization of these Black values, which also include undying love for Black people, the recognition that all Black people are Africans, that the spirit of *Ujamaa*—loving cooperation—is the natural spirit of Black people and that security, respect and equality shall be the foundation of Black life.

The Black Education Program also proposes to encourage Black people to understand the disciplines of science, mathematics, and other technical areas, as it applies to a liberated Black existence. It will seek to provide an arena for the perfection of those skills necessary for the maintenance of a Black Nation. No nation can be built on love alone and our people must thoroughly understand that the study of, and involvement in, science is a cornerstone to our eventual liberation. We must *reclaim* our facility in mathematics and science which were, in fact, originally creations of our people.

The functions of education are twofold: one, to sustain the culture of a nation; and two, to develop skills which will satisfy the needs of the nation.

The Black Education Program will take a total rather than a fragmented approach to the education of Black people. This necessarily means constant and thorough involvement of all levels in the Black community, both locally and worldwide: Afro-American (locally) or in a Pan-African (worldwide) context.

The Black Education Program realizes that the necessity of control is vital to every level of Black *endeavor*. There is no substitute for Black control in the movement of Black people toward liberation.

In essence, we will, through Black Education, define for ourselves the relationship between our history as a people and our present situation, so that we may better understand how we must create our future.

The main emphasis of the Black Education Program will have to be toward liberation of Black people. As Junebug Jabbo Jones says, "Those who are oppressed cannot look to those who oppress them, in this case the American Nation, to deal in any way with the nature of their oppression."* Since education should serve to expand the minds and spheres of action of the people involved in it, Black Education must prepare Black people for the most complete self-expression which must, in fact, be liberation and self-determination.

The question of liberation, however, cannot be dealt with concretely until the people seeking it are prepared to effectively separate themselves—in terms of attitude, basic social structure, and technology—from the oppressive and draining forces which surround and permeate them. The Black Education Program must then be dedicated to preparing Black people for the ultimate state of separation which must exist in order to assure liberation and maintain it—once it has been gained.

*Pool Hall Address, In It, Mississippi, 1961, "Keep Your Pool Stick Chalked."

Black Education will take the position that the logical extension of separation must be the construction of a durable and productive nation—a nation which must survive the dying spirit of a society which has both encased and dispersed its people, its energies, and its potential for centuries. Nation-building, then, must be the end-product of Black Education and the beginning of a lasting and meaningful Black peoplehood. Whether that nation is to be a collection of enclaves or a geographical location, existing within or without the United States, is a question we must ultimately answer as a people. Yet, the Black Education Program recognizes the necessity for Black people to be prepared to face and decide that question in the foreseeable future.

Undying Love Among Black People

The Black Education Program shall seek to develop a relationship among Black people that manifests itself as service to the Black community. The Western selfish individual concept of "me first" must be superseded for an African cooperative family concept of *Ujamaa.* Blackness must change its emphasis from that which is seen, such as Afros and dashikis, to that which is necessary, such as living and working with Black people to achieve our goal of liberation.

Those Black persons who are trained for various professions must come to see themselves as members of a family whose interest supersedes their own.

A Black doctor would distinguish himself from his white counterpart by working in the Black community that most desperately needed his talents. The Black doctor would seek *only to make a living* and not accumulate great amounts of wealth, and in turn the Black community would support him, and he would serve that Black community.

A Black doctor would also devote himself to encouraging Black youth to become interested in medicine and serving the Black community. The Black community in return would pay for the education and training of the doctors who would come back to serve them. The same model would apply to all technical and professional areas—architecture, engineering, food processing, biology, chemistry, etc.

We Are Africans All

"We are an African people whether we live on the continent of Africa or in the outlying areas of the American continent, Europe, the West Indies, etc." (Junebug Jabbo Jones, Buttermilk Bottom Address, Atlanta, Georgia, 1957)

It is essential that Black Education provide a setting—both physical and emotional—for the strengthening of current vaguely perceived ties between Black people throughout the world. This will mean the institution of methods of communication and vehicles of exchange which will serve to bring together the information and talents of all Black people everywhere. Methods of communication could include use of independent media to project an accurate image of various sectors of Black life and the interrelation of those sectors. Plays, documentaries, films, and literature will be televised and otherwise broadcast with a central theme of "We are Africans all"—emphasizing the common need for and active participation in the movement toward liberation.

Various kinds of exchange programs between African, Caribbean and North and South American Blacks will lead to a knowledge of —and, more importantly—an empathy political, cultural and economic, with Black People in those countries.

The Black Education Program will include in its activities a series of group-travel plans through which students will be able to visit, work and learn in various areas of this country—Black cooperatives in the South, for example—and the rest of the Black world—e.g., the Caribbean, Africa and Latin America.

In this way, real contact will be established and maintained between Black people in countries around the world and Black people in America. For participants in the Black Education Program, the physical exposure to other Black populations will make the study of Black people much more concrete, and will reinforce the importance of techniques and principles used in struggles of liberation all over the world.

Many aspects of Black culture have been lost or transformed through time. One of these very important aspects which can be seen among Black people is in our homeland. We can never achieve liberation and nationhood for ourselves as a people until we adopt *Ujamaa* as a guiding force in our daily lives.

We must live and cooperate with our brothers in our daily activities if we ever are to build a nation. No individual by his personal merits will ever accomplish the goal of Black liberation. This goal can only be achieved by a concerted, cooperative, and enduring struggle by our people.

Security, Respect and Equality

Meaningful education for Black people must insure security; for without security, no other achievements can have meaning. Black security must mean security from hunger, sickness, and shelterlessness. Black security also includes a psychological well-being. As a family, we must show love to all family members and thereby express a love which brings security.

Respect represents a basic principle which, through the Black Education Program, must be strengthened as a key aspect of the Black Nation. The showing of respect for all people also increases the dignity and security of the nation.

The Black Education Program will stress the equality of all brothers and sisters realizing that the strength of the Nation depends on mutual love, respect and dignity.

Technical Skills

There are certain technical areas vital to the building of a Black Nation which will be included in the Black Education Curriculum. Biology, Chemistry, Engineering, Mathematics and Architecture will all be taught with the goal of providing Black people with the resources necessary to structure, improve, and maintain a self-sufficient Nation.

Community

Historically, the official instrument of education has been kept separate from the lives of the people in the community it is supposed to serve. The alienation of brothers on the block from any kind of isolated approach to education is a depressing reminder of this separation. The Black Education Program will move toward expressing itself in terms of the total Black community, rather than limiting its activities to the students who are taking academic part in its construction and development. This will mean the institution of a carefully designed segment of the Program dealing specifically with such areas as participation by students and staff in projects being carried on by Black schools, political organizations, businesses, churches, etc. The community, then will become a crucial part of the Black Education Program, and the Program will become equally important to the lives of the people in the community.

Control

The Black Education Program recognizes that control is a critical issue within the Black Education Program as well as the community as a whole. The control of the Black Education Program must be kept in the hands of Black people. Decisions on whether any white teacher should teach a Black Education course and other such matters are tactical questions which would be decided by the Black Education Committee, but the issue of control of the Black Education Committee is substantive, therefore must be in Black people's hands.

The fallacy of coalition has been a hard-learned lesson for Black people. The necessity for having both representatives who are responsible to the Black community in addition to having an independent source of power has become very clear. The Black Education Program accepts the principles of control as fundamental to the building of a Black Nation and the self-respect of a people.

The Black Education Program will, in essence, be at once a cultural and educational vehicle for creating awareness, confidence and determination in Black people in order to achieve liberation, self-sufficiency and Nationhood. It will provide the interaction and cooperation necessary for an atmosphere of productivity and unity which must exist in order to insure the meaningful and lasting bringing together of brothers whose Blackness will help define and support the creation of a new world.

The specifics of a Black Education Program are implied in our general proposal. Further refinement, i.e., courses and curriculum must, and will, be determined by those instructors who will teach in the Black Education Program.

The Independent Black Institution

The California Association for Afro-American Education, Nairobi College

The California Association for Afro-American Education and Nairobi College jointly sponsored a *Workshop on the Independent Black Institution* on August 17–19, 1970, in East Palo Alto, California. The purposes of the workshop were: (1) to review and analyze developing models for the Independent Black Institution, (2) to establish a viable communications link among Independent Black Institutions, and (3) to develop a conceptual plan for implementation of a nationwide system of Independent Black Institutions. The workshop agenda included the following working sessions: *Financing the IBI, Defining the IBI, Black Priorities in Education, The National System of IBI's, Curriculum* (Pre-school through Higher Education), *The Black Student, Teacher, Counselor and Administrator,* and *Building a Communications/National Network.* In accordance with the wishes of conference participants, the workshops on Financing of the IBI and The National System of IBI's were combined. Further, participants preferred to spend an entire day in plenary session discussing The New African Man/Values—Pan-Africanism and, thus, the latter three working sessions mentioned above were not convened.

Fifty persons representing the following institutions attended the workshop: Uhuru Sasa School (Brooklyn, New York), CCED School (Roxbury, Massachusetts), Martin Luther King On-Campus School (Syracuse, New York), Malcolm X Liberation University (Durham, North Carolina), Foundation for Community Development (Durham, North Carolina), Malcolm X School (San Francisco, California), Martin Luther King School (San Francisco, California), Academy for Black and Latin Education (Harlem, New York), Center for Black Education (Washington, D.C.), Community Institute (Pittsburgh, Pennsylvania), Black Planning Institute (Harlem, New York), California College for Arts and Crafts (Oakland, California), Nairobi College, Nairobi High School, and Nairobi Day School. Additionally, several persons attended who were not directly involved in the development of an Independent Institution.

The workshop was convened with a powerful and inspiring keynote address by Brother James Lee, Operations Office, Malcolm X Liberation University. Following the keynote address, participants were involved in a plenary session entitled *A Look at Selected IBI's*. The purpose of this session was to provide an in-depth review of an elementary, secondary and higher education institution, particularly in relation to its development, governance, staffing, curriculum, and major successes and failures. Throughout the next three days, indicated workshops were convened and charged with responsibility for developing a conceptual framework and/or plan of action in each area of concern. The workshop concluded with a day-long working session moderated by Brother St. Claire Drake, Director of Black Studies, Stanford University. Thus, following two days of creative thinking, pointed discussion, and intensive *work*, participants had the rare opportunity to interact with Brother Drake, one who has made the resolution of international Black problems his life's work. It is likely that the day-long session with Brother Drake was the most interesting, informative, and beneficial of all the working sessions.

The Keynote Address, Brother James Lee, Operations Officer, Malcolm X Liberation University, Durham, North Carolina

Although it is impossible to recapture the inspirational message delivered by Brother James Lee, following are summary highlights of his address:

> The concept of the Independent Black Institution can only be viewed as a revolutionary concept. Among its implications are the following: (1) recognition of what the educational process is or should be, a process which prepares people to fit into a society and serve that society, particularly in relation to the survival of the society and the individual; (2) recognition of the contemporary social, political, economic, and educational context in which Black Americans must function and recognition that racism is a pervasive phenomenon within and throughout American social institutions; (3) recognition that the Black American is functionally ignorant, that is, he is either "overeducated" (educated to serve a society too technically advanced for the needs of our people) or "miseducated" (not educated for community development); (4) recognition that poverty and social evils do not come about because of laziness, unemployment, and poor education, but rather result from an economic system designed to maintain poverty; (5) recognition that traditional solutions to the "Black Problem" (e.g., integration) have not been functionally appropriate; (6) recognition that the *concept of independence* implies the building of an independent society through the development of independent social institutions—which by necessity involves the acquisi-

tion of land and power through struggle, revolution, and, if necessary, war.

Developing solutions to the problems of African peoples requires a broader analysis of our history and our contemporary social context. Such study should recognize that culture, economics, and politics are *inseparable,* that the political, economic, and cultural motifs of the United States are European, and that these European motifs are inseparable. Throughout history, European educational systems have advocated white supremacy/white racism, justified social institutions and practices on the basis of this cultural perspective, and supported a competition model (survival of the fittest) undergirded with a philosophy of exploitation as a law of nature. One outgrowth has been the creation of an industrial complex dependent upon the exploitation of Africa, Asia, and Latin America for its survival, that is, upon exploitation of the Third World. Yet, we are living in an era of liberation and nationalism, and Black people throughout the world are struggling to control their land and its resources. Consequently, the competitive, exploitative model of the European is in conflict with the liberation/nationalistic mold of African peoples. Africa and Europe are on a collision course and, if we are Africans, we too are on a collision course.

White/European nationalism is now sweeping the world and Billy Graham, among others, is its foremost evangelist. As the imminent confrontation between Europe and Africa burgeons, African peoples in the United States *will be identified by White America* as African, regardless of whether or not we choose to do so ourselves—witness the Japanese-*American* experience during World War II. The question, then, becomes one of survival since, like it or not, the American European will define and treat us as African people to the extent that Africa is able to thwart the raping and plundering of its resources. African people in the United States must therefore develop institutions which operate from the "cradle to the grave" and which are based upon the *survival* needs of our people.

We must be wary of viewing the problem of Black people from a class context rather than a racist one because, among other reasons, racism has no ideological boundaries. Yes, we are an African people and thus must be about the business of the survival of African peoples throughout the world. We must forever remain cognizant of the Ashanti proverb which states,"I am because we are and since we are therefore I am."

If we are ready to realistically assess our political position in the world, if we are prepared to broaden our perspectives beyond the borders of our own little communities, if we are prepared to deal with the needs of our people from the cultural to the military and to achieve a balance based on *need,* not ease of implementation, then and only then are we prepared to come and sit together to talk about the Independent Black Institution.

It should be clear that Brother Lee set a mood and tone which prevailed throughout the remaining days of the workshop.

Following are summary minutes for each working session which was convened at the workshop.

Defining the IBI

This workshop developed a philosophical framework for functional definition of the Independent Black Institution. Participants identified and delineated the minimum characteristics of the prototype IBI in reference to the following topics: ideology, definition (minimum characteristics for classification within the system of IBI's), purpose, objectives, organizational structure, research, and relationship to traditional Black and white educational institutions.

The ideology of the Independent Black Institution must include but is not necessarily limited to six fundamental concepts: (1) the concept of *communalism*, (2) the concept of *decolonization,* (3) the concept of the *African Personality,* (4) the concept of *humanism,* (5) the concept of *harmony* between the individual and his environment, (6) the concept of *nation-building. Communalism* represents the antithesis of competitive individualism, that is, a set of human relationships based upon cooperativeness, cohesiveness, and concern for African peoples transcending self. *Decolonization* emphasizes the acquisition of ownership and control by African people of the political, economic, social, and educational institutions which are rightfully their own. Though as yet fully undefined, the *African Personality* as embodied in the New African Man is representative of a set of attitudes, values, and behaviors which are necessary for the development, maintenance, and perpetuation of African peoples throughout the world. The concept of the African Personality includes but is not limited to respect for ancestors and the African heritage, identification with Africa and African people throughout the world, concern for the unification of all African people, positive self-identification, and faith and trust in Black people. *Humanism* is in essence an attitudinal and behavioral perspective which stresses *distinctively* human rather than material and profit concerns. *Harmony* between the individual and his environment suggests a functional relationship between man and his natural surroundings and stresses functional congruency between man and his environment. Nation-building is an evolutionary process involving the utilization of human and material resources for community development, service, ownership, and control—survival. These six concepts, though not mutually exclusive nor exhaustive, are deemed to fulfill the minimum requirements for a sound conceptual framework of the Independent Black Institution.

Participants defined minimum institutional characteristics for classification within the system of IBI's to be:

1) *Governance*—Black people must be in exclusive control of institutional decision-making, particularly in the areas of policy control, curriculum, staffing, and budget—except when it is deemed beneficial to involve other Third World people in governing processes; composition of the community people at *all* educational levels.

2) *Finance*—Financial resources may be obtained from any source (the Black community, government, foundations, philanthropists, etc.) but such resources must be received on terms *defined by the institution.* Under no circumstances must an institution compromise its principles to obtain financial support. Further, institutions must place primary emphasis upon developing financial resources from the Black community-at-large.

3) *Ideology*—The institution must subscribe to the ideology delineated above.

4) *Staff*—All staff are required to be of African heritage unless deemed beneficial to utilize other Third World students.

5) *The Black Community*—Primary emphasis in all institutional activity should be directed toward serving the needs of the Black community unless deemed beneficial to assist other Third World communities.

These five components define the minimum characteristics of the prototype IBI and serve as the basis for classification of institutions within the system of Independent Black Institutions.

The overall purpose of the Independent Black Institution is to control the *development* of the mind and consciousness of the Black people, that is, to control the socialization process through directing and channeling thought patterns. Its primary function is to educate the pure, and to de-educate the contaminated, those who have been "overeducated" or "miseducated" as a consequence of enrolling in traditional institutions. The primary objectives of the IBI include but are not limited to the following: (1) to serve the needs of African people throughout the world with primary attention given to Africans residing within the geographical boundaries of the United States; (2) to stop the process of cultural, physical, economic, political, and social genocide (survival); (3) to teach the history and culture of African people, to develop an awareness of the contemporary political, social, and economic context in which African peoples live, and to train for nation-building and community development, organization, service, ownership, and control; (4) to create a new type of individual who is able to build new social institutions through the application of analytical and practical skills; (5) to offer new inducement for attaining the "good life" as determined by the operational definition of the African Personality.

After reviewing and analyzing various organizational models, participants offered the following suggestions regarding organizational structuring of the IBI. The organizational structure should be one which is self-determining with task force units rather than bureaucratic hierarchal structures. To the extent possible, it should provide for team decision-making based upon a broad communal-family concept. The organizational structure should provide for broad representation of students, staff, and community people throughout its governing processes and provide for broad distribution of power among these groups. There should be a system of institutional checks and balances based upon harmony rather than conflict and designed to develop trust among the various constituencies, all of whom *must* endorse the ideology of the institution. Finally, the organizational structure should provide for multiple role functions for each person involved in whatever capacity in the institution.

Participants defined the role and responsibility of the IBI in the area of research to be practical as well as analytical. Research must be utilized to develop curriculum and supporting materials (texts, maps, bibliographies, etc.). It must be used for internal program review and evaluation. Research must be directed toward the obtaining of data to increase knowledge of and enhance understanding of our own Black communities and must serve to counter fallacious findings prevalent throughout research conducted by white researchers.

Since the overwhelming majority of Black students are presently enrolled in traditional institutions, the Independent Black Institution has a definite responsibility to facilitate, to the extent possible, change in traditional institutions. Primary and foremost emphasis must be given to institutions (public and higher) presently enrolling large numbers of Black students. The IBI must assume responsibility for organizing the Black community to "move on" existing schools and personnel serving large numbers of Black students. The IBI also has some responsibility for organizing student leadership in traditional institutions so that Black students begin to focus efforts upon community development and nation-building rather than upon "making white institutions over in their own image." Further, IBI staff should serve as consultants to traditional institutions but *only* with financial compensation and only when such compensation is to be received by the IBI.

Following this report is a checklist whereby institutions can evaluate the extent to which they meet requirements for classification within the system of IBI's. Each recipient of this report is asked to complete this checklist, and, if necessary, to get on his job in developing an institution which meets these requirements.

The National System of IBI's

This workshop focused upon one of the most perplexing and critical (yet heretofore least dealt with) areas, that of developing a coordinated thrust in producing sound, viable educational institutions and programs for the Black community. Primary attention was given to the development of a plan of action for structuring a loose federation of IBI's throughout the country. This plan of action encompasses a set of activities to be completed during the next year and includes two regional meetings, a national meeting, and development of plans for establishing a national coordinating body with a supporting central office and staff. The outcome of these planning activities will hopefully be a finite, though flexible, series of proposals for structuring a loose federation of IBI's and for establishing a national coordinating body with its central office.

In early December, two regional meetings will be held for purposes of developing concrete plans for regional and national coordination of existing IBI's. Institutions west of Kansas City, Kansas, will attend a meeting hosted by Nairobi College; institutions east of Kansas City (includes Kansas City) will attend a meeting hosted by Uhuru Sasa School. Host institutions for the regional meetings are responsible for disseminating information, establishing a specific meeting date in December, preparing an agenda, and assuming general responsibility for coordination of meetings. Additional information can be obtained from either Robert Hoover, President, Nairobi College, 1627 Bay Road, East Palo Alto, California, or Yusef Iman, Uhuru Sasa School, 10 Claver Place, Brooklyn, New York. Each IBI is expected to send at least one representative to a regional meeting.

The purposes of the regional meetings are, among other things, to develop concrete plans for establishing a regional organization of IBI's and a loose national federation, to review and evaluate institutional progress in terms of meeting requirements for classification within the system of IBI's, and to develop proposed agenda topics for the national meeting.

In early February, Uhuru Sasa School will host the second national meeting of IBI's. The purposes of the national meeting are to finalize plans for establishment of a national coordinating body and national federation, to develop a set of operational guidelines for the federation, to specify the broad functions and responsibilities of the coordinating body, and to establish a central coordinating office. Presently, proposed functions for the federation and coordinating body include the implementation of pilot programs, the development of a communiversity, the establishment of guidelines for expanding the number of IBI's at each educational level, the identification of a cadre of human resources to assist and support the IBI federation, the development of guidelines for accreditation of IBI's, the determination of the location of the central office (it was proposed, for example, that the central office rotate annually to different institutions), and the coordination and maintenance of a communications network for IBI's.

Each IBI is asked to assist the host institution for the national meeting (Uhuru Sasa School) by forwarding the addresses of IBI's not in attendance at the Nairobi Workshop. Ths host institution will disseminate an interim report on the regional meetings plus materials about any single IBI not greater than three pages in length to all Independent Black Insitutions.

Financing the IBI

This workshop developed a plan of action for obtaining continuing financial support for IBI's. Primary attention was directed toward the establishment of a National Black Education Foundation with central responsibility for fund-raising and receiving and disbursing funds, funds which would be used to supplement financial resources obtained through institutional fund-raising efforts.

The workshop proposed a "*working model for policy structure*" for the National Black Education Foundation. The IBI federation (see the National System of IBI's) would consist of all identified IBI's, and its *voting* membership would include one representative from each IBI. The Foundation Board would be directly responsible to the IBI federation, its membership elected by and from the voting membership of the federation. The three standing committees of the foundation would be the Fund-Raising Committee, the Program Committee, and the Disbursement Committee, each responsible to the Foundation Director, a full-time person with supporting staff. Membership on standing committees would include persons either appointed or elected from among the membership of the Foundation Board. All decisions of the Fund-Raising and Program Committees would require Foundation Board approval. Some decisions on disbursement of funds would not require Foundation Board approval because of the infrequency of Board meetings, but the Disbursement Committee would be bound by guidelines established by the Foundation Board and *held accountable* for its decisions. Eligibility for grants would not necessarily be dependent upon membership in the National Federation, but this issue has not yet been resolved.

Suggestions for disbursement procedures include the following: (1) At least three months prior to the beginning of the foundation's fiscal year, each IBI would project and submit its annual operating budget (excluding special projects) including a statement of anticipated expenditures and income. The initial request for foundation support would be limited to dollar differences between income and expenditures. (2) The Disbursement Committee would meet to review all initial requests simultaneously and would determine on the basis of its current (not projected) assets whether all IBI requests could be approved. If not, each IBI would receive a pro rata share of available funds. (3) If the assets of the foundation were greater than the total amount requested, surplus funds would be used to support requests from non-federation institutions or to support special programs/projects of federation members. Decisions on expenditure of surplus funds *would require* approval of the Foundation Board.

The exact specifications of the structure, governance, and functions of the National Black Education Foundation remain to be finalized at the upcoming regional and national meetings. An interim task force has been assigned responsibility for developing further recommendations.

Sources of funds for the National Black Education Foundation would be obtained through payroll deductions, benefits by Black entertainers, Black athletic events, and various kinds of gift programs. Individual institutions would be advised to seek funds from the Black community at large, churches, Black organizations, Black professionals, speakers' bureaus, consultant services, foundations, government, business and industry, individual donors, investment portfolios, entrepreneurships and business enterprises, special events, extralegal sources, and the National Black Education Foundation.

Black Priorities in Education

Virtually all IBI's are being pulled in many directions in attempting to respond to the needs and wishes of the communities which they serve—perhaps this is as it should be. Yet, the IBI cannot be all things to all people and must set some priorities, priorities which flow from the political, social, economic, and educational problems which confront the Black community—locally, regionally, and nationally. This workshop attempted to sort out the problems and issues and establish a set of guidelines for the IBI in relation to Black priorities in education.

The foremost priorities of the IBI should be: (1) *development and perpetuation of the ideology* which encompasses the concepts of communalism, decolonization, the African Personality, humanism, harmony between the individual and his environment, and nation-building (see page 4); and (2) training to meet the needs of African peoples in their quest for independence through community development and nation-building. Beyond these broad areas, further delineation of priorities is dependent upon the nature and purpose of a particular Independent Black Institution. All aspects of cultural, economic, political, and military training are relevant to the struggle of building a nation. A contribution by any IBI in any of these areas is by definition a contribution to all other IBI's and to the struggle. Each IBI must then establish its own unique priorities in terms of what it wants to contribute to the struggle. *It is imperative, however, that every IBI realistically assess whether or not it is actually making contributions to nation-building.* Each IBI should continually evaluate *why* it exists, *what* it is doing, *how* it is functioning, *what* it is producing, and determine whether it qualifies as an IBI by addressing itself to the needs of nation-building. It is important to recognize that any type of institution which is Black *can be* relevant to nation-building provided that it functions on the basis of the above mentioned priorities and provided that its product endorses the ideology and becomes involved in nation-building activities. It is not enough, for example, for a pre-school to teach students that Black is beautiful if these students ultimately are trained to serve the interests of the oppressor—by definition this school is *not* fulfilling its responsibilities for nation-building. That an institution is Black, therefore, *does not automatically* qualify it to deal with independence and nation-building.

There should be several kinds of IBI's joined together by an ideology of *independence* and by commonality of life styles among people who are developing IBI's, particularly in terms of their relationships to the worldwide African community. There should be a functional balance between different types of IBI's, each dealing with different aspects of the development of African people. Suggested types of IBI's include those which focus upon (1) *acculturation* (defining the socialization process for African people in American culture, developing understanding of Africanisms, African life styles, etc., and developing creative motifs through the fine arts), (2) *technical training* (providing skills required for African people to be about the business of nation-building), (3) *leadership and organization skills development* (training a cadre of people with organization, leadership, and communication skills), (4) *research and curriculum development* (preserving and transmitting our ideology and culture), and (5) pre-school and/or elementary training. Regardless of priorities, each IBI should establish educational programs which include physical fitness, first aid, survival techniques, nation-building skills, and provide for a learning process based upon communal cooperation with students assuming collective responsibility for learning among students. IBI's should look toward establishing functional relationships with traditional institutions serving large populations of Black students when such relationships *can* facilitate program development within the IBI (e.g., use of funds, facilities, and faculties).

Curriculum Workshops (Pre-School through Higher Education)

There were three simultaneous working sessions on curriculum—pre-school/elementary curriculum, secondary curriculum, and higher education curriculum. Each working session reviewed and analyzed the curriculum of each institution represented at the workshop, identified the necessary components of the core curriculum at each educational level for an IBI, and established mechanisms for sharing information about curricular approaches among different institutions. Participants did not attempt to bring positive or negative sanctions against representative programs but rather sought to communally review and evaluate each curriculum and to offer guidelines for improvement. Since much time was devoted to information sharing, each participant was given an in-depth understanding of curricular programs at each represented institution. The following report on curriculum working sessions does not include a description of each institution's curriculum but rather is limited to suggested core curriculum at each educational level and other summary highlights.

Pre-School/Elementary Curriculum

This workshop defined curriculum as the total experience of a learner as he interacts with his environment. In developing a pre-school/elementary curriculum institutions should understand that learning experiences involve each of the following: (1) the needs of the learner, (2) learning objectives (knowledge, skills, and values), (3) specific learning activities, (4) evaluation of the learning process, (5) parental reinforcement of school activities, and (6) resources and materials. The fundamental learning principles which should undergird each pre-school/elementary curriculum are the concepts of (1) liberation (the power to be free, the power to be human, and the power to be self-determining) through decolonization and nation-building; (2) establishing control over the development of the minds of Black children through a directioning and channelling of thought patterns; (3) communal-cooperative learning; (4) creation of the African Personality/the New African Man; (5) humanism; and (6) human relationships particularly in relation to male/female consciousness of roles and functions.

The core curriculum in a pre-school/elementary program should include but is not limited to the following: (1) language skills development (reading, writing, speaking, and listening), (2) math-science skills development, (3) African life styles/Our Story, (4) physical fitness training, health and nutrition, (5) socio-cultural studies, and (6) political training. Suggested media for obtaining educational objectives include the use of plays, poetry, dance, music, arts and crafts, songs and games, comic books, cards and dice, and *anything which works.*

Secondary Curriculum

Participants in this workshop reviewed and evaluated the curriculum of each represented institution. Such an analysis led to the identification of fundamental principles on which the secondary curriculum should be structured: (1) it should be geared toward the needs of Black people; (2) it must provide for the development of skills in leadership and problem-solving, the development of knowledge of Black people, and the development of an understanding of the relationship of African people throughout the world; (3) it should require and maintain a high level of performance among staff and students at all times—a maximizing of abilities; (4) it should provide for the development of intellectual and creative skills necessary not only for comprehending the abstract but also for translating the abstract into meaningful, productive, relevant programs for Black people; (5) it should enable students to develop a sense of responsibility and commitment to the Black community; (6) it should provide for development of skills in the art of self-defense; (7) it should serve to provide a smooth transition from the elementary to the higher educational levels within the system of IBI's.

Participants defined the following as comprising the core curriculum of the secondary IBI: math-science skills development, communication skills development (language, arts, reading, writing, speaking, and listening), political education (the political, social, and economic aspects of African peoples' lives), community skills development (student activity in community organizations involved in community problem-solving), cultural development (music, dance, dress, art, customs), development of awareness and consciousness, and Our Story (not history). Each IBI is expected, however, to implement the core curriculum in terms of its own individual purposes and the needs of the community which it serves. IBI's must remain cognizant that they will be confronting numerous problems in implementing a curriculum including (among others) allocation of roles and responsibilities among students, staff, and community people, lack of relevant teaching materials, and identification and recruitment of staff who endorse the ideology of the IBI.

Higher Education Curriculum

This workshop reviewed and evaluated the curriculum of each represented institution. Further, attempts were made to assist each institution to better structure its curriculum in light of its established purpose. For example, Malcolm X Liberation University is primarily a technical institute with comparatively less emphasis on the fine arts. Suggestions on usage of graphics/graphic design, photography, film, and videotape were shared in attempting to assist Malcolm X to strengthen its curriculum. Thus, the report for this workshop is limited to suggested core curriculum for each higher educational IBI. That core curriculum should include but is not necessarily limited to communication skills development (reading, writing, speaking, listening), science/math/technical skills development, community problems and community skills development, self-defense (all forms), physical education, first aid, and development of consciousness and awareness.

The New African Man/Values—Pan-Africanism

It is virtually impossible to provide a summary description of this workshop although it was deemed by many to be the most informative and productive of all. Participants met in plenary session for an entire day with Brother St. Claire Drake, Director of Black Studies, Stanford University, the moderator of this session. Brother Drake shared valuable information about the history of the concept of Pan-Africanism, the functional role of Kwame Nkrumah in the development of the concept of Pan-Africanism, the history of the liberation of the free African states, and the contemporary status of African peoples throughout the Third World. This work session can perhaps best be described as an informal "give and take" between participants and Brother Drake on significant issues pertaining to the theme of the working session.

APPENDIX I

Independent Black Institutions Workshop

The California Association for Afro-American Education (CAAAE) is a statewide organization composed of students, parents, paraprofessionals, professionals and, most importantly, community people representing organizations in the Black community. CAAAE is primarily concerned with the liberation of Black people through continuing improvement in the quality of Black education in California. The long-range goal of CAAAE is the development of a system of Independent Black Education Institutions throughout the State of California. Its most recent statewide meeting was convened the weekend following the Nairobi IBI Conference. One of the working sessions at the CAAAE meeting was on the Independent Black Educational Institution. The following is a brief summary report on that working session.

The working session received a report on the Nairobi IBI workshop and subsequently discussed the following topics: (1) relationship of California IBI's to traditional (white-controlled) institutions, (2) role and responsibilities of students, faculty, and administrators in the IBI,

(3) relationship of California IBI's to the Black community, and (4) establishment of a system of IBI's in California (k–12).

The IBI has a definite *functional* relationship to establish with traditional institutions in California. It can provide a community power base for effective change in traditional institutions, develop feasibility models of new teaching methodologies, and provide opportunities to expand and apply skills learned in traditional institutions to further development of Black social institutions and the Black community. In addition, the IBI can maintain a research center for Black students enrolled in traditional institutions, serve as a center for extension and correspondence courses for these students and for community people, and, under certain conditions, provide in-service training for traditional-oriented teachers, training for new teachers, and other consultant services in developing its financial resources.

Participants viewed learning as a continuous process and thus classified all persons involved in an IBI as students. Much stress was placed upon utilizing older students to teach younger students and upon shared cooperative responsibility for individual learning (inter- and intra-classroom). IBI's must create small-team relationships based upon the family concept within and throughout the institution.

Much stress was given to talent utilization as opposed to role stratification (building institutions around individual talents rather than fitting individuals into bureaucratic roles). The IBI must place maximum emphasis upon broad *distribution* of roles and responsibilities rather than upon stratification.

Regarding the Black community, the IBI can provide human and material resources to affect the life style of Black people. Since the IBI exists to meet the needs of the Black community, it can assist in the development of community resources (social, political, economic, religious, educational, physical, and human), examine Black values, work toward a reordering of the Black value system through reinforcement of positive values and elimination of negative values, and work to develop functional unity among diverse ideologies in the Black community. The IBI must remain cognizant that the *community* is its power base and, thus, its effectiveness in serving the Black community is the primary criterion for its legitimacy.

Much attention was given to the establishment of a system of IBI's in California. The establishment of such a system will be dependent upon our effectiveness in each of the following areas: (1) conversion of traditional institutions serving large populations of Blacks into IBI's; (2) establishment of new IBI's with initial emphasis directed toward lower educational levels; (3) assisting existing institutions endorsing the IBI concept to become true IBI's in reality. Three traditional institutions serving large Black constituencies have been identified as target institutions for conversion. Task forces have been established to develop a plan of action for rendering these three traditional institutions into functionally operating IBI's. A fourth task force was established to identify all institutions in the state presently endorsing the IBI concept, to assist these institutions to the extent possible, and to develop plans for establishing new IBI's in selected regions in the state, particularly at the pre-school and elementary levels.

APPENDIX II
A Brief Look at Selected IBI's

Uhuru Sasa School, 10 Claver Place, Brooklyn, New York

Uhuru Sasa School presently is governed by a board composed of students, faculty, administrators, and community people. To the extent possible, group consensus typically undergirds the decision-making processes of the school. Its primary purpose is to develop a New African Man possessing the values, skills, and knowledge necessary and sufficient for the process of nation-building. Uhuru Sasa School presently has a staff of sixteen persons and seventy-five students ranging in age from four through eighteen. Its curriculum is varied and cuts across all major problems and issues related to the Black experience.

Martin Luther King School, 632 Oak Street, San Francisco, California

Martin Luther King School has a governing board comprised of teachers and community people. Institutional decision-making is typically vested in the governing board. The purpose of this school is to provide a meaningful, relevant, and viable education for Black youth. It has been operating for several years and its varied and comprehensive curriculum is designed to produce Black youth trained to deal effectively with the problems and needs of the Black community.

Malcolm X Liberation University, P.O. Box 251, Durham, North Carolina

Malcolm X Liberation University has from its conception been guided by the ideology of Pan-Africanism with nation-building as the concrete action for making this ideology a reality. Malcolm X has a governing board composed of students, faculty, administrators and community people with a system of institutional checks and balances for decision-making based on a family-communal concept. Its purpose is to create an educational process which is based on a revolutionary ideology that projects self-awareness, disseminates necessary concepts and techniques, provides the technological know-how with which to engage in a struggle and develop a nation. Its curriculum emphasizes three things: ideology, skills, and a positive attitude toward physical work. The ideological component of the curriculum includes study of Independent African Civilization, Colonialism, Neocolonialism, and Pan-Africanism. Technical studies (skills areas) include the teacher corps, bio-medics, engineering, communications technology, and food science. The physical work aspect of the curriculum includes, among other things, a full day's work each week on the school farm.

Morgan Community School, 1773 California Street, N.W., Washington, D.C.

Morgan Community School has a governing board comprised of students, teachers, and community people. The purpose of the school is to move youngsters, educationally, from the affective to the cognitive domain by dealing with objective reality, thus bringing about qualitative changes in the educational program for oppressed people. The school presently has a staff of sixty-two persons serving more than 700 students. It offers a varied curriculum including all academic areas and the fine arts.

Dr. King On-Campus School, 107 Waverly Avenue, Syracuse, New York

The major purpose of this school is to identify the major agents of socialization for Black youth, to develop a viable program of ego development for students, and to develop forms of schooling which enhance values of Black self-determination. Its staff of nine works with more than 100 students in math, science, fine arts, Afro-American studies, reading, language arts, music and other activities.

Academy for Black and Latin Education, 73 West 105th Street, New York, N.Y.

The school is a non-accredited Street Academy registered with the state as a nonprofit organization. Its student body is composed of dropouts who are drug addicts. The curriculum includes courses in English, math, Hispanic history and culture, Black history and culture, Spanish, political science, and economics. Emphasis is upon utilizing community persons in teaching positions and students in community projects. Future plans include establishing programs for oppressed brothers released from prison.

The Black Institute/California Center for Arts and Crafts, Broadway and College, Oakland, California

The Institute is focusing upon the role of the Black artist in the struggle. It is attempting to revolutionize art form, content, and the form of distribution of art to Black people. Community people are actively involved in the institute and it has established several programs for bringing Black art to the people.

Atlanta Center for Black Art, 1532 Gordon Street, S.W. Atlanta, Georgia

The Atlanta Center for Black Art has a governing board composed of teachers and community persons. The governing board establishes institutional policy, but such policy is developed with participation by all persons involved in the Center. The purpose of the Center is to continue the long struggle to build an African nation. It presently has a staff of fourteen and serves approximately thirty students. Its curriculum is varied with primary emphasis given to the Black arts. Its student population includes junior and high school-age students who are recruited through the mass media and visits to schools and homes. As with other IBI's, its curricular program is in the developmental stages, but much optimism prevails among the staff.

Nairobi College, 1627 Bay Road, East Palo Alto, California

Nairobi College has a governing board comprised of equal numbers of students, faculty, and community people. Its governing processes place heavy emphasis upon student involvement in decision-making. The purpose of Nairobi College is to provide a relevant education for people of color, to develop skilled persons and leadership in communities of color, and to offer a viable educational alternative for students of color. The College presently has forty-two volunteer instructors and expects a full-time staff of approximately twelve beginning in September. Its curriculum is varied with course offerings in each academic discipline. Student enrollment is expected to exceed 200 during the next academic year.

Nairobi High School, 1189 Saratoga, East Palo Alto, California

Nairobi High School has a governing board composed of twenty community people plus an advisory community board. The primary purpose of the school is to develop through community-nation-oriented education a group of young Blacks who have the skills with which to solve the problems in Black communities. It presently has a staff of twenty-three full-time, part-time, and volunteer persons who serve approximately fifty students. Its curriculum includes courses in mathematics (from arithmetic through calculus), chemistry, physics, communications, writing, journalism, language, sewing, and the fine arts. The high school has a program which serves the total educational needs of its students.

APPENDIX III

The institutions listed below are defined as Black Independent Schools—either in physical, legal, or psychological terms. The list was produced by the Action Library of Afram Associates, 103 E. 125th Street, New York, New York. HAVE YOU written a check for the IBI in your community? If not, review the following list of IBI's and GIVE TO THE INSTITUTION OF YOUR CHOICE.

Atlanta Center for Black Art
1532 Gordon Street, S.W.
Atlanta, Georgia

New School for Children
6 Bradshaw Street
Dorchester, Mass.

CCED School
54 Roxbury Street
Roxbury, Massachusetts

Uhuru Sasa School
10 Claver Place
Brooklyn, New York

West 80th Street Day Care Center
Hotel Endicott
80th St. and Columbus Avenue
New York, New York

Store Front Learning Center
90 West Brookline Street
Boston, Massachusetts

Postal Academics Program
12th and Pennsylvania Avenues
Room #2119
Washington, D.C.

African Free School at
Robert Treat School
131 13th Street
Newark, New Jersey

Sasa Educational Foundation
939 Peach Tree Street, N.E.
Washington, D.C.

The Liberty School
Bergen County Headstart Program
Palisades and Teaneck Avenues
Englewood, New Jersey

Arthur M. Schomburg Learning Center
Community School #39
216 East 126th Street
Harlem, New York

Roxbury Community School
1-A Leyland Street
Dorchester, Massachusetts

Children's Community Workshop
565 Columbus Avenue
New York, New York

Dr. King On-Campus School
107 Waverly Avenue
Syracuse, New York

Highland Park Free School
42 Hawthorne Park
Roxbury, Massachusetts

Operation Bootstrap
4171 So. Central Avenue
Los Angeles, California

Georgetown Black and Proud School
8000 Powell Road Drive
Jackson, Mississippi

African Free School
33 Sterling Street
Newark, New Jersey

Albany Nursing and Community School
P.O. Box 1024
Albany, Georgia

Community Participation in Education Project
110 E. 125th Street
New York, New York

Escuela Espana
18 Avenue D
New York, New York

Harlem Educational Program
275 W. 145th Street
Harlem, New York

School of Common Sense
949 Marcy Avenue
Brooklyn, New York

Concord Elementary School
833 Marcy Avenue
Brooklyn, New York

Harlem Parent-Teachers Association
P.O. Box 547
Clewiston, Pennsylvania

Southeast-East San Diego Day School
c/o Dave Crippens KEBS-TV
San Diego State College
San Diego, California

Black Institute
California Center for Arts and Crafts
Broadway and College
Oakland, California

Architects Renewal Committee in Harlem
221 W. 116th Street
New York, New York

School for Retarded Children
14921 Kunsman Road
Cleveland, Ohio

S.O.U.L. School
522 N. Freemont Avenue
Baltimore, Maryland

METCO
178 Humbolt Avenue
Roxbury, Massachusetts

W. E. B. Du Bois Institute
1249 Griswold #619/519
Detroit, Michigan

The Academy: New York City Mission Society
531 W. 155 Street
New York, New York

Freedom Library Day School
2064 Ridge Avenue
Philadelphia, Pennsylvania

New Approach Method
22 General Greene Avenue
Trenton, New Jersey

Ocean Hill-Brownsville Demonstration School District
249 Hopkinson
Brooklyn, New York

Malcolm X Liberation University
P.O. Box 251
Durham, North Carolina

Malcolm X College
8259 St. Lawrence Avenue
Chicago, Illinois

Venice Community Improvement Union
617 Broadway Street
Venice, California

Martin Luther King School
532 Oak Street
San Francisco, California

Malcolm X School
540 McAllister Street
San Francisco, California

Harlem Street Academies
c/o New York Urban League
202 W. 136th Street
New York, New York

Martin Luther King, Jr. School
1331 Sharon Street, N.W.
Atlanta, Georgia

Black Communiversity
700 E. Oakwood Blvd.
Chicago, Illinois

Freedom Library Day School
2064 Ridge Avenue
Philadelphia, Pennsylvania

ABLE
Academy for Black and Latin Education
73 West 105th Street
New York, New York

Nairobi College
1896 Bay Road
East Palo Alto, California

Nairobi Day School
1189 Saratoga Avenue
East Palo Alto, California

Nairobi High School
1189 Saratoga Avenue
East Palo Alto, California

Pomona Day School
240 E. 11th Street
Claremont, California

Morgan Community School
1773 California Street, N.W.
Washington, D.C.

I.S. 201 Community School District
103 East 125th Street
Harlem, New York

T.W.O. Experimental Schools Project
6253 S. Woodlawn
Chicago, Illinois

Center for Black Education
1435 Fairmont St. N.W.
Washington, D.C.

Institute of the Black World
Atlanta University
Atlanta, Georgia

Communiversity
1168 E. 105th Street
Cleveland, Ohio

APPENDIX IV

Checklist for Independent Black Institutions

Does your institution meet the requirements for classification within the system of Independent Black Institutions? Complete the following checklist to determine whether it qualifies. If not, then the IBI workshop encourages you to be about the business of qualifying.

YES	NO	
		I. *Governance*
____	____	A. Are Black people in exclusive control of decision-making, particularly in the areas of policy control, curriculum, budget, staffing—unless the involvement of Third World people in governing processes is deemed beneficial?
____	____	B. Are students, staff, and community people represented on the governing board?
		II. *Finance*
____	____	A. Are financial resources received on terms defined by the institution?
____	____	B. Has the institution compromised its principles to obtain financial support?
		III. *Ideology* Does the institution endorse the following concepts?
____	____	A. Communalism
____	____	B. Decolonization
____	____	C. The African Personality
____	____	D. Humanism
____	____	E. Harmony between the individual and his environment
____	____	F. Nation-building
		IV. *Staff*
____	____	A. Are all staff of African heritage unless utilization of Third World staff is deemed functionally beneficial?
		V. *Students*
____	____	A. Are all students of African heritage—unless involvement of Third World students is deemed functionally beneficial?
		VI. *The Black Community*
____	____	A. Does the institution direct primary emphasis toward the needs of the Black community?

YES NO

VII. *Purposes*

____ ____ A. Does the institution endorse the purpose of "control of the development of the mind and consciousness of Black people, i.e., control of the socialization process"?

VIII. *Function*

____ ____ A. Does the institution endorse the primary function of "education of the pure and de-education of the contaminated?"

IX. *Objectives*

Does the institution endorse the following objectives?

____ ____ A. Serving the needs of African people throughout the world

____ ____ B. Stopping the process of genocide—all types

____ ____ C. Teaching history, culture, and understanding of our social context and training for nation-building and community development

____ ____ D. Creating a new type of individual who can build new social institutions

____ ____ E. Offering inducements for attaining the "good life" as reflected in the African Personality

X. *Research*

Has the institution established research programs in one or more of the following areas?

____ ____ A. Curriculum development and development of supporting materials

____ ____ B. Internal program review and evaluation

____ ____ C. Collection of data on the Black community to increase knowledge about and understanding of the Black community

Post this checklist above your desk and review it weekly to assess your progress.

Education and Teaching in Pre-Colonial Black Africa

Staff, Center for Black Education

I. Education in Pre-Colonial Black Africa

Despite the great ethnic diversity of the populations of Black Africa and the variety in forms of social organization, reflecting differences in the level of economic, political and social development attained before the colonial conquest, one finds in the educational domain a certain number of common traits which clearly demonstrate the cultural unity of the African peoples. In every region and geographical zone, and in all the clans, tribes and ethnic groups, traditional education in Black Africa is characterized by the following:

1. The great importance which is attached to it, and its collective and social nature.
2. Its intimate tie with social life, both in a material and spiritual sense.
3. Its multivalent character, both in terms of its goals and the means employed.
4. Its gradual and progressive achievement, in conformity with the successive stages of physical, emotional and mental development of the child.

Many facts point to the importance accorded to education in precolonial African society. First of all, the parents and the family (in the African sense of the word) have a sharp sense of their responsibilities in this area, not only toward the child but toward the entire community. On one level, in the framework of a highly developed sense of self-respect and sensitivity, corollaries to an ancient and somewhat pigheaded tradition of honor rooted in traditional African society, the family of a child considers itself, and is considered by others, responsible for education. The importance given to education is seen also in the fact that the whole community takes part in it in various ways: the individual intervention of any adult in the education of any child, or the management of various aspects of education, in varied and carefully defined circumstances, by elected or designated members acting in the name and for the benefit of the community. In the social sphere, even in the feudal societies of pre-colonial Black Africa, education was considered far more valuable than even high birth or fortune, to the point where the title of "man" was inseparable from a certain number of traits linked to education.

It is essential to realize that children occupy a central place in the life of the African family, despite the very deceiving appearance of numerous attitudes in the behavior of African parents. Life in an African household, monogamous or polygamous, is to a very large degree conditioned, if not determined, by the possibility or impossibility of having children. One marries to have children, or divorces in order to remarry and have children. The childless woman is looked down on, and she makes every conceivable effort and spends all her money on consultations and treatments from medicine men or marabouts in order to bear more children. There are few countries where childbearing is such an overriding preoccupation as it is in Black Africa (pre-colonial as well as contemporary), for husband as well as wife, married couples as well as their families, families as well as the entire community.

Care of the infant is in the mother's hands during his infancy. She feeds him and cares for him, and it is not an exaggeration to say that the African child is an integral part of the mother's body. This is not only because, like all mothers, the African woman is intensely sensitive to everything that concerns her child, but also because she breast feeds him for a long time, makes a great fuss over him, puts him to sleep beside her and carries him everywhere on her back. Later she watches over his first movements, and it is at her side that he says his first words and learns to name the things surrounding him. Until he attains the age of six to eight, the African child remains in the shadow of woman (at the foot of a tree, as it were). Everyone who has observed the African mother has been struck by the innumerable little efforts she makes for her child: the way she calms him or puts him to sleep singing soft lullabies; the way she literally chews his food before giving it to him; the ways she spends her meager resources to get him protective amulets to ward off a bad fate, sorcerers or evil spells, or to provide for the medicines, powders, concoctions and various other mixtures to cure illness.

When a child reaches the age of six or eight, the mother, in the case of a girl, the father if it is a boy, assumes the main responsibility of his education. The child enters the next phase of his education by helping with the work of one of his parents. A lot has been written to the effect that the child is a domestic during this period by those who apply the economic categories of middle-class capitalistic society to pre-colonial society. In the latter, along with the social relations of a feudal type, there coexisted many strong traits of the primitive community: collective ownership of land, hereditary division of labor (castes), and an economy based on the family. Such writers also and more importantly entirely miss the significance of African tradition, where the mother or father in fact fulfills the functions of a teacher, the child those of a disciple. The obedience of the latter is inseparable from the responsibilities and solicitude of the adult. It is the duty of the father or the mother to guide the infant when he makes his first contacts with the society around him (work and social intercourse with others), to help him benefit from their own experience through his effective participation, according to his capabilities, in the workings of the community. The father teaches his young boy how to become a man, just as the mother teaches her daughter everything relating to the role of the woman and mother. If under circumstances the heavy demands made by parents on their child influence the nature, intensity and manifestations of affection they have for him and vice versa, it is only natural. Those who consider these demands as springing from a supposed inhumanity and the child as an "instrument" who performs various tasks to satisfy adult needs, lose sight of the fact that in traditional African education school and life are one. The consequences of the behavior of the child and the adult have a far greater import than they have when learning takes place between the four walls of a classroom.

It is well known that the child is considered part of the common wealth in traditional African society, and that the adult life of a man only starts with marriage and children. One has only to listen to everyday conversations and observe various events to realize that no one has the full right to be called an adult man until he has reproduced, and that the celibate is treated with a mixture of scorn and pity; to hear, when a child is delivered, the ritual question, "What have we had?"; to see the importance given to the ceremony of baptism, in which the entire community participates, in order to appreciate and understand the vital role played by the child in the life and preoccupations of traditional African society.

As soon as the child is old enough to leave his family and house, his education is in large measure the business of everyone. In the beginning, when he is at the age of "running errands," the child considers it very natural to be called and sent away by an adult or older child, scolded, corrected, or advised, consoled, revenged or rewarded by them. Later, when it is time for his initiation, it will be under the direction of members of the community chosen for their knowledge, wisdom and experience that he will learn the first elements of what he must know, physically and intellectually, to start the life of an adolescent. As a young man, he will complete his training by listening to and observing the "elders," at community "palavers," and by taking part in the different aspects of social life to which he is admitted, just as when as a child he listened with the other children to the stories, legends and riddles told by the adults. Thus, during his entire physical growth and intellectual and emotional development, the child and later the adolescent is closely followed by the entire collectivity, in a direct or indirect fashion.

Starting at the age of six or seven years, the child begins to participate in varied ways according to his capacities in productive activity. First of all, a whole series of tasks on the household level falls to his lot. The boy will cut the grass for the horse or goat, provide water for them, accompany his father to the field, carrying the flask of water or his father's hoe, or watch over the family's animals. The small girl will fetch water with her mother, go with her to market and carry the purchases, light and tend the kitchen fire, grind the seasonings, take care of her young brother or sister, sweep, or wash the dishes. Later, a little at a time, the range of activities widens and takes the child beyond purely familial tasks. He becomes more and more involved in production (including produce destined for the marketplace) and starts to make his own independent relationships with members of the community. The boy will start to work his little plot of land, watch over the field, chasing animals and birds, and can on occasion go to gather food or collect wood or grass, which he can sell for his own profit. The girl will weave little articles of basketry, cook certain dishes, grind with her mother, go shopping at the market or sell homemade products (fitters, basketry, cola nuts), make different objects (basketry, embroidery on leather) and will start gathering food or making things on her own that she can sell for her own profit. Adolescent boys and girls participate fully in production with increasing independence and responsibility. In sum, it is by accomplishing productive tasks that the child and an adolescent familiarize themselves with adult jobs and are initiated into different social aspects of their future lives.

However, participating in production for the benefit and under the supervision of adults, with ever-increasing independence is not the only form of liaison between traditional African education and productive activity. Certain children's games have an important role in this respect, even if they are only an imitation without apparent significance. Boys imitate various adult activities, such as hunting or fishing, basket-weaving, jewelry-making, leather work, or simply make toys, which familiarizes them with practical problems. Girls play at being housewives, shopkeepers, seamstresses or potters. They are certainly not helping with production, but at least they are preparing to do so, both on the material level (contact with practical aspects of production) and on the psychological level (liking for work, particularly manual). It is a kind of pre-apprenticeship carried on without adult interference.

As in all educational systems, the child's initiation into adult society simply means in the beginning learning how to behave well and be polite. But quite early on (and this is one of the characteristics that contributes to its originality), traditional African education involves the child concretely in more complex and meaningful relationships with the members of his community. The child is an intermediary between adults during the first phase, mostly by running errands. However, he picks up a good deal of information about the relationships between adults in society and their relative standing. When he starts to participate in production his own status is gradually transformed; in an increasingly independent manner he enters into relationships with other men: he sells the products of his own labor, buys for himself or for his family, takes part in various social activities; in brief, he acquires his own experience of various aspects of social life, of the relations that it implies between individuals, and of the differentiation and stratification inherent in it.

Through his daily activities the child and later the adolescent is gradually made aware and comes to understand the material and the spiritual fundamentals of social life: values, customs and traditions, world view, and the meaning of life. At the same time he is assuming more and more of the responsibilities and duties which fall to him. Ties of solidarity and fraternity between children in the same age group are woven and reinforced in childhood groups determined by age, later during the initiation ceremonies, but these ties also exist between children and their elders, and between them and the entire community.

However, it is in learning his job with adults, which involves the transmission of the experience and heritage of his ancestors (in the framework of the division of society into castes or discrete groups, which communicate family, tribe or clan secrets) that the adolescent-become-man will enter into his social function fully, and at the same time, the community itself.

Finally, as in all other aspects of traditional African education, games play a definite role in the initiation of the child and adolescent into social life. Children play together according to their age in traditional African society. The collective aspect of playing is like a duplication of adult social life in the relationships it creates and develops among the participants. The child learns to live with children in the same age group, to fill a determined role, to appreciate and esteem his friends, to judge his own capacities and those of others in practice, and to work with others as a team. A large number of games, particularly the games of initiation, are imitations of real social life, and games involving different kinds of work reproduce the relationships between adults of different professions. Dolls are "married" to little boys in the same age group as the little girl who is the "mother," or little boys and girls play at being married. It is undoubtedly true that while amusing themselves children learn a great deal about behavior that is related to actual social life.

Thus a whole series of facts shows that the child is educated and educates himself in the bosom of society itself, in the "school of the family" and in social life with his age group, and is constantly in contact with the various aspects of adult life.

In the examination of the different traits of traditional African education one of its most striking characteristics, which deserves special attention, is its multivalent nature, embracing all sides of the personality of the child and the adolescent.

1. The Development of the Physical Aptitudes of the Child Is Stressed Right from the Beginning. Children's games are often very active, and some of them are completely devoted to athletics. Whether it is pretend horseraces with millet or sorghum stalks, or competitive individual or group games (jumping, races, climbing, balancing, swimming), acrobatic dances, or the many others which combine different physical exercises, the child not only develops his body but also his agility, endurance, physical resistance and ability to use his body in different circumstances and for different purposes. From this point of view initiation is a special period in his life. Composed of a series of tests among which sports competitions play an important part, initiation is in a way a systematic recapitulation. Because of its length it allows the child to strengthen the skills he has previously acquired, in a highly competitive framework.

On the other hand, many utilitarian tasks assigned to the child help considerably in his physical development. They involve many of the physical movements used in different sports: running, walking, jumping, climbing and balancing. Furthermore, because he is obliged to do them, the child is made more aware of the physical movements he accomplishes, particularly since there is always a precise objective whose significance and utility are clear to the child or adolescent.

2. Molding character and providing moral qualities are primarily objectives in traditional African education.

Almost all the different aspects of education of the child and adolescent aim toward this goal, to a greater or lesser degree. In the family, parents concern themselves with the bearing, manners, honesty, courage, solidarity, endurance, ethics and above all the concept of honor which are, among others, the moral qualities constantly demanded, examined, judged and sanctioned, in ways which depend on the intellectual level and capacities of the child and adolescent.

Here again, initiation plays a very special role, not only because of the many tests to which the child is submitted, but also because of the atmosphere in which it takes place. Because all children of the same age group take part, initiation takes on, in the same way as the games, aspects of collective and social life, to the point where it is no longer a matter of playing, but of leaving the world of games and childhood insouciance, with all the gravity such a step entails, and entering the world of adult care and responsibility.

In a more general fashion, all the useful activities of a child enable the members of the community to exercise their influence on the formation of his character, especially by the relationships they establish between the child and his friends of the same age group, his elders, adults and the elderly of the community. This occurs either through the direct intervention of a member of the community regarding the behavior of the child in predetermined conditions, or indirectly by the personal observations that the child learns to make in the framework of a social life. In the same way, hearing stories and legends contributes to the character formation of the child. Stories are an inexhaustible source of teaching about the behavior of the individual, through the animals and men they bring to life. They describe, laugh at or ridicule certain faults as they praise, glorify or make the child appreciate and love various other qualities. As for the legends, the events they tell of and the deeds of their heroes are always an occasion to stress a character trait or a vile or glorious act. In this way stories and legends are part of the teaching arsenal that seeks to influence the character of the child and instill in him the moral values of the community.

3. Traditional African education, because of the degree of economic and social development of pre-colonial African society, does not seem to emphasize the intellectual training of the child as heavily as other aspects of education. Definite attention, however, is given to intellectual training. From the point of view of general knowledge, intellectual training touches on a limited number of areas: history, geography, knowledge of plants and their attributes, development of reasoning and judgment, and the acquisition of elements of philosophy. The above is true in non-Moslem African societies. In Moslem countries or regions, until the eve of colonial conquest, there were a large number of schools and university centers which provided education in Arabic, and the various fields of knowledge and abstract thought held an important place in them. Along with teaching in the Arabic tongue, literature developed in Peuhl, Hausa and Kanouri which used the Arabic script. Although the importance of the Islamic schools should not be exaggerated as regards intellectual training (because of their pedagogical techniques, the small number of these

schools, and, above all, their strictly religious goals and the partial and limited course of study given the great majority of students), it is still true that they played an eminent role in pre-colonial Black Africa on the intellectual level.

In any case, it is incontestable that traditional African education includes the intellectual training of the child and the adolescent. An important place was reserved for mastery of the language (community discussions, narrations, stories and legends) and to abstract thought, in admittedly limited ways such as riddles and proverbs, and discussion of various problems. In particular, certain adult and adolescent games, such as *dara* or *dili*, *wouri* or *awele*, are real exercises in mathematics, which involve geometry, combinations, and the properties of numbers. At the same time, the acquisition of the ability to reason and form solid judgments was considered extremely important. Certainly much has been said about the "wisdom" and the "philosophy" of the elders in Black Africa. However, it has been said more to "lay the foundation," "establish" or demonstrate a certain number of these relative to the "irrationality" or the "primitiveness' of "Negro thought" than to examine objectively the relationships and implications that can result from such circumstances in traditional African society.

Outside the area of religious phenomena (and here, let it be said in passing fetishism and animism have nothing on Christianity when it comes to cults of images, statues and relics—no doubt they have enough in common with it to explain the success of missionaries in areas of religious animism), traditional African education, through a whole series of processes, develops logical reasoning and the critical spirit (the riddle games, debating contests, mathematical games). A great number of questions and problems demonstrate, to anyone willing to reflect on them, that concepts of classical logic were not unknown to the Africans: this can be seen in the "oral tests" of the type, "which is the most . . ." (rapid, clever, foolish, greedy, et al.). Finally, although the transmission of general knowledge is not systematic and organized as in modern education, nevertheless in traditional African education it is effected through practical experience and through the oral teaching given the child and adolescent in historical recitations and discussions.

4. It is scarcely necessary to point out that traditional African education constantly combines manual activity with intellectual activity. This has emerged clearly from the above discussion.

With the means available to it, and in the framework of the limits imposed on it by economic, political and social conditions, traditional African education thus sought to mold men, in the largest and fullest sense of the word.

The existence of clearly defined age groups is a widespread phenomenon; despite differences in detail, such as the precise number of groups, the three following groups are always found:

1. First age group: birth to six or eight years. During this period, which corresponds to the first and second infancy, the education of the child falls mainly to the mother, and takes place within the framework of the family. The father has relatively little to do with children during the first years.

2. Second age group: six to ten years. When they are six, children are separated according to sex, the boys being answerable to the men and the girls to the women. Children participate more and more in work, but a large part of their time is devoted to games with boys or girls in the same age group.

In Moslem countries the children go to the Koran school in the morning and in the evening, which in no way prevents their doing other things the rest of the day.

3. Third age group: ten to fifteen years. Children of both sexes are increasingly involved in the life of men and women, respectively, and called on to accomplish adult jobs in a more complete manner. They are gradually given more and more independence, with its attendant responsibilities. They are allowed to attend more and more of the various public affairs, and to see and hear more about the problems of daily life. They lead a collective life with their contemporaries in the same age group and of the same sex, which strengthens their solidarity. They learn an occupation, which may be a hereditary one, in their own families with a father or uncle, or in professional groups.

Initiation takes place after a child reaches fifteen or sixteen, and varies according to the region and whether or not the community is Moslem. It signifies the passage from adolescence to adulthood, to the moment when the child, until then considered as being outside the adult world, is admitted to it. In animistic religions ritual and group ceremonies take place during initiation, and in some Islamic communities it involves the marriage of the young man in a special ceremony.

Generally speaking, circumcision is performed during initiation, and constitutes the essential part of the ceremony for Moslems. The young men live in an isolated group of thirty or forty, under the care of elders who give them instruction. They undergo physical exercises for endurance and litheness, dances and various games. They develop the spirit of comradeship and solidarity among themselves.

The beginning and the end of this turning point in the life of adolescents is marked by grandiose ceremonies, for which they wear special dress. When the young men emerge from initiation, they are men, and as such allowed to participate more fully in the life and social activities of adults. In general, a young man is willing to have his parents choose his first wife, and after his marriage he takes full part in the life of the community.

II. Teaching in Pre-Colonial Black Africa

Among non-Islamic African peoples, the child in the course of his development generally acquires all his knowledge from family and social life. On the practical level, he does this by observing and imitating adult behavior and work, and by playing many different group games. On the theoretical level he learns by listening to his older friends and the "elders," questioning them in the course of daily activities or during evenings spent in conversations, telling stories, legends, riddles and proverbs. Later, his intellectual "equipment" is completed when he sits in on the "palavers" and the various ceremonies and public occasions. Lastly, at the time of his initiation, he acquires general knowledge concerning areas as diverse as plants or religious and sexual life, which completes the knowledge he has acquired day by day during the preceding periods of his development.

In Moslem areas, in addition to the aspects of education described above, the Koran is taught. This is done by marabouts, starting when a child is six or seven, and consists essentially in learning the Koran by heart, and absorbing enough Arabic to read, write and sometimes speak it, but above all to be able to explain and comment on the Koran. This teaching lasts three to five years, according to the methods employed, and is completed by secular knowledge drawn from various treatises on law, history, geography and others, on an elementary level. At the end of the cycle, which is marked by an important ceremony, the adolescent acquires the title of *Malam* or *Alfa* and is entitled to teach. If his studies have been interrupted he will at least know how to say his prayers correctly. The new "graduate" can pursue what corresponds to higher education with his own marabout, or with marabouts with a scholarly reputation, who surround themselves with numerous disciples. Universities existed in a certain number of famous cities: Timbuktu, where the renowned University of Sankore had a great reputation in the Muslim world; Dinguiray in Futa, Sokoto in the Hausa country, Jenne in the loop of the Niger, and many others. Several of the teachers from these universities have remained celebrated for their reputation and scholarly output: Ahmed Baba, Muhammad Koti El Timbuktu and the Sheik Usuman dan Fodio of Sokoto.

The process of learning an occupation, or apprenticeship, follows practically the same pattern in all the regions of Black Africa.

At a very early age the child is taught to cultivate by following his father to the field, or tending his own little piece of land, or to watch sheep or goats, later herds of cattle, either by helping an adult or on his own. Apprenticeship for most of the other occupations takes place within professional groups, of blacksmiths, woodworkers, cobblers, weavers or whatever. In the case of hereditary occupations, the family hands down to the child the techniques and secrets of the trade, which he in turn will pass on. The important secrets are usually only revealed to the oldest of the male children, or sometime to the child judged most worthy to receive them, utilize them and keep them in the family.

Apprenticeship continues for a long time, and it is not rare to see young married men still working under the aegis of their elders, continuing to perfect their skills.

III. Some Remarks About Traditional Education

Pre-colonial African education responded to the economic, social and political conditions of pre-colonial African society, and it is in relation to these conditions that it must be examined and analyzed.

Pre-colonial African society (one might say African societies) was feudal society, at least in the most advanced areas, in which clans and tribes coexisted or persisted side by side. Generally speaking, they were small feudal communities, both in terms of land area and population, a fact closely related to the disastrous consequences of slave trade. Nevertheless, there was great historical continuity (to which I would like to draw the attention of the African reader) in the Sahelian zone of Black Africa, which was the scene of incessant efforts to regroup the little fiefs into great empires, under the leadership of men as different as Mansa Musa, Sundiata, Askia Muhammad I, El Hadj Omar and Usuman dan Fodio. As Dr. W. E. B. Du Bois has pointed out, the drastic effects of the slave trade on the historical evolution of the peoples of Black Africa can never be fully measured. First of all, because of the massive depopulation it entailed (estimated at about one hundred million people during the four centuries of the trade), it emptied Black Africa of its best and most vital men and women, thus sapping the potential demographic development of African societies. The artificial maintenance of permanent internecine warfare between the peoples of Black Africa was one of the most serious obstacles to the process of national unification, notably by transforming all the feudal wars into commercial enterprises to supply slaves to the treaty market, and by making any large state composed of small fiefs unstable. As a result, African society stagnated in the feudal stage, or regressed toward a state of slavery.

Traditional African education, as described above, was fully capable of supplying the necessary elements to maintain in all its essentials the level attained by African society (before the slave trade) in the economic, social, technical and cultural spheres. In this sense, one can say that it fulfilled its objectives, if the regressive effects of the slave trade are taken into account. Even today, the technical achievements, political and economic organization, works of art, the striking personality of older Africans and the intact vitality of the peoples of Black Africa bear witness to this fact.

But it is not enough to simply state the fact. The success must be explained, and from the analysis of the content of traditional African education, it will be seen that its proven effectiveness stems from a certain number of characteristics.

In its general conception, traditional African education never separated education, in the large and real meaning of the word, from instruction in the precise, limited sense. These two aspects of all attempts to "mold" human beings are constantly and intimately connected, to the point where it is often necessary to resort to abstract analysis to separate the factors relating to one or the other.

Traditional African education, as we have seen, embraces character-building, as well as the development of physical aptitudes, the acquisition of those moral qualities felt to be an integral part of manhood, and the acquisition of the knowledge and techniques needed by all men if they are to take an active part in social life in its various forms. In all this, its objectives do not differ from those of education in other societies living in other parts of the world.

The effectiveness of this education was possible because of its very close relationship with life. It was through social acts (production) and social relationships (family life, group activities) that the education of the child or adolescent took place, so that he was instructed and educated simultaneously. To the extent that a child learned everywhere and all the time, instead of learning in circumstances determined in advance as to place and time, outside of the productive and social world, he was truly in the "school of life," in the most concrete and real sense.

From another point of view, the pedagogy of traditional education reveals a profound knowledge of the physiology of the child and adolescent. The different age groups correspond generally to the different stages of mental and behavioral development of the child. Pedagogical methods employed in each of these stages show striking evidence of adapting to the physical and psychological potential of the child, which necessarily requires knowledge and understanding of the fundamental characteristics of "personality" at each different stage of a child; an evolution.

From birth to six or seven years, the child is educated in the family, by the mother, on whom he depends both physiologically and materially. The father is involved only emotionally, or as a complement to the mother.

Starting at the age of six or seven, games occupy an important place in the education of children, in conformity with the awakening of intense mental activity and of egocentrism, which characterizes his mental life. Listening to stories and legends and hearing riddles help to build up and feed his powerful imagination and give him a solid basis for clarifying his ideas. The small tasks he performs help to limit his egotism. All his activities have a physical aspect essential to his development.

Between ten and fifteen, with the development of his ability for abstract thought and reasoning, and the development of his personality, the child is more and more closely associated with social life, both actively in production, and as a passive spectator of social relationships and public affairs. At the same time he is given a certain amount of independence in the family, along with increased responsibilities. It is during this period also that he will start his apprenticeship in some occupation.

At around fifteen years the child undergoes puberty and becomes an adolescent, with all the anxieties this change entails. It is precisely at this moment that the period of initiation comes, and its content, as regards educational value, fully responds to the circumstances. The emphasis it puts on physical exercises, sexual education, awareness of responsibility and the harmonious acceptance of the child into the community should be stressed with especial force. The ritual ceremonies and impressive spectacles indicate the intense interest shown by the entire community in this event in the life of the adolescent.

After initiation, the adolescent is prepared for life, and completes his training with his elders and with the "elders" of the village. He perfects his craft, accumulates experience, and in participating more fully in social life, assumes more of his responsibilities as a man toward other men. When he marries, he will pass through the final door to complete adulthood.

I have already pointed out that judging by results, traditional African education for the most part attained the objectives required in the economic, political, social and cultural context of pre-colonial Black Africa.

In the economic sphere, it trained and supplied the peasants and artisans (blacksmiths, weavers, shoemakers, et al.) in sufficient numbers to supply in normal times the goods and supplies needed for pre-colonial African society, in the framework of trading on the African market, or even with foreign countries.

In the political, social and cultural spheres, enough has been written on different aspects of the political and social life (the empires and kingdoms in Ghana and Mali, the Songhai, Sokoto, Benin) and of the cultural life (oral and written literatures, works of art and music) in pre-colonial Black Africa, particularly during the period preceding the spread of the slave trade, to demonstrate the effectiveness of traditional African education.

However, this relative success calls for a certain number of observations:

1. First of all, the potential and effectiveness of this system of education, and its practical translation into reality, are intimately connected to the economic and social context, and the importance and extent of the heritage to be handed down to the child. In a relatively backward society (although this was not always true in relation to European societies of the same period), where production and trading had just begun to expand and a market come into existence, and where techniques were purely artisan, there could be no separation between the theory and practice of phenomena and their application. Knowledge and technology were essentially empirical, and could only be acquired through actual experience. Since writing was practically unknown (aside from Arabic which was monopolized by the marabouts) no other way to transmit human experience, whether individual, social, technical or scientific existed except the means used by traditional African education. It is for this reason that intellectual pursuits occupied such a small place in this education, at least in the sense they were advanced societies: the systematic teaching of theoretical and practical subjects, with no concrete relation to production.

2. The organization of education is very embryonic, fragmentary, and localized, rarely operating outside the village framework. It can only be effective in an agrarian economy and a society where crafts are transmitted from father to son, where techniques are not very advanced, or where occupations are of an artisan nature and can be learned right on the spot. (This is not to say that important and interesting discoveries cannot be made in various fields.) The organization of the system of education is a reflection of the economic, social and political structures of pre-colonial Black Africa.

There are many traits in traditional African education common to all agrarian and feudal societies or civilizations, whatever their geographical or historical framework. But there are unique aspects also, primarily its very real and concrete collective nature. The significance of this phenomenon should be emphasized, relative to the social and human content of education, particularly as the involvement of society (aside from classical forms of involvement, direct or indirect, through social relationships, habits, and customs) in this case means the direct physical intervention of individuals. It is hardly necessary to observe that no other social organization of the kinds known elsewhere—whether under the aegis of the government or of educational vocational or religious institutions—can claim to do as well in the areas of human relationships and contact.

3. The preceding remarks set down the assets and the inadequacies of traditional African education. Very effective when it is simply a matter of handing down experience from generation to generation, when techniques are relatively backward and essentially empirical, it nevertheless offers no possibility for progress through the assimilation and spread of new experiences and knowledge, because facts had to be transmitted individually, and therefore in isolation. It was condemned to repeat itself and remain immutable, unless there was social upheaval or important political changes which brought on social upheaval.

It remains true, however, that in seeking the qualities needed for any system of education in a given society—adaptation to concrete conditions and desired goals, foundation on a profound knowledge and rigorous observation of the laws and characteristics of child development, richness of human and social content, sufficient flexibility to allow of subsequent changes—as well as in seeking the faults and pitfalls to avoid—traditional African education is a rich source of information, worthy of creative reflection. This is particularly true now, when all of Black Africa is faced with the crucial problem of creating an educational system which answers to the aspirations and needs of our people and at the same time is worthy of the great future which can be ours.

Resolutions

by Preston Wilcox

The Education and Black Students' Workshop divided up into eight divisions as follows:

1. Early Childhood Materials Development
2. Independent Black Institutions
3. Black Studies Programs, Black Colleges, and Black Student Unions
4. Teachers and Administrators in Public Schools: Toward a Community Union
5. Education in Confined Settings
6. A Federal Funding Apparatus
7. The Language of Humanism: Need for a Dictionary
8. Community Control of Schools

The workshop discussions were directed toward the end of determining *what* must be done, *how* it must be done, *who* was going to do it, *when* it was going to be done, and to *whom* the *doers* would be accountable. We accepted white institutional racism, colonialism, capitalism, and imperialism as a basic condition and as different forms of the same kind of oppression. Another basic assumption was that we exist as a nation of people of African origin suffering from common experiences wherever we reside and that there was a need to raise the level of consciousness around the actual existence of that nation and to create the institutions which will give that nation the forms required for its survival, restoration and liberation.

This report will stress the highlights of the reports from eight divisions and identify several general themes that threaded themselves throughout the Thursday period. The general themes were as follows:

1. All Black educators (teachers, students, parents, administrators, and community residents) should be held accountable to the Black community.
2. The education of Black people should be controlled by Black people whether it takes place within a white setting or within a Black setting.

3. Education is a political act; its goals are people-building, community-building, nation-building. It should be directed toward the transmission of skills, knowledge, culture, and values designed to produce the new African man.
4. There is a need to define what we mean by Black-controlled institutions, how to create Black institutions, how to subvert white institutions, how to convert white institutions into Black institutions, how Black people can learn how to look out for each other, how to communicate with each other and to determine how education can be applied as a tool in the nation-building process outside of formal educational institutions.

Early Childhood

The early childhood division will survey, screen and evaluate all known educational materials available for use in Black educational settings. It will also develop materials in four areas: African deity, Our Story, Black myths and fables, and reading readiness. This program will be coordinated with offices of African embassies in America.

Community-Controlled Schools

Successful community-controlled school efforts will be analyzed and summarized. The findings will be disseminated to areas that intend to engage in such efforts. An effort will be made to develop a Black educational service in such communities. A final effort will be made to develop a directory listing the legislative and legal powers already available to local districts. A request will be made to the Community Organization Workshop to develop a manual on how to capture your school.

Independent Black Institutions

The major recommendations of this workshop are as follows:

1. The priority goal is the establishment of a nationwide system of independent Black institutions through . . .
   a. creating new IBI's
   b. strengthening old IBI's
   c. converting traditional institutions into IBI's (community control)
2. Hook up to the developing system of IBI's, i.e., the CAAAE/-Nairobi College Workshop.
3. Write a manual on "How to Set Up an Independent Black Educational Institution." The manual will have the following sections: definition, purpose and objectives, institutional planning (the community, curriculum, staff, students, finance struc-

ture, evaluation, defense). The target date for this item is January 1, 1971.

Black Student Unions

The Black student unions viewed their responsibilities as follows: expanding the development of IBI's, to make Black studies programs accountable to the Black community, to volunteer their services to the people, and to insist that all IBI's become accountable to the Black community.

Black Studies Programs

The Black Studies Program staff resolved to develop models for comprehensive educational programs at the local level and then to develop a process and procedure for knitting existing IBI's, Black Studies Programs, Black Community Educational Programs into a single Comprehensive Black Educational System.

Black Teachers and Administrators in the Public Schools: Community Union

The recommendations of this particular workshop are:

1. That there should be the organizing of a Black community union by Black people and for all Black people regardless of their skills or positions. The participants should come from every social institution in the Black community such as the home, church, civic groups, schools, colleges, bars, pool rooms, etc.
2. These Black community unions must create an apparatus and/or methods for the participants of the Black community unions to build a trust level of solidarity. This should involve a financial base.
3. One of the top priorities of each Black union should be about the business of getting every Black brother and sister out of every white-controlled union.

Education in Confined Settings

An effort will be made to identify those confined settings (prisons, the military, orphanages, detention homes, residential treatment centers, and the like) where Black people are being held and to develop ways and means of exposing them to Black history, literature, and materials.

Language of Humanism

An effort will be undertaken to develop a Dictionary or Directory on Language of Humanism as a tool to facilitate communication among Black people on a human level.

Federal Funding

An effort will be undertaken to compile and disseminate information on federal appropriations for education and to develop a plan and design for a Black Education Foundation.

A Council of the Education and Black Students Workshop was selected and held its first meeting on September 7, 1970.

We began laboring for a nation on Labor Day, 1970, Atlanta, Georgia. Our first task was to complete this summarization *together.*

COMMUNITY ORGANIZATION

Resource Papers

Community Organization

by Sultani Mtetezi Weusi

The main references upon which this paper is based are the ideology of CFUN and the experience we have gained working in our community. We recognize that our emotional commitment is to Africa but our rational commitment is to our experience in America. So our ideological frame of reference is based upon AFRICAN TRADITION *AND* REASON. We don't believe that what we have is better than what others have. We just believe it is better for Blacks, as we learn at CFUN.

We have written that we must reject individualism for we are all Black men. We are Joe the sharecropper, John the janitor, and Mose the miner. When they catch hell, we catch hell. We have said that nothing in language is accidental. So, we find that in the word *community* (by community we mean the coming together of people who share the same values) we find the word UNIT-Y-oneness—the oneness of many. And in the word *organization* we find another together term, ORGAN—a part composed of several tissues and adapted to the performance of a specific function or functions. So, when we speak of community organization we are talking about all of us Black tissues coming together in unity to perform functions that will benefit us all —the entire ORGAN of Black people.

We must be organized to do what we will for if we do not band together we will most certainly die alone. And perhaps the white nation will treat us as it did the Indian—kill us and put our heads on nickels as an eternal monument to our ignorance. We must be organized no matter what it is we propose to do. It takes organization to give a tea party and a bus ride as well as to fight a war. The brother who thinks that he can put on a bus ride successfully without first organizing those who are to help him is just as unrealistic as the brother who shouts "pick up the gun" and expects that (a) Black people will do it, and (b) that once they do so they will know how and whom to shoot. We must be organized because that is what it has always been about—WHO IS THE BEST ORGANIZED—not who has the most men (the French learned a hard lesson and now the Americans are getting theirs in Vietnam). The only way we will liberate ourselves is to be better organized than those who would seek to oppose our liberation. But where do we begin? Can we organize from jump street or is there something else we must do first? There are at least two things that must be done before we would seek to organize our people—mobilization and nationalization.

By mobilization we mean that we must get our people moving, from in front of the TV sets, out of the bars, out of the thirteenth floor of that housing project. We must mobilize them around issues that affect them, i.e., the maximum number of people in a given area. Examples would be ineffective poverty programs, spending 65 percent of the budget on salaries to create a comfortable corrupt buffer of bourgeois kneegrows or a school system whose highest ranking official is an alcoholic (it has been said that those who control the schools control the minds of your children and therefore the future of your nation).

The next move is to nationalize the people. We must get them to think of themselves as a nation—that is, a group of people with a common past, a common present and hopefully a common future, based upon a common way of life. One of the most effective means of nationalization is through pointing out the contradictions in the system. But it must be a part of the system that the community knows about and can relate to. Take the police department. In NewArk, New Jersey, of 1,400 policemen on the force, there are about two hundred Blacks, one Puerto Rican, and recently a Filipino became the first of his group to join this illustrious outfit. About 65 percent of NewArk's 405,000 people are Black. Some 10 percent are Puerto Rican. That leaves at best 25 percent of NewArk white, while 85.61 percent of the police department are white. Similar statistics can be produced for the fire department, administrative and teaching staffs of the public schools and the various boards and commissions. All of this topped with the fact that most of the jobs have a NewArk residency requirement attached to them while more than half of these jobholders do not live in the city. We ask ourselves that if this is a democracy and democracy means majority rule, then why do these situations exist? Is it coincidence? Have we been overlooked (mistakenly of course)? Hardly. We are Black and that is the reason. And that is the ultimate reality that we must face. It has been said that we must deal with the enemy on the level he deals with us. Hence, since it is as a nation that we are enslaved, it is as a nation that we must move to liberate ourselves.

It is through nationalization then that we succeed in winning the minds of our people. Once the mind is won, the body must follow and we must organ-ize. We must organize different personalities and organizations into one gigantic clenched Black fist thrusting forward and striking down all obstacles. An important concept in the organizing process is operational unity. Unity without uniformity "allowing for the diversity of groups and personalities and stressing the unity of purpose." During the recent political campaign in NewArk, we were able to put together a cadre of diverse persons and groups such as Bill Cosby and Adam Powell, and S.C.L.C. and the Young Lords, all for the purpose of electing our brothers to office and bringing Black Power to NewArk for real.

So we have isolated three things we must do in our thrust for national liberation:

1) Mobilize around issues that affect the maximum number of people in the community.
2) Nationalize them by pointing out the system's contradictions.
3) Organize, using the concept of operational unity.

If we are to seriously embrace the slogan "by any means necessary" then we must ask ourselves, is politics a means and is politics necessary? But first we should clarify what we mean when we say politics. Politics is the gaining, maintaining and the use of power. Power is the ability to create and define without obstacles. Together the definitions say that politics is the gaining, maintaining and the use of our abilities to create and define without obstacles.

There are at least four areas of political power:

1) Public Office
2) Community Organization
3) Alliances and Coalitions
4) Disruption.

We will discuss each in the order given. Perhaps the most legitimate area of political power in America is public office. The two kinds of public office are (a) elective and (b) appointive. This is an area in which we have begun to move effectively, primarily because voting and elections are what the majority of *active* Black people think is happening. It is up to the nationalist to channel this thinking into action that will benefit the maximum amount of Black people. Witness NewArk and Gary. Does this mean we believe in American politics? No, not necessarily, but even if we do or think we do, the minute after we took control of it, it would cease being American politics. Our ethos would see to that and the position of the office would legitimize our thoughts and actions.

The second area is community organization. Here we speak specifically of organizations in the community. These organizations serve as power bases to move to get things done. They represent the community or at least an aspect of it, for they are of the community. With whatever skills and resources the community organization has, it serves to keep the enemy on his toes and on the defensive for he knows that the community organization is a vehicle through which the entire community can be aroused to action.

The third area is alliances and coalitions. An alliance is a long-term agreement which for us can be made only with people of color. This is not to say that we can make alliances with *all* such people for there are some whom we all know are beyond salvation or trust (some Toms just like the name). A coalition on the other hand can be made with anyone or anything for it is a short-term agreement that is made to achieve a specific goal and then it's " *'sante sana and tutaonana.*" Of course here we are talking about noncolored peoples. We can make coalitions with scorpions but that does not mean that we must crawl under the rock with them.

Through alliances and coalitions we expand our power base, increase our resources and enhance our effectiveness and legitimacy in the community. At the same time the various skills of each group can be learned by the other, thereby further strengthening each group. Moreover, (in the case of alliances) the longer the groups work together they will find that they have more in common than indifference.

The fourth and final area of political power is disruption. There are two kinds: (a) threatened (b) actual. A Chinese philosopher has written, "To fight a hundred battles and win is good. But to win a hundred battles without fighting is better." Many times a show of force obviates your having to use it. But when it must be used, disruption may go from filibustering to all-out war, which is the highest form of disruption. For to disrupt is simply to stop the orderly process of. For example, if the Board of Education sees fit to deny that Swahili be taught in the school system that is 85 percent Black and you have tried all other three areas of political power to change the Board's mind and failed, then you may see fit to prevent the Board from conducting any other business at its meeting until you get what you want. You can do this by getting large numbers of speakers to address the Board on the same topic one after another into the early morning hours (we've done this in NewArk); or you can shout down opposition speakers or the Board members themselves so they can't communicate. Imagination is the only limiting factor in determining other things that can "stop the orderly process of."

The four areas of political power then are:

1. Public Office
   a) elective
   b) appointive
2. Community Organization
3. Alliances & Coalitions

4. Disruption
   a) threat of
   b) actual

We must use them whenever, wherever, and however we can as vehicles to our goal of National Liberation.

Are Community Relations and Public Relations relevant to this discussion? What things are involved with Community Relations? What is the difference between Community and Public Relations? We answer the last question first and then answer the others during the rest of the discussion. Community Relations is ideas and problems relating to Black people sharing the same values. While Public Relations concerns itself with all others, there are three things involved with Community Relations:

1. Influence
   a) Simple
   b) Programmatic
2. Involvement
   a) Voluntary
   b) Involuntary
3. Control
   a) Economic
   b) Institutional
   c) Coercive

To put it straightforward, to influence someone is to get him to do what you want him to do. When we speak of simple influence we speak of the people picking up your program and ideology without your directly programming them. Our organization is guided by Seven Principles—Unity, Self-Determination, Collective Work and Responsibility, Cooperative Economics, Purpose, Creativity, and Faith, which we call our value system. Without having attended any of our classes, thousands of Black people in NewArk have become aware of and embraced our first two principles (Unity, Self-Determination) and to some extent our seventh one, Faith. (For an in-depth discussion of these Principles see *A Black Value System* by Imamu Amiri Baraka, Jihad Productions, Box 663, NewArk, New Jersey, 1970.) By us being around each other, they have picked up our ideas.

The second kind of influence is programmatic, by which is meant getting the people to do what you want them to do through lectures and examples. Our organization, CFUN, has developed its congregation of rational fanatics into speakers who are able to run down various aspects of our doctrine in small groups or before large audiences. Every Sunday we have what is called a Soul Session at which we do this. It's free and many Black people, young and old, attend to learn something. (One sister, about fifty-five years old, told us that she likes to come because she learns a lot of "cute sayings" which she writes down. If memory serves me correctly, one such saying was "Individualism is a white desire; cooperation is a Black need.") Recently, we have taken our Soul Session to different parts of the city, spreading our ideology. However, often it is necessary to show a sermon as well as deliver one. To this end we at CFUN have not merely talked unity and self-determination, we practice it in our daily lives, providing models for the community to emulate. Since everybody likes a winner, the more we succeed while portraying what the community would be were it conscious of itself the more the community will identify with our thoughts and actions or in a word, us.

The next thing involved with community relations is involvement. The more involved people are, the more they have invested and hence the more easily they are handled or controlled. So we must get them involved on whatever levels we can use them and they are willing to be used. Many people will become involved because they *want* to be a functioning part of the movement. We call this voluntary. Then there are those who are around for very personal reasons (a sister wants to get next to a brother or vice versa; another dude is doing his Master's thesis). Whatever their motivation though we must develop ways to make use of their talents and skills. If they have none we must teach them some so that the involuntary ones will become more useful to the movement. It's highly likely that the involuntary ones will become voluntary as their emotional commitment to the movement is deepened.

The third and final thing involved with community relations is control. The first kind of control is economic. We must move to control the various anti-poverty programs by getting the votes on their Trustee Boards ourselves or programming those who are already on them. Next we have to get jobs for community people in these programs and use these agencies to build and develop the community's economic base. We must build and maintain in a cooperative effort our own stores, shops and other businesses and profit together from them. We must seek maximum profit for the maximum number.

The second kind of control we should seek to get is institutional. For it is through our institutions that we legitimize ourselves and sustain and perpetuate our way of life. A good example is schools. It was stated earlier that whoever controls the schools controls the minds of the youth and therefore the future of the nation the youth represent. Other examples are the police and the courts.

And finally, there remains coercive control, to simply gorilla your way, which unfortunately becomes necessary from time to time. We must learn to defend our programs and ideology mentally, spiritually and physically. If we cannot defend what we develop it will be taken away from us. Or just as bad, we may have the best program but the poorest warriors. (How many football games did your school win only to lose the fight afterwards?) Don't sell a wolf ticket if the buyer can make you eat the receipt later.

We see then that community organization is a useful tool in our efforts to obtain National Liberation. We have tried to point out that community organization involves several things. We summarize them.

1. Make the correct choice of issues and
   a) Mobilize
   b) Nationalize
   c) Organize
2. Use the four Areas of Political Power
   a) Public Office
      1. elective
      2. appointive
   b) Community Organization
   c) Alliances and Coalitions
   d) Disruption
      1. threat of
      2. actual
3. Three things involved with Community Relations
   a) Influence
      1. simple
      2. programmatic
   b) Involvement
      1. voluntary
      2. involuntary
   c) Control
      1. economic
      2. institutional
      3. coercive

What we have attempted to provide here is a specific and common framework out of which we all can work. It has worked and is working with the Committee for Unified Newark in our work in NewArk, New Jersey. It is hoped that something of value or beauty discussed here will prove useful to the rest of the African peoples of the world.

Malcolm X in the Military

by CMSgt. Milton White

To the American armed forces, Malcolm X was born March 10, 1970. That was the day two Air Force chief master sergeants took a document bearing his name into the office of a white commanding officer, setting off a reaction that reached from that room to the White House.

Much of what happened afterward was characterized by paranoiac racism, deceit and cowardice. First there had been approval of the organization we call the Malcolm X Association. But suddenly—on the strength of paternalistic intuition and the advice of "good" Negroes[1]—the white power establishment decided that such an organization could challenge its totalitarian prerogatives.

But the two Black men, CMSgt. Mayanard Jordan III, and the writer, were convinced that the organization had to be, whatever the risk. Like many Black noncommissioned officers we were beginning to feel an incompleteness. Jordan and I were two of a handful who identified this incompleteness as an inability to meaningfully relate to Black America. This was brought home by the lack of any kind of meaningful dialogue between us and the younger Black airmen just entering the military system, fresh from the revolutionary civilian society outside. We were disgusted and ashamed about the house nigger typecasting we as leaders and middle management (the military's great bourgeois class) had been automatically and resentfully consigned to by many of these alert and sensitive young Black men and women.

Black commissioned officers too have been acutely aware of a failure in communicating with other Black persons, but they are by disposition and training less inclined to a revolutionary commitment.[2]

[1] In this analysis "Negro" refers to Blacks of predominantly white value-orientation, while "Black" refers to those inclined to nationalism, except as otherwise indicated by context.

[2] But Black officers seem more comfortable with their lack of identification mainly, I suspect, because of the compensating power of greater status and a deeper inculcation of political religion, which develops at least a mild chauvinism.

While these officers and noncoms had been looked up to before the national renaissance of the Black Liberation Movement, we were now symbolically spat upon. Before any of us wearing an armful of stripes or a shoulder heavy with brass even has a chance to speak to represent himself individually, he is immediately seen as a General Davis, or a General James, men who go through brilliant personal careers, but whose only contribution to the Black masses has been to model what a *Black might* become.

There are recorded many acts of individual rebelliousness, like the Army specialist fifth class calling an officer a white bastard.[3] However, acts of this sort are unorthodox since they represent just one nigger gone crazy. But when the Malcolm X Association showed the capability for organization and cohesiveness, as well as followership that did not require white leadership and approval, it thereby became anathema to the establishment. It was this sort of thinking that forced a reversal of their original approval and the base commander's forbidding our organizing on-base and even discouraging participation by military people off-base.

Sometimes history is made quietly and accidentally. It is doubtful that Mrs. Rosa Parks understood the impact of her deed when she helped change the historical relationship between law and segregation in America with the words, "No. I'm tired." Similarly, Jordan and his associate were not fully cognizant of the revolutionary substance of our deed in informing this commander that the Malcolm X Association would be formed without his blessing. We were simply afraid to go back to our young Black brothers and inform them that we had done what white America has come to expect of its Blacks and what the military, particularly Strategic Air Command, demands: "The man has said no, so we'd better cool it for a while."

So Malcolm lives in the military, near Vandenberg Air Force Base —a huge tract of land centered on a California coastal promontory from which Strategic Air Command test-fires missiles halfway around this world and lofts satellites partway to others. To keep him alive the brothers and sisters dig into their pockets to rent a hall for meetings in the adjacent town of Lompoc (pending a decision as to whether we have been deprived of rights and property, since taxpayers and other organizations have access to the morale and welfare facilities and funds).

So much is discipline the eros of armed organizations that their administration can be no less than totalitarian. We call this totalitari-

[3]The incident, which was tried at Ft. McPherson sometime during 1968, ended in the soldier's acquittal.

anism "command" and we are taught that command allows no corporate decisionmaking or "democratic" participation. The only influential decisional input to command is the technical advice invited and accepted by the commander.

Strategic Air Command is necessarily more totalitarian than the rest. What with generally older, more conservative officers and a sense of supreme importance this is not surprising. SAC was handmade by Governor George Wallace's running mate in the 1968 presidential race, General Curtis LeMay, a further indication of its lingering conservatism. Another striking feature of this command is its quality in the man-machine context, conservatism in matters of personnel and progressivism concerning hardware.

While the Air Force (that is the Air Force outside SAC, for though SAC is theoretically part of the Air Force it is actually a special elite entity directly under the President and the Joint Chiefs, enjoying special privileges unknown to others) was concentrating on humanizing its "people" programs, SAC was polishing its hardware. It is a command uncommonly gifted in the art of making absurdities believable, e.g., its slogan "peace is our profession," when everybody knows its "piece" is kept oiled for war. SAC is a killer in the tradition of Hiroshima and Nagasaki and has since, resourcefully and steadily upgraded its capacity to kill—no, they had to invent a word for what it can do: "overkill."

It is little wonder that the Malcolm X Association didn't set too well with SAC. We wanted a militant organization of persons interested in promoting awareness and understanding of Black America. By militant we meant that we weren't prepared to wait while generals and colonels considered and considered until they considered us out of existence. But mutiny, insurrection and political disobedience wasn't our thing. We had to keep the conflict dialectically abstract. Once it became a material thing SAC could deal with it; and if you think Hiroshima looked bad, think of how SAC would powder a bunch of insurrectionist niggers.

Immediately after the Malcolm thing hit Vandenberg, a dearth of *The Autobiography* struck. Buyers were officer and noncom leaders who suddenly found the need to know more about a Black philosopher, people of color who couldn't decide whether it was more opportune to be Negro or Black at this juncture, as well as a number of deeply committed Blacks who simply weren't up on Malcolm of Harlem.

A crop of Malcolm experts quickly emerged. Negroes who weren't reinforcing their misgivings about the brother's ultra-militancy were coming to the guarded admission that "some of his stuff is good." Whites were beginning to observe that you can accept the creativity of a life without subscribing to everything it represented. Liberal integrationist whites still couldn't see how Malcolm was together at all in the days when he was preaching Farard's Allah, but equipped with some social translation by the Malcolm X Association they could appreciate that Malcolm was talking heavy American political philosophy, even heavier than Thomas Jefferson in relevance to Black folk.

To those of us who think we really understand the relevance of Malcolm to twentieth-century America, Jefferson was not even a comparison much less a reference point. But whites, including most white liberal intellectuals are just as brainwashed as Negroes (they are affected by the same analytical "black-out" of Blacks in contemporary as well as classical American history), naturally go to a white standard. And what better standard to them than Jefferson, the revolutionary architect of the folk content of the American democracy. But whites, and not a few people of color, had to be taught comparisons like this. Of course a one-to-one comparison of Malcolm to Jefferson is nonsense, but we gave them a little chronological exercise that even a racist mind could handle: Jefferson, the bad-dude-turned-good, *used* to own slaves but outlived that disgrace to become the advocate of egalitarianism[4] compared with Malcolm the self-sufficiency advocate who *used* to be a racist.

Still Malcolm was too much. The liberals told us we would have a better chance of establishing a Black identity organization if we changed the name. Malcolm had hurt the feelings of too many during his television time on earth. The old guard might be willing to go along with something like a Martin Luther King Association or perhaps Blacks Unlimited. But not Malcolm. Justify and Jeffersonize all day, but the white man, particularly the SAC white man was not about to permit the Malcolmization of niggers.

But we could not compromise on the name. The decision to use Malcolm was the imperative. The contents of this imperative were five:

(1) Dignity—It was ours so it was groovy.

(2) Indignation—Since it was groovy and ours, the man's telling us we would have to off it meant we couldn't possibly do so.

(3) Independence—We didn't have to get the man's approval; actually if the name we gave our organization was to be legitimate we would neither ask for such approval nor accept it if it were volunteered.

(4) Utility—Saying just what we felt, Malcolm was the most appropriate symbol.

[4]General history is typically about this side of Jefferson's life. I know of nothing to substantiate conclusively that he ever washed his hands of slavery.

(5) Revolution—Only the ideas of Malcolm were sufficiently suggestive of the continuing struggle for change, cultural mobilization of the brothers and sisters and prevention of our going back to sleep.

A SAC base was both a good and bad model for introduction of the sort of progressivism identified with Malcolm. As a microcosm of the American community, it had its wives and children along with its military persons, and its residences, schools and churches along with its missiles and airplanes. It was in short just a miniature version of Anytown, U.S.A.

As such, it provided a good deal more flexibility than could exist in a purely military compound. It seems safe to speculate that were it not for the participation of dependent wives (that magnificent Black woman again) in the organization most of the men would be in jail or shipped out and were it not for the need of Black Studies in the area schools with Black (and white) children there to legitimize this need, a louder command, much more difficult to neutralize, would have been yelled by the establishment.

The great disadvantage of a social movement on a SAC base is the distinctness of class lines. In a command which is task-oriented as well as hardware-oriented the pre-eminence of class is clearly suggested. Even a day's seniority in rank is precious. This affects Blacks gravely in SAC, for even in less elitist, less-conscious outfits, Uncle Tom is a friend of the family. Army Major Lavall Merritt, a forty-one-year-old Chicago brother, said in Saigon, Vietnam, in late 1968 that Black officers constitute the largest group of "identifiable accommodationists" (Uncle Toms) and that they should recognize this and "start acting like men."[5]

Merritt's point seems to hold true for the Air Force, according to the limited experience of the Malcolm X Association. Even after we were investigated and found to be "clean" in terms of insurrectionary objectives, only two among a score of officers would actually commit themselves to total participation, although several contributed in ways that did not involve putting their careers on the line. But there are proportionately as many noncoms, secure in their class and still unwilling to support what they feel to be the side that will inevitably lose.

Blacks in the armed forces have a notable record of moving up by themselves. Some say privately that they are helping the other brothers and sisters by doing their thing as individuals, that by maximizing their personal careers they serve as examples. But they don't seem to care that these examples serve, not as incentives to other Blacks, but to assist white officers in explaining away prejudice and/or a lack of

[5]"Negro Major Charges Army." *The New York Times,* Oct. 14, 1968, p. 3.

sensitivity to the special wants and needs of Blacks. For instance, when Jordan and I confronted the base commander with the original Malcolm X proposal, he showed us an article on Lt. Gen. Benjamin O. Davis Jr. (now retired). He was tokenizing the general with the customary "everybody can make it." We told him that not "everybody" had the only Negro general's special talent.

Imagine for a minute the possible influence of a gifted Black military theoretician who had spent thirty years speaking out powerfully and pridefully (in concert with other Blacks who were as militantly unsilent as they were technically resourceful) for the mobility of the masses of brothers, instead of in the soft, safe tenor of *equality*-mindedness or "in his own quiet way." It's possible that had they spoken out they would have never become the senior officers and chief noncoms. It is also possible that given their leadership and technical resources, they would have been *higher* officials as it was recognized that they had a Black following. In any case the average Black could not help but benefit.

The average Black is the *victim* of equality, the whole concept of which is wrong because it is based on imitation rather than cultural self-sufficiency, and because it subtly retains a status quo based on deceptive proportionality. Says Merritt:

> The American people have for years been told that the military leads the nation in breaking down and eliminating all vestiges of segregation and discriminatory treatment of minority groups. This is a blatant lie.[6]

Armed forces integration is merely a shallow social arrangement for getting the job done rather than any sort of genuine exchange of fundamental group values. Lasting cooperation can come about only through a cultural partnership, that is, the Black man's being a cultural broker in his own right.[7]

There is much evidence that the military establishment will not allow on-base establishment of the Malcolm X Association before a drawn-out battle in the federal courts.[8] But in the meantime it cannot

[6] *Ibid.*

[7] Cooperation seems more relevant here than the notion of "integration" or "assimilation."

[8] The writer preferred court-martial charges against the commander of Vandenberg Air Force Base, accusing him of depriving the Malcolm X Association of the right of peaceable assembly and use of their property (as taxpayers, the public land, i.e., the air base belongs to them), without due process of law. As of this writing, the senior commander, a general, had dismissed the charges, but the writer is now petitioning a higher authority for reinstatement of the charges and authorization for the commander and himself to undergo lie detector (polygraph) examinations.

prevent its off-base activities and the attending growth of cultural awareness. The positive rethinking of the role of Blacks in the military, which has already begun, will therefore result largely from activities such as this.

A Report on Racism in the United Service Organization (U.S.O.)

by Louis J. Gothard

". . . we in the churches and synagogues have a continuing task while we urge our government to disengage itself from a disgraceful commitment. We must continue to raise our voices if our nation persists in its perverse ways in Vietnam. We must be prepared to match words with actions by seeking out every creative means of protest possible."

Dr. Martin Luther King, Jr.
From an address given at Riverside Church Meeting, New York—April 4, 1967

I. History

In a day when the problems of militarism and racism are eroding American society, the United Service Organization (U.S.O.) continues to perpetuate these two problems: it fails to meet the responsibilities incumbent on every American social institution, and to fill the needs of its clients.

Among the facets of the present protest against the war in Vietnam and against growing racism in the nation as a whole, one of the culpable agencies most unscathed is the U.S.O.—United Service Organization.

The U.S.O. remains, with its Ping-Pong and happy hostesses, untouched and smugly self-righteous. The agency has rested on its laurels, earned over twenty-nine years, on and off, of direct services to the military men. It has become a multimillion-dollar adjunct to the U.S. program of genocide against colored and colonized peoples of the world. While we will not deal here intensively with the policy and value questions which are raised by the Vietnam war, we will at the outset consider the following premises as operational for the purposes of this monograph:

1. The war in Vietnam is an illegal, immoral intrusion into the affairs of other sovereign nations.
2. It is racist in effect and in intent.

3. Afro-American men have never had the freedom for which they are supposedly fighting in Vietnam.

4. The U.S.O. in its present form is a willing accomplice and conspirator in the racist practices of the military and in America's warlike foreign policy.

How did it happen? When did this seemingly innocuous, patriotic, social service agency become the racist monster it is today? How could an agency formed for the "duration" of the Second World War find itself committed to a policy of perpetual war?

Let us begin by examining briefly the era which produced the Second World War, the U.S. Army as a world instrument of might, and a civilian population which could find no nobler cause than "supporting our boys overseas," and that support was needed.

The terror of Hitler's siege of Europe had, by 1940, thoroughly convinced the American populace that the policy of isolationsim was less and less expedient. The attack on Pearl Harbor made instant volunteer soldiers out of hundreds of thousands of men. The civilian response, while not entirely pro-war, was at least pro-defense. The economic upsurge that the war had engendered brought thousands of jobs to white Americans, and gradually, when manpower needs became pressing, many defense jobs went to Blacks. By 1944 a million more Negroes were employed in civilian jobs than in 1940.

In the military, most Blacks were placed in unskilled, service-oriented, noncombat duties, until the combat needs became so great that military expediency dictated integration of the fighting forces. It is in this context of patriotism and defensive fervor that the U.S.O. was born. The needs were clear. Communities throughout the nation were experiencing enormous stresses as masses of military personnel moved in and out, straining social services of all kinds. In industrial areas, influxes of defense workers posed housing and living space problems on an unprecedented scale. After several months of negotiations, six social agencies agreed to attempt a coordinated approach to meet these various needs. The founding members of the U.S.O. were:

Young Men's Christian Association
Young Women's Christian Association
The Salvation Army
National Catholic Community Service
National Jewish Welfare Board
Travelers Aid Association of America

These early attempts at coordination were something less than successful, beset as they were with institutional parochialism. In August 1941, the agency came under fire in *The Nation,* in an article by Jonathan Daniels.

> As in some other details of defense, the government itself has been slow in building the recreation centers in which some of us understood that Y.M.C.A. secretary, priest, rabbi, and Salvation Army officer would be concerned only with giving the soldiers the services and the welcome they need in a crowded town. Go look at the crowded towns now. The United Service Organizations are less in evidence as a united body than in their separate stands competing with one another for the soldiers and their souls. The Salvation Army has its special boom-town complement of drums beating by its special boom-town hall. The Catholics have their center by the bus station. The Y.M.C.A. is operating across the street. The Jewish center is open in the hall over the hardware store. The unity that was shown in raising cash does not seem so evident in the spending of it. There is, in some defense centers, little more competition among the honky-tonks that [sic] among the good-deed-doing organizations which so recently marched under one banner to do one job.

He concluded:

> . . . None of these organizations are so important as the job intrusted to them. It ought not to be intrusted to them for another year unless they prove in this first one that they understand that the money was meant for the men and not for the organizations, united or not.
>
> The boys have shown that they could take more brotherhood than they are getting. I think America and its good-doing organizations could, too.[1]

Like the paradoxes of the military (American) attitude toward race, and human rights, the U.S.O. also existed in the midst of self-contradiction. On March 16, 1942, President Franklin D. Roosevelt wrote to Harper Sibley, the President of U.S.O.:

> Not by machines alone will we win the war. Unitedly, unstintingly, and without interruption or delay, we have solemnly promised to give our men a mounting tide of guns, tanks, planes, and ships.
>
> We shall keep that promise, and one promise more—that we shall preserve for them, wherever they may be, and *without regard to race, creed or color,* [italics mine] the moral and spiritual values of the democratic ideals and freedoms for which they are now fighting.
>
> Because the U.S.O. is unitedly dedicated to that high purpose, and because that high purpose is a vital part of the job of winning this war, the U.S.O. should be supported by everybody—cheerfully, generously, and now.[2]

In the memorandum to foundations that year, 1942, the U.S.O. described its operations: "U.S.O. is now operating in 310 cities and towns in the United States, and in twelve territories, possessions, and offshore bases. On April 20, 1942, U.S.O. operations numbered 671 in all. This total included 57 *units for colored troops.*"[3] [italics mine]

Hence, while the U.S.O. was using the Presidential endorsement ". . . without regard to race . . ." et cetera, to raise its $33,000,000 budget, it was in practice as racist as any other existing institution, a bastion of segregation. Like other American institutions, it was a fraud.

Nor could the U.S.O. be accused of taking leadership in the field of race relations. One reporter noted that at one point, the opportunity to do so was presented. Writer Rex Stout, Chairman of the Writers War Board, submitted a pamphlet called "The Races of Mankind" to be distributed in the reading rooms of U.S.O. member organizations. The pamphlet was written by Professor Ruth Benedict and Dr. Gene Weltfish of the Department of Anthropology of Columbia University. In essence, the pamphlet refuted many of the fallacies and superstitions about racial characteristics and differences. It sought to undermine the bases of racism and prejudice by pointing to such factors as the 1917 A.E.F. intelligence tests, in which Northern Blacks did better than Southern whites. The pamphlet was personally withdrawn from circulation by the then President of U.S.O., Chester I. Barnard. Elmer Rice, in a letter to Barnard soon after the incident, wrote (May 4, 1944):

> I have read very carefully your memorandum on the suppression of "The Races of Mankind" by the U.S.O., and I regret to say that it confirms my impressions that your action is a concession to those backward elements in our population who persist in maintaining, both in theory and practice, the vicious and un-American policy of "white supremacy . . ."
>
> . . . It looks to more than one observer as though you were more interested in the sensibilities of your Southern contributors than in the preservation of those principles of democracy for which we are presumably fighting this war.[4]

When, in the late 1940's the U.S.O. did in fact integrate its services, it managed to continue to bow to local pressures by holding segregated dances and other social events, either in separate facilities or at separate times. Consistent with American racist social practices, it remained wholly unacceptable to the white male ruling class for "socializing" to occur between Black men and white women.

> The sexualization of racism in the United Sates is a unique phenomenon in the history of mankind; it is an anomaly of the first order. In fact, there is a sexual involvement, at once real and vicarious, connecting white and black people in America that spans the history of this country from the era of slavery to the present, an involvement so immaculate and yet so perverse, so ethereal and yet so concrete, that all race relations tend to be, however subtle, *sex* relations.[5]

Since the social service volunteer class has traditionally been made up of middle-class white women, the number of less affluent Black women volunteers in the U.S.O. has always been small. The problem of sexualized racism has been pervasive. To this day, it poses some of the most serious problems of U.S.O. administration, from simple arguments to riots in U.S.O. lounges in this country and other parts of the world. It is well known that the military provides one method by which America exports its racism.

The likelihood that the U.S.O. brand of racism will persist seems guaranteed by its Board of Directors, a peculiar combination of colonialist, social and religious agencies together with hand-picked members of the military-industrial complex. Together, they have carved out a feifdom over great chunks of territory—in the form of millions of dollars' worth of facilities, purchasing power, government favors (they are a quasi-governmental agency) and a virtual monopoly over the entertainment and reading of millions of servicemen.

While the American public as a whole is defrauded and debased by this process, there can be no doubt that Black, brown, and red Americans, women and the servicemen themselves are by far the most exploited and abused by this system, as by America as a whole.

II. The Politics and Economics of Racism

There are several working definitions of racism extant. It may be useful to discuss them here briefly. Extensive discussion is unnecessary since both groups, the racists and the victims of racism, know well what is meant by the term. Carmichael and Hamilton defined it thus:

> By 'racism' we mean the predication of decisions and politics on considerations of race for purposes of subordinating a racial group and maintaining control over that group. . . .
>
> Racism is both overt and covert. It takes two closely related forms: individual whites acting against individual blacks and acts by the total white community against the total black community. We call these individual racism and institutional racism. The first consists of overt acts by individuals which cause death, injury or the violent destruction of property. . . . The second type is less overt, far more subtle, less identifiable in terms of specific individuals committing the acts. But it is no less destructive of human life. The second type originates in the operation of established and respected forces in the society, and thus receives far less public condemnation than the first type.[6]

This exhaustive definition, particularly as it relates to the "second type" or institutional racism, will be the most relevant for our discussion here.

Another, simpler definition posed by the Committee for One Society, is this:

> The definition of racism used by COS is broad—any institution that works to the advantage of white people and to the disadvantage of black people is a racist institution. The same test applies to individual policies. Whether those institutions and policies are consciously racist or unconsciously racist is not the issue. If the results are disadvantageous to blacks, it is racist; the burden of proof rests on behavior and not attitudes, on results and not opportunity. In order to have a non-racist institution, black people must not only have equal opportunities in employment, but there must be equality of results in all aspects of the operation including employment, ownership and control, and relations with the larger community.[7]

While the white, liberal establishment agrees in substance with both definitions, it develops a peculiar blind spot when implementation questions arise, as for example in the Kerner Report. The report, also known as the Report of the National Advisory Commission on Civil Disorders, popularized the concept of white racism as a causative factor in today's racial crisis, but reverted back to its shaky premises of mild reforms, "blaming the victim," and asking for reallocation of resources. This document typifies the reaction of the liberal establishment and while conservatives brand such token, attitudinal posturing as radical, even revolutionary, Blacks and radicals see it as doctrinaire liberalism.

In a society in process, therefore, there is no "objective" definition of racism. There is only the victim's view and that of the perpetrator. It is possible therefore for a Barry Goldwater to talk about "Equality under Law" in the *Congressional Record,* September 20, 1963.

> Conservative thought demands a legal and political structure which insures free competition, redress for injury, fair trial, equal rights of participation, and the right of a citizen to protect his home and property. We do not believe in any kind of second-class citizenship, nor in restricting people in any way for reasons of race, color, or hereditary characteristics.[8]

Yet it is not apparently unusual to Mr. Goldwater that of the staff and board of U.S.O. the percentage of Black and brown people approximates .05 percent while in the general population we are close to 25 percent. Nor would he, in all likelihood, attribute the disparity to conscious or unconscious racism, but to the inability of minorities to convince the agency of their worth.

In another statement, a part of his *Congressional Record* "Conservative Creed" statement, Mr. Goldwater focuses on the "monopoly of power." Item 7 of that statement was:

A Belief In The Dispersion Of Power

Our belief in the checks and balances of our republic impels us to regard any concentration of governmental, economic or social power as dangerous to the society. For this reason, conservatives would cut down any monolithic, arbitrary power over the whole of the society whether it resides in the government, the state, the church, in a company, a union or association.[9]

It becomes obvious that he prefers to exercise this censure against unions than against a "voluntary" (or quasi-governmental) association like the U.S.O.

The italicized statements below are Goldwater's specific criticisms of "monopolistic union power," from *The Americanism of Barry Goldwater.*[10] The commentary in parentheses compares the U.S.O. to unions in the context of Mr. Goldwater's assertions.

1. *Almost total immunity under the anti-trust laws.*
   (U.S.O. is wholly immune from anti-trust laws, as are most nonprofit corporations.)
2. *Immunity from taxation.*
   (The U.S.O., as other nonprofit and/or "charitable" organizations is tax-exempt.)
3. *Immunity from injunctions by Federal Courts.*
   (The U.S.O. enjoys a peculiar type of immunity which, though recently challenged by several states, still persists in a number of states.)
4. *Authority to use union funds for purposes not related to collective bargaining even where union membership is not compulsory.*
   (Under the façade of emergency and contingency funds, the U.S.O. maintains a reserve, in marketable securities of over $1,000,000, using the pretext that the demand for services fluctuates with the shifts in American foreign and military policy.)
5. *Power to compel workers to join the union as a condition of continued employment.*
   (As a monopoly, the U.S.O. has at any given time a captive audience for its inane entertainment and pseudo-services.)
6. *Power to compel the employer to bargain exclusively with the majority union.*
   (As the exclusive agency serving the military the U.S.O. has charter from the U.S. Government and reports directly to the President.)
7. *Absolute authority to deny union membership to workers employed in the bargaining unit, on any grounds or for no reason at all.*
   (Screening procedures for U.S.O. volunteers are such that

political beliefs, as well as all phases of background are open to question, and persons may be excluded without a reason.)

8. *The right, in some situations, to invade the privacy of workers, even against their wishes. This deprives them of a legal right enjoyed by all other members of society.*

   (U.S.O. camp-shows and college performers must submit to security clearance by the F.B.I., which may include questioning of friends and neighbors, employers, et cetera, which may occur unbeknownst to the applicant.)

9. *The right, in some situations, to compel employers to make available for union use the private property of the employer.*

   (The Federal Government has made available to the U.S.O. numerous facilities for its own use, as well as providing transportation for various performances, utilizing public, tax-supported facilities.)

10. *Unions are immune from the payment of damages for personal property and property injuries inflicted on employers or others by union members engaged in activities such as strikes or picketing. And this stands even in situations where such activities have been officially authorized by the union.*

    (Under the laws of most states, nonprofit corporations, *qua* corporations, are immune from certain legal actions, as criminal acts which would require imprisonment, since a corporation cannot be imprisoned. Only individuals may be imprisoned.)

III. History, The Military and Woman

The following quotations from *Prostitution in Europe and The Americas* may give some insight into the historical forebears of the U.S.O. and into the woman's role as it has historically related to the military.

> CAMP FOLLOWERS
>
> As we have seen, both lay and clerical life were involved with prostitution—throughout the Middle Ages. But there was another important section of the population which developed its special kind of sexual service—the Army.[11]

The German medieval poem *Parsifal* describes these women of the Army.

> Of women, too, one saw enough;
> Many bore the twelfth sword girth
> As pledge for their sale of lust
> They were not exactly queen;
> Those same paramours
> Were named women of the war canteen.[12]

> Bodies of men constantly marching and counter-marching across Europe far from their homes and womenfolk demanded companionship. It was not merely a question of the satisfaction of sexual needs though this was important—there were other duties (p. 55) which only women could properly fulfill. A sixteenth-century account of the duties of a camp follower brings this out very clearly.
>
> "Item, when a regiment is strong in numbers, then the camp followers also are not few; there should be appointed by the colonel, an official . . . [who] . . . must know how to order and lead such troops just as ordinary or straying troops have to be kept in order and led."
>
> "He must see to it that they do not hinder the troops on the march, and that they do not come into camp before them, where they would take away everything usable from the combatants. Besides, he must see that whores and loose fellows keep clean the latrines, and further:
>
> "That they wait upon their masters faithfully and that they are kept occupied when necessary with cooking, sweeping, washing . . ."
>
> "Under the officer for the harlots is a provost, whose duty it is to establish peace and order, when he cannot make peace by other means, he has a conciliator about the length of an arm with which he is authorized by their masters to punish them."[13]

The specifically sexual function of the camp follower has been recognized since the inception of fighting forces. Sometimes the recognition is open and unabashed as in the medieval period, or shamefaced as in more modern armies.[14]

We point to these factors simply to emphasize the demeaned historical role of women in wars. We suggest that women reassess this role in the light of the Women's Liberation Movement—and that Black women begin to look at their role in terms of the Black liberation struggle.

IV. Implications for the Black Nation

While white radical military organizing has progressed apace, Blacks have made do with informal organizations and reliance on white radical organizational benevolence. While informality and anonymity can be a distinct advantage, there comes a time when Black people must make a direct and unequivocal input into the plight of the Black soldier. This means that there must be ways and means developed to counter the multiple institutional forms of racism which impinge on the Black soldier (the armed forces themselves, the American Red Cross, U.S.O., Uniform Code of Military Justice, informal barracks racism, etc.)

It means further that Black communities must learn how to relate, as an ongoing part of our community organizing programs, to the Black soldier, Black draftee and potential draftee. Many Black communities are carrying forward the fight against the United Way-

United Fund structure in their areas—that pose institutional alternatives to the white-dominated United Fund Structure.

Similarly, we must pose institutional alternatives to the para-world of military and quasi-military structures.

Recommended Reading

Robert Sherrill, *Military Justice Is to Justice as Military Music Is to Music* (New York, Harper and Row, 1970).

Dan Wakefield, *Supernation at Peace and War* (Boston, Bantam Books, 1968).

John M. Swomley, *The Military Establishment* (Boston, Beacon Press, 1964).

Gerald Leinwand, *The Draft* (New York, Pocket Books, 1970).

Kenneth Cole, *Military Counseling Manual* (National Lawyers Guild Los Angeles Regional Office, 507 N. Hoover, Los Angeles, California).

Thana Wentworth Higginson, *Army Life in A Black Regiment* (Crowell-Collier Publishing Company).

Notes

1. Jonathan Daniels, "A Native at Large, The 'Unity' of the U.S.O.," *The Nation* (August, 1941), p. 143.
2. United Service Organization, *Memorandum To Foundations* (1942), p. 8
3. *Ibid.*, p. 1
4. Elmer Rice, "The U.S.O. and 'The Races Of Mankind,' " *Saturday Review* (July, 1944), p. 13.
5. Calvin C. Hernton, *Sex and Racism in America* (New York, Grove Press, Inc., 1965), p. 7.
6. Stokely Carmichael and Charles V. Hamilton, *Black Power* (New York, Vintage Books, 1967), pp. 3–4.
7. Committee for One Society, Report of the Committee, *An Action Research Project* (Chicago, Illinois, 1968), p. 1. Unpublished manuscript.
8. Frank R. Donovan, *The Americanism of Barry Goldwater* (New York, Macfadden Books, 1964), p. 53.
9. *Ibid.*, pp. 53–54.
10. *Ibid.*, pp. 144–145.
11. Dr. Fernando Henriques, M.A., *Prostitution in Europe and The Americas* (Citadel Press, New York, 1965), p. 54.
12. H. H. Ploss, M& P. Bartels, *Woman*, E. J. Dingwall, ed. London, 1935, Vol. II, p. 108.
13. L. Fronsperger, *Kreigssbuch*, Frankfort, 1958.
14. *Ibid.*, p. 56.

Resolutions

by Lou Gothard

The Community Organization Workshop dealt with questions pertaining to the general community organizing needs throughout this country and the Third World.

We agreed that these needs were not substantially different. We recognized that the area of Black fund-raising institutions, that is, organizing resources, is key to the survival of Black organizations throughout the world. We recognized ideology as the basis of all general organizing processes. Further, we saw the area of relating Community Organizing skills to the problems of the Black military man as a sorely neglected study area.

The following sub-section reports constitute the final document of the Community Organization Workshop; while the implementation process is not complete, the structure for completion is included in our council design. We are prepared to "labor for a Nation."

Section I: General Community Organization

The Community Organization Workshop's Recommendations To The Congress of African Peoples:

1. All Community Organizations must relate to the Liberation of Africa, and before we can properly and ideologically organize, we must have a value system. This value system must create behavioral changes. Therefore, we accept the seven Principles as the value system:

   UMOJA (UNITY)—To strive for and maintain unity in the family, community, nation and race.

   KUJICHAGULIA (SELF-DETERMINATION)—To define ourselves, name ourselves, and speak for ourselves, instead of being defined, and spoken for by others.

   UJIMA (COLLECTIVE WORK AND RESPONSIBILITY)—To build and maintain our community together and to make our brothers' and sisters' problems our problems and to solve them together.

UJAMAA (COOPERATIVE ECONOMICS)—To build and maintain our own stores, shops and other businesses and to profit together from them. This must include the concept of land and bread.

NIA (PURPOSE)—To make as our collective vocation the building and developing of our community in order to restore our people to their traditional greatness.

KUUMBA (CREATIVITY)—To do always as much as we can, in the way we can in order to leave our community more beautiful and beneficial than when we inherited it.

IMANI (FAITH)—To believe with all our heart in our parents, our teachers, our leaders, our people and the righteousness and victory of our struggle.

These Principles must be:

The foundation for each Community Organization operating under the Congress of African Peoples. Endeavors pursued by each organization must be consistent with the value system which provides us with these functions:

A. Predictability of behavior

B. Serve as an ultimate authority

C. Give us a means of security

2. That we emulate successful African models in determining the direction that each Community Organization should follow. These models must be in accord with the value system stated above. Models should include, but not be limited to, those provided by the Ujamaa Village in Yakima, Washington; Committee for a Unified NewArk; Tanzania, Guinea and any others.
3. All Congress of African Peoples' Community Organizations must work with the ultimate goal for the Liberation of all African Peoples. (This includes the hemispheres, continents and all other places where Black people find themselves.) We also recognize that this work will mean the destruction of racism and imperialism.
4. All Community Organizations must deal with the reality of the forces of violence, control of goods and services and educational processes enslaving our people.
5. The exact locations of these Community Organizations will be established in conjunction with the institutions set up by the Political Liberation Workshop.
6. We strongly urge all African peoples concerned with the struggles of the Congress of African Peoples to read books and papers by such people as:

   Mwalimu Julius Nyerere

   Sékou Touré

Kwame Nkrumah
Kenneth Kaunda
Imamu Baraka
Odinga Odinga
and Hayward Henry. This is a minimum requirement.

Section II: Fund-Raising

The Community Organization Workshop was assigned the responsibility of resolving problems of funding of the organizational arms of the Congress of African Peoples, in the present and future.

It is necessary to produce this internal mechanism in order that our institutions will be independent and not rely on the traditional funding agencies in the past to solve the problem of Black people in America.

In the past, white and pseudo-Black funding agencies have given monies to support Negro organizations which protected, projected and perpetuated their systems. We, the Congress of African Peoples, acknowledge that Black people striving toward Nationhood will not fit within the confines of that accepted definition.

It is for this reason the fund-raising committee is proposing a mechanism to perpetuate and support our institutions.

This vehicle will be ours to use as a source of direct funding for the Congress of African Peoples. The structure of a National Black United Fund is needed to provide:

A. Recruitment and training for fund-raisers to function
B. Data and research on funds and resources
C. Campaign seed funds
D. Staff of local and National Congress units produced and channeled through National Congress, must be applied to the ongoing survival of the (structured) congress. The fund-raising structure must be built into the congress three ways:
(1) as a basic Black fund-raising commission
(2) as a vehicle related to the work units of the congress
(3) as a vehicle related to the local units of the congress

7. Continued existence and funding of the Congress of African Peoples. We must consider:
The uniqueness of the concept in its relationship to Africa. Therefore its goals should include the following:
A. to be a primary vehicle by which Black people relate to Africa economically.
B. to be the primary vehicle by which U.S. institutions, government, church international organizations, business and industry, relate to Africa in the field of philanthropy and aid.

Function:

It may function as a coordinating vehicle, a resource funnel, an economic lobby within the U.S. for African states. It will relate to economic investments in Africa, philanthropic investments in Africa, and government policy toward Africa, regarding trade development of underdeveloped countries in providing technical assistance, resources, etc. and government military policy which affects Africa.

Funds:

It will therefore endeavor to tap all funds within the U.S. related to international development.

The Congress of African Peoples will promote and program the concept of "Investing in *Ujamaa*"—its role will perpetuate its existence and produce resources by which it relates to its own people. Therefore it will offer mechanisms by which emerging Black enterprises, white industry, and corporations make that investment, for the benefit of Africa, themselves, and Black people.

Funds:

Concessions and promotional sales will be contracted to Black enterprises and Black-related enterprises that practice the principles of *Ujamaa* (Cooperative Economics). Contracted agreements should state that the abovementioned enterprises will stipulate non-exploitation of goods and services in the Black community.

Black Professional Organizations:

will be encouraged to develop investment and pension funds to be utilized solely in investments in Africa through the Congress of African Peoples' mechanism and will also be asked to contribute and assess amounts to the C.A.P. (Note in re: fraternities = Congress of African Peoples should replace the old Pan-Hellenic Council.)

Based on their recognition of their African Heritage	e.g., Fraternities Sororities Masons Elks Links, etc.

Technical assistance should be provided by the Congress of African Peoples to these organizations in order to set up pension and investment pools. Continued organizing of congresses (local) and implementation of its several programs emerging from this meeting.

Churches–White and Black:

will be requested to channel "Foreign Mission Funds," through the congress. (At least $100,000 per year for the conference itself, committed to five years until a regenerative process is stabilized.)

Funds–Individuals

Membership	Investment in Africa	Industries, Corp. Tax
5	5	5–10% Income
10	10	
25	25	
	50	
	100	
	1000	

8. With respect to the immediate situation:
   Sunday Appeal
      Black churches
      White churches–foreign missions collections as a responsibility of the local councils.
   Request: $1.00 donations from church memberships
      $5.00 pledges with $1.00 paid

Assess each delegate and related person $5.00 based on the need to develop a new value and principle system within the Black community toward the financing of their institutions and processes. $5.00 should constitute commitment, the minimum pledge, with no limitations on the maximum.

Recommend that local councils develop a 5 percent tax on income for local and national (congress) survival funds.

Support efforts in conceptual development of Black United Fund or Black United Appeal as one approach to the needs of locals to raise funds.

9. Efforts at this congress meeting
   A. $500.00 was raised on Sept. 4, 1970 from the 100 members of the Community Organization Workshop
   B. $1000 in personal pledges were raised from the workshop coordinators
   C. The planning and implementation group has been developed by the Community Organization Workshop
   D. Additional funds were raised in each workshop. Commitments for pledges exceeded $5000 both from individuals and from organizations
   E. It has been established that our entire conference deficit can be removed by total participation by each workshop
10. Each workshop has been asked to provide the names of two persons to Brother Lou Gothard as fund-raising liaison persons. Several workshops have complied.
    It was agreed that there are definite models that must be implemented by the Congress of African Peoples.

Section III: Community Organization and Black Military

A. Potential Draftees and Volunteers

1. Research and set up subcommittee to deal with keeping brothers and sisters out of United States military
2. Set up a National Committee to deal with the question of the military
3. Deal with Black brothers and sisters in the U.S. in a Pan-African context
4. Deal with the Pan-Africanists movement throughout the world, for example the Pan-African Brigades
5. Form a United Front with other Liberation struggles in America and on an international scale

B. Structural Change Recommendation:
That there be a national committee on the military set up to deal with the question of the military and the Congress of African Peoples

C. The Community Organization Council of Twenty-five shall:
1. Whenever possible use already established organizations as the "Congress of African Peoples" delegate
2. Pay for consumable items plus phone and conferences expenses
3. Establish new community organizations in cities with large African populations. We will utilize existing organizations to implement the congress's objectives. The council will work with units established by the Political Liberation Council Workshop
4. These organizations will be administratively responsible to the Community Organization Council of Twenty-five. This council will also work and study in conjunction with the Political Liberation Council to further develop ideology for these institutions. This ideology should receive its direction from various success models: Committee for a Unified New-Ark, Ujamaa Village in Yakima, Washington, and many others.
5. These organizations should begin operating within ninety days of September 8, 1970 with the council reconvening within thirty days after September 8 to discuss implementation plans, or an executive committee at least meet.
6. Raise $26,000 within six months of September 6, for the purpose of allocation to congress units that have been successful in the implementation of mobilizing, nationalizing, organizing process set by this body. Consideration of the organizational performances in accord with the Black population of the cities that the delegates represent.

D. Structure of the Council of Twenty-five is:
Chairman–Leonard Harrison
Co-Chairman–Sultani Mtetezi

Program Director–Brother Fred Johnson
Budget Director–Brother Bob Woodley
Field Director–Brother George Chaka
Fund Director–Brother Michael Wilson
Research Director–Brother Erle Jones
Communications Director–Brother Uba Eei
National Coordinating Committee of the Congress of African Peoples

The Community Organization Workshop selected Sister Carole Smith and Brother Fred Johnson to be their representatives on the Coordinating Committee. Alternates were selected as well: Brothers Sultani, Chaka, and Dillon.

LAW AND JUSTICE

Coordinator's Statement

Justice

by Raymond Brown

We justify the perpetuation of this social anachronism by reference to the holy principle of justice. I am told that Justice Oliver Wendell Holmes was always outraged when a lawyer before the Supreme Court used the word *justice.* He said it showed he was shirking his job. The problem in every case is what should be done in this situation. It does not advance a solution to use the word justice. It is a subjective emotional word. Every litigant thinks that justice demands a decision in his favor.

I propose to demonstrate the paradox that much of the laborious effort made in the noble name of justice results in its very opposite. The concept is so vague, so distorted in its applications, so hypocritical, and usually so irrelevant that it offers no help in the solution of the crime problem which it exists to combat but results in its exact opposite—injustice, injustice to everybody. Socrates defined justice as the awarding to each that which is due him. But Plato perceived the sophistry of this and admitted that justice basically means power, "the interest of the stronger," a clear note that has been repeated by Machiavelli, Hobbes, Spinoza, Marx, Kalsem, on down to Justice Holmes.

Contrast the two ways in which the word is commonly used. On the one hand, we want to obtain justice for the unfairly treated; we render justice to an oppressed people, we deal justly with our neighbor (cf. Micah). We think of justice in terms of fair dealing and the rescue of the exploited and we associate it with freedom and social progress and democracy.

On the other hand, when justice is "meted out" justice is "served," justice is "satisfied" or "paid." It is something terrible which somebody "sees to it" that somebody else gets; not something good, helpful, or valuable, but something that hurts. It is the whiplash of retribution about to descend on the naked back of transgressors. The end of justice is thus to give help to some, pain to others.

What is it that defeats and twists the idea of justice in its legal applications? Is it our trial court system? We would like to think of our courts as reflections of our civilization, bulwarks of public safety, tribunals for the insurance of fair and objective judgement. Should we revert to some earlier process of investigation of the alleged offender? Or is it that people confuse justice with the elimination of dangerousness from human misbehavior? Is protection from violence something obtained with the aid of justice or in spite of it?

Resource Papers

Will You Survive America?

by Kasisi Sadikifu Nakawa

It is now 1970. Maulana Karenga pointed out back in 1965 that this would be the year when there would be a fine line drawn between Black and white. When things would clarify more than ever and you would really be able to dig the division.

We find ourselves here in September in Atlanta, Georgia, for the convening of the Congress of African Peoples, the evolution of the Black Power Conference. Our purpose here is to develop viable institutions that will develop us and bind us together as a nation; for we realize now that it is "Nation Time" and that we must labor for our nation.

This paper is an example of the institutions we seek to create. This is a proposal for a center for the conscious development of our African youth. It is an example of progressive perfection that we in the priesthood of Kawaida have been developing for the last few years. It is entitled "Who Will Survive America?" and we say that the Black man will survive for we are African people.

Imamu Amiri Baraka, poet and definer of our struggle, has raised the question of survival and who will survive, "Who will survive the heat and fire of actual change?" What will enable you to survive? The correct information will allow us to survive. The information that tells us who we are, what we must do, and how we shall do it. The information that gives us identity, purpose and direction. Keeping us on the righteous path. When that information is correct, it will also be inspirational. We say that inspiration and information are the two components of education. This education will make us dig our *need* for survival, it will sustain our *belief* that we will survive, therefore developing the *will* that is essential to our survival.

When we speak of survival, we point out the repression and genocide that America is dropping on us, the African peoples. America, the sea of madness being led by madmen who spread misinformation causing brothers to commit suicide and say that is revolutionary. As many niggers that have died here in this, there is certainly nothing revolutionary about death in this entrapment. So now we talk about creating institutions, more specifically survival institutions. These institutions that will expand/awaken the consciousness of our brothers. Our brothers who possess the Blackness of our color, the soul of our culture, but who lack the consciousness that awareness, acceptance, and practice of our African identity, i.e., life style, gives us so fruitfully. That life style that gives us a value system that makes us predictable. "We need a value system to be predictable in our behavior," Maulana has said. "Predictable, meaning stable, pointed toward a single goal. The liberation of our soul, mind, and body."

We who live in the life style of the Kawaida faith have accepted and practiced our value system. And in our acceptance and practice, we have become predictable moving toward our liberation of soul, mind, and body. We have said that we will not violate our value system, that we shall survive. That we will not fight the wars of our oppressors. That we will not struggle against ourselves. We are a creative people and war violates our religious code of morality, the *Nguzo Saba.* War violates our Sixth Principle, *Kuumba* (Creativity) and war violates our Second Principle *(Kujichagulia).*

So now we call upon all African peoples to unite *(Umoja)* come together and say that we shall determine our destiny, we shall not commit suicide, that our youth shall be creative and develop for the nation. *Kuumba Kwa Kujichagulia,* Creativity through Self-Determination. That shall be our motto and the military will no longer kill, maim, and misuse the children of our nation. We shall build institutions of consciousness to eliminate this. We shall expand the consciousness of our people. We speak of conscious development, amending conscientious objection. We say it's Nation Time and we must provide identity, purpose and direction.

1. Selective Service and Military

The Selective Service, America's distortion of conscription which can only be distorted in this kind of oppressive system. For a "nation is a group of people who share a common value system, a common past, a common present, and hopefully a common future," Maulana points out in the doctrine. Therefore, we are not actually part of this nation; we do none of these things with these people.

The purpose of Selective Service is to speedily at any given time fulfill the military manpower needs of the nation. The Selective Service maintains a tap on the resources of the nation. It functions in two ways: programming and fear (of punishment). You are faced with submitting to induction and being the "redblooded American boy" or refusing to submit and being the criminal, evader, rebel, fugitive, etc. Once again, we face the oppressive legal system.

The other way you become part of the military madness is volunteering to serve. Actually for African peoples, there is no volunteering to serve, for we are either programmatically coerced or directly coerced. When we speak of programmatic coercion, we speak basically of four areas:

A. *Loyalty/patriotism*—brothers who have actually been mentally assassinated by the massive communication monster, i.e., newspapers, TV, radio, schools, etc. They actually believe in America and have no concept of themselves as an African people. It is not hard to imagine that they believe in Tarzan, Superman, Batman, etc. They are simply unconscious and it is our collective responsibility *(Ujima)* to raise them.

B. *Occupational/educational opportunities*—these brothers are also mentally assassinated by white media. They are existing in some kind of Disneyland, they are not dealing with reality because as Maulana points out in the *Quotable,* "The problem is not economics or social status, it is racism." Look around, brothers on all levels are crying discrimination.

C. *Escape to respectability*—to some brothers a uniform and medals of "dishonor" are all that they require of life. Actually, uniforms will wear out and medals will rust in the jungles of Vietnam with their "soul, mind, and body."

D. *No alternative*—these brothers are suffering from naive realism because life is always an alternative to death. Even a prison term is better than death.

All of these could be solved through expansion of their consciousness, through work and communication. When we speak of direct coercion, we simply mean the brothers who become directly confronted with the Selective Service and respond. Rather than seek an alternative, they begin to rationalize that the service is not that bad. Only when they are stopped by a bullet in Vietnam or are subjected to some form of racism do they realize their miscalculation.

Over the past few years with the emergence of a strong antiwar/-draft movement, the power structure has decided to develop a few smokescreens to calm down the dissent. We deal with the two most commonly discussed. The first one, the lottery, is now a law, with the second one, a voluntary army, supposedly coming in the future.

First the lottery, which was supposed to cut down on the inequities of the system, is fine for white boys, but really does not concern us. For we speak of self-determination *(Kujichagulia)* and creativity *(Kuumba).* So whether our number is in a capsule or in a space capsule, it makes no difference, the war still violates our principles. The second smokescreen, voluntary service, will probably never become a reality and its primary tactic is that of a diversion for the purpose of rhetoric.

For as we stated in the beginning that the primary function of selective service is to speedily meet the military manpower needs by tapping all the nation's resources, so if there was a voluntary army and a manpower shortage or emergency arose there would have to be some form of conscription.

More than anything when discussing the Selective Service and military we must realize who we are. We are an African people seeking to build a nation. We realize the *need* for that nation, we *believe* in that nation, and we have the *will* to build that nation. So once more we say that our motto is *Kuumba Kwa Kujichagulia* (Creativity through Self-Determination). We must say it's Nation Time, let's labor for a nation. We must build survival institutions. Since the draft is an instrument of the oppressive legal system that is committing genocide/repression on us, we propose the building of an institution that will allow us to speak for ourselves and say we are not going to war, we shall create for the nation. We say that we shall aspire to a value system that will make us predictable as Maulana has said, and to quote Imamu Baraka, "predictable, meaning stable, pointed toward a single goal. The liberation of our soul, mind, and body." We must develop consciously, not only conscientiously object.

2. *Center for Kuumba Kwa Kujichagulia*

If you can visualize that today, 1970, five years after the death of Malcolm and the fires in Watts, brothers are still fighting and believing in America and that this maniacal system is seeking to "eventually" grant us total freedom and equality, then you can see the need for this center. If you can't grasp that, then think of the fact that the main institutions for guidance, education, job placement of our youth are in those same hands that guided us in our youth. From these two examples I'm sure that you will realize that it is our collective work and responsibility *(Ujima)* to build this center.

The center for *Kuumba Kwa Kujichagulia* is designed to provide:

A. Military Counseling—to counsel our brothers and secure their future.

B. Guidance Program—to counsel and guide our brothers into schools, jobs, and careers essential to nation-building.

C. Job Placement—to place in jobs essential to career development and nation-building.

D. Tutorial Program—to prepare them for jobs and schools through tutorial and remedial program.

E. Cultural Education—to expand their level of consciousness to aspire to a Black value system and to see their needs in respect to the nation as one.

The center would be broken down into these five areas. The responsibilities for these areas would be:

1. *Draft and Military Counseling*
   A. Counseling on Selective Service and military
   B. Information/Communications concerning Selective Service and military
   C. Alliances with churches, politicians, community organizations
   D. Legal and medical referrals and assistance
2. *Guidance Program*
   A. Guidance counseling
   B. Information and contacts on colleges, vocational schools
   C. Information and contacts, scholarships/financial aid
   D. Directing towards the interests of persons and needs of the nation.
3. *Job Placement Responsibilities*
   A. Source of jobs
   B. Information and contacts in job development programs
4. *Tutorial Program*
   A. Tutors for students having problems in specific areas
   B. Remedial reading program
5. *Cultural Education Program*
   A. Program based on Seven Criteria of Culture
   B. Designed to give brothers identity, purpose, and direction
   C. Classes to be conducted evenings and weekends

The New Well: "Operation Coat Puller"
by George Hicks

The Right Door
—Roland White

Ah, the head once bowed,
now rises from a stupored sleep,
with a new-found peace of well-being,
and a determination of Faith to keep,
The Faith of my peers in this common bond,
who does walk the upright path of abstinence
New-found!

They who abstained from the Opiate Menace,
with outstretched arms they implore:
"Pray come, my brethren, to the New Well's Door;
and we shall show you the Way,
to overcome your addiction Forever More,
Forever more."

A common plea for a Social Ill,
Where until now the results were nil,
So with outstretched arms, we implore:
"Pray come to the New Well's Door!
So your problems can be defeated;
and the Battle be won."

You can also raise a Proud Head,
come to Life from the Living Dead.
A stupored sleep is a cheat to Life;
and as human beings, pray—
do not make such a sacrifice!

For our young, let us set the Pace,
of Pride and Dignity in the Human Race.

That where once was addiction,
in its place,
We shall fill that void with a lasting Grace.

Goals

Our program's specific goals are the following:

1. To recruit patients through the machinery of personal contact made by already rehabilitated addicts. These contacts will "pull the coats" of addicts in the streets—informing each of them of the Well's facilities for detoxification and related services, without the hospitalization under federal "jail" sentence they have come to expect and fear.

   The recruiters will, in search of addicts needing help, go into alleys, abandoned buildings, cellars, roofs, taverns, poolhalls or wherever else they suspect would be a breeding ground for addiction. The recruiters will work around the clock, seven days a week, seeking known, unknown and potential addicts among both adults and teen-agers. The recruiters will attempt to interest the addicts in the Well's program—encourage them to enroll, participate in the detoxification portion of the program, accept help in rehabilitating themselves, accept training and go back themselves and recruit others for the program.
2. To train ex-drug addicts in public speaking, how to effectively participate in panel discussions and meetings, and how to best interest the community in the rehabilitation of drug addicts. This kind of training is necessary in order to articulately reeducate the general public to the dangerous evil of narcotics addiction, and to the urgency of prevention and rehabilitation.
3. To provide and maintain an actual facility (center), and to offer preventive and rehabilitative programs to the community.
4. To offer to addicts a complete, well-rounded rehabilitation program in which they can feel the greatest amount of confidence.
   a. Detoxification
      (with close medical supervision).
   b. Intensive group therapy and private counseling where necessary.
   c. Help in reestablishing family ties.
   d. Assistance in job retraining, employment referrals, etc.
   e. Assistance in problems dealing with housing, welfare, etc.
5. To maintain a liaison between Operation Coat Puller and as many as possible other elements in the community—agencies administering job training, employment, housing, welfare services, and religious establishments and groups. The cooperation of the above-mentioned groups will be sought as each addict

participating in the program needs their help while he readies himself for replacement in the mainstream. Those agencies and groups will serve a vital need in assisting the addicts to become productive, self-respecting individuals again.

6. To provide a complete and extensive Speakers' Bureau and Information Service, which will be available to any community organizations requesting information regarding the myriad problems related to drug addiction.
7. To inform the community why and how it can and must cooperate in our effort to prevent addiction, and to restore good health, pride and dignity in the men, women and children already caught up in the misery and horror of addiction.
8. To reduce the high rate of crime in the ghetto and outside it. Through implementation of our program, many, many men who would otherwise be forced to steal, will be off the streets and performing as productive citizens.

The Well's logical contention is that there are no better qualified rehabilitation workers than ex-drug addicts, to work at the recruitment of, counseling of, and administering of services to addicts. An ex-addict who has made it without drugs is living proof that a complete and permanent cure is possible. An ex-addict is respected and accepted as sincere by addicts whom he encounters. He's not regarded as a "do-gooder" who may have no real experience, knowledge or feeling for the plight of the addict. The ex-addict has "been there," and can best relate to where "there" is.

The United States Bureau of Narcotics lists New Jersey fourth among the states highest in incidence of narcotics addiction. Newark is listed among the ten cities with the greatest number of known addicts. Essex County alone has 2,216 registered addicts, and since 1963 over 300 addicts have been treated in the Essex County Penitentiary.

The Bureau of Narcotics statistics must be realistically considered modest, however, because they are based only on opiate use. New Jersey has no real accurate statistics for publication. We do know that the great majority of addicts are poor, that most addicts admitted to the New Jersey Neuro-Psychiatric Institute are between the ages of eighteen and twenty-five, and that community workers with anti-poverty agencies all through the state have consistently reported regular contact with surprising numbers of addicts in slum areas. Particularly in the northeastern part of the state, there appears to be a recent great increase in addiction. This is attributed by some to the passage of a tough addiction law recently applied in the state of New York, driving many of New York's addicts to New Jersey.

This impression has not been statistically substantiated, however.

For many years there has been evidence of an increasingly serious drug problem in New Jersey, and the problem has been avoided, for the most part, by government. The need grows greater every day for a meaningful, intelligent statewide program to prevent and combat drug addiction. Fear is the obstacle in the way to much progress in our state. The public is ignorant of the problem, has no understanding of it at all except to fear an addict's breaking into homes, or perhaps dealing physical harm to the community. This fear prevents the location of treatment centers in residential areas, and closes people's mind to any possible solutions to addiction.

The Well will attempt to reduce and eliminate that fear, and to encourage the interest and support of the community.

Program Personnel for the period 12/1/67 to 3/1/68

The current staff includes two licensed physicians, one registered nurse, ex-drug addicts, and one non-addict who serves as administrative assistant to Mr. Hicks.

MEDICAL STAFF	Eugene R. Sims, M.D. Harry W. Kingslow, M.D. Audrey Jackson, R.N.
DIRECTOR	George Hicks Age 34, addicted 9 years 1950–59 Golden Gloves Champion 1952 Professional boxer 1956–59 Bartender 1961–67 Police Community Relations Program 1967 New Jersey Community Action Training Institute 1967 Rutgers University Community Action Intern Program 1967
ADMINISTRATIVE ASSISTANT	Lester Gilbert Age 39, non-addict Army Air Force 1946–48 Central Institute New School for Modern Music Amateur boxer, truck driver, salesman Worked closely with George Hicks in planning "Operation Coat Puller"; is staff supervisor.
OFFICE MANAGER	Charles Benson Age 37, addicted 22 years 1946–67 Vocational school, through 3rd year

	Army 1951–54 Remco Industries, Foreman 1954–63; Quality control inspector 1964–66 Works seven days a week, twelve hours a day with The New Well—at the Center; intake of new applicants, set up doctors' and counseling appointments, etc.
REHABILITATION SPECIALIST	Euther Presha Age 46, addicted 22 years Dale Carnegie Course in Public Speaking Army 1942–45 Full day with the New Well; group therapy, speaking engagements, individual counseling, recruiting.
REHABILITATION SPECIALIST	James Way Age 39, addicted 20 years 1947–67 High school graduate Air Force 1948–52 Five–six hours a day with New Well; screening, clerical work, speaking engagements, etc.
REHABILITATION AIDE	Walter Zegler Age 24, addicted 7 years High school graduate Western Electric 1961–65 Kleen-Stik Company 1965–67 Five–seven hours a day with the New Well; counseling, clerical work, screening and field work.
REHABILITATION AIDE	John Williams Age 45, addicted 19 years Army 18 months Salesman, counterman Five–six hours a day with the New Well; counseling, screening, clerical work, field work.
REHABILITATION AIDE	Thomas Sims Age 27, addicted 11 years Earned high school equivalency certificate Works seven–nine hours a day with the Well; speaking engagements, community relations, recruiting & counseling young people.
REHABILITATION AIDE	Jesse Smitherman Age 35, addicted 18 years

	High school graduate Works four–five hours a day with the New Well; group therapy, field work.
REHABILITATION AIDE	Mitchell Kelley Age 44, addicted 20 years Varied work history Four–five hours a day with the New Well; group therapy leader, screening, individual counseling.
REHABILITATION AIDE	Norman Bell Age 35, addicted 20 years Varied work history Four–five hours a day with the New Well; field work, screening, individual counseling.

The Detoxification Process

Detoxification is supervised by two doctors, and a part-time registered nurse. The process begins after the addict patient has been interviewed and accepted for treatment by the Screening Committee.

The physician in attendance administers 10 mg. of methadone four times a day for a period of four days. The patient is required to visit the doctor on each of the four days under methadone treatment in order to be examined, and in order to receive his prescription for the treatment drug.

The medical staff has determined that 160 mg. of methadone is adequate dosage with which to carry the patient through the withdrawal period with some degree of comfort.

Visits with the staff physician are continued following withdrawal, for the purpose of reinforcing the patient's emotional stability, and for prescribing such drugs as may be necessary to assist the patient in his successful return to a normal life. Additional and supportive medication consists of tranquilizers, sedatives and other drugs designed to relieve the symptoms of other diseases which have been previously marked by the use of heroin.

A physical examination is performed prior to the issuance of medication, and again at completion of withdrawal. Any medical problems aside from addiction are either treated by staff physicians, or the patient is referred to an appropriate clinic. Under no circumstances is a patient maintained on the methadone drug beyond withdrawal. (The aforementioned four-day period.)

In the experience of Dr. Sims (one of our doctors), we note evidence that approximately 90 percent of addict patients have gone through "cold turkey" withdrawal at least once in one of the many correctional institutions (both voluntary and involuntary) in the United

States, only to return to use of heroin either immediately or soon after release from the institution. Dr. Sims feels that the therapy most helpful to the addict is treatment *within the community* where he lives, and can receive some support, emotionally, from family and ex-addicts at the New Well. Dr. Sims feels that the realistic rehabilitation of the addict must include full community participation, from both agencies and individuals.

The Well has been in existence for about eighteen months. It originated in downtown Newark, on Ferry Street, and was sponsored by the Ironbound Council of Churches. After a year of operation in Ferry Street, the Well moved to the basement of the State Employment Service offices at Washington Street, Newark.

The move to Washington Street put the Well out of the target area, and it became more difficult for servicing the greatest number of addicts. In order to get to the downtown area for receiving treatment, the addict had to travel through what was for him an alien neighborhood. He stuck out like a sore thumb, in the business/shopping downtown section of Newark.

The Well program had required that an addict, in order to get treatment, be accompanied by an adult relative who would be held responsible for the administering of his prescribed medication. In addition, this sponsor would see that the addict attended meetings, or always showed up at the Well for doctor appointments, etc. The sponsor proved to be a real problem for most addicts—to produce a member of his family was a problem, as most addicts, when they begin to steal from their families, and abuse them in other ways, because of having to satisfy the need for the drug, alienate themselves. In any case, the families of most of these addicts were poor people, and they were concerned with many problems other than addiction itself. Primarily, they're worried where their next meal is coming from. They would much rather lament and withdraw from the problem of addiction. They have a feeling of hopelessness about addiction, anyhow. They feel that the professionals have done little to solve the problem of addiction, and logically, feel that they, as nonprofessionals can offer no solution, that they cannot cope with the problem.

The Well, upon moving to 18th Avenue, under new direction, decided it would no longer compel an addict to produce a sponsor, but would initiate a new approach to the problem of administering medication—an issuance of a daily prescription, under supervision of the medical staff, of course.

On December 1, 1967, recognizing that the state and county had funds available for the establishment of narcotics rehabilitation programs, the Ironbound Council withdrew its support from the Well operation. George Hicks, employed at the old Well as a rehab counselor, and a few friends worked together to find a new facility, where the work of the old Well could be continued, and expanded. The new location is in the heart of the Central Ward, Newark, where the city's greatest concentration of addiction is found.

The facility at 18th Avenue is a building with three floors—with much work to be done on it. Ex-addicts, with no money and lots of brawn, have renovated the first floor into what is used as a reception area, with meeting facilities. We are currently using the second floor for staff meetings, and the Screening Committee meets there. We use the second and third floors for cooking, and ex-addicts who have no homes live-in there.

The "Operation Coat Puller" at the New Well is making a, so far, successful effort to prove that narcotics addiction can be licked, and that narcotics *addicts can rehabilitate each other.*

George Hicks, Director of the New Well, and an ex-addict himself, defines the purpose of the New Well this way:

> We want to re-educate the community to the problem of addiction. We want to "pull their coats" to the fact that they've got to take the time to be concerned about heroin addicts, because these addicts are their own brothers, sisters, mothers and fathers, sons and daughters. If the community had, many years ago, implemented a program like the Well, we would certainly not have the large number of addicts we have today.
>
> We've got to talk to parents, and let them know what symptoms to look for, so that so many of their kids don't wind up with a needle in their arm.
>
> We want to provide a facility where an addict can come for help when he makes up his mind he's had it with heroin. A place where he knows he won't have to go to jail in order to get treatment.
>
> *We're doing these things with "Operation Coat Puller."* We're getting to the community, and we're providing asylum and help for the rejected, dejected drug addict. What we need is more community and agency support—it takes money, and lots of it, to operate a real, meaningful, WORKING rehabilitation program for drug addiction.

Contrary to popular belief, drug addiction is not a problem that does NOT strike suburban youth, but its main concentration is within the ghetto areas of our large cities. And it's a problem that affects our lowest-income Negro and Puerto Rican people in particular. From *Reader's Digest,* November, 1967: ". . . There is virtually no heroin in any of our colleges. Heroin is a problem of the high school dropout. It is a problem of the areas of decay within our large cities. Some 65 to 70 percent of all heroin users are Negroes and Puerto Ricans. . . . There is not one whit of evidence that heroin users are given to man-to-man violence. Their crimes are more against property. In New

York City, some 20 to 30 percent of property crimes are committed by heroin addicts; it has been estimated that they steal up to one billion dollars' worth of goods each year to support their habit."

It is Mr. Hicks's feeling that the community, if for no other reason than to protect itself from outrageous theft, should wholeheartedly support the Well's efforts to clean up the heroin addict.

Mr. Hicks contends, logically, that ex-addicts are the best equipped persons to help others overcome addiction. And so, the Well's staff is made up of almost all ex-addicts. From intake to recruitment to speaking engagements to screening to job development, ex-addicts operate the program.

The New Well's philosophy is that no one is better qualified to rehabilitate an addict than an ex-addict. A tired addict always relates to an ex-addict like he could to no one else. He's receptive to being helped by a man who's proven it can be done; a man he's gotten high with, stolen with, gone to jail with, was hungry and cold with, or perhaps has slept on rooftops or in alleys with. The addict feels that the ex-addict really knows the problem with all its agonies, and he can accept the fact that the ex-addict is sincerely interested in dealing with the overall problem.

The ex-addict, then, is living proof that permanent withdrawal is a real, attainable goal, that it can be accomplished, and that he, himself, is the addict's greatest hope for salvation.

Once he acquires the determination, and can be assured of supportive services, the addict can be successfully treated. We hope to be able to do this at the New Well.

No one knows better than an ex-addict that a user will do anything to get that heroin. He'll steal from his family, from the church, from a hospital—he'll even steal his own babies' milk money. But stealing from one avenue won't feed that habit, so every addict has a number of ways to make money fast. By the Black addict's being more or less confined to the ghetto where he lives, the people who suffer most from these stealing methods are the very people who live in the community.

At our group sessions, we try to get across to the addict patient how much hell he is forcing his people to catch. This thing that makes *him feel so good* is making him hurt his people. These people don't enjoy that good feeling, but they are having to support *his* feeling good. His sisters and his brothers, his mother and father, his wife and his own children—all the people who love him, and whom he loves, are having to pay dues for the feeling he gets. We stress the importance of his being conscious of *himself,* and himself in relation to other people, at these group sessions. If the addict doesn't get to know himself, understand his behavior, and establish pride in himself, he will not stay clean.

We feel it is important to tell teen-agers that if they begin that road by sampling other drugs—or smoking marijuana, they're going to end up with heroin habits, anyhow. We tell them that of every addict we've treated, fewer than 2 percent could say they hadn't sampled other drugs before heroin. We try to impress upon them that once they start shooting heroin, they will have no more control over themselves. That means that everything and everybody GOES before that habit—EVERYTHING.

The addict under treatment is always aware that our doors are open to the police. He knows he cannot come to the Well unless he's clean. We tell them that we're there to HELP them, not to HIDE them.

Of the 218 addicts who have received treatment at the New Well, we can be absolutely SURE of the whereabouts and behavior of at least twenty. We can account for their not using drugs at all, and can attest to their being gainfully employed outside the project. Follow-up by our own recruiters indicates that many other ex-addicts who received treatment at the Center, but do not return frequently to let us know what they're doing, are indeed, clean, but because they are engaged in seeking employment and trying to rebuild their family relationships, they just have time to come around and visit us on rare occasions.

We have at least fifteen ex-addicts who are rehabilitated and do attend group sessions, and/or visit the Center daily. These rehabilitated addicts, in our estimation, are saving the community in the neighborhood of $1,200 a day, as it is believed that every addict steals around $150 worth of merchandise each day in order to support his habit.

Although the New Well has been in operation since December, 1967, it has yet to be funded. No person on staff is salaried—even its director is not being paid. Since its inception, the New Well's monthly rent ($150) has been paid by Robert Curvin, Director of the Rutgers Community Action Intern Program, of which Mr. Hicks is a graduate. Mr. Curvin has donated monies himself, and has raised money from friends for the purpose of helping the Well meet its rent.

Fuel costs in the neighborhood of $700 so far, and $150 has been paid on that account to date. Electricity and gas runs about $30 a month. The phone bill for the Well averages $50 a month.

The Well has a dedicated Intake Worker, who works twelve hours a day, and has received no salary yet. Six volunteer rehabilitation counselors work both full-time and part-time—without pay. Unsalaried also are five volunteer rehab aides. The Business Manager has given thousands of volunteer hours without regard for the lack of funds to compensate him.

Each addict patient accepted for treatment by the Screening Committee is asked to contribute $10 to the maintenance of the Well. This $10 contribution from each registrant has enabled the Well to operate so far on the modified basis it has, in terms of finances.

It is moderately estimated that Newark has 12,000 narcotics addicts. (Newark area includes surrounding portions of Essex County.) The New Well has already reached 218 of these addicts, with treatment. Theoretically, with proper and adequate funding, we can expect to reach *half* the addict population in the city of Newark within one year.

We feel that if the community had had an educational program dealing with narcotics addiction, realistically approaching the problem, years ago, we would not have nearly the monumental number of addicts we have today. We want to establish facilities to operate regular education meetings for the entire community. We plan to divide the participants into three groups: teen-agers, adult evening groups, and adult daytime groups. These meetings, in addition to staff members' outreach work, will help acquaint people with the drug problem, and help them to understand how they can avoid addiction in their own families.

We hope to be able to renovate the third floor of our building to make facilities for office space that would accommodate persons from various community agencies like the Urban League, State Employment Service, training programs and welfare or social service organizations. We would want to see this kind of outside agency participation because they offer the kind of supportive services that make a significant contribution to the effectiveness and the permanence of rehabilitation.

We have found the employment (or lack of it) situation a serious one. With funding, we hope to be able to use both the Employment Specialist and perhaps one or two other staff people to deal with job development and placement.

Looking back at the records we have kept, we discover that we have helped many kids in school, who have been able, after treatment at the Well, to continue their studies. That is one of our most gratifying statistics. We have helped people who lived in much more comfortable home situations than most of us in the ghetto. We have helped husbands and wives whose spouses never knew about their addiction. Many cases are similar, but few are ever the same.

The Well has proven how well ex-addicts can work with addicts. The ex-addict knows the problem AND the people who have the problem—like the back of his hand. When he is dealing with the problem—counseling an addict patient or recruiting him for the program—he does not convey a "social worker attitude," he does not impress shame upon the addict, and the addict cannot dismiss the offer of help because it comes from another one of these "do-gooders." He KNOWS the ex-addict is for real.

Ile Elegba

The Committee from Pittsburgh

Proposal

Ile Elegba means "House of Elegba." Elegba is an ancient African god known as the "guardian of the crossroads." He is the protector of our children at the crossroad into this life, and the protector of our elders as they again approach the crossroads into the other life.

This is particularly significant of the drug addict who desires to get to the crossroads and enter a new life—a drug-free life.

Rationale

We believe that the fundamental *cause* of narcotic addiction in the Black community rests entirely in the fact of WHITE RACISM and subsequent colonization (dehumanization, deculturalization, and political enslavement). But we further believe that narcotic addiction is only one of the many *effects* of RACISM and colonization. Others include such things as self-rejection, Black rejection, demoralization, deterioration of human values and the desire to look, talk, dress, walk and be like the oppressor or the most like facsimile. (If you light, you all right; if you brown, stick around; if you Black, stay back.)

A young Black child starts out in this world (America), for the most part, concerned about himself and his playmates, engrossed in discovering new things and having fun. But all too soon, his little world enlarges. His new discoveries become fewer and his fun becomes tragedy. It usually starts with the local brainwashing clinic (public school). As he grows, he becomes able to recognize the discrepancies between the images imposed at school and the REALITIES in his home and in his community. They are the exact opposite of each other. And, as he grows, so grow the discrepancies. All around him he observes the reactions and survival tactics used by the members of his family and the members of his community. On the bases of these observations and other experiences in his life, he begins to form his own habits, attitudes, personality and, above all, goals.

From then on, it's clear sailing. Right into a brick wall, and then another, and another, and another. And it's not as though we don't see them big white walls. The problem is that we are not the ones in control of our own flight and destination.

The walls are, also, very clearly labeled: Poverty, Unemployment, White education, Self-hate, White-love, Jail, Broken homes, Kill your brother, Sell you sister, Sell yourself, D.P.A., Poverty programs, etc. On one of the walls Death is misspelled . . . D-O-P-E.

But the time has long since passed for Black people to take control of our own flight; and to reduce those walls to ashes; to plant our feet firmly on the ground, united in the true knowledge of our true selves, ready and able to live or die TOGETHER! Like a strong nation is spoze to do.

We believe that real addict rehabilitation *for Black people* MUST mean a complete revolving of 360 degrees. Not merely to the point of decreasing narcotic intake, or substituting one narcotic for another, nor merely eliminating drugs completely, only to usher Black people right back into the bloodstream of American democracy. No. All Black people must *revolve* the complete cycle, back to the point of departure from our naturally Black and Beautiful selves. And to be Black (color, culture, consciousness) today involves, among other things, an inherent, immediate responsibility to join, totally, in the struggle for Black survival, for reculturalization, rehumanization, remoralization, reeducation and reBlackenization of our brothers and sisters, for whom we claim a newfound love. That's what rehabilitation has to mean for *us.*

On that basis, we therefore submit, that there is presently a critical need for a *real* rehabilitation program for Black drug addicts in Pittsburgh, one that deals with the problem, rather than the symptom of the problem. One that results in a non-addicted (physically and psychologically) new Black man and woman.

Structure and Administration

Black community of Pittsburgh is, in this case the highest degree of authority. It is to the Black community that we owe the fact of our existence. It is to the Black community that we owe primary accountability. And it is the Black community that we serve.

The Board of Directors of *Ile Elegba* will be responsible for the overall effective operation and receiving and dispersing of money and other assets for *Ile Elegba,* and proper record-keeping of such. The Board will act as the ultimate decision and policy makers. The Board will hire a director who will be held accountable to the Board.

The director is responsible for the overall administration and operation of the house, and the periodic reporting of such to the Board of Directors.

His responsibilities include:

1. Hiring and firing of administrative and clerical staff personne
2. Proper recording of all financial matters concerning the house
3. Major clinical decisions concerning the residents, in conjunction with other staff members
4. Acceptance of new residents into the house
5. Maintaining an image of responsibility, concern, emotional growth and maturity and all responsibilities or aspirations expected of the residents

Operation

Facility

Our physical facility will be a large house, containing:

Sleeping area
Central dining area
Orientation center
Interview room
Large meeting room, convertible into a lounge area
Library and reading room
Medical room
Staff offices

Therapeutic Communal Living

The residents of *Ile Elegba* will live and relate very much like a family. Everyone will have a specific job function that is necessary for improvement and maintenance of the house. Jobs will vary in terms of degree of physical labor, responsibility and status. The residents who hold the jobs of less physical output, greater responsibility and higher status are all ex-addicts who have demonstrated the trustworthiness, responsibility and emotional growth necessary to hold down the job. With each step up, the responsibility, status and pressure increases. So the residents in those positions represent an achievable goal, which serves as a strong motivational factor for new residents.

Deliberate model behavior will be demanded of all staff and residents at all times, except when otherwise permitted by the director.

Absolutely no drugs, marijuana, alcohol or any chemical of that nature will be tolerated, at any time, inside or outside of *Ile Elegba*

Education and Redevelopment

Seminars

Seminars will be held daily for all residents. The scope of the seminars will be broad, covering such things as political, economic, and social issues confronting the community, sex, religion, culture, values, dope addiction, hygiene, Black psychology, etc.

Seminars will also take several forms:
- Guest speakers
- Staff speakers
- Resident speakers
- Resident debate teams
- Resident panels
- Guest panels

Question-and-Answer sessions will follow speakers in all seminars.

Encounters

The Encounter is the setting where the character-overhauling actually takes place. It is the focal point, around which all other activity in the house revolves. An Encounter may be said to be a highly specialized type of group therapy. It usually involves about eighteen to twenty people in a large room and comfortable setting. There is no official group leader.

All participants are encouraged to honestly and openly verbalize feelings and criticism of the people in the room or of the program itself. The criticism may address itself to personal attitudes and behavior or criticism of how one is carrying out his assigned responsibility in the program.

This kind of verbal exchange offers a counter-balance for the model behavioral relationship that is demanded of staff and residents at all times, except in an Encounter.

The whole group focuses on one person at a time. In other words, anyone in the room who wishes to express feelings to or about the person who is, at the time, the object of criticism (target), will say any and all of what he wishes to say before another person becomes the target. Also, if anyone thinks the criticism to be invalid or too harsh, or not harsh enough, he will immediately come to the defense of the target or compensate with added criticism whichever is called for.

After the points have been made and it appears that the target realizes his unacceptable behavior (usually about fifteen to twenty minutes), someone (anyone) in the group fires at another target and the group's focus switches, allowing a rest and emotional recuperation period for the former target.

Thus, with twenty people digging down into your very being and watching, with cat-eyes for any implicating reaction one might display (which might just be uncrossing your legs, or a sigh), it is almost impossible to hide or camouflage any guilt, or weakness or hang-ups, no matter how deep or how old they might be.

The Encounter opens you up and everyone, including yourself, can take a look inside and see what *really* makes us tick. This is something that is extremely rare among people in this and other Western influenced countries. Once we can look squarely at our hang-ups, without guilt and fear, then we can begin to *deal* with them in a manner that will eliminate them rather than bury them deeper. Hence we start to relate differently to ourselves and to others and the differences is called HONESTY.

Neither titles, or position or anything else spares you from the skin tight, bone-deep scrutiny and probing of an Encounter. The only effective defense is honesty.

Usually, everyone in the room will, at one time or another, or several times in the session, be the *target* of an Encounter. No holds barred, except physical violence.

Individualized rapping (counseling) sessions will be available on a regular basis for anyone who wishes to take such advantage, or who may need such. These sessions may be between staff, or between staff and residents or between the residents alone. They may be called by whoever wishes the session and will be held in the privacy of the Interview Room.

Formal and informal classes will be available both on a voluntary and mandatory basis, depending upon the desire or need as determined by the staff and/or residents. All classes will consist of courses relevant to the program or to the community.

Audio-Visual Program

Films, slides, records and tapes of things educational and entertaining will be made available as often as possible.

Library

A collection of relevant literary material and a quiet study area will also be available, and its *overuse* will be encouraged.

Field Trips (educational) and *Group Outings* (recreational)

Trips and outings to places of relevance and recreation will be well planned and implemented as frequently as is practical.

Advanced Program

After the residents have demonstrated success consistently enough, to the satisfaction of the director and staff, advanced programs will be made available, such as,

1. Technical training sponsored by the Bureau of Voc. Rehabilitation that is relevant to the needs of the community *and* that enables him to earn a living.
2. Scholarships and an open enrollment program, for graduates

from the program, will be sought with the local colleges and universities.

3. On-the-job training in the program as assistant to the administrative staff, from which he will hopefully move toward the salaried, staff position as director.
4. Involvement in some kind of activity (political, social, economic, cultural, etc.) in and with the community.

This advanced phase of the program actually prepares residents to re-enter the community as a functional Black man or woman. When he has been in the advanced phase long enough that he and/or the staff thinks he doesn't need the therapeutic community situation any longer, he will be booted out of the program with all the blessings and best wishes of all the people who have, of late, been his *family*.

Rehabilitation Cycle

Point A represents the point at which a person starts in the program. It may mean that he simply walks into the office to ask about the program. He will receive information about how the program is run, both in the form of literature and verbally. At the same time he is given a very clear and frank picture of future alternatives if he doesn't immediately begin to get himself together, such as, still hustling in the streets (at best), or in some hospital or jail (if he's lucky) *or death* (most likely) or O.D. or bullet or heart failure or hepatitis, etc.

If he indicates that he is motivated to deal with his problem and desires to enter the program, then certain necessary statistical information about himself will be asked for (which will be strictly confidential), whereupon he is admitted to the indoctrination phase of the program.

Orientation (Phase I)

The addict is required to come to the orientation center every day at 9 A.M. From 9 A.M. to 11:30 A.M. and from 1 P.M. to 4 P.M. orientation groups (lightweight encounters) are held. Here he learns about how the program works, the techniques used in the encounter games, and he is constantly told that he will have to cut down his habit considerably or detoxify completely before he will be admitted to the second phase of orientation. He is also urged strongly to begin to speak up in the groups and try to honestly relate to his *feelings*. After two or three weeks of daily attendance at the center and if he has satisfactorily shown motivation and sincerity he will be admitted to the Day Care unit of the house. By this time he will have kicked his habit—cold turkey. If his habit is such that he must be withdrawn in a hospital, then he will be admitted to the narcotic withdrawal ward of ________ Hospital, and then admitted into the Day Care unit of the house.

The Day Care unit of *Ile Elegba* is an extremely important part of the program. It acts as a bridge between Orientation, Phase I and Treatment. It has been found that the intense pressure that goes on in treatment is too radical a change for the average addict coming out of Orientation. Therefore, a simulated treatment facility of less intense pressure and responsibility will bridge the gap.

In the Day Care unit, the addicts will attend daily from 9 A.M. to 5 P.M.; the daily schedule will be:

(1) Morning meeting
(2) Work
(3) Lunch break
(4) Seminar
(5) Work—Tuesday and Thursday
or
Encounter—Monday, Wednesday, Friday

The minimum time spent in the Day Care unit is four months. The maximum will vary according to the individual.

Treatment (Phase II)

As a new member to the household he will be in a very limited situation and under very close observation by staff and other residents of the house. His privileges are few. He is not allowed visitors, nor is he allowed to leave the house without the permission and accompaniment of superiors. He is also not allowed to possess or receive money or valuables from outside the program. The money or valuables he may have upon entering the program must be relinquished and then earned. And he must earn the privileges of visitors and freedom to leave the house without the permission and accompaniment of superiors.

Upon entering the house, he is assigned a bedroom and a job in the house. He will also receive the rules and regulations of the house, and a schedule of activities he is expected to attend (seminar encounters, individual rapping classes, film showings, etc.). He will be introduced to the other staff and residents of the house and his immediate supervisor. Forward progress in the program is judged on the basis of many things, such as:

1. Ability and eagerness to carry out assigned responsibilities
2. Relating to the other people in the house in the manner expected (model behavior)
3. Respecting and obeying house rules and regulations and the people in position of authority
4. Participation and interest in house programs beyond mere attendance

5. Promptness
6. Personal appearance and hygiene
7. Awareness
8. Adaptability
9. Ability to honestly relate to his feelings in Encounter games, and his ability to effectively use the Encounter techniques.

As these values are acquired and as openings become available new residents move up in the program in terms of responsibility and status.

Treatment

Job functions in the house are varied and job changes are frequent, as mentioned earlier. As residents develop they are assigned new job functions appropriate for their level of growth and automatically the more advanced jobs are seen as bringing more status in the house.

The departments are, from bottom up:

1. Service Crew
2. Kitchen Crew
3. Maintenance Crew (light repair work)
4. Building Crew (heavier repair work and renovation)
5. Commissary and purchasing
6. Photography—interior decoration—graphics art department
7. Department head of 1–6
8. Education Department
9. Community Relations Department
10. Acquisition Department
11. Administration Department
12. Expeditor
13. Chief Expeditor
14. Trouble Shooter
15. Coordinator

Each department has a crew and a department head, who is accountable to the coordinator.

Re-entry Candidacy (Phase III)

The meaning of this phase is implied in its title. After one has satisfactorily progressed in the Treatment Phase, he becomes a candidate to graduate from the program. But, as stated previously, complete rehabilitation for Black people must mean finally that one is a functional Black (color, culture, consciousness) man or woman, that is, functional for Black people and himself.

Therefore, phase III will concentrate on the re-entry candidate becoming technically and ideologically prepared to re-enter the Black world, devoid of the need to escape its reality and committed and equipped to CHANGE that reality.

Re-entry

The re-entry phase also serves to "detoxify from the therapeutic community" life. We know that life in the outside world is much different from life in the therapeutic community. And, by this time, it will have been a long time since we really confronted the outside on a daily basis. So, without relinquishing the values and honesty of the therapeutic community, residents must slowly learn how to deal with the other world, this time without becoming a victim of it.

We conclude this part of our proposal by reiterating that the two most essential factors in the success of such a program as this are:

1. Motivation of the addict, and
2. the aformentioned operation and supervision of the house must be carried out primarily by capable ex-addicts.

If we have said anything of value and of beauty all praise is due to Black people, and all mistakes have been ours.

Resolutions

Law and Justice—Survival Institutions, Prisons, Narcotics

by Raymond Brown

The American legal system has been, is presently, and will continue to be an instrumentality through which colonized peoples throughout the world are suppressed, controlled, dictated to, castrated and eliminated. We, the members of the Congress of African Peoples, engaged in charting new directions for the course of Black people, find it imperative and of the greatest urgency that we issue the following proclamation.

Traced to its origin, American law evolved out of European common law. The rights which grew out of this common law were rights to control, possess and be protected in the ownership of property. The rights of the individual man to pursue happiness and to control his own destiny were always secondary to the rights of property owners.

This is the law Europeans used as a shield for imperialism as they raped, pillaged and stole the land of our heritage. The rights of the property owner and capitalist to be protected by the law justified the suppression of the indigenous population.

It was these same principles of capitalism which protected the colonizers of this country. It was this same law which protected the slave property of the plantation owners and traders. These same property laws prevent the Black man today from establishing an economic tool to help him deal with the capitalist lawmakers, or to achieve justice in a criminal law system infected by racism and economic bias.

Because capitalism has always come before democracy in this country, because the laws and the complexity of the legal system serve to perpetuate the landlords, entrepreneurs, and industrialists of this society, because our people have no stronghold in the elite of this structure, and because the property-biased laws and principles of capitalism do not protect or extend rights to Black people—these laws therefore require no respect or compliance from Black people.

Individual rights were created by the Magna Carta, state and federal statutes. Individual rights however, were likewise created for and on behalf of white people. Black people were not included in or consulted on the creation of these constitutional rights. Black people were not considered human and thereby not entitled to human rights. Black people know that constitutional amendments and liberal high court decisions are nothing but crumbs from a table which are swept away by omnibus crime bills, fascist police "no-knock" laws and the manipulation of legal terminology and justice.

Black people realize this country is a liar. When this nation can verbally denounce the rampant racism of South Africa and Rhodesia but fails to censure them economically or politically through the United Nations (where America is one of the leading proponents of world peace and brotherhood), then this country is serving to perpetuate the very racism which it denounces.

This country is deceiving us when whites place Black people in their legal and political institutions as puppets and yet continue to control the decision intimately.

Where this country preaches love and brotherhood but deliberately institutes programs of genocide through murder, dope, birth control, abortion and draft in our communities, then this country is a criminal and should be dealt with as such.

Where this country through ignoring and violating principles of international law is responsible for re-continuation of the scourge of war across the face of this globe, and where the highest court in the land is sworn to uphold the Constitution for all the people but refuses to deal with or rule on the legality of a war that is killing dark-skinned peoples, then the court and legal system is lying when it purports to be concerned about the human rights, freedom or justice of Black people.

Therefore, let it be known that Black people will no longer accept the crumbs of justice. Black people have no commitment to obey or respect laws which were designed to suppress them and their children. The Black people have stopped waiting for this country to wake up. We are building a new nation. Intrinsic in our new nation will be a new code of morals and legal ethics.

We must reject the European value system based on materialism, and accept and practice a new one based on certain principles, in harmony with African communalism. Since a value system shows one's appreciation of life and determines how one shall live, these principles should be internalized and not contradicted in thought, speech, or action.

1. Unity: African people must have unity on all levels—self, family, community, nation, race, world. This is our belief that unity must be one that will start with program and move to ideology.

2. Self-determination: We must determine for ourselves what we must do and what we want. We must govern for ourselves, speak for ourselves, define for ourselves. Our government shall be respected and defended by all African people.
3. Economics: We will build, maintain, control and protect our own economy. This economy must be based on collective and cooperative concepts from which we shall all share.
4. Purpose: Our purpose is a collective purpose of nation-building. We realize our ultimate goal is owning and controlling our own land. First, we must set up institutions that will prepare and guide us to this land and power.
5. Collective Work and Responsibility: We must build a nation through a collective effort and a collective need. We must all face and solve our problems together. Every African is responsible not only to himself but to and for his African brother.
6. Creativity: We are a creative people by nature and we shall create for ourselves concepts and precepts by which we will realize self-determination and nationhood. It is a monument to our African strength that we have remained creative here in America.
7. Faith: Our faith binds all these principles. We must by precept and example carry on our struggle of nation-building. For this faith is a legacy handed to us by our ancestors who have carried out our righteous struggle.

Respect for human values over property values must be our fundamental concern. To accept the value system which has, inherent in it, respect for the worth of the Black man and his right to realization of his full potential as a human being.

We as members of the Congress of African Peoples call upon all Black law students, lawyers, judges, probation and parole officers to cast off the puppet strings which are tying us to an unjust and immoral legal system. Free ourselves of the oppressor who is using us to suppress our own people in order that he might exploit them through our work.

We call upon all Black people in the legal professions to accept this code of legal practice for Black people in our communities, courtrooms and jails. Our new law must be geared to our people to help them survive in this white system until the total concept of Black unity is practiced in the Black community.

The following conditions are seen as the basis for the need to develop survival institutions:

1. The extreme exploitation of our community by the established law enforcement agencies.

2. Absolute failure of police departments to protect the rights of our people, their life, limb, property, etc.
3. The ever presence of threatening and destructive influences (such as drugs).
4. The absence of genuine and legitimate political institutions grounded in our community.

The survival institution committee of the Congress of African Peoples declares a definite need for survival institutions. However, the need for absolute followup and maintenance of an ongoing communications system must be developed, recognizing the following conditions and expressions of this workshop as only a bandage approach to the total and real problem.

Preliminary alternatives for dealing with these conditions are suggested as follows:

1. Decentralization of today's present system of the police department functioning in the Black community so that they are under full control of a community-based organization; for example, the policemen assigned to a given Black community would be under the authority of a board (comprised of) or elected by the residents of that community. This board should have hiring and firing power.
2. Staffing of precincts and patrol forces within the Black community by Black officers, especially key decision-making personnel.
3. The organization and establishment of a community security force to maintain peace, protect and give service to the citizens of the Black community. This force shall be made up of and be governed by the community.
4. (Elevation) recruitment of more Black personnel in high level positions within police department.
5. To expose police atrocities committed under the banner of upholding the law.

Be it resolved that we as Black people propose that the following steps be instituted in the Black community to combat the serious drug problem:

1. It is alleged that methadone is a detoxic with limited usefulness in the treatment of drug addiction; therefore we consider the tactic of maintaining Black people on the narcotic called methadone to be an act of aggression against the African race in this and all countries because of its addictive nature.
2. That the Congress of African People supports the concept of the African rebirth cycle, which is a system of a communal living situation, re-education, re-culturalization, re-direction and community self-defense against drug traffic in the Black Com-

munity consistent with the ideology of Black liberation; which also encompasses involvement of the total Black community including the school systems, churches, colleges, etc., engaged in a war against drugs in our bodies and in our minds.

Law and Justice

Republic of New Africa

Whereas; prisons in this country are designed to perpetuate a certain economic base and

Whereas; it is the most atrocious penal system in the world and

Whereas; it is big businesses in this country and

Whereas; the population of prisons are mostly Black and

Whereas; prisons are necessary to the existence of this system and

Whereas; prisons reduce inmates to sub-human tendencies through sub-human treatment and

Whereas; prisons do not punish for crimes but make inmates criminal and

Whereas; inmates return to society broken mentally, spiritually, physically, socially, and psychologically and

Whereas; inmates are denied the natural functions of sexual release and are made to react in an abnormal way and

Whereas; poor rehabilitation programs exist that are not helpful or related to the inmates.

Therefore, there should be a citizen review board for existing prisons:

1. TO REVIEW PRISONERS' SENTENCING
   a. political prisoners
   b. antisocial prisoners
2. TO ALLOW COMPANIONS' VISITS TO SECURE NATURAL SEX FUNCTIONS
3. HUMANE TREATMENT OF PRISONERS

There should be no prisons at all but the creation of a city where inmates move about freely in a natural state, with programs geared to their special needs, and also they should have been given a choice to say what they wanted to do with their lives, and whereas; proper indemnity or reparations should have been paid to them to afford them a fresh start as due any bonded people, and whereas; to make sure that our people receive full justice, a thorough second look at the Fourteenth Amendment is required and lawyers should raise the question of our citizenship in all of their cases, when they go into the court of the United States and whereas; only through Nationhood could a people ever hope to be free with full equality, dignity, and justice.

Therefore, be it resolved that this Congress of African Peoples support the Republic of New Africa's struggle for National Liberation and Independence in the Western Hemisphere and our claim to land in the five-state area of South Carolina, Georgia, Alabama, Mississippi, and Louisiana, and our right to hold a plebiscite before the world declaring that we are forever free and must determine our own destiny.

HISTORY

Resource Papers

History

by Dhati Changa

To raise Black people to our traditional greatness is the aim of National Liberation. But in order to know where we are going, we must know where we are coming from. That is to say, we must know our history before we can go a step farther. If we know our history, we can anticipate history and if we can anticipate history, we can make it.

Our aim in this workshop should be to give our people a history that will give us identity, purpose and direction. A history that will define you, let you know who you are; a history that gives you a reason and a desire to exist; a history that gives you a way to follow in order to fulfill your purpose.

History is defined as a continuation of mythology or religion in more human terms. That is to say that mythology, which would give you the origin of things and is necessary for a good self-concept, is taken a step farther. History is a record of images, issues and events that reinforce a good self-concept.

There are two types of people who write history, the history writer and the historian. We have to make a distinction between history writers and historians. History writers write that which the power structure dictates. Historians create concrete ideas. The historian writes the history of his own people to build and reinforce their good self-concept. Only a people can write its own history. Therefore, Blacks must write their own history and develop their own heroic images and heroic deeds. When we say that Blacks must develop their own heroic images, we mean exactly that. For instance, to the white boy, Marcus Garvey was a failure . . . to us he was perfect for his time and context. To the white boy Malcolm X was a hate teacher . . . to us he was the highest form of Black manhood in his generation.

Being that a people think no more of themselves than their history permits, it becomes imperative that we write our own history. A step toward giving us a true identity as African people is to rectify the inaccuracies and distortions about us and the role we have played in the making of world history.

Four points which we consider basic for this workshop to accomplish are:

1. the history of other workshops at the Congress of African Peoples
2. the building of Black institutions that would analyze and examine
   a. books
   b. Black studies programs
3. creation of Black textbooks, periodicals, movies and other educational materials
4. historians taking activist roles in protest of maps, charts, books, lectures, presidents' speeches and any other type of distortion of our history

A history of the workshops at the congress would be a history of the people. That is to say, a brief history of these areas—economics, political liberation, religious systems, education, Black technology, social organization, creativity, etc.—would be a record of all aspects of our life. The role of the historian is clearly designed for him . . . which is to expose the distorted histories of our people as being exactly that, distorted and inaccurate.

Therefore, our main purpose in the history workshop should be that of raising the consciousness of our people through the study of a history of Blacks written by Black historians.

Guide to the Study of African History Based on the Works of Basil Davidson

by John Henrik Clarke

This course* is designed as an introduction to African history that will stimulate a continuous study of the subject. In the fifteen lectures, African history and its relationship to world history will be explained. The course will start with an examination of the evidence that tends to prove that mankind originated in Africa. Special attention will be paid to all of the main currents of African history such as: Africa at the dawn of history and the beginning of organized societies, the early empires of the Western Sudan, West Africa, and the grandeur of African civilization before the coming of the Europeans, the decline of the great nation states of Africa and the development of the slave trade, colonialism and African resistance, and Africa in the twentieth century.

Session 1

Africa and the origin of man. The beginning of organized societies in Africa. The early migrations within Africa.

REFERENCES

A Guide to African History, 1965, pp. 1–10.
A History of East and Central Africa, 1969, pp. 1–27.

Session 2

Africa at the dawn of history. North Africa, the relationship of its history to the other parts of Africa, mainly Ancient Egypt and Kush.

REFERENCES

Africa in History, 1969, pp. 1–14.
The Lost Cities of Africa, 1959, pp. 1–47.

Session 3

The early empires of the Western Sudan (West Africa). The An-

*The main writings of Basil Davidson on African History are listed at the end of this Guide.

cient Ghana from 300 A.D. to the Abu Bekr conquest during the reign of Tenkamenin in the year 1076 A.D.

REFERENCES

A History of West Africa to the Nineteenth Century, 1966, pp. 1–49.

The Lost Cities of Africa, 1959, pp. 51–81.

Session 4

The decline of Ancient Ghana and the rise of Mali. From the year 1076 A.D. through the reign of and death of Mansa Musa in 1332 A.D.

REFERENCES

Africa in History, 1969, pp. 82–91.

A History of West Africa to the Nineteenth Century, 1966, pp. 53–60.

Session 5

The Empire of Mali after the death of Mansa Musa, and during the reigns of Mansa Maghan, successor to Mansa Musa, and Mansa Suleiman (1336–1359), who was king of Mali during the visit to Mali of the famous Arab traveler and writer, Ibn Battuta, in the year 1352.

REFERENCES

The Lost Cities of Africa, 1959, pp. 90–98.

Africa: History of a Continent, 1966, pp. 108–114.

Session 6

The rise of the Empire of Songhay, from the reign of Ali Kolon (the first Sonni Ali, 1335) to the death of the second Sonni Ali in the year 1492 (the year Columbus discovered the New World).

REFERENCES

A History of West Africa to the Nineteenth Century, pp. 120–129.

The Lost Cities of Africa, 1959, pp. 98–104.

Session 7

The Empire of Songhay during the reign of El Hadj Mohammed Et-Touré (Askia the Great), 1493–1528.

REFERENCES

Africa in History, 1969, pp. 82–91.

A History of West Africa to the Nineteenth Century, 1966, pp. 122–129.

Session 8

The decline of the Songhay Empire after the death of Askia the Great, 1538 to the invasion and collapse of the Western Sudan in the year 1591 and a hundred years afterward.

REFERENCES

Africa in History, 1969, pp. 91–108.

The Lost Cities of Africa, 1959, pp. 117–124.

Session 9

The smaller kingdoms and states of the Western Sudan. Brief histories of the Mossi Empire, the Fula or Fulini Kingdom of Massina (17th and 19th centuries), the Tukolor Empire of El Hadj Omar and the Mandingo Empire of Samory. The rise of the Ashanti Kingdom, 1700–1895, from the reign of Osei Tutu to the exile of Prempah, 1896, the state of Nupe (in Eastern Nigeria) and the inland kingdoms of Housa, Bornu, Kanem, Baghirmi and Wadai or Wadah.

REFERENCES

Africa in History, 1969, pp. 170–194.

A History of West Africa to the Nineteenth Century, 1966, pp. 65–117.

Session 10

The coming of the Europeans to West Africa and the beginning of the slave trade.

REFERENCES

Africa in History, 1969, pp. 144–159.

Black Mother: The Years of the African Slave Trade, 1961, pp. 1–60.

Session 11

The civilizations, nations and kingdoms of East and Central Africa. Old Uganda, Ethiopia, the Empire of Monomatapa, Zimbabwe, the old Congo and the rise and decline of the East Africa city states of Mogadiscio, Kilwa and Sofala.

REFERENCES

A History of East and Central Africa to the Late Nineteenth Century, 1969, pp. 203–215.

The Lost Cities of Africa, 1959, pp. 131–139.

Session 12

The formation of South Africa, the coming of the Boers and the English and the beginning of the Zulu Wars in the latter part of the eighteenth century. The rise of the Zulu Empire under the leadership of Chaka, the death of Chaka in 1828 and its effect on the rest of South Africa.

REFERENCES

The Lost Cities of Africa, 1959, pp. 43–69.

Africa in History, 1969, pp. 127–139.

Session 13

South Africa after the death of Chaka, the other Zulu Wars and the nature of the Africa's resistance to European rule in other areas of South Africa, such as Bechuanaland, Slaziland and South West Africa.

REFERENCES

Africa in History, 1969, pp. 227–239.

The Lost Cities of Africa, 1959, pp. 317–332.

Session 14

The early manifestations of nationalism in West Africa and the nature of the African's resistance to European rule as reflected in the Ashanti Wars in the Gold Coast (not Ghana), the rise, fall and exile of the famous warrior chief, Jaja of Eastern Nigeria, the war against French rule of Dahomey, the war against the French in Guinea, led by Samary Touré, grandfather of Sékou Touré, the present President of Guinea, and the emergence of a new type of non-warrior African nationalist at the end of the nineteenth century.

REFERENCES

Black Mother: The Years of the African Slave Trade, 1961, pp. 214–238.

Africa in History, 1969, pp. 240–275.

Session 15

Africa in the twentieth century. The rise of the new leadership, the independence movements and the impact of Africa and the world; such personalities as Julius Nyerere of Tanganyika, Sékou Toúré of Guinea, Tom Mboya of Kenya, Tafewa Balewa of Nigeria, Kwame Nkrumah of Ghana, and others.

REFERENCES

Africa in History, 1969, pp. 276–297.

Which Way Africa, 1964, entire book.

MAIN WORKS OF BASIL DAVIDSON RELATING TO AFRICAN HISTORY:

The Lost Cities of Africa. Boston, Massachusetts: Atlantic-Little, Brown Co., 1959. (Also in paperback.)

Black Mother: The Years of the African Slave Trade. Boston, Massachusetts: Atlantic-Little, Brown Co., 1961. (Also in paperback.)

The African Past: Chronicles from Antiquity to Modern Times. Boston, Massachusetts: Atlantic-Little, Brown Co., 1964.

"Africa: The Face Behind the Mask," *Horizon* (March, 1963).

Africa: The History of a Continent. New York, N. Y.: Macmillan and Co., 1966.

African Kingdoms. New York, N. Y.: Time and Life, 1966.

A History of West Africa. New York, N. Y.: Doubleday Anchor Books, 1966. To the late nineteenth century.

Africa in History. New York, N. Y.: Macmillan and Co., 1969.

A History of East and Central Africa. New York, N. Y.: Doubleday Anchor Books, 1969.

A Guide to African History. New York, N. Y.: Doubleday Zenith Books, 1965.

Which Way Africa. The Search for a New Society. New York, N. Y.: Penguin Books, 1964.

The Liberation of Guinea. New York, N. Y.: Penguin Books, 1969.

Dimensions of the Black Experience Bibliography

by John Henrik Clarke

The new interest in Africa and Afro-American History has inspired a number of new writers to address themselves to this subject. The subject is not new, nor is the long neglect of its importance. Up to a few years ago most books on this subject did more harm than good. With the rise of modern African independent nations, and the phase of current Afro-American History known as the Black Revolution, this situation changed radically without completely losing all of its old unpleasant features.

For this bibliography, I have selected what, in my opinion, are some of the best new books on African and Afro-American History. I have purposely selected books that are easy to read and easy to obtain. Most of the books selected are in general circulation.

The bibliography is in three main parts. The first part consists of books on African History and are not difficult to use as basic texts in teaching this subject. Books on Africa are being published faster than they can be counted and most of them leave a lot to be desired. Unfortunately, very few of the new books written on African History by African writers and teachers have been published in this country.

The second part of this bibliography consists of books on Afro-American History and Culture. Most of these books are recent and reflect a more enlightened point of view than the books that were written ten or twenty years ago. The cry for "Black History" and "Black Power" has had some good effects.

The third part of this list consists of general references relating to the community of Harlem. This part of the bibliography was compiled in order to call attention to the rich body of material that is available on Harlem—the world's most famous ethnic community.

Africa

Images of Africa. A report on what American school students know and believe about Africa. Compiled by Barry K. Beyer and E. Perry Hicks. Carnegie-Mellon University, Pittsburgh, Pennsylvania, 1968.

Africa South of the Sahara. A resource for secondary school teachers. Edited by Barry K. Beyer. Carnegie-Mellon University, Pittsburgh, Pennsylvania, 1968.

African Affairs for the General Reader, compiled by the African Bibliographic Center for the African-American Institute, New York, N.Y., 1967.

Africa South of the Sahara, edited by Kenneth M. Glazier. The Hover Institution, Stanford University, Stanford, California, 1964.

Handbook of American Resources for African Studies, edited by Peter Duignan. Hover Institution, Stanford University, Stanford, California, 1967.

Checklist of Paperbound Books on Africa, compiled by Paul Rosenblum, 1965

Afro–America

The Negro in America. A bibliography, compiled by Elizabeth W. Miller. American Academy of Arts and Sciences. Harvard University, Cambridge, Massachusetts, 1966.

A Layman's Guide to Negro History, compiled and edited by Erwin A. Salk. McGraw-Hill, New York, N.Y., 1967.

The Negro in the United States. A research guide, by Erwin K. Welsch. Indiana University Press, Bloomington, Indiana, 1965.

Teacher's Guide to American History, edited by William Loren Katz. Quadrangle Books, Chicago, Illinois, 1968.

General References on African History

African Glory. The story of vanished Negro civilizations, by J. C. de Graft-Johnson. Walker and Co., New York, N.Y. Reissued 1966. 211 pages, $4.95.

Africa: History of a Continent, by Basil Davidson. Macmillan and Co., New York. 320 pages, $25.00.

African Kingdoms, by Basil Davidson and the editors of Time-Life Books, New York, N.Y. 192 pages, $3.95.

The Lost Cities of Africa, by Basil Davidson. Little, Brown, and Co., Boston, Massachusetts, 1959. 366 pages, $6.50.

The World and Africa, by W. E. B. Du Bois. International Publishers, New York, N.Y., 1965. 368 pages, $5.00.

The Pharaohs of Ancient Egypt, by Elizabeth Payne. Random House, New York, N.Y. 191 pages, $1.95.

Ancient African Kingdoms, by Margaret Shinnie. St. Martin's Press, New York, N.Y., 1965. 126 pages, $4.95.

The Splendor That Was Egypt, by Margaret A. Murray. Hawthorn Books, New York, N.Y., 1963. 354 pages, $8.50.

World's Great Men of Color 3000 B.C. *to 1946* A.D., by J. A. Rodgers. Rodgers Publishers, 1270 Fifth Avenue, New York, N.Y., 1947. 296 pages, $4.50.

The African Background Outlined, by Carter G. Woodson. Associated Publishers, Washington, D.C., 1936. 478 pages, $7.00.

African Heroes and Heroines, by Carter G. Woodson. Associated Publishers, Washington, D.C., 1939. 251 pages, $2.60.

The Negro in Our History, by Carter G. Woodson. Associated Publishers, Washington, D.C. Revised edition, 1962. $8.33. See early chapters, page 1 through page 140.

Capitalism and Slavery, by Eric Williams. Russell and Russell, New York, N.Y., 1961. 285 pages, $6.00.

Black Cargoes. A history of the Atlantic Slave Trade, by Daniel P. Mannix and Malcolm Cowley. Viking Press, New York, N.Y., 1962. 306 pages, $6.95

Black Mother. The years of the African Slave Trade, by Basil Davidson. Little, Brown and Co., Boston, Massachusetts, 1961.

Africa, the Politics of Independence, by Immanuel Wallerstein. Vintage Books, New York, N.Y., 1961. 173 pages, $1.25.

Africa, the Roots of Revolt, by Jack Woddis. The Citadel Press, New York, N.Y., 1960. 285 pages, $4.50.

Africa, the Politics of Unity, by Immanuel Wallerstein. Random House, New York, N.Y., 1967. 273 pages, $4.95.

The African Awakening, by Basil Davidson. Jonathan Dape Ltd., London, 1955. 258 pages, $6.00.

A History of West Africa to the Nineteenth Century, by Basil Davidson and F. K. Buah. Doubleday Anchor Books, New York, N.Y., 1966. 342 pages, $1.45.

African Nationalism in the Twentieth Century, by Hans Kohn and Wallace Sokolsky. Van Nostrand Co., Inc., New York, N.Y., 1965. 191 pages, $1.45.

Nationalism in Colonial Africa, by Thomas Hodgkin. University Press, New York, N.Y., 1956. 216 pages, $3.75.

"The New Image of Africa." Special Africa issue of *Freedomways* magazine, Fall, 1962.

Topics in West African History, by Adu Boohen. Longmans New York and London, 1964.

The Rise of the Nation States. A history of the West African Peoples 1800–1964, by F. Agbodeka. Nelson and Co., New York and London, 1965.

Africa Since 1800, by Roland Oliver and Anthony Atmore. Cambridge University Press, New York and London, 1967.

Zamani—A Survey of East African History, edited by B. A. Ogat and J. A. Kieran. Longmans, New York and London, 1968.

Great Rulers of the African Past, by Lavinia Dobler and William A. Brown. Zenith Books, Doubleday and Co., New York, N.Y., 1965.

A Glorious Age in Africa, by Daniel Chu and Elliott Skinner. Zenith Books, Doubleday and Co., New York, N.Y., 1965.

A Guide to African History, by Basil Davidson. Zenith Books, Doubleday and Co., New York, N.Y., 1965.

The Dawn of African History, edited by Roland Oliver. Oxford University Press, New York and London, 1961.
The Middle Age of African History, edited by Roland Oliver. Oxford University Press, New York and London, 1967.
A History of West Africa—1000–1800, by Basil Davidson. Longmans, New York and London, 1965.
East and Central Africa to the Late Nineteenth Century, by Basil Davidson. Longmans, New York and London, 1968.
Africa in History, by Basil Davidson. Macmillan and Co., New York, N.Y., 1968.

Suggested Reading for a General Survey Course in Afro-American History

This list represents a rich body of fact and interpretation essential to an objective understanding of how, historically, the Black and white population in the United States have influenced each other. This is a small sampling of the large body of material that is available on this subject. The material listed here ranges from informative books for young readers (that are also suitable for adults) to exciting works or original scholarship. The books have been arranged in order to create a self-teaching course in Afro-American History.

KEY: (P)—Paperback
(H)—Hardcover
(L)—Available in local library if not readily purchasable
(*)—Titles marked (*) are for advanced reading

General History

Aptheker, Herbert, *The Negro People in the United States; A Documentary History.* Citadel (P), $2.25.
Bennett, Lerone, *Before the Mayflower: A History of the Negro in America.* Penguin (P), $2.45.
Cash, Wilbur J., *The Mind of the South.* Vintage (P), $1.65.
Duberman, Martin, *In White America.* Signet (P).
Franklin, John Hope, *From Slavery to Freedom.* Knopf (H).
Ginzberg, E., and Eichner, A., *The Troublesome Presence.* Mentor (P), 75¢

Hughes, Langston, and Meltzer, Milton, *A Pictorial History of the Negro in America.* Crown (H).
Logan, Rayford, *The Negro in the United States.* Van Nostrand (Anvil Books) (P), $1.45.
Meier, A., and Rudwick, E., *From Plantation to Ghetto.* Hill & Wang (H).
Quarles, Benjamin, *The Negro in the Making of America.* Collier (P), 95¢.
Redding, J. Saunders, *They Came in Chains.* Van Nostrand (P).
Woodson, Carter, and Wesley, Charles, *The Negro in Our History.* Associated Publishers (H).

1619–1861

Cowley, Malcolm, and Mannix, Daniel, *The Slave Trade and the New World.* Black Cargoes; a History of the Atlantic Slave Trade. Viking (Compass) (P), $1.85.

Du Bois, W. E. B., *The Suppression of the African Slave Trade to the United States.* The Slave Trade (H).

Du Bois, W. E. B., *The World and Africa.* New World (P), $1.95.

Williams, Eric, *Capitalism and Slavery.* Capricorn (P).

1619–1861—Slavery as an Institution

Botkins, B. A., *Lay My Burden Down.* A folk history of slavery. Phoenix (P), $1.65.

Douglass, Frederick, *Life and Times of Frederick Douglass.* Collier (P), $1.50.

Kemble, Fanny, *Journal of a Residence on a Georgian Plantation.* (L) 1863.

Litwack, L., *North of Slavery: The Negro in the Free States—1790–1860.* University of Chicago Press (Phoenix Books) (P), $2.45.

Stampp, Kenneth, *The Peculiar Institution: Slavery in the Ante-Bellum South.* Vintage (P), $1.95.

Sterling, Dorothy, *Forever Free.* Doubleday (H).

Tannenbaum, Frank, *Slave and Citizen: The Negro in the Americas.* Vintage (P), $1.45.

1619–1861—Resistance and Struggle Against Slavery

Aptheker, Herbert, *American Negro Slave Revolts.* New World (P), $2.95.

Buckmaster, Henrietta, *Let My People Go.* Beacon (P), $1.95.

Du Bois, W. E. B., *John Brown* (a biography). New World (P), $2.25.

Foner, Philip, *Frederick Douglass.* Citadel (P), $2.45.

Nelson, Truman, *The Sin of the Prophet* (a historical novel about John Brown). Little, Brown (H).

1861–1900—The Negro and the Civil War

Cornish, D. T., *The Sable Arm.* Negro Troops in the Union Army. Norton (P), $1.75.

Franklin, John Hope, *The Emancipation Proclamation.* Doubleday (H).

Higginson, T. W., *Army Life in a Black Regiment.* Collier (P), 95¢.

McPherson, J., *The Negro's Civil War.* Pantheon.

Quarles, Benjamin, *The Negro in the Civil War.* Little, Brown (H).

Rose, V., *Rehearsal for Reconstruction.* Bobbs Merrill (H) (L).

Sterling, Dorothy, *Captain of the Planter.* Doubleday (H).

1861–1900—Reconstruction

Buckmaster, Henrietta, *Freedom Bound.* MacMillan (H), $3.75.

Du Bois, W. E. B., *Black Reconstruction.* Meridian (P).

Fast, Howard, *Freedom Road* (historical novel). Crown (P), $1.45. Pocket Books (P), 35¢.

Franklin, John Hope, *Reconstruction: After the Civil War.* University of Chicago Press (P), $1.95.
Stampp, Kenneth, *The Era of Reconstruction.* Knopf (H), $4.95.
Wharton, Vernon L., *The Negro in Mississippi (1865–1890).* Harper (P), $1.75.

1861–1900—The Era of Re-oppression
Chalmers, David M., *Hooded Americans.* The First Century of the Klan. Doubleday (H), $5.95.
Logan, Rayford W., *The Betrayal of the Negro.* Collier (P).
Meier, A., *Negro Thought in America: 1880–1915.* University of Michigan Press (H) (L).
Randal, W. P., *The Ku Klux Klan.* Chilton (H), $5.95.
Woodward, C. Vann, *Reunion and Reaction.* Little, Brown (H). Anchor Books (P), $1.25.
Woodward, C. Vann, *The Strange Career of Jim Crow.* (Galaxy Books) Oxford University Press (P), $1.50.
Woodward, C. Vann, *Origins of the New South: 1877–1913.* Louisiana State University.

1900–1941—The New Resistance
Du Bois, W. E. B., *Souls of Black Folk.* Fawcett (P).
Du Bois, W. E. B., *Dusk of Dawn.* Harcourt (H) (L).
Hughes, Langston, *Fight for Freedom:* The story of the N.A.A.C.P. Berkley (P), 50¢.
Cronon, E. David, *Black Moses:* The story of Marcus Garvey. University of Wisconsin Press (P), $1.95.
Ginzberg, Ralph, *100 Years of Lynching.* Lancer (P), 75¢.
Johnson, James Weldon, *Along This Way.* Viking (H).
Meltzer, Milton, and Meier, August, *Time of Trial, Time of Hope: 1919–1941.* Doubleday-Zenith (P), $1.45.
Orvington, Mary White, *The Walls Came Tumbling Down.* Harcourt.
Sterling, Dorothy, *Lift Every Voice.* Doubleday-Zenith (P), $1.45.
Washington, Booker T., *Up From Slavery.* Several paperback editions, less than $1.00.
White, Walter, *A Man Called White.* Viking (H).

1900–1941—From South to North
Bontemps, Arna, and Conroy, Jack, *Any Place but Here.* Hill & Wang (H).
Drake, St. Clair, and Clayton, Horace, *Black Metropolis.* Harcourt Brace (H). Also (P) Torch Books, 2 vols., $2.45 each.
Johnson, J. W., *The Autobiography of an Ex-Colored Man* (A sociological statement in fictional form). Hill & Wang (P), $1.45.

1941–1967—Yesterday, Today, Tomorrow

Baldwin, James, *Nobody Knows My Name.* Dell (P), 50¢. Also Dolta-Dell, $1.65.
Baldwin, James, *The Fire Next Time.* Dell (P), 50¢.
Bates, Daisy, *The Long Shadow of Little Rock.* McKay (H).
Belfrage, Sally, *Freedom Summer.* Viking (H).
Bennett, Lerone, *The Negro Mood.* Ballantine (P), 60¢.
Braden, Anne, *The Wall Between.* Marzani & Munsell (P), $1.85.
Clark, Kenneth, *Dark Ghetto.* Harper & Row (H), $4.95.
Farmer, James, *Freedom When?.* Random House (H).
Frazier, E. Franklin, *The Black Bourgeoisie.* Collier (P), 95¢.
Freedom to the Free, Report of the U.S. Civil Rights Commission, 1963. U.S. Government Printing Office, $1.00.
King, Martin Luther, *Stride Toward Freedom.* Ballantine (P), 50¢. Also Harper & Row (Perennial Library), 65¢.
King, Martin Luther, *Why We Can't Wait.* Signet (P), 60¢.
Lewis, Anthony, *Portrait of a Decade:* The Second American Revolution. Bantam (P), 95¢.
Lincoln, Eric, *The Black Muslims in America.* Beacon (P), $1.75.
Lomax, Louis, *The Negro Revolt.* Signet (P), 75¢.
Malcolm X, Autobiography of Malcolm X. Grove (P), 95¢.
Peck, James, *Freedom Ride.* Grove (P), 95¢.
To Secure These Rights, Report of the President's Committee on Civil Rights. U.S. Government Printing Office, 1947.
Silberman, Charles E., *Crisis in Black and White.* Vintage (P), $1.95.
White, Walter, *How Far the Promised Land?.* Viking (H).
Young, Whitney, *To Be Equal.* McGraw Hill (H).
Zinn, Howard, *SNCC: The New Abolitionists.* Beacon (P).

Selected List of Recent Books on Afro-American History

Black Power, U.S.A. The human side of reconstruction, 1867–1877, by Lerone Bennett. Johnson Publishing Co., Chicago, Illinois, 1967.
Pioneers in Protest, by Lerone Bennett. Johnson Publishing Co., Chicago, Illinois, 1968.
Black Protest: History, Documents, and Analyses—1619 to Present, edited by Joanne Grant. Fawcett Book (paperback), 1968.
Chronicles of Negro Protest, edited by Bradford Chambers. Parents Magazine Press, New York, N.Y., 1968.
Black History, edited by Melvin Drimmer. Doubleday & Co., New York, N.Y., 1968.
From Slavery to Freedom, by John Hope Franklin. Alfred A. Knopf Co., New York, N.Y., 3rd edition, 1967.
White Over Black, American Attitude toward the Negro, 1550–1812, by Winthrop D. Jordan. Penguin Books, New York, N.Y., 1969 (P).

To Be a Slave, by Julius Lester. Dial Press, New York, N.Y., 1969.
Negro History and Culture, A bibliography for the young, edited by Miles M. Jackson, Jr. The University of Pittsburgh Press, Pittsburgh, Pa., 1968.
Black Abolitionists, by Benjamin Quarles. New York, Oxford University Press, 1969.
Reconstruction, edited by Staughton Lynd. Harper & Row, New York, N.Y., 1969.

General References Relating to The Harlem Community

A History of Negro Slavery in New York, by Edgar J. McManus. Syracuse University Press, Syracuse, N.Y., 1966.
"The Negro in New York, 1783–1865," by Leo H. Hirsch, Jr. *Journal of Negro History,* Vol. XV (1930).
The New York Plot of 1741. Henry H. Ingersoll. "The Green Bag," XX, 1908.
The New World A-Coming, by Roi Ottley. Houghton Mifflin Co., Boston, Mass.
Harlem: A Community in Transition, edited by John Henrik Clarke. The Citadel Press, New York, N.Y., 1964.
The Negro in New York, by James Egert Allen. New York, Exposition Press, 1964.
"Race Riot, 1900: A Study of Ethnic Violence," by Gilbert Osofsky. *The Journal of Negro Education,* Vol. XXIII, No. 1 (Winter, 1963).
"New York Negroes and Employment, 1625–1920," by Herman D. Bloch. *Inter-racial Review,* June, 1964.
The Negro 1775–1861, by Simon Anekwe. Special issue Amsterdam News Progress Report on the Negro in New York, April 23, 1966.
Harlem: Negro Metropolis, by Claude McKay. E. P. Dutton & Co., Inc., New York, N.Y., 1940.
Black Nationalism: A Search for an Identity in America, by E. U. Essien-Udom. Dell Publishing Co., Inc., New York, N.Y. (P), 1962.
Black Moses: The story of Marcus Garvey and the Universal Negro Improvement Association, by Edmund David Cronon. University of Wisconsin Press, 1957.
Garvey and Garveyism, by Jacques Garvey. Published by the author, 1963, at 12 Mona Road, Kingston 6, Jamaica, W.I.
The Negro at Work in New York City, by George E. Haynes. New York, 1912.
Booker T. Washington and His Critics, edited by Hugh Hawkins. D. C. Heath & Co., Boston, Mass., 1962.
The New Negro, edited by Alain Locke. Albert & Charles Boni, Publishers, New York, N.Y., 1925.
Harlem: The Making of a Ghetto, by Gilbert Osofsky. Harper & Row, New York, N.Y., 1965.
Adam Clayton Powell and the Politics of Race, by Neil Hickey and Ed Edwon. Fleet Publishing, New York, N.Y., 1965.

Negro Capitalist, by Abram L. Harris. The American Academy of Political and Social Science, Vol. XII, 1936.

Mayor's Commission Report on the Condition of Harlem (1936), New York State Temporary Commission, Second Report on the Condition of Colored Urban Population, Feb., 1939.

"The Relationship of Afro-Americans to African Nationalism," by E. U. Essien-Udom. From *Freedomways,* Fall, 1962, Vol. 2, No. 4.

"The Nationalist Movement of Harlem," by E. U. Essien-Udom. From *Harlem, A Community in Transition,* edited by John Henrik Clarke, 1964.

"The New Afro-American Nationalism," by John Henrik Clarke. *Freedomways,* Fall, 1961, Vol. 1, No. 3.

Chief: The Story of A. Philip Randolph, by Anna B. Hildebrand. Associated Publishers, Washington, D.C., 1965.

The Black Muslims in America, by C. Eric Lincoln. Beacon Press, Boston, Mass., 1961.

My Face Is Black, by C. Eric Lincoln. Beacon Press, Boston, Mass., 1964.

When the Word Is Given, by Louis Lomax. World Publishing Co., New York, N.Y., and Cleveland, Ohio, 1963.

Malcolm X Speaks, edited by George Breitman. Merit Publishers, New York, N.Y., 1965.

The Autobiography of Malcolm X, written with the assistance of Alex Haley. Grove Press, New York, N.Y., 1965.

"Behind the Harlem Riots." Two articles from *Spartacist Magazine,* New York, N.Y., 1965.

Hunger and Terror in Harlem, by James Ford. Prepared for the Mayor's Commission on Conditions in Harlem, April, 1935. Pamphlet.

Harlem: Dark Weather-Vane, a report on the Harlem Riot of 1935, by Alain Locke.

Dark Ghetto, by Kenneth B. Clark. Harper & Row, New York, N.Y., 1965.

"The Negro and American Entertainment," by Langston Hughes. From *The Negro American Reference Book,* edited by John P. Davis, Prentice-Hall, Inc., New York, N.Y., 1966.

"When the Negro Was in Vogue," by Langston Hughes. From his book *The Big Sea.* Alfred A. Knopf, New York, N.Y., 1940.

Blues People, Negro Music in America, by LeRoi Jones. William Morrow & Co., New York, N.Y., 1963.

The Meaning of the Blues, by Paul Oliver. Collier Books, New York, N.Y., 1963.

The Negro in American Culture, by Margaret Just Butcher. The New American Library, New York, N.Y., 1956.

The Book of the Blues, edited by Kay Shirley and Frank Driggs, Crown Publishers, Inc., New York, N.Y., 1963.

"Jazz at Home," by J. A. Rodgers, from *The New Negro,* edited by Alain Locke. Albert and Charles Boni, New York, 1925.

What Made Harlem Famous, by Howard Brown, Monograph prepared for the Community Action Institute, 1966.

"Harlem Nightclub," by John A. Williams, from *Harlem, A Community in Transition,* edited by John Henrik Clarke. Citadel Press, New York, 1964.

"The Music of Harlem," by William R. Dixon, from *Harlem, A Community in Transition,* edited by John Henrik Clarke. Citadel Press, New York, 1964.

"Harlem." Special issue of *Time* magazine, July 31, 1964.

"Harlem: Hatred in the Street." Article in *Newsweek* magazine, August 3, 1964.

Pickets at the Gates, by Estelle Fuchs. The Free Press, New York, N.Y., 1966.

Notes of a Native Son, by James Baldwin. Beacon Press, Boston, Mass., 1955.

Nobody Knows My Name, by James Baldwin. Dial Press, New York, N.Y., 1961.

"Social Agencies in Harlem," by Ray Rogers, from special Harlem issue of *Freedomways,* Summer, 1963.

Harlem-Upper Manhattan, published by the Department of Church Planning and Research, the Protestant Council of the City of New York, 1962, 2 volumes.

South in the Ghetto: A Study of the Consequences of Powerlessness and Blueprint for Change, compiled by the Research Department of HARYOU, published by HARYOU, 1964.

The Negro in New York, An Informal Social History, edited by Roi Ottley and William J. Weatherly, The New York Public Library & Oceana Publications, Inc., publishers, Dobbs Ferry, N.Y., 1967.

New York Past, Present, and Future, by Ezekiel P. Belden, G. P. Putnam, New York, N.Y., 1949.

"The Negroes of New York in the Emancipation Movement," by Charles H. Wesley, *Journal of Negro History,* January, 1939.

Narrative of the Life of Frederick Douglass, an American Slave, written by himself, The Anti-Slavery Office, Boston, Mass., 1845.

The History of the Negro Church, by Carter G. Woodson. Associated Publishers, Washington, D.C., 1921.

Immigrant Gifts to American Life, by Allen H. Eaton, Russell Sage Foundation, New York, N.Y. 1932.

The New Negro, by Alain Locke. Albert & Charles Boni, New York, N.Y., 1925.

Resolutions

by John Henrik Clarke and
Yosef ben-Jochannan

The History Workshop realizes that the recognition of our traditional greatness is an important factor in National Liberation. To know where we are going, we must know where we are coming from. That is to say, we must know our history before we can go a step farther. If we know our history, we can anticipate history; and if we can anticipate history, we can make it.

This workshop sought to give our people a history that will give us identity, purpose and direction; a history that will define us, let us know who we are; a history that gives us a reason and a desire to exist; a history that gives us a way to follow in order to fulfill our destiny.

The History Workshop makes the following resolutions to the 1970 Congress of African Peoples:

1. That the attempt be made to facilitate contact and cooperation between African historians in Africa and in the Diaspora for the purpose of using our collective historical experiences to help with our liberation.
2. That in conceptualizing the history of African peoples, it is imperative that we see ourselves as one African people, no matter where we are located in the world, and that this history be referred to as AFRICAN history.
3. That a commission of Black scholars from every nation represented at the congress, and others not represented, produce within a suggested period of two (2) years from this date, a comprehensive world history of the African peoples entitled, *The African Peoples in World History.*
   A. That a comprehensive annotated bibliography be produced for use in all Black institutions, so that the distortions will be identified and corrected.
   B. That educational materials on history of all ranges from pre-kindergarten children to high school seniors, with illustrations by Black illustrators, be compiled.

4. That there be established a Congress of African Peoples publishing house.
5. That a Black controlled and directed Research and Information Dissemination Center be established.
   A. The congress should establish a committee to evaluate existing Black institutes, societies, associations and organizations.
   B. The congress should consider the possibility of forming a consortium of those institutes, societies, associations, etc., that are qualified to serve as an accrediting entity in the field of historical scholarship for African people (e.g. the AHSA, Institute of the Black World, etc.).
6. That white dominated and controlled African studies programs and institutes should not control information relative to African people. The only legitimate African studies programs and institutes for African peoples are those manned by African scholars.
7. That Black History be presented as the unfolding of the social heritage of Black people everywhere and not as adjuncts to other people's history.
8. That contrary to present usage, colonialism and slavery be developed as episodes in the general history of the African Motherland. The European contacts must be seen as incidents in the African canvas.
9. That the predominant social institutions of Africans abroad be traced to their historical origins in the African heritage.
10. That the Congress of African Peoples co-opt the assistance of Black colleges to research selected topics and areas of Black History for the benefit of the Black community.
11. That Black colleges be encouraged to develop community projects for the study of the history of local Black institutions and local Black communities. This type of community research should be action-oriented, and primarily for student involvement.
12. That a commission be established by the congress to describe in pamphlet form the basic aspects of our culture as a guide for thought and action.
13. That the congress establish procedures to rebut distortions and to provide clarifications on misinterpretations of life and culture of African peoples in the movies, television, radio, newspapers, magazines, and above all, advertisement.
14. That the congress establish affiliations with the following Black scholarly research organizations:
    The Institute of the Black World and African Heritage Studies Association.

COMMUNICATIONS

Coordinator's Statement

by Tony Brown

The traditional use of mass communication in this country has been for the purpose of oppressing nonwhites and entertaining whites. The result of this vicious misuse of communications has been a general disrespect and misunderstanding by whites about Blacks and Blacks about themselves.

The general categories of communications are as follows:

Electromagnetic (TV and Radio)
Print (newspapers, magazines, and various forms of publication)
Verbal and Non-Verbal ("grapevine" transmission of popular folklore)

All of the above-stated categories of transmitting information have enslaved the Africanoid peoples on this continent much more effectively than the police, the army or any form of force currently available to the vested interest groups that own the United States. The psychological phenomenon of repetition compulsion has created among our people a vicious cycle of self-hate. Its manifestations are subtle yet damaging to our sense of worth without which freedom is impossible.

An understanding of the environmental supports such as the church, the police, the school and media will lead us to the understanding that the entire frame of reference for white racism is taught directly through the institutions of communications. An example of the use of environmental institutional support is offered as follows:

> A white man and his son standing in front of a school building. The man explains to his son that the broken windows and the garbage littered around the building are the results of a people who have no respect for themselves or others. Also he points out that the average I.Q. of students in this all-Black school is 40 points below the average of students in an all-white school. Because of the manner in which the white racist educational system reinforces white racism and a general hostile environment develops a sense of frustration among Blacks, the breaking of windows and strewing of garbage are quite

> understandable as an outlet for hostility. The I.Q. test is an instrument to measure one's ability to relate to and understand a middle-class white racist mentality because the standardized group for the I.Q. test was composed of upper middle income WASP's.

In the above example if the environment were void of I.Q. tests for whites being used to test the mentality of Blacks and if the circumstances which lead to the breaking of windows and the strewing of garbage were not present then the white man could not successfully teach white racism through an institutional support to his son who in turn will use it to continue the oppression of Black people. Succinctly, white racism created the pathology of this society, condones it and perpetuates it through the use of the mass communications media.

In the context of the ideological statement of the Congress of African Peoples by Brother Imamu Baraka, the use of mass communications should be placed in perspective to Black liberation, survival and nation-building. Communications must be in the hands of Blacks for the purpose of developing a Black identity through which national liberation can be achieved. It must advance our respective religions, recapture and explain our true history, aid in the education and use of political, economic, social and community organizations. Alliances should be advanced along the lines of short- and long-term goals and coalitions used as temporary arrangements for short-term goals. A communications network interrelating *all* forms known or to be discovered must reinforce each of the segments of our culture as above stated. As an immediacy we are to understand that a Black consciousness of Nationhood must be taught to those Africanoids who have not yet come to the realization of true self and heritage. They must be appealed to in the broadest possible sense so that rhetoric can be replaced by Nationhood.

This congress must result in the formation of instruments and mechanisms in the area of communications that will counter the monopolization of thought and expression which characterizes the current lessons of white racism which kills the minds of Black people. Television and print outlets have created the imagery of a racist society in which Blacks are invisible and when portrayed are seen in fairytale situations for the purpose of soothing white America's guilt, or are not situated at all, both of which are equally damaging.

Television is the principal source of communications in this society and the most effective brainwashing tool ever devised. "Television is the Message." In this country fifty-five percent of 200,000,000 people depend on the six o'clock news to understand what is going on; children spend an average of six and one-half hours a day watching a black duck who unlike the white ducks is an oddball non-swimmer or an asexual Buckwheat in "Our Gang" whose mother cannot distinguish between "it" and a monkey at feeding time. This is the lesson Black children receive more hours in the year than they spend in the classroom. This is the lesson of the electromagnetic spectrum which has two-thirds of all American households watching its one-eyed white racism between the hours of seven and ten P.M. every night. Blacks watch it an average of fourteen hours a day and are more selective viewers than whites on (UHF) Educational TV. There is not one television station in the United States, its possessions or territories that has a Black general manager and no Blacks are involved in decisions of programming. The commercial TV stations use the airwaves to transmit their racist messages with the approval of the Federal Communications Commission, allegedly acting as a regulatory agency in the public's "interest, convenience and necessity." The airwaves belong to the public and licensees of commercial stations (VHF) receive this largest single capital investment in their operations absolutely free.

A succinct analysis of the above paragraph will quite clearly lead one to the conclusion that we have a monetary investment in the very system that systematically teaches us to hate what we are and to love what we are not.

Television, and print to a lesser extent, creates the basic conceptual foundation of every child in this society; if it does not change to reflect our Black life style, liberation will remain rhetoric.

Of some two hundred educational television stations all of which are directly or indirectly supported through state and federal taxes, not one has a Black general manager and all have less than three percent employed in any capacity. In a petition recently filed with the FCC asking for the removal of the right to broadcast from the Alabama Educational Television Commission, the National Association of Black Media Producers and Black Efforts for Soul in Television, advised the Commission as follows:

> Petitioners do not contest the fact that by the standard generally employed by "commissions" dominated by whites, some of the material contained in these programs may be objectionable. But petitioners do not accept any inference that the majority of the material is objectionable by any standards and that the vast majority of these programs are ill-suited for broadcast by educational television stations. However, whether the material is offensive to either the AETC or the Commission is essentially irrelevant to the issue at hand. The primary concern here is not the sensibilities of "commissions" but the education of Black children and Black adults in Alabama. *The educa-*

tion of Blacks cannot be furthered if the standards of white individuals —whether at the AETC or at the Commission—are used to measure the value of educational television programs for Black individuals.

Indirectly, citizens throughout the United States support the AETC. Without their tax dollars, neither the Federal nor the state government would have the resources to provide the assistance essential to AETC sustenance. Only recently the AETC received five grants under Public Law 87–447 totalling $1,000,000; the AETC also has pending with the Department of Health, Education and Welfare ten similar grants totalling $2,761,213. The AETC has demonstrated a financial dependence on the public which requires extra diligence in meeting its responsibilities to all segments of the community.

There are some seven thousand radio stations, but only ten are Black-owned. The majority of "Soul" stations that "make your knees freeze and your liver quiver" are owned by whites.

Ownership by Blacks is nonexistent in television and extremely negligible in radio. This fact must have absolute priority in the development of mechanisms to develop Black consciousness and combat white racism. Communications is the cornerstone in the struggle for our survival.

The systems discussed above—television, radio, and the print medium—are "old" systems. New systems such as cable which utilized a coaxial for transmission over, through, under or around anything and EVR (Electronic Video Recording) which will revolutionize communications dramatically must be controlled by Blacks. Cable systems require the approval of local politics (city hall) and a possible timetable for erection of the systems can follow the pattern of Black political control at the municipal level.

There is already some print control (the Black press) and Blacks working in white press situations, both of which need support and relationships to the Nation.

Resolutions

by Lou House

Communication is the exchange of, transmittal, reception and dispersal of information.

For the Congress of African Peoples, communication is a primary need in the movement for national liberation and the building of a Black nation.

For a movement to succeed it must have both an ideology, a framework in which to place all ideas and problems dealing with the community, giving us identity, purpose and direction, organization, which we are structuring at this Congress of African Peoples, resources, and most important communications which addresses itself to the need of the congress to mobilize, nationalize and organize Black people, and raise the level of consciousness. This is the role of communications in supporting Black nationalism and Pan-Africanism.

For these reasons the Communications and Systems Analysis Workshop proposes the creation of a communications network system that expresses and moves to fulfill the needs of the Congress of African Peoples.

Communication Network System for Dissemination of Information

1. Economic
2. Political Liberation
3. Creativity
4. Religious System
5. Education
6. History
7. Law and Justice
8. Black Technology
9. Social Organization
10. Community Organization

A. National Coordinating Committee of the Congress of African Peoples
B. Council on Communication and System Analysis of the Congress of African Peoples
C. Creative
D. Supportive
   a. Printed Media
      Support and expand UMOJA as official publication of the Congress of African Peoples
   b. Electronic Media
      Submit proposals for acquiring education TV channels
   c. Training Institution
      Institute drawing up proposals for funding of training institution for skilled media personnel
   d. Emergency Network
   e. News service/information center
   f. Public Relations
   g. Communication Task Force to monitor existing media
   h. Technical Assistance
      Reclaiming of stations and station-challenge information center be established
   i. Regional Congress of African Peoples Communications office

The communications council will meet within ninety days to draft detailed plans for the implementation of the Congress of African Peoples Communications network.

Representatives to serve on National Coordinating Committee of the Congress of African Peoples: Lou House and Laini ya Fundi.

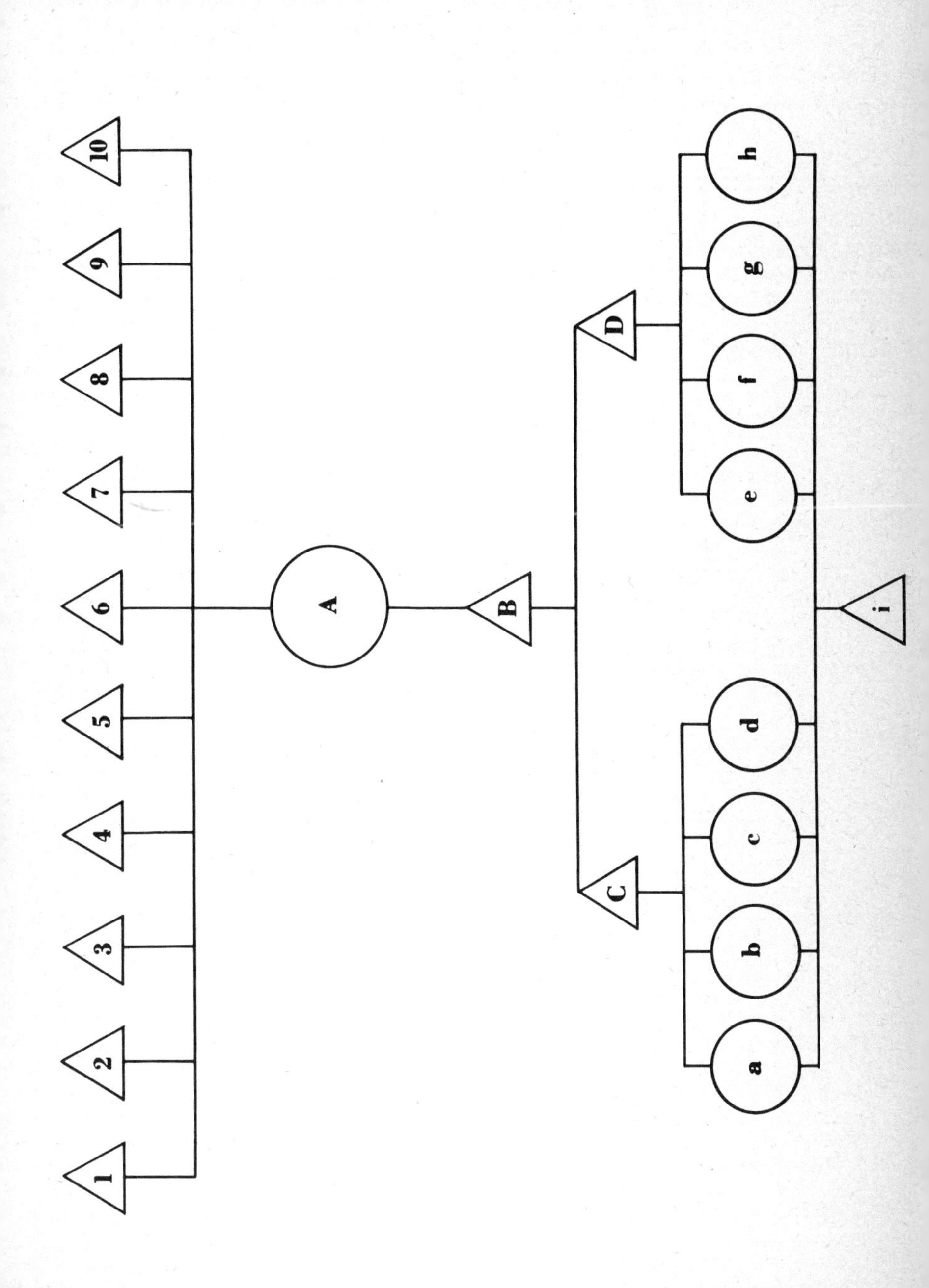
1
2
3
4
5
6
7
8
9
10
A
B
C
D
a
b
c
d
e
f
g
h
i

ECONOMICS

Coordinator's Statement

by Dunbar S. McLaurin

This paper represents the position of one of the coordinators of this workshop, Dunbar S. McLaurin, and does not necessarily represent the position or Mr. Robert Browne, my co-coordinator. Under our division of responsibility, I have taken the workshop for Friday, and he has taken it for Saturday, with a rap session jointly on Sunday.

Partially because of the nature of the subject, and partially because it represents only one half of the workshop, this position paper is brief. Its purpose is to set forth a guideline for discussion by the workshop.

The almost absolute lack of participation in the American economy by American Blacks has been too well documented to be repeated here. We constitute 21 percent of the population, but own less than 3 percent of the businesses. These tiny mom and pop shops—beauty parlors, barber shops, groceries, bars, undertaking parlors, etc.—are not only completely insignificant, but are practically irrelevant to the basic American economy. Even the 3 percent of the businesses which we own numerically, financially constitute less than .01 percent of the assets of American business—a figure almost too small to be measurable. Any single one of the five hundred largest American corporations has assets greater that all of our businesses put together, including our banks and insurance companies.

So much for repeating the obvious. What do we do about it? It is the position of this paper that our time these two short days should be spent not in repeating the problem, and in high-flung rhetoric decrying the white man and the way we have been shut out of the economy. This problem was not created in two days, nor will we solve it in two days.

Nor, in my view, should we spend our time here attempting to fashion some solution for which there is no follow-up; and upon which there can probably be no agreement.

I pose the following practical problem to this workshop: Let's solve our own economic problem. If we cannot solve the economic problem of *this conference* how can we solve the economic problem of the Black Economy?

I therefore propose that we devote our time in this conference toward devising practical means whereby this congress can be put on a permanent self-supporting basis, with a full year-round staff. This to me would be the greatest contribution at this session which this workshop could make, namely to come up with a plan for self-financing of this organization so that we would not have to beg, borrow and steal to have this meeting. This approach has been discussed with Mr. Jones and the Steering Committee, and I believe they are in agreement.

Beyond serving the purposes of the conference itself, I believe that this approach would basically also serve our own greatest purposes. For it would mean that we shall have created an instrument which would work on a year-round basis on economic problems also. We would have a secretariat and a functioning economic staff which could follow through on the recommendations for economic empowerment which we developed at this conference.

In the special August issue of *Ebony,* my article on Economic Liberation begins with the quotation of an old African proverb:

> "If you don't know where you're going—
> Any road will take you there!"

I believe that before we can know where we are going we must have a stable organization as an instrumentality to take us down that road. We then will be able to choose our road and chart our course.

I therefore commend to you that we discuss ways and means for economic empowerment of this conference before we go forward to save the Black World!

Brothers and Sisters, I say
Fight on, and Right on!

Resolutions

by Robert S. Browne
and Dunbar S. McLaurin

We define economic organization as a ways and means of providing goods and services. The problem is that we don't control the economic machinery in the space in which we live. There are two basic historical reasons for this: 1) the industrial revolution which took place in the West; and 2) racist, imperialist aggression upon African peoples by European nations.

All African people suffer from these historical facts, or to put it in more concrete terms, all African peoples suffer from some form of economic colonialism. A man who is not economically free is still a slave. You can't be equal to a man who owns four houses, and you still live in his apartments.

There can be no political power without an economic base. The white power structure (which is international in scope) controls the economics of Africans all over the world, whether they be in Harlem, Watts, South America, Central America, Asia, or the Motherland itself. All peoples of African descent suffer economic oppression and exploitation at the hand of the European slave master.

Black Economic Autonomy is a concept that must be actualized in the real world. If we wish to be free, we must establish and control our own economic institutions; the problem is however a scientific one. We must seek ways and means of neutralizing or defeating Western imperialism. We must discuss, analyze, and come up with sound ideas and solutions that are realistic.

Let us deal with the problem in a twofold manner:

1. Seek ways and means to break the economic straitjacket that African people suffer from, i.e., capitalism.
2. Build and maintain viable Black economic institutions that will provide the community with an alternative.

Black economics must benefit all Black people. Capitalism is based on the belief that competition is more valid than maximum cooperation. We believe that Blacks work better with the maximum amount of cooperation. Black people can only reach a stage of economic force through a cooperative economic system. *Ujamaa*—Cooperative Economics—is the only solution through which we can achieve this end. *Ujamaa* in plain, simple terms, means to build and maintain our own institutions, businesses, stores and shops, and to profit from them together. Therefore, we see that *Ujamaa* is not only traditional, i.e., part of African people's life style, but very reasonable for the goal we wish to accomplish, since it benefits all Black people.

Economic activity, as we defined earlier, has to do with the provision of goods and services. It must function in two circles on two different levels. The first level of economic activity is *Internal.* It should provide us with the maximum provisions not maximum profits. Local and national economics should progressively become more interdependent so that it includes political power. There could be an exchange of goods and services with Afro-Asian nations, attempting to satisfy a new standard for international market, in a word, to create an alternative world market.

The circle of international economic activity must deal with the circle of external activity but not with the same principles, i.e., cooperative economics, but with the principles of the external circle. We should not try to practice communalism with capitalists, but within ourselves. We must adjust to the level of our major audience. If we provide goods and services for the external circle, it must be along the lines established, and we must learn to compete, giving our resources and skills as best as we can with that external system. That is a principle, but it is here that it is practical reality. We withdraw from it internally, but externally we must deal with it.

Economic activity on one level would deal with society. This has to do with the concept of the U.S. as a society, i.e., a political expression where we don't have the same values, but we share goods and services. In a community, we share values first, then goods and services. What we can get in terms of goods and services from the external society that would profit us, we must get it. We must stay away from neophytism that says we don't want anything from white people meaning that we don't want technology. We must not try to produce everything for ourselves when we can get others to make them for less effort and expenditure. We must learn to use others for resources to our advantage with the least complications for us.

International would deal mainly with trade with Afro-Asian countries that have resources that we need.

Our first step, in order to achieve these institutions, must be to re-educate ourselves; to regain our former attitude of mind.

Economic Principles

1. Be it resolved that the concept of *Ujamaa*—cooperative economics—be fostered in all Black activities, and to specify the concept of *Ujamaa* as a permanent economic policy.
2. A research coordinating committee should be established to utilize and organize all available resources that would implement the concept of *Ujamaa* and develop some sort of "*Ujamaa* Fund" that would benefit all Black people.
   A. This resolution was based upon the fact that in order for African peoples to survive America, we must create a complete alternative to the white racist system now existing.
   B. We reject the whole concept of capitalism because it is based on the belief that competition is more valid than cooperation. We believe that man works better with maximum cooperation.
   C. Since economic organization is essential for every culture all that we do to implement the concept of *Ujamaa* should be based on tradition and reason, i.e., part of African peoples' life style, and applied to the concrete needs of Black people in America.
   D. We define economics as a ways and means of providing goods and services, that is to say, what will benefit the maximum amount of Black people.
   E. Also, all institutions set up should perpetuate Black Nationalism, that is Black people making up a Nation. This would give the people a cultural education as well as a political education.

There has to grow out of the effects of the congress, particularly the Economic Autonomy section, the founding of a new economic process, a new process that begins to deal with the problem of the Black people of this and other countries. A new process based on a new set of values which stress self-determination, self-respect, self-responsibility and above all self-sufficiency. This is invalid, however, unless you see yourself as part of the Black Nation, that is through "groupism" rather than individualism.

To do this, we must accomplish a series of interim goals:

1) Equip Black people with the management tools necessary for running an efficient and viable business.
2) Provide, through Black collective ownership, financial institutions that will reverse the "balance of payments" drain in the Black communities.
3) Provide jobs and a self-sustained labor force.
4) The congress should establish international trade centers in the

following sections for the purpose of promoting Black-produced products: New York, Los Angeles, the Midwest and the South. The congress should also establish a mechanism to teach Black people about international trade. But Black people refuse to deal with oppressive states or corporations which oppress Black people.

5) The congress should help all organizations which advocate Black awareness through a Pan-African concept, with financial aid, talents, and other resources.
6) The congress should form a national Black labor union and/or an alliance of Black labor unions.
7) The Economic Autonomy Workshop adopts the position paper of our workshop Co-ordinator as the basic position paper of this workshop.

Banking

1. The congress should establish itself as a tax-free foundation whose main purpose would be to coordinate, direct, and finance a Black Nation, and it should utilize a holding company concept as a vehicle to channel funds any way necessary.
   A. Specific Project: have Black students immediately address themselves to some problems that we need solved by doing research papers, master's and doctoral theses in these areas.
2. The congress must be on a permanent self-supporting basis with a full, year-round staff.
3. The congress will function as a holding company for various local organizations that will be concerned with building a Black Nation.
   A. These organizations will operate basically on cooperative systems.
   B. These organizations will channel funds into the congress.
4. The congress skill banks will establish a communication network that will make available a resource of knowledge from Black economists, accountants, lawyers, etc., whose expertise can be utilized at any time.
5. The congress will set up a means whereby Black students can do research papers, and theses on specific areas in our nation-building effort.

Manufacturing

1. The congress should establish a communications network to disseminate information to persons interested in manufacturing products and related areas. The Congress of African Peoples

should support the manufacturing of special products; the formulation of a research talent bank and the exporting and importing of products produced in all Pan-African countries and marketing facilities to handle all products produced.

Rural Development

The congress should address itself to achieving the following goals:

1. Development of land already in the hands of Blacks by assisting Black landowners and utilizing their land for industrial development, agricultural production, home usage, i.e., total community development. The congress should start out by selecting a particular region. We propose that the New Communities project region in Southwest Georgia be the starting point.
2. Setting up a central and local land bank program that would acquire more land for Black people to utilize and develop. These banks would have departments of information, development and planning, and others as the need arises. These banks would be owned and controlled by the members of the congress.
3. Setting up an Institute for Land Development to study, research and coordinate efforts at achieving these goals.

Finance

1. To get funds immediately from the delegation. Some suggestions are as follows:
   - A. $5.00 contribution from each member of the congress.
   - B. An appeal to the body of the conference to make them aware of the economic needs.
   - C. In terms of showing collective concern for unity of purpose it was suggested that those conference members who have contributed to this cause be recognized by either a stamp or seal or any kind of marking which would indicate that they have contributed. It is not an attempt to badger or impose upon participants, but rather an attempt to acquire more funds.

Financing the "Year-Round Congress Concept" that has been proposed:

1. An attempt to enlist pledges from both public and private corporations with specific attention directed toward Blacks in those corporations.
2. Publications—Suggestions for forming a newsletter entitled *The Congress of African Peoples' Newsletter* with membership fees. With this idea those who have registered with the congress

would pay five to ten dollars less (because of registration fee).

3. Marketing of products—As with the newsletter we are attempting to see what sources can be used as a distribution arm for the sales of Black products. Some of the suggestions were:
   A. A specific steering committee designed for the purpose.
   B. The utilization of professional Black athletes to contribute to the above project (Black Financing).

ORGANIZATIONS REPRESENTED AT CONGRESS OF AFRICAN PEOPLES SEPTEMBER 3–7, 1970—ATLANTA, GEORGIA

Akron, Ohio
  Black United Front
  WANTU
Albany, New York
  T.W.L.F.
Aligruppa, Pa.
  AEA
Atlanta, Georgia
  Black Unity Association
  Black Methodist for Church Renewal
  Institute of Black World
  SCLC
  New World Development
  Afro-American Police
  CORE
  Southern Rural Action
  Urban East Housing
  Black National Association of Social Workers
Berkeley, California
  Association of Black Psychologists
Bloomington, Indiana
  Afro-American Student Association
  IVAA Student Association
Bloomfield, New Jersey
  B.S.O.
Boston, Massachusetts
  Black United Front
  Black Unitarian Caucus
  Community Health Organization
  Boston University Martin Luther King Jr. AA Sc.
  Afro-American Institute
  National Directors of Faison & Norton Research
  Harambee 13
  Unity Bank & Trust Co.
Bronx, New York
  NAAAE
  Society of Black Engineers, *NYU School of Engineering & Science*
  Soul Liberator
  National Association of Black Students
  HARYOU Act
  CORE
  National Black Theater
  Blackfrica Promotions

Brooklyn, New York
- Juvenile Economic Progress Unit
- Model Cities
- New York Solidarity Council
- School of Common Sense
- Black Unity
- Ft. Greene Community Corp.
- Young Warriors Party
- Bedford Stuyvesant Youth
- Puerto Rican Eagles
- FANKO
- Black Arts Alliance
- Tom Skinner Association
- EAST (A.S.A.)
- Yan Sanna Gallery
- Aware Communication Network
- Ocean Hill Brownsville C.E.C.
- BPRSC
- Bushwick Hylan Community Center
- Youth in Action

Buffalo, New York
- Black Students Union, SUNY

Cambridge, Massachusetts
- Afro-American Committee

Camden, New Jersey
- BEE

Chicago, Illinois
- PBAC
- University Unitarian
- BUUC
- Woodlawn Experimental School Project District
- Lutheran Church in America Board of American Missions
- Council for Bio-Medical Careers
- Chicago Defender–Pittsburgh Courier
- FMO
- Black Student Association, Roosevelt University

Cincinnati, Ohio
- United Black College Organization
- B.S.U.

Cleveland, Ohio
- U-Jammi-Din
- Black Humanist Fellowship of Liberation
- Black Liberation Front
- Black Action Training

Columbia, South Carolina
- Black United for Action & Blocks

Dallas, Texas
- Afro-American Student Union
- BLAACS

Dayton, Ohio
R.N.A.
Delray Beach, Florida
Citizens for a Better America
Detroit, Michigan
Young Socialist Alliance
Association of Black Students
Pan-African Congress, U.S.A.
East Lansing, Michigan
Black United Front
East Orange, New Jersey
100 Day Care
Elizabeth, New Jersey
Organization for Black Liberation
Freehold, New Jersey
Monmouth City Coalition for Human Relations
Central Jersey Community Co-op
Greensboro, North Carolina
GAPP
Greensboro Association of Poor
Brothers & Sisters in Blackness, Guilford College
Student Organization for Black Unity
Houston, Texas
UHBSU
The Faith Essence
Africans in America for Black Liberation
Ithaca, New York
Africana Studies & Research Center, Cornell University
Jackson, Mississippi
Jackson Human Rights Project
Federation of Southern Co-ops
Jacksonville, Florida
Florida Black Front
UHURU-Youth for Human Dignity
Jamaica, Long Island, New York
OMNI Committee
Jamaica Plains, Massachusetts
Tenant Management Corp.
Kansas City, Kansas
Center for Human Dignity
Black Student Union, Kansas University
Knoxville, Tennessee
Committee for the Development of the Black Community
O.I.C.
East Tennessee Progress Association for Economic Development
Lancaster, Pennsylvania
Community Action Group

Lexington, Kentucky
- Black Student Union, University of Kentucky

Los Angeles, California
- CORE
- Center for Extending American History
- Watts Summer Festival
- CAAAE

Louisville, Kentucky
- BSU, University of Louisville

Madison, Wisconsin
- U.W. African Center
- Inter-Varsity Christian Fellowship

Miami, Florida
- Center for Urban Studies, University of Miami

Milwaukee, Wisconsin
- B.S.U., University of Wisconsin

Montclair, New Jersey
- Glenfield Grassroots
- B.O.S.S., Montclair State College

Nashville, Tennessee
- Afro-American Heritage Society

NewArk, New Jersey
- Urban League
- Black Freedom Society
- BOS, Rutgers University
- Committee for Unified NewArk
- Soul Markets, Inc.
- African Free School
- Jihad Productions
- Spirit House Movers

New Haven, Connecticut
- United Newhallville Organization
- Community Progress, Inc.
- Black Coalition Alderman
- Afro-American Inc.

New Orleans, Louisiana
- Republic of New Africa
- A.A.S.U. Xavier University
- International Relations Club, Xavier University
- Free Southern Theater
- Sons of Desire (SOUL) Xavier University
- KBCPC, Dillard University
- SGA, Xavier University

New York City
- Marco, Inc.
- African Students Organization
- N.A.R.C.O. II
- Association of Black Social Workers

YMCA
NABSW
NAACP Legal Defense Fund
Cerberan Society
Local 1199 Drug & Hospital Union
St. Mary's Community Service
Blackfrica Promotion, Inc.
IFCO
T.N.G.
Urban League
Togetherness Productions
National Council of Churches

Norfolk, Virginia
Progress Association for Economic Development

Orangeburg, South Carolina
Black Community Development Committee

Palo Alto, California
Nairobi, California

Paterson, New Jersey
W. E. B. Du Bois Memorial Library

Peoria, Illinois
AFRAM

Petersburg, Virginia
Afro Society

Philadelphia, Pennsylvania
SCLC
UMOJA
Universal Negro Improvement Assn.
USTI
RNA
RTI
National Progress Association for Economic Development

Pittsburgh, Pennsylvania
Black Action Society, Univ. of Pittsburgh
United Black Front

Raleigh, North Carolina
Africana Arts

Roanoke, Virginia
Kuumba
Kuamka-Center for Black Education

Rochester, New York
FIGHT

Roxboro, North Carolina
Person County Voters League
NCCU & PTI

Saginaw, Michigan
Poverty People's Alliance

San Diego, California
- EOC
- Southeast San Diego Communications Complex
- Kuumba Foundation

San Francisco, California
- Young Adults of San Francisco

Sarasota, Florida
- Black Studies Assn. (New College)

Savannah, Georgia
- Pan-African Liberation School

Schenectady, New York
- Schenectady Community Action Program

South Ozone Park, New York
- Community News Service

Springfield, Massachusetts
- Pan Afro

St. Albans, New York
- National Black Science

St. Louis, Missouri
- National Black Liberation

St. Paul, Minnesota
- B.L.A.C. of Macalester College

Stamford, Connecticut
- West Main Community Center

Surinam, South America
- African Organization

Syracuse, New York
- People Equal Action & Community Effort, Inc.

Vauxhall, New Jersey
- Vauxhall Neighborhood Council

Warrenton, North Carolina
- Warren County Youth Council

Washington, D. C.
- The Washington Post Company
- D. C. Veterans Association
- Black UU Caucus
- Freedmans Hospital
- Black Peoples' Union
- Pride, Inc.
- Youth Pride, Inc.
- Columbia Heights Community Association
- Nia Kuumba
- Peoples Involvement Corp.
- Pan African Committee
- NSF MRC
- Joint Center For Political Studies
- Service Corporation, Federal City College

West Haven, Connecticut
  Black Out Loud
Wichita, Kansas
  Black Student Union, Wichita State University
  Black United Front
Wilmington, Delaware
  People Settlement Association
Youngstown, Ohio
  Freedom Inc.

INDEX

Index